GW00771590

HIDDEN

FOUNDATIONS

OF THE

GREAT INVOCATION

Also by the author

Sacred Vessel of the Mysteries
Seven Ray Energy Cards
The Daily Seven Ray Energy Journal

HIDDEN
FOUNDATIONS
OF THE
GREAT INVOCATION

John Berges

PLANETWORK PRESS

ISBN 0-9641549-3-5

First Edition, October 2000

Library of Congress Card Number: 00-191188

Printed in the United States of America

Inquiries about other Planetwork publications may be sent to the above address.

Permissions

I would like to thank the following publishers and authors for permission to quote from their previously published material: Lucis Publishing Co., Peter Dawkins, Karl Hollenbach, Penn Leary, and Michael Taylor.

Credits:

Lucis Publishing Co.: All excerpts from the books of Alice A. Bailey, Foster Bailey and Mary Bailey may not be reprinted except by permission of Lucis Trust 120 Wall St., 24th floor, New York, NY 10005, which holds copyright.

The Second Cryptographic Shakespeare, by Penn Leary is available directly from: Westchester House Publishers, 218 South Ninety-fifth, Omaha, NE, USA 68114 for $15.00 prepaid.

DEDICATED TO THE MASTERS
RAKOCZI AND DJWHAL KHUL

THE SACRED CIRCLE
OF THE
INVOCATION FOR POWER AND LIGHT

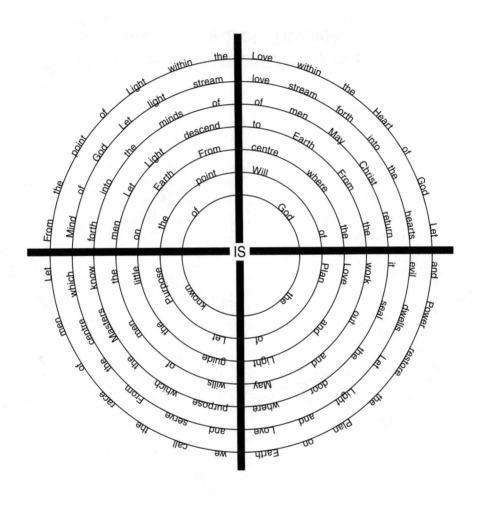

CONTENTS

List of Illustrations   x
List of Tables   xii
Preface   xiv
Acknowledgments   xvii
Note to the Reader   xviii

Introduction   1

1. The Great Invocation   8
   The Writings of the Tibetan Master, Djwhal Khul   8
   The Immediate Plan of the Hierarchy   10
   The English Translation of the Great Invocation   12
   Sacred Vessel of the Mysteries   13
   How It All Began   14
   Notes   18

2. The Master R: Enigma of the Hierarchy   19
   Master R   19
   Francis Bacon   22
   Francis Bacon and Shakespeare   26
   Dr. John Dee   27
   Francis Bacon's Mysterious Birth   29
   Francis Bacon and Ciphers   30
   Master R and Current Literature   33
   Notes   38

3. Ciphers and Numbers   40
   Modern English Gematria   44
   Elizabethan Gematria Methods   47
   Other Cipher Methods   52
   Notes   55

4. Traces of the Master R   56
   The Rose   57
   Athena   59

The Signature of Sirius   62
Bacon, Napier, and Zeros   64
The Ship Metaphor   69
Notes   77

5. Mediocria Firma   79
    The Middle Letter of the Great Invocation   91
    The Middle Word of the Great Invocation   92
    Names of the Masters   95
    Notes   97

6. From Shakespeare to Egypt   98
    The Number of the Human Soul   104
    Three Letters   107
    Notes   107

7. Seeking Francis Bacon   108
    Francis Bacon Word Search   120
    Notes   125

8. A Cryptic Message   126
    "A Word from the Master"   126
    Sirius   130
    1993   131
    Capitalized Words   135
    The Final Five Words   140
    Emergence of Ray Five   148
    Notes   150

9. Word Weaving   151
    The Heart of the Lion   157
    Notes   163

10. The Synthetic Triplet   164
    Synthesis   164
    Notes   173

11. God of Light Within   174
    Summation   180
    Notes   183

12. The Primordial Light of the World 184
    Sanat Kumara and Sirius 190
    Sanat Kumara and Leo 192
    Sanat Kumara and Gemini 197
    The Three Cosmic Crosses 201
    Hermes Trismegistus: Human, Planetary, and Cosmic 208
    Summation 212
    Notes 218

13. 113 The Hidden Key 219
    The 113 Unit Cycle 219
    A Redemptive Event in Progress 227
    Notes 233

14. 555 Restore the Plan on Earth 235
    The Human Cycle of 113 239
    The Fifth Root-race 247
    Summation 251
    Notes 256

Appendices:
    Appendix A:
        1. Psalm 46 260
        2. The Great Invocation 261
        3. "A Word from the Master" 262
    Appendix B: Symbolic Number Glossary 263
    Appendix C:
        Chapter 1 of *Sacred Vessel of the Mysteries* 269
        Chapter 2 of *Sacred Vessel of the Mysteries* 285
    Appendix D: Star Chart with Signature of Sirius 297

Glossary 298
Works Cited 309
Index 311

LIST OF ILLUSTRATIONS

1.1.	Master R with Maltese/Templar Cross	17
3.1.	Elizabethan Use of U and V	48
4.1.	Rosy Cross of the Great Invocation	58
4.2.	Septenary Cross of Athena	62
4.3.	Signature of Sirius	63
4.4.	Titlepage of Shakespeare's *Sonnets*	65
4.5.	Bacon's Titlepage from *The Advancement of Learning*	71
5.1.	Bacon's Family Motto, *Mediocria Firma*	80
5.2.	George Wither's Janus Epigram	83
5.3.	Gematria List of Psalm 46	85
5.4.	The Three Middle Words of Psalm 46	89
5.5.	The Three Middle Words of the Great Invocation	89
5.6.	Gematria Crosses of the Great Invocation	93
5.7.	Gematria Cross of Rakoczi	94
6.1.	To the Reader and Number 287	99
6.2.	Heart of the Cross—Number 157	102
7.1.	Bacon's Cross	109
7.2.	Final Left and Right Pages of the First Folio	110
7.3.	Arithmetic of 993	111
7.4.	Key Word Lineage	115
7.5.	Bacon in *King Henry the Fourth*	118
7.6.	Francis Bacon Word Search	123
7.7.	Master R, Lord of Civilization	124
8.1.	Master Rakoczi is Known	129
8.2.	My Essence is Silence	142
8.3.	Bacon's Cross	147
9.1.	Number 52 Links Three Works	153
9.2.	Word Weaving	155
9.3.	The Heart of the Lion	159
10.1.	The Mind of Master R	171
12.1.	Mission of Sanat Kumara	196
12.2.	Triangle of the Cosmic Christ	201
12.3.	Numbers Related to Sanat Kumara	206
12.4.	The Fixed Cross	206
12.5.	Planetary and Cosmic Hermes	210
12.6.	Sanat Kumara and Hermes	212

12.7. Three Levels of Hermes   214
12.8. Energy Alignments of Sanat Kumara   217
13.1. Divisions of the Cosmic Planes   221
13.2. Divisions of a Planetary Scheme   222
13.3. Divisions of a Chain   223
13.4. Descent of Sanat Kumara   226
13.5. The Great Invocation and Root-race Overlay   230
13.6. The Cross of Sanat Kumara   232
14.1. Divisions of a World Period   239
14.2. 113 Branch-races   242
14.3. The Great Invocation and Branch-race Overlay   243
14.4. 2401 Branch-races of the Fourth Round   245
14.5. Races 333 to 555   246
14.6. The Fifth Race of Mind Development   250

LIST OF TABLES

3.1. Modern AN Values   45
3.2. Modern RAN Values   46
3.3. ESC AN Values   49
3.4. ESC RAN Values   49
3.5. ERC Values   50
3.6. RKC Values   51
5.1. Middle Word of Psalm 46   86
5.2. Middle Word of Great Invocation   88
5.3. Multiples of 19   91
7.1. Three Middle Words of Psalm 46   112
7.2. Key Word Lineage Gematria   116
7.3. R at the Middle   117
7.4. Summary of Francis Bacon Word Search   124
8.1. RAN Method   127
8.2. "My name is a cipher"   128
8.3. Separation of Sirius A and B   132
8.4. Capitalized Words in "A Word from the Master"   135
8.5. Gematria of Capitalized Words   136
8.6. Cipher Message of Final Five Words   141
8.7. Final Five Words of the Great Invocation   144
8.8. Final Five Words of "A Word from the Master"   144
8.9. Total Value of Two Sets of Final Five Words   146
8.10. Synthesis of Two Sets of Final Five Words   148
9.1. Three Mottos   157
9.2. First, Middle, and Last Essence Values   161
9.3. First, Middle, and Last Word Values   162
10.1. 417 Words   165
11.1. God of Light Within   175
11.2. Numbers 22 and 44   178
14.1. Restoration of the Plan   237

ABOUT THE AUTHOR

John Berges, M.Th. is a student, writer, teacher and lecturer of the Ageless Wisdom. He lives in Egg Harbor Township, New Jersey, where he, his wife, and coworkers utilize meditation and the teachings of the Ageless Wisdom in service to humanity. He is also the author of *Sacred Vessel of the Mysteries*, creator of the *Seven Ray Energy Cards,* an intuitive counseling system based on the seven rays. He and his wife, Darlene, are also the creators of *The Daily Seven Ray Energy Journal*, a journaling accessory to the *Seven Ray Energy Cards*.

PREFACE

When I finished writing my first book, *Sacred Vessel of the Mysteries*, I was greatly relieved that such a large project was finally completed. Although I knew that some further material related to the hidden codes of the Great Invocation might be mined from its words, I did not foresee the direction which my future work would take me, and I certainly did not think that I would be immediately immersed in new research. The thought that I would soon be delving into the life of Francis Bacon, Shakespeare, and the little known work of Master R was the furthest thing from my mind. Yet, three years later, here is a new book about the Great Invocation indicating another hidden layer of meaning related to Master R.

Although I am a student of the esoteric and subjective aspects of life, I approach such ideas with a critical mind. I believe that the intuitive ideas we receive must be weighed with reason and logic. I believe this is the best way to judge their value in relation to the universal principles of the Ageless Wisdom already laid down for us by past teachers. My reason for mentioning this is that I have felt pulled or drawn into the writing of this book by outer events and the findings of other people; whereas, the writing of *Sacred Vessel* was primarily based on subjective impressions. I have told my closest associates that while researching and writing *Hidden Foundations*, I felt like a fish on a hook being reeled into a net. This idea really struck home when I realized halfway through the project that the words in Peter Dawkins' poem (purportedly from the Master R) were actually describing the process which I was following to write the book! Consequently, logic and reason are gently invited to hold their proper place in the greater Scheme of the Universe which is far beyond their ability to fathom. Logic and reason will help you understand the mysteries presented in these pages, but only if they are made to serve within the larger sphere of intuitive and spiritual perception which sees wholes rather than parts. It is in this spirit that I invite you to consider the ideas presented in this book.

During the course of this study, I often refer to my first book. Please don't interpret these references as self-centeredness, but simply as a means of establishing the parallels in numbers, symbols,

xiv

and themes between my new findings and the material recorded in *Sacred Vessel*. As my research continued, I was continually amazed by these connections.

As you will read, I came into contact with the "right people" or "right" information which provided the clues to the next leg of my journey of discovery. What started out as a tiny bit of intriguing information rapidly expanded into a highly charged, magnetic center drawing me inexorably into its field of influence. Soon, it was obvious that enough information had come into my hands and mind to write another book. When this became clear to me, I was not sure I was ready to wade into the countless details of putting another book together, especially so soon after *Sacred Vessel*. Yet, the knowledge provided by the clues which I had assembled acted as an irresistible force which would not be denied a hearing. Thus was born *Hidden Foundations of the Great Invocation*.

Just as with *Sacred Vessel of the Mysteries*, you must judge the worth and integrity of the information presented within these pages. As in my first writing, I have simply explored certain ideas and theories through the esoteric Law of Correspondences. Within the context of this law, my chief tool is gematria and number symbolism.

The results of my efforts have expanded my understanding and appreciation of the Great Invocation and the inner workings of the masters of the spiritual Hierarchy. Some of the ideas presented here, especially in the final three chapters, are challenging to grasp; but if you take the time to examine them carefully, I am confident they will provide you with a wider horizon of spiritual understanding. I say this because that has been their effect on me and I don't consider myself much different from any other modern explorer of esoteric ideas. Always being a slow learner, I believe that if I can "get it," so can you. And what you will "get" is, I believe, the occult key to understanding the unprecedented era in which we live.

Our planet is on the verge of spiritual greatness and the emerging Light will forever change our view and experience of the world. This 100 year period, from 1925 to 2025, is of such paramount importance in our planet's spiritual evolution, that the composers of the Great Invocation ingeniously encoded the symbolism of this time period in its words. Indeed, according to one great teacher of the Hierarchy, this is the time period for which the spiritual Intelligences of our planet have been preparing for millions of years. They are ready to implement great changes in the nature and qual-

ity of life on Earth. They now wait for humanity to respond by showing its willingness to establish right human relations. We are very
close to making this happen. You may be that special human being
who, by some kind deed or thought, will tip the balance just enough
to allow the spiritual Forces of Light to flow into our waiting world.

Hidden Foundations is not only about the codes hidden in the
Great Invocation, but also about who put them there. Hence, it is a
mystery story and a revelation of humanity's spiritual destiny all
rolled into one. I hope you enjoy it, but more importantly, I hope it
deepens your awareness of the spiritual dimensions of life and
inspires you to add the Light of your soul to the ever increasing Light
of the World.

ACKNOWLEDGMENTS

I want to thank Michael Taylor and Peter Dawkins for aiding my understanding of the life of Francis Bacon and the activities of his inner circle of writers and poets. Their studies of the Master R have also served to enhance my understanding in this area, thus enabling me to shed new light on the origin of the Great Invocation.

Especially in the area of the Bacon/Shakespeare question, I wish to thank Karl Hollenbach and Penn Leary for their insightful and valuable contributions .

Many thanks to my friend and colleague Roger Stair for his advice on various questions of gematria and other esoteric matters. His knowledge of numbers always provides a reliable sounding board for my ideas whenever I seek his counsel.

Additionally, I want to thank Lucis Trust for their permission to quote freely from the books of Alice A. Bailey. Their continued support is greatly appreciated.

Much gratitude goes to my good friend, Mary Ann Casalino of the Seven Ray Institute who is always there to lend support when needed. It should also be noted that these ideas were first presented as a master's thesis for the University of the Seven Rays.

Closer to home, the work of putting this book together and getting it into print could not have happened without the help of my associates in spiritual study and service. My heartfelt recognition and gratitude for their hours of help go out to Suzanne Coia, Karen Cooper, Patricia Johnson, Kathy Sakson, and Tony Sakson.

I especially want to thank my family for patiently listening (I think they were listening) to my theories, explanations, and "mad professor" excitement over things most often esoteric to their ears.

As always, I can never thank enough my wife and spiritual partner, Darlene, for her patient listening to the many abstract ideas and concepts which must be dealt with in the process of researching and writing a book. Her wise advice and counsel these past years, including her physical support, have proven invaluable to me and this work. They stand as a testimony to the profound place which spiritual partnership can hold when giving supplants grasping and mutual sacrifice gives birth to right relationship.

NOTE TO THE READER

For those readers who have not read my first book, *Sacred Vessel of the Mysteries*, or anyone not familiar with the work of Alice A. Bailey and Djwhal Khul, I strongly recommend that you read appendix C before proceeding. This section is a reprint of the first two chapters of *Sacred Vessel*. It provides the basic information necessary for understanding the material presented here.

Additionally, I have taken the liberty of capitalizing terms which I consider significant according to the context of the material.

INTRODUCTION

*The one thing which humanity needs today
is the realisation that there IS a Plan.*

The Externalisation of the Hierarchy, 670.

The present volume is a continuation of some of the ideas examined in my first book, *Sacred Vessel of the Mysteries*. The material contained in that book uncovers number patterns and codes based on gematria in the Great Invocation. These codes strongly suggest a deliberate effort to place a message within the message of the Great Invocation.

This second work extends some of that material and it also introduces new findings concerning the possible identity of the individual who translated the Great Invocation into English. Running parallel with this information, however, is an underlying, less visible, stream of numeric clues of even deeper meaning illuminating the hidden foundations of this great Word of Power.

As documented in my previous work, the Great Invocation is more than a mere translation of spiritual concepts into words. It is a composition, an arrangement of words, into a specific pattern containing profound symbolic meaning about our world and humanity's place in it.

It is obvious to most of the people on our planet that the world is in the midst of unprecedented growth and change. Most attribute

1

this change to the rapid increase of man's knowledge, with the resulting advance of science and technology. As a result the world has been rapidly transformed in little more than one hundred years. Many hesitate to guess what the discoveries of science will bring to the world in the next one hundred years.

One of the fundamental questions raised in this book is this: Does civilization simply sprout up randomly, through haphazard forces or events or is there a plan behind the growth of civilization? In many ways this question also underlies *Sacred Vessel of the Mysteries*. The philosophy underlying the material in the present book and my previous work is based on the Ageless Wisdom, sometimes referred to as the Perennial Philosophy. This Ageless Wisdom is the main root from which all the major religions and philosophies have grown throughout history.

Generally speaking, the Ageless Wisdom is a storehouse of esoteric knowledge concerning the nature of the cosmos and the role of our planet Earth in the universe. It is also about the nature and role of humanity within the world and the cosmos. This Wisdom posits the existence of a Plan which governs the purpose of life at every level. A direct quote from the Ageless Wisdom is appropriate here. It comes from a member of the Hierarchy named Djwhal Khul (more about him shortly):

> You might here ask and rightly so: What is this plan? When I speak of the plan I do not mean such a general one as the plan of evolution or the plan for humanity which we call by the somewhat unmeaning term of soul unfoldment. These two aspects of the scheme for our planet are taken for granted, and are but modes, processes and means to a specific end. The plan as at present sensed, and for which the Masters are steadily working, might be defined as follows:—It is the production of a subjective synthesis in humanity and of a telepathic interplay which will eventually annihilate time. It will make available to every man all past achievements and knowledges, it will reveal to man the true significance of his mind and brain and make him the master of that equipment and will make him therefore omnipresent and eventually open the door to omniscience. This next development of the plan will produce in man an understanding—intelligent and cooperative—of the divine purpose for which the One in Whom we live and move and have our being has deemed it wise to submit to incarnation.[1]

This extract from a book by Alice A. Bailey tells us much. It states that the Plan can be seen in two ways. First, there is the general plan of evolution for our planet. At the risk of oversimplifying a complex subject, our planet is a world in which spiritual entities gain experience at the physical level of existence in order to expand their awareness of the larger scheme of evolution beyond the Earth. This process includes all forms of life. The specific form of life called "humanity" advances through what is referred to above as "soul unfoldment."

The second point regards a more specific Plan (note the capitalization). This Plan has a goal of producing "a subjective synthesis in humanity" and "creating a telepathic interplay which will eventually annihilate time." This certainly appears to be describing the internet, wireless telephones, and satellite communications. All of these devices and technologies are annihilating time—and this technology is only in its infancy.

The third point made in the above extract is the most mysterious. It says that the next phase of the Plan involves our intelligent and cooperative understanding of the purpose for which God "has deemed it wise to submit to incarnation." Without getting too far ahead of ourselves, the Ageless Wisdom states that the Being Who created the Earth is actually living on the Earth in some state of embodiment just beyond the range of our physical senses. This involves a tremendous sacrifice on the part of this Being. We will have much more to say about this later.

The point is that the Plan exists in phases. Its comprehension by any given individual grows in proportion to that person's expanding consciousness—the soul unfoldment mentioned earlier. In addition to an individual's ability to fathom deeper levels of the Plan, there is the implication that masses of humanity can experience a new understanding of the Plan through revelation. The word "revelation" is usually associated with religion; however, in modern terminology we can refer to such a revelation as a paradigm shift. This term is familiar to many and it simply means that people see the world in a new way. This shift is the result of the rapid growth of knowledge which subtly changes humanity's perceptions of the world in terms of meaning, values, opinions, beliefs, etc. The Ageless Wisdom teaches that these shifts are driven by Intelligences Who are literally managing our planet's development through a phased Plan. The most important point to grasp now is that humanity's free will is never violated in this process.

The Plan is said to originate in the Mind of God in higher dimensional levels within the Earth's scheme of evolution. This concept expands the envelope of life on Earth beyond the physical dimension of existence into dimensions of consciousness beyond our five senses. Viewed from this angle the Plan transcends the human world, yet humanity is the focus of the Plan at this time in planetary history. Consequently, the Ageless Wisdom teaches that the work of bringing God's Plan to fruition is occurring on various planes of existence simultaneously. It involves intelligent Beings from the highest level of our planet's infrastructure to human beings working in the world everywhere.

At the same time, the Plan for our world is part of a greater Plan encompassing our entire solar system. In turn, our solar system is governed by a higher order of Lives from the star Sirius. We will have much to say about Sirius later, but for now I will mention that Sirius is very close to our solar system in terms of cosmic measurements. Considering that our galaxy is 100,000 light years in diameter, Sirius is almost on top of us—being only 8.6 light years from Earth.

Returning to the main point, we are not simply floating haphazardly through time and space as accidentally created creatures on a planet orbiting an ordinary star. No. The Ageless Wisdom, which is found all over the world in various forms, teaches that humanity is on this planet for good reason. We are here to fulfill some greater purpose of which, at present, we know nothing. The Plan for humanity is the means for fulfilling God's purpose.

We are told that humanity is almost to the point of psychological maturity. Consequently, we can now begin to learn about God's purpose and how that purpose can be implemented through the Plan. Part of the reason we are at the stage of psychological maturity is that, prophets, messengers, saviors, and avatars have come to the world throughout the centuries to guide our growth.

These spiritual Teachers come from a dimension of consciousness which the Ageless Wisdom calls the Hierarchy of Souls. These Messengers and Teachers were once human beings like ourselves. Through many lifetimes of trial and error they overcame the cause and effect factors which lead to continued incarnation. As a result, they achieved liberation from what the Buddhists call the wheel of rebirth. Many of these liberated human beings—these "Masters" of human living—choose to stay on Earth to help the world overcome its suffering. They work in all the primary fields of human endeavor: politics, religion, commerce, art, science, and education. Their work in these areas is to stimulate and inspire the minds of the millions of people found in these fields.

The ultimate goal is to create a world in which the Light, Love, and Power of God are free to circulate throughout the Earth. Here is another quotation from Djwhal Khul:

> The first aim and the primary aim is to establish, through the medium of humanity, an outpost of the Consciousness of God in the solar system...

> To found upon earth (as has already been indicated) a power-house of such potency and a focal point of such energy that humanity—as a whole—can be a factor in the solar system, bringing about changes and events of a unique nature in the planetary life and lives (and therefore in the system itself) and inducing an *interstellar activity* [emphasis mine, JB].[2]

Before such a stupendous condition as this can occur, the material substance which composes all the life forms on Earth must be refined. Quite simply, this means that the human kingdom will become the saving force of the planet. Through continued advances in knowledge and understanding of the natural world, humanity will form a seamless mediating relationship between the kingdoms of nature below it and the kingdoms of spirit above it. Granted, no one knows what such a world will be like. This description of humanity's future destiny on Earth and beyond certainly lies far in the future. According to the Ageless Wisdom, however, after millions of years of evolution, humanity is now ready to *consciously* participate in this planned goal.

We, a rapidly integrating humanity, are now consciously entering (for the first time) into that stage mentioned earlier, in which some of God's purpose and Plan will be revealed to mankind. It is this critical juncture of planetary history which this book seeks to magnify. I believe this Plan and the unique position and opportunity of humanity today are deeply emphasized in the subtle coding of the Great Invocation. *Sacred Vessel of the Mysteries* broke the ground in this area. *Hidden Foundations* carries that message further.

As mentioned at the beginning of this introduction, a great deal of this book touches on the work of one of the Masters of the Hierarchy who has been instrumental in fanning the flames of growth in Europe and America for the past 500 years. To some, this Master is known as Saint Germain. In the books of Alice A. Bailey, he is referred to as Master Rakoczi or Master R. These latter two names will be used in this book. Although some general information about Master R appears in this work, the primary focus of our investigation is the Great Invocation and Master R's possible role in its composition.

Most students of the Ageless Wisdom assume that the Master Djwhal Khul translated the Great Invocation into English, but this may not be the entire story. The projects initiated and inspired by the members of the Hierarchy for advancing human development often extend over many centuries and utilize the various fields of religion, science, and art. In order to accomplish these large projects the Masters of the Hierarchy work in a highly integrated and cooperative manner. This is borne out by the evidence assembled in these pages which suggests that the Masters Rakoczi and Djwhal Khul collaborated in composing and translating the Great Invocation into English. It is an accepted fact among students of the Alice Bailey material that the Master Djwhal Khul dictated the Great Invocation to Alice Bailey and that he commented on its meaning quite extensively. Embedded within the words of the Great Invocation, however, are many clues suggesting that the Master R had much to do with its creation behind the scenes and, as we shall see, this silent method of work is very characteristic of the Master R's style.

Djwhal Khul states that one of the Master R's incarnations was that of Francis Bacon. Therefore, we will examine the interests of Bacon and his possible involvement with the works of Shakespeare. Many people believe Bacon wrote those works and left coded messages within the plays and sonnets attesting to this fact. Our primary interest is the fact that Bacon employed codes in his writing, not whether he wrote Shakespeare.

We will also investigate a poem written in 1993 by Peter Dawkins, a philosopher and researcher into the life of Francis Bacon and the Master R. Dawkins claims that his poem was directly inspired by the Master R.

In particular, we will compare the gematria codes found in the

Great Invocation with similar codes found in Psalm 46 (which contains the words "shake" and "speare"), several Shakespearean writings, and Peter Dawkins' poem, "A Word from the Master."

These various clues are a prelude to a much greater theme encompassing our entire planet; for the clues are not only meant to identify the author of the writings in question, but are designed to teach us and lead us into reflection on the Author and Creator of our world. That divine Author writes His words with Light, not ink, and the subject of His work is Man through which the Plan of Love and Light can be restored on Earth.

The presentation of the Great Invocation to humanity is the culminating phase of a Plan stretching back into the night of time before humanity existed on Earth. The latter chapters explore this fundamental, originating phase of the Plan. What is termed the "immediate Plan" of the Hierarchy (the past five or six hundred years) represents what I believe is a climaxing phase of a much larger cosmic Plan encompassing twenty million years of planetary evolution. Granted, this is a very long time from the human standpoint. But from the vantage point of Those Who Instituted this Cosmic Plan, twenty million years might be compared to one year of human activity.

Notes

1. Alice A. Bailey, *A Treatise on White Magic*, 403-4.
2. Alice A. Bailey, *Esoteric Psychology*, vol. II, 217.

THE GREAT INVOCATION

This Invocation, which I have lately given to you,
is the group prayer of all humanity in the Aquarian Age.

Discipleship in the New Age, vol. II, 179.

THE WRITINGS OF THE
TIBETAN MASTER, DJWHAL KHUL

In the year 1919 an English-born woman, living in California, named Alice A. Evans (born as Alice La Trobe-Bateman and soon to be wed to Foster Bailey and thus be known by the now more familiar name of Alice A. Bailey) was contacted telepathically by a Tibetan teacher of wisdom named Djwhal Khul (also known as DK or the Tibetan). He asked her to write a series of books dictated by him which were to be a modern foundational rendering of the Ageless Wisdom. After some trepidation Alice Bailey agreed and the beginning of a thirty year project was initiated, resulting in one of the most complete and sophisticated metaphysical presentations of spiritual truths ever given to humanity.

In the midst of transmitting this series of books came the Great Invocation. The Great Invocation is a prayer meant to be used by all of humanity regardless of their religious background. Although the word "Christ" appears in it, this term is meant to be interpreted as the universal anointed spiritual Teacher of the human race. The Great Invocation follows.

From the point of Light within the Mind of God
Let light stream forth into the minds of men.
Let Light descend on Earth.

From the point of Love within the Heart of God
Let love stream forth into the hearts of men.
May Christ return to Earth.

From the centre where the Will of God is known
Let purpose guide the little wills of men—
The purpose which the Masters know and serve.

From the centre which we call the race of men
Let the Plan of Love and Light work out
And may it seal the door where evil dwells.

Let Light and Love and Power restore the Plan on Earth.

The Great Invocation is a beautiful and inspiring prayer; yet, it is much more. It is a word of power, a mantram, or hermetic sound formula. These three synomynous terms describe a specific group of words scientifically formulated to produce one or more specific results. When these words are sounded with an attitude of selfless service, powerful spiritual energies are released which benefit humanity as well as oneself. Like all prayers, its effectiveness is based on the faith of those who use it. Beyond this, however, the Tibetan was explicit in his writings that the Great Invocation was the most powerful prayer ever given to humanity and that its use represented a cosmic event; therefore, the Great Invocation is in a category all its own in terms of spiritual power, meaning, and significance. According to the Tibetan, in the year 1945 the Christ made a decision that, at some future date, He would once again become a public figure by incarnating in physical form. This event is referred to by DK as the "reappearance of the Christ." Because He decided to reappear, the Christ was given permission to use the

Great Invocation by the Lord of the World, identified by the Tibetan as Sanat Kumara. Apparently this powerful prayer had never been used by the Christ or any member of the Hierarchy prior to 1945. DK reports the following:

> The agony of the war, and the distress of the entire human family led Christ, in the year 1945, to come to a great decision—a decision which found expression in two most important statements. He announced to the assembled spiritual Hierarchy and to all His servants and disciples on Earth that He had decided to emerge again into physical contact with humanity, if they would bring about the initial stages of establishing right human relations; secondly, He gave to the world (for the use of the "man on the street") one of the oldest prayers ever known, but one which hitherto had not been permitted to be used except by the most exalted, spiritual Beings. He used it Himself for the first time, we are told, at the time of the Full Moon of June, 1945, which is recognised as the Full Moon of the Christ, just as the Full Moon of May is that of the Buddha. It was not easy to translate these ancient phrases (so ancient that they are without date or background of any kind) into modern words, but it has been done, and the Great Invocation, which may eventually become a world prayer, was pronounced by Him and taken down by His disciples.[1]

This tremendous spiritual event culminated some 600 years of planning by the Hierarchy and 2,000 years of preparation by the Christ. (For an explanation of this and other esoteric terms see the glossary.)

THE IMMEDIATE PLAN OF THE HIERARCHY

Around the year 1400 A.D. the Hierarchy recognized the development of a difficult situation regarding humanity's growth. Humanity had become too separative in its political and religious views and practices. According to the writings of the Master Djwhal Khul, the spiritual Hierarchy observed the situation for about 100 years. About 1500 A.D., the Masters met once again to decide how to accelerate the integration process in the human kingdom in order to promote a cooperative spirit in human relations. Although the urge toward union and integration is a fundamental universal law, this urge had been artificially thwarted by the desires of individuals who wanted to amass power and wealth. Selfish desire and the protection of territory in the physical, political, and religious fields ruled the day. As the Hierarchy saw it, separatism and prejudice, if allowed to continue, would destroy humanity. The other problem which needed to be addressed was that of mental growth. The minds of human beings were becoming more powerful, but needed to be trained and refined spiritually. The Hierarchy recognized that the divine Plan could not move forward without improved mental capacity, but at the same time realized that knowledge without wisdom and a sense of brotherhood was dangerous.

There was a gap in social and cultural development in Europe following the collapse of the Roman Empire. The Byzantine Empire was flourishing, but the great learning and knowledge which it possessed was spreading too slowly into Europe. One of the decisions made at that conclave was to inspire the more evolved souls of that era to awaken people to a higher quality of life based on a more cooperative spirit of personal and social relationships. Apparently this resulted in the appearance of experienced souls on the European scene who began that cultural and scientific movement known as the Renaissance. What began in Italy through the incarnation of older and wiser souls soon spread throughout the continent and eventually to England. By the twentieth century the steady growth of this group of individuals led to the creation of what the Tibetan calls the New Group of World Servers. This is not an objective organization in the physical sense, but a subjective group of souls affiliated along spiritual lines whose "members" now exist in every country of the world. They are characterized by their willingness to set aside their personal beliefs in order to meet the primary goal of helping people in need no matter what racial, ethnic, religious, or political background they have.

This twentieth century phase of the Plan was implemented by creating four distinct areas of service for these committed souls. These four groups include the cultural, political, religious, and scientific fields. The Tibetan points out that recently the philosophical, psychological, and financial groups have emerged. Thus, seven distinct groups now exist as part of the field of service for the New Group of World Servers. As an example of the effects of these groups in the earlier stage, DK points out that the cultural group produced the poets of the Elizabethan age and the musicians of Germany and the Victorian period.[2] One of the most influential members of this group during the Elizabethan era was Francis

Bacon (1561-1626). Although he is recognized as the father of the Western scientific method, Francis Bacon's writings spanned the philosophical, fictional, and poetic spheres of expression.

THE ENGLISH TRANSLATION OF THE GREAT INVOCATION

According to Djwhal Khul, the Master Rakoczi once lived in human form as Francis Bacon. Bacon was already quite an advanced soul at that point in time. In his final incarnation in Europe during the eighteenth century, he was known as Count Saint Germain. It is assumed by many esoteric students that this was his final incarnation in the human kingdom prior to his becoming a Master of the Hierarchy under the name Master R. For the purposes of this study we will focus mainly on Master R's lifetime as Francis Bacon.

Bacon is known to have written and worked with codes or ciphers[3] and is recognized as a major contributor to the growth of the English language. The Great Invocation is a prayer containing ingenious number codes and the symbolic placement of words and phrases in a manner similar to the methods used by Francis Bacon. It is logical to reason, therefore, that the Master R may have influenced the wording of the Great Invocation because, according to DK, the Master R is closely involved in aiding the Christ in His planned reappearance. Furthermore, because we are told that the Great Invocation is the most important tool for humanity to use in fostering the Christ's reappearance, it is fair to extend our thinking and to raise the question as to whether the Master R aided in or single-handedly translated the Great Invocation into English.

It is commonly accepted by the great majority of esoteric students studying the books of Alice A. Bailey that the Great Invocation was transcribed in English by Alice Bailey in the exact words given to her telepathically by the Master DK (appendix C). Further clues however, have come to light which strongly suggest the possibility of influence by the Master R. He works secretly, but deliberately leaves behind subtle clues in order to give those "with eyes to see or ears to hear" the opportunity to discover evidence of his influence. His methods are designed to teach by providing hints and clues which lead the seeker to greater discoveries.

SACRED VESSEL OF THE MYSTERIES

Before explaining how this theory was born, it is necessary to briefly explain the subject matter of my first book, *Sacred Vessel of the Mysteries*. That book details the presence of symbolic coding hidden within the Great Invocation, strongly suggesting deliberate design by the Master Djwhal Khul. (Obviously, the information which has now come to light may change the theory that Djwhal Khul was solely responsible for that coding.) According to Alice Bailey, the Tibetan transmitted this prayer to her via telepathy sometime during April of 1945, although no exact date of transmission appears in her books.[4]

This prayer for humanity is glorified beyond the measure of its words alone because of the profound esoteric information placed within it. Metaphorically, a beautiful vessel has been designed to hold some of the most sacred and precious details of our planet's role in the Greater Life of God. Since people never think to look for "the pearl of great price" in obvious places, great truths have often been concealed directly in front of the "collective eyes" of the public. Ancient monuments and great cathedrals often contain universal mathematical proportions and symbols of divine mysteries built into their very structures. The Great Invocation is the centerpiece around which the spiritual Hierarchy and humanity gather in meditation for furthering the next stage of the Plan for planet Earth. What better place to code esoteric symbolism than this modern "cathedral" of prayer.

Sacred Vessel of the Mysteries uses the exact form of the Great Invocation (shown at the beginning of this chapter) as published in the books of Alice A. Bailey. It is my contention that Djwhal Khul wanted the Great Invocation presented in this exact form in order to preserve the symbolic meaning of the number of stanzas, lines, words, letters, and the positions of particular words and phrases within the text. The coding techniques and the information resulting from those techniques will be used to investigate the possibility that a similarity of coding style and technique exists in the writings of Francis Bacon and the Great Invocation. As mentioned already, Bacon is important because his was one of the incarnations of the individual now known as the Master R, one of the leading Masters of the Hierarchy.

HOW IT ALL BEGAN

The issue of the original "authorship" or translation of the Great Invocation has come up due to certain events which occurred in October, 1997. That year I went to a conference in New Zealand to present my newly published book, *Sacred Vessel of the Mysteries*. I am not an enthusiastic traveler, and even though I was going to an exotic far-off land, the trip represented more of a duty than a vacation. Added to this was a nagging sense of, "Why all the way to New Zealand?" As I thought about this, I realized that although I was obviously flying there, it was strangely symbolic that I was carrying a load of books, each depicting on the cover a mystical ship traveling across a vast expanse of "cosmic" ocean; and here I was flying above a vast ocean enroute to a rather remote island nation only a hop-skip-and-a-jump from Antarctica.

After the conference began I was mildly excited about a presentation on the subject of the Master R, which was going to be given by a man named Michael Taylor, author of the book *Master R: Lord of Our Civilization*. I attended the lecture and my interest was piqued when Mr. Taylor explained the mysteriousness of the Master R and how this Master enjoys teaching others through the presentation of riddles, hints, and clues. The Master R's early talent for playing hide and seek was especially obvious in his incarnation as Francis Bacon. Several startling factors then came to light as Taylor went on to describe how Bacon used codes to hide his identity during Elizabethan times. He loved to play games with words and sentences and may have been the true author of the Shakespearean works, or at least headed a group of writers and poets who produced these works under the collective name of Shakespeare. Bacon's favorite Muse and inspiration was the goddess Athena. One of Bacon's symbols was the even-armed cross. He was probably the head of the Rosicrucians, and the rose at the center of this cross was therefore another symbol important to him. He was very much interested in establishing the English language as the leading language of the world. The numbers 1.9 and 9.3 were also of importance in Taylor's presentation. I immediately realized many of the details that Mr. Taylor was enumerating had a direct correspondence to discoveries I had made concerning the Great Invocation. I had uncovered many of the same facts prior to ever meeting Mr. Taylor. What's more, I had very little interest in the Master R and Francis Bacon; I knew little about the former and close to nothing about the latter. Suddenly, I found myself telling him and those present that I had just written a book about the Great Invocation and its secret coding; from the information he was conveying, I had a strong sense that the Master R aided the Master DK in constructing the Great Invocation.

After his presentation, Taylor and I spoke briefly and I showed him my book. He was amazed to find that much of what was in it reminded him of Bacon's word and number play. He also noted that Sirius had some connection with the Master R. Added to all this, he then related that the city of Christchurch, where the conference was being held, was linked to the Master R in some way.

After returning home I began gathering information about the Master R and Francis Bacon. Taylor recommended I correspond with Peter Dawkins, a specialist on the Master R/Bacon connection. I soon obtained several of Mr. Dawkins' books which contain some of the material discussed by Taylor, plus a great deal more. Studying this material impelled me to broaden my research and I soon found myself searching the Internet for more information. Thus began another venture into the uncharted waters of the origins and creation of the Great Invocation—its hidden foundations.

This mysterious connection to Christchurch reappeared almost two years later. While on vacation, my wife and I were explaining some of the details of this current book to two close friends. As we began, Jerry (not his real name) jumped up and ran off to another room to get some handouts he had saved from a numerology class he had taken several years earlier. The handouts were copies of drawings of various Masters of the Hierarchy. Such pictures do not impress me very much, but when he showed me the drawing of the Master R, I immediately noticed a medallion hanging from the Master's neck. It was in the form of a Maltese cross, but without the notches in the outer lines of the arms. I had used the exact type of cross to depict the Great Invocation in my first book (figure 1.1).

We eventually tracked down Edmund Harold's book, entitled *Master Your Vibration*, from which the drawings were copied. To my astonishment his drawings originated in Christchurch, New Zealand. They were drawn by a female artist who wanted to remain anonymous. In his preface Mr. Harold relates that while on a lecture tour in New Zealand in 1981, an incident occurred which led him to write his book. Harold explains: "During this segment, as I held up a rough sketch of the Master R, a colleague in the audience who is possessed of an exceptional clairvoyant ability, perceived the said Master begin to manifest behind me."[5]

His friend went on to tell Harold that he was to write a book about the various Masters and the use of number vibrations. The book was also to have drawings of the Masters within it. For more than eighteen months Harold searched without success for the right artist to do the drawings. It was during another lecture tour of New Zealand that he began getting a strong impression that he should begin working on the book. By the time he reached Christchurch, located on the southern island of New Zealand (also named Christchurch), he heard about a woman living there who had been suddenly impressed to start painting pictures of the Masters. Harold was unimpressed and it was not until a week later, at the further urging of his friends, that he relented and agreed to meet this "artist." He describes the meeting in this way:

> I am uncertain which of us had the greater shock, for the artist—a shy, retiring woman—had been receiving communications that she was to work with me—indeed, was to meet me within days. It was not unitl later that I found she had received the instruction to purchase paint for the project at precisely the same time as I had received my own "manifestation," but neither had been advised of the other's task until that moment in time. It should also be known that the artist has not received any professional training during this current lifetime, although the works are completed in oils. She is also quite insistent that her name be omitted from the credits.[6]

All four of us were amazed at the strange coincidence between Edmund Harold's experience in Christchurch and my rather reluctant journey there to introduce my new book. If I had not gone, I may never have begun researching the possible role of the Master R in the writing of the Great Invocation. If Edmund Harold had not returned to Christchurch, he may never have located the anonymous artist who painted the pictures of the Masters, and especially the one of Master R with that Maltese-like cross (see glossary).

As figure 1.1 shows, the cross worn by Master R is identical in shape to the cross of the Great Invocation appearing in *Sacred Vessel of the Mysteries*, published in 1997, and which I have reproduced

Figure 1.1. Master R with Maltese/Templar Cross.[7]

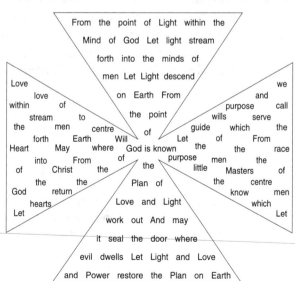

here. This cross motif containing the Great Invocation actually dates from 1995 when I first discovered it and I have used this image as an overhead in public presentations for five years.

This story describing my discovery of this drawing of the Master R is one more incident which could be termed coincidence. I am left with the feeling, however, that there is more than coincidence operating here. Nevertheless, without fully comprehending how or why, I now find myself at a point where I must report on the findings of my investigation since the results suggest the distinct possibility that the Master Rakoczi was involved at some level in the composition and translation of the Great Invocation into English. Did he collaborate with the Master Djwhal Khul in the design and translation of the Great Invocation into the English language? Did he design the Great Invocation himself and then pass it on to DK who in turn gave it to Alice Bailey? Did he consult with the Tibetan on ways of encoding certain information into it, but then have nothing to do with the actual design, translation, and final product?

No matter what his level of involvement might be, the question is whether the Master R had anything at all to do with the design and coding of information into the Great Invocation. Evidence of this may appear as similarities in technique as well as specific data, such as particular numbers, names, or symbols, related directly to Master R or his life as Francis Bacon. With these preliminary thoughts complete, let's examine more closely the background and work of the Master R and Francis Bacon.

Notes

1. Alice A. Bailey, *The Reappearance of the Christ*, 30-31.
2. Bailey, *A Treatise on White Magic*, 408.
3. Cipher is a term for a letter, number, or symbol which is substituted for the original character.
4. Alice Bailey wrote eighteen books with Djwhal Khul from 1919 until 1949, the year in which she died. Detailed information about their work together can be found in the book, *The Unfinished Autobiography*, published by Lucis Trust.
5. Edmund Harold, *Master Your Vibration*, 7.
6. Ibid., 8.
7. This is a Templar cross according to *Coil's Masonic Encylopedia*.

THE MASTER R:
ENIGMA OF THE
HIERARCHY

The work of the Master R. has always been recognised as of a peculiar nature and as concerned with the problems of civilisation.

The Externalisation of the Hierarchy, 274.

MASTER R

Of all the Masters of the Hierarchy, the Master R is one of the most mysterious and influential with respect to the growth of human civilization and culture. He appears to be the guiding force behind much of the development and direction of Western civilization for the past 1,700 years. Apparently, it was this vast experience which led to his appointment as Lord of Civilization. Although he is now the Lord of Civilization under the third ray, he was originally a Master on the seventh ray. The Tibetan offers the following:

> The Master R. is upon the seventh Ray, that of Ceremonial Magic or Order, and He works largely through esoteric ritual and ceremonial, being vitally interested in the effects, hitherto unrecognised, of the ceremonial of the Freemasons, of the various fraternities and of the Churches, everywhere. He is called in the Lodge, usually, "the Count," and in America and Europe acts practically as the general manager for the carrying out of the plans of the executive council of the Lodge.[1]

This extract from *Initiation, Human and Solar* was written between 1919 and 1922. This same idea is expanded upon in a message dated December 1919 from the book *The Externalisation of the Hierarchy*:

> As the seventh Ray of Organization and of ceremonial work is now coming into prominence and manifestation, the work of the Master on that ray is that of synthesising, on the physical plane, all parts of the plan. The Master Rakoczi takes of the general plan as it is outlined in the inner Council Chamber and approximates it to the possible. He might be regarded as acting as the General Manager for the carrying out of the plans of the executive council of the Christ.[2]

These two extracts show how the Master R, prior to his becoming Lord of Civilization, was already recognized as a pragmatic manager and implementer of the Plan in terms of physical plane manifestation of tangible results. In the later writings of Djwhal Khul, he notes the following changes:

> This shifting and interchange is taking place all the time. When, for instance, the Master R. assumed the task of Mahachohan or Lord of Civilization, His Ashram was shifted from the seventh Ray of Ceremonial Order to the third Ray of Active Intelligence.[3]

As Lord of Civilization, the Master R holds huge responsibilities in preparing a global infrastructure which transcends the old national boundaries and blockages which obstruct the free flow of trade and commerce. This third ray activity is most obviously seen in the current world economy with its international markets, global corporations, and the powerfully sophisticated communications networks spanning the globe.

In his book, *Master R: Lord of Our Civilization*, Michael Taylor suggests that St. Alban, a Gnostic Christian martyred around the year 303 A.D., was the first known appearance of the soul now identified as Master R. Mr. Taylor describes the various lives of the Master R throughout history. Most of these appear to be based on descriptions given by C.W. Leadbeater in his book *The Masters and the Path*. Here is an extract from that book:

> The Head of the Seventh Ray is the Master the Comte de St. Germain, known to history in the eighteenth century, whom we sometimes call the Master Rakoczy, as He is the last survivor of that royal house. He was Francis Bacon, Lord Verulam, in the seventeenth

century, Robertus the monk in the sixteenth, Hunyadi Janos in the fifteenth, Christian Rosenkreuz in the fourteenth, and Roger Bacon in the thirteenth; He is the Hungarian Adept of The Occult World. Further back in time He was the great Neoplatonist Proclus, and before that St. Alban.[4]

Leadbeater was not the only source of this information. DK offers the following concerning Master R:

> The Master Who concerns Himself especially with the future development of racial affairs in Europe, and with the mental out-growth in America and Australia, is the Master Rakoczi. He is a Hungarian, and has a home in the Carpathian mountains, and was at one time a well known figure at the Hungarian Court. Reference to Him can be found in old historical books, and He was particularly before the public eye when he was the Comte de St. Germain, and earlier still when he was both Roger Bacon, and later, Francis Bacon. It is interesting to note that as the Master R. takes hold, on the inner planes, of affairs in Europe, His name as Francis Bacon is coming before the public eye in the Bacon-Shakespeare controversy.[5]

With respect to the Master R, a large portion of this chapter focuses on his life as Francis Bacon due to Bacon's ingenius use of ciphers and codes during the Elizabethan era. The Shakespearean literature contains word clues and ciphers suggesting that the author of the plays may have been Francis Bacon because similar ciphers and word-play appear his own writings. This information serves our purposes by providing possible clues to Bacon's cipher styles, but it should be made clear that the Shakespeare author-ship question is not our primary concern. If some of this evidence suggests a similarity between the coding techniques found in the Great Invocation and coding techniques found in Shakespeare, then that is icing on the cake. Furthermore, the works of Shakespeare catapulted the English language to new heights with the tremendous addition of hundreds of new words. These factors in the life of Francis Bacon are indications that the Master R (through the Bacon lifetime) has experience working with words, language, and codes, not to mention Bacon's contribution to the growth of science and learning.

FRANCIS BACON[6]

If Francis Bacon's life and accomplishments are taken into account solely on the basis of his exoteric life, he was certainly a gifted individual. An entirely new dimension of possibilities opens up when his life is considered from the esoteric angle as well, for as Djwhal Khul tells us, the Master R was once Francis Bacon.

Bacon was born in London on January 22nd, 1561. His father was Sir Nicholas Bacon, a man of great integrity, and counselor to Queen Elizabeth I. His mother was Anne, daughter of Sir Anthony Cooke. Anne was very learned and skilled in both Greek and Latin. Thus, both parents were of high caliber in the social, ethical, and educational standards of the times.

In 1573, Francis was sent to Trinity College, Cambridge after receiving a strong foundational education at home. While at Trinity College he was under the tutelage of John Whitgift, who later became the archbishop of Canterbury. However, after 32 months Bacon came down with the plague which, although he survived, cut short his education at Trinity College. According to the records, he later told William Rawley, his first biographer, that his university stay created a strong dislike for Aristotle and his philosophy. This bit of information may say something about Bacon's psychospiritual development, because Aristotle's philosophy forms much of the basis of the modern Western worldview which abandons the more mystic and poetic idealism of Plato in favor of the more scientific, sense-based logic of Aristotle. If we posit the advanced spiritual development of Francis Bacon, then it is reasonable to assume that he would have an innate repulsion toward a purely left-brained approach to the universe. This is rather ironic, because Bacon became the "father of modern science" through his new approaches to scientific observation and research. If the secretive, esoteric aspect of Bacon's life is considered, however, then we see a more balanced picture of the left and right-brained, holistic philosophy of an enlightened soul.

In any event, following Francis' return from Trinity College, his father decided to send him to Paris to serve with Sir Amias Paulet, ambassador to France. Bacon stayed in Paris from 1576 to 1579. Apparently, there is sketchy information about his exact duties while in Paris, but it is presumed that he was learning statecraft and was performing diplomatic duties, such as the rudiments of coding sensitive political documents.

During his stay in Paris, Bacon's father died (1579) and he was forced to return home. Because Francis was the second son of a second marriage, his father had not settled the terms of his inheritance which left him with no land, position or income. Somehow he found the means to study law and he advanced with remarkable speed, graduating in 1582 at age twenty-one. He was so talented that he became a "bencher" or magistrate by 1586, and a "reader" or what would now be known as a professor by 1588 and a "double bencher" (Ph.D., perhaps) by 1600. In the meantime, while in the middle of his law career, Bacon had begun a career in Parliament in 1584—a political career which lasted until 1621. Thus, for most of his life, Bacon was involved in the legal and political professions at a high level.

Bacon ran afoul of Elizabeth I when he opposed in Parliament what he thought was an excessive and unfair tax. Because of his stand, Bacon's star was permanently tarnished in the queen's court. His influence in the English court did not reach its full power until James I took the throne in 1603. He was knighted in 1603, became the king's counsel in 1604, solicitor general in 1607, attorney general in 1613, privy counselor in 1616, lord keeper in 1617, and lord chancellor in 1618. Later in 1618 he took the title of baron Verulam and created viscount St. Alban in 1621. (Here may be some indication of his attraction to the former life of St. Alban.)

None of this was due to political favors alone (although as the record shows, what a difference a monarch makes), for Bacon was considered a gifted counselor by his contemporaries. His peers celebrated his great forensic skills, his memory of legal cases and procedures, and his capacity to grasp all the complexities of the issues involved. Furthermore, he was in great demand as a reporter of complicated parliamentary proceedings, where his clear thinking showed through at its best.

Despite these skills, Bacon was not his own person. He had to accede to the political demands of the English court, especially under James I. Yet, he was able to pursue an entirely different area of interest in which he did have some independence. This avocation was in science and philosophy. In spite of such a demanding public career, Bacon managed to produce a prolific body of writing in the sciences and philosophy. From 1603 to 1610 he had assembled enough research to produce the first part of his multi-volume book series, *Great Instauration* (Instauratio Magna—Great Restoration), which was entitled *The Advancement of Learning*. This was the first part of a grand work which he never completed, namely the reformation of the arts and sciences. The second part of this work took the form of his *Novum Organum*, which made Bacon famous as a scientist. It is here in this "great instauration" that we see the possibility of a seventh ray influence, because it is ray seven which restores and renews. (Recall that Master R originates on the seventh ray, but now works with the third ray as the Lord of Civilization.)

Although Francis Bacon wrote a great deal about science, it is noted by Brian Vickers that Bacon was out of touch with the scientists and theories prevalent in his time: Copernicus, Kepler, and Galileo. Vickers points out that Bacon never really understood the importance of mathematics in relation to physical laws. Instead, we see him devoting much of his life to law and to the restoration and reordering of scientific inquiry. Law was the line of least resistance for Bacon. He took to it naturally, and as we have seen, had an innate ability to recall and reason the details and complexities of legal matters with great logic. Bacon was certainly interested in science and law, but his real interest was the reformation of laws (seen in his work in Parliament and as a magistrate) and the restoration of knowledge and science to their proper place in society. Bacon states in his *Literary and Professional Works*, vol. VIII:

> ...for I have taken all knowledge to be my province; and if I could purge two sorts of rovers [misleading, confusing trends], whereof the one with frivolous disputations...and the other with blind experiments...hath committed so many spoils, I hope I should bring in industrious observations, grounded conclusions, and profitable inventions and discoveries; the best state of that province. This, whether it be curiosity, or vain glory, or nature, or (if one take it favourably) philanthropia, is so fixed in my mind as it cannot be removed.[7]

Here we see that although Bacon is interested in all knowledge, he considers it of little worth unless it is put to practical use.

The following remarks by Vickers describe the eclectic and far-reaching genius of Francis Bacon:

> [He possessed] Intellectual penetration coupled with imagination and eloquence.

> Bacon's whole lifework was one of persuasion, whether as lawyer or parliamentarian, counselor to the monarch, or advocate of the new science. He was the master rhetorician of his day.[8]

In fact, Bacon's intellectual talents were so extensive that some researchers believe he was appointed chief editor of what is now known as the King James Bible. Manly Hall quotes William T. Smedley's statement that, "It will eventually be proved that the whole scheme of the Authorized Version of the Bible was Francis Bacon's."[9]

In 1594 Bacon set to writing from memory 1,655 proverbs, quotations, metaphors, and pithy speeches in his book *Promus.* In 1624 he wrote *Apophthegms,* another similar collection. If we set aside the theory that he was the actual author of the Shakespearean literature, Bacon's most imaginative writing was the *New Atlantis.* This is an unfinished story about a utopian society which exists on an island somewhere in the Pacific Ocean. Bacon used this story to convey his ideas about future science and technology. He does this through a description of a school on this mysterious island called the "College of the Six Days' Works." It is dedicated to the study of nature and the discovery and invention of devices for the betterment of society. Bacon even describes "underground laboratories for coagulation, refrigeration, and conservation, to study that valid connection between cold and the preservation of food."[10]

Ironically, the accepted story is that Francis Bacon died of a chill while investigating the effects of cold on vegetation. The date of his death is on Easter Sunday, 1626. Some, however, dispute this date of death. Michael Taylor reports:

> Bacon was buried in a tomb at William Rawley's St. Michael's Church in St. Albans. But when the tomb was opened 100 years later by the second Lord Verulam, nothing was found, no bones, no valuables, *not even a coffin.*[11]

Taylor goes on to say that Manly P. Hall believed Bacon faked his own death so that he could go to Europe and continue working to strengthen the Freemasonic lodge. Taylor also suggests that Bacon may have secretly published the Rosicrucian literary material of the seventeenth century. In light of the influence of mystical and occult ideas on many thinkers and scholars throughout history, these are not such far-fetched ideas.

FRANCIS BACON AND SHAKESPEARE

It is not my intention to explore in detail whether or not Francis Bacon was the actual author of the Shakespearean works; however, in order to make valid comparisons between parallel coding techniques and specific numbers common to both Francis Bacon and the Great Invocation, we will briefly discuss the Bacon/Shakespeare controversy here. This will prepare the way for the various numbers and codes which we will explore later.

For this we will first turn to Manly P. Hall, who explains that there are only six examples of Shakespeare's handwriting—all signatures. These signatures are written as "Shakespere" (note the missing "a"). "The scrawling, uncertain method of their execution stamps Shakespeare as unfamiliar with the use of a pen."[12] Furthermore, although no signed manuscripts of his plays have ever been found, the *Folios* and *Quartos* are signed "William Shakespeare" with the added "a."

There is no evidence that Shakespere ever had a library nor did he leave any books in his will. The sheer scope of knowledge contained in the plays suggests that the author had to be familiar with court politics, many languages, foreign lands, cultures, and philosophies. Hall goes on to point out that various Shakespearean plays contain philosophical viewpoints that only a "Platonist, Qabbalist, or a Pythagorean" would know.[13] Hall continues by mentioning that Francis Bacon had a massive library containing the necessary books to write such information into the plays. Hall concludes his thoughts on this controversy with the following:

> Scores of volumes have been written to establish Sir Francis Bacon as the real author of the plays and sonnets popularly ascribed to William Shakespere. An impartial consideration of these documents cannot but convince the open-minded of the verisimilitude of the Baconian theory....Sir Francis Bacon, the Rosicrucian initiate, wrote into the Shakespearean plays the secret teachings of the Fraternity of R.C. (Rose Cross, JB) and the true rituals of the Freemasonic Order.[14]

Manly Hall's final remarks on Francis Bacon fit well with the account given by the Tibetan concerning the Renaissance period *circa* 1400 through Bacon's time. Hall concludes that Bacon was "...a link in that great chain of minds which has perpetuated the secret doctrine of antiquity from its beginning."[15] This remark by Hall shines a brilliant light on the claim that Francis Bacon was an initiate later to appear as the Comte de St. Germain in the eighteenth century and eventually as the Master Rakoczi.

DR. JOHN DEE

Hall's comment concerning the great chain of minds perpetuating the "secret doctrine of antiquity" can be best illustrated through the life and influence of Dr. John Dee, who may have deeply affected the development, direction, and methods of the Rosicrucians and the Freemasons of the sixteenth century. Born on July 13th, 1527, Dee (apparently a genius) was an avid student. By the age of twenty-three he had already earned degrees in science, mathematics, Master of Arts, and finally Doctor of Hermeticism, and Cabala. He became a noted teacher of cabalistic, hermetic, and magical theory—particularly relating to numbers—and having settled in Paris, was sought out by some of the greatest thinkers of Europe. Dawkins points out that Dee, after returning to England in 1551, eventually "...became associated with the proponents of religious reform at court" and met Geronimo Cardano, "a Renaissance *magus* of the highest order, who profoundly influenced Dee."[16]

Cardano himself was a tremendous thinker, a philosopher, physician, scientist, and mathematician. He wrote 131 books and developed the first treatise on the Theory of Probability. He wrote on every conceivable topic of his day, but he is best known for his stenographic system of cryptography, known as the "Cardano grille" method. This is where Bacon and his cipher knowledge enter the picture. Commenting on Cardano's cryptographic systems, Dawkins writes:

> This is an almost perfect cipher system which Dee learnt and taught to his pupils, and which Walsingham used in his Intelligence Service. This "Cardano grille" system was later adapted and improved upon by Anthony and Francis Bacon, and used in their printed works.[17]

Between 1562 and 1564, Dee traveled throughout Europe and eventually wrote *Monas Hieroglyphica*, a treatise summing up his philosophy and wisdom of accumulated knowledge. This book apparently was so advanced that it was attacked by the academicians of

the day because they did not understand it. Queen Elizabeth I, however, defended Dee's work and protected him from attack.

By 1583 Dee owned the largest and most comprehensive library
in Elizabethan England (4,000 volumes). According to Dawkins, a
study of the literary collection of Dee's library reveals the:

> major part that poetry, drama, architecture and occult mathematics
> played in the whole scheme. This cannot be stressed enough. Occult
> mathematics is really the scientific basis of Cabala, which links num-
> bers with letters (and hence geometry and numerology with language
> and culture)....
>
> Occult mathematics is the rational basis of all Gnosis, or Gnostic
> teaching, of whatever language, culture or religious teaching. It is the
> foundation that underlies and holds together, for instance, the
> Hebrew, Greek and Latin Bibles. After John Dee's and Francis
> Bacon's work was completed, this was also true of the English Bible...
>
> Dee and those directly associated with him, used cryptographic
> methods in all that they published, and in their associated pro-
> gramme to usher in a Golden Age.[18]

These extracts not only show the breadth of Dee's knowledge, but
also focus particularly on his interest and development of ciphers and
cryptographic methods which later emerge in the works of Francis
Bacon, as well as other poets, writers, and scholars of the day.

Dee formed his own academy of learning where he generated
interest in the arts and sciences. Dee's academy was at his residence,
geographically located along the Thames near the English Court, in
a place called Mortlake. Because he was often at court, many of the
courtiers were constantly found at Mortlake. According to Dawkins:
"Sir Francis Walsingham, Adrian Gilbert and Edward Dyer for
instance, constantly visited Dee, as also did the rest of the group of
scholar-poets that became known as the English Areopagus."[19]

This group of men believed they could usher in a new Golden
Age through a reformation and renaissance of the arts and sciences.
Dawkins suggests that the activities of this group headed by John
Dee and later by Francis Bacon eventually led to the formation of the
Rosicrucian Fraternity and Freemasons in England. From the infor-
mation offered by Djwhal Khul, this English movement initiated a
great part of the effort to create a global civilization and culture
which is still rapidly forming today, 500 years later. DK states:

Today, as a result of a spiritual awakening which dates from 1625 A.D., and which laid the emphasis upon a wider, general education and upon a revolt from the imposition of clerical authority, the radiation from the world of souls has greatly intensified and the Kingdom of God is becoming a corporate part of the outer world expression, and this for the first time in the long, long history of humanity.[20]

FRANCIS BACON'S MYSTERIOUS BIRTH

According to Karl F. Hollenbach in his book *Francis Rosicross*, Francis Bacon learned cryptography at the London school of Francis Walsingham, who was the Secretary of State under Elizabeth I.[21] Walsingham learned cryptography, among other things, from John Dee and thus we see the indirect (at first) influence on Bacon due to the teachings of Dee's academy. While working in the English embassy in France, Bacon began inventing his own cipher system. Some Baconians have suggested that he wanted to secretly record his own life history because of his discovery that he was the illegitimate son of Queen Elizabeth I and Robert Dudley, Earl of Leicester. This story of Bacon's birth and parentage is alleged to have come from information which Bacon himself encoded in the text of the 1623 First Folio of Shakespeare's plays. (The name "First Folio" is commonly used to describe what is actually entitled *Mr. William Shakespeare's Comedies, Histories, & Tragedies*. This is an anthology of scripts.) Although this coding theory was later disproved, it is worth mentioning here because of the persistent rumors and controversies which surrounded Elizabeth I in regard to her suitors and the political ramifications of her romantic intrigues. In any case, here is the supposed story as it was worked out by Dr. Orville W. Owen, an American cryptographer.

It seems that Elizabeth and Dudley fell in love at some point and were secretly married while they were held prisoners in the Tower of London by Mary Tudor (*circa* 1557). Robert Dudley, however, was already married at the time.

Elizabeth became queen in 1558. Two years after ascending the throne, she found herself pregnant with Dudley's child. Either through Elizabeth's order or by Dudley's own initiative, he either murdered his wife, Amy, or had her killed prior to the birth of this illegitimate child. The Queen and Dudley were then secretly married once again by Sir Nicholas Bacon with one of the two witnesses being Bacon's wife, Ann. On January 22nd, 1561 Francis was born and discreetly adopted by Sir Nicholas and Lady Ann Bacon.

Elizabeth was never to publicly acknowledge her marriage to Robert Dudley and she therefore denied the existence of any offspring, including another son named Robert who was born in 1566 and adopted by Walter Devereux, Earl of Essex. Eventually Dudley abandoned his relationship with the Queen and married Lettice Knollys, ironically the widow of Walter Devereux who had adopted his son Robert.

When Francis was approximately fifteen years of age, he was at the Queen's court with his cousin, Robert Cecil, who was twelve. Because Cecil did not like the maid, he deliberately caused a stir by shouting that the maid had said something to dishonor the Queen. When Elizabeth demanded to know what was said, Cecil related that the maid said the Queen bore a son by Robert Dudley. Infuriated, the Queen attacked the maid. Francis, upon trying to stop her, incurred the wrath of the Queen who said, "How now wilt thou forsake thy mother? Fool. Unnatural, ungrateful boy! Does it curd thy blood to hear me say I am thy mother! Trouble me no more. Speak thou not of this that thou has heard, but go. I desire thee to know no more."[22]

This incident certainly must have had a major impact on the life of Francis Bacon. If true, this knowledge was incentive enough for him to devise a method of communicating it to others and recording it in history since it was certain he could never ascend to the throne.

FRANCIS BACON AND CIPHERS

Dr. Orville W. Owen published his findings (upon which this story of Bacon's true birth was based) in his book, *Francis Bacon's Cipher Story* (1894). In it he explains what he believed to be the word cipher of Francis Bacon. As briefly explained by Taylor:

> ...the word cipher is constructed by stringing together words, lines and passages from various Elizabethan works using key words as starting points. These keywords were *Fortune, Nature, Honour, Reputation* and *Pan.*[23]

Owen's book is one source of the events related to Bacon's birth and true parentage. Later, his assistant, Elizabeth Wall Gallup, published her own findings based on Bacon's Biliteral cipher,[24] which Bacon explains in his book, *Advancement of Learning*. Gallup applied this cipher method to the First Folio of Shakespeare's plays and obtained a story similar to Dr. Owen's which tells of Bacon's confrontation with the Queen and her admission that she was his mother.

Michael Taylor explains that two of the best cryptologists who ever lived, William and Elizabeth Friedman, worked with Gallup on deciphering the messages in the First Folio, but they later found that she had made many deciphering errors. In 1957 they published their findings in *The Shakespearean Ciphers Examined*. Quoting Taylor:

> Many chapters were devoted to Gallup's deciphering, proving that she was misguided in her method. Nevertheless, the Friedmans harbored the view that it was entirely possible Bacon had planted ciphers in the First Folio. It had not yet been conclusively proven, however.[25]

Beyond the Word cipher and the Biliteral cipher there is the Sixth Line Word Cipher. This coding technique was discovered by Edward D. Johnson and published in his book, *Francis Bacon's Maze*, in 1961. According to Taylor:

> Part of this cipher however suffers from the same problem Gallup's application of the Bi-literal cipher suffers from; it cannot be duplicated. But there is one part of the cipher which works consistently and brilliantly; the acrostics (where the first or last letters of lines of type spell a word) spelling the word "Bacon."[26]

The following is a simple, but accurate example of an acrostic.

Anyone
Can see the
Really
Outstanding value of
Simplifying an example with
The
Information provided here on this
Coding technique called the "acrostic."

Note that the first letter in each line spells "acrostic." Quoting directly from the Friedmans' 1957 book, Taylor notes:

> We should not be surprised if it is claimed that acrostics appear in Shakespeare's works, for they abounded in the literature of the time; nor should we be surprised if these devices concern the authorship of the works, for they have often been used to this end. We should even be tolerant of variable and erratic spelling, for this was to some extent a common Elizabethan practice.[27]

Johnson illustrates many instances of acrostics which indicate various forms of "Bacon" in the First Folio. He explains the sixth line cipher as follows:

> He chose the sixth lines because he never missed an opportunity of showing the numerical seal or count or [sic] the name Bacon, which is 33. When planning the lay out of the First Folio he decided that each full column should contain 66 lines, as 66 is double 33, and the number 33 represents his name. Looking at the number six six he though [sic] it would be a good idea to insert cipher messages in the sixth line counting down and the sixth line counting up the columns, but as this would not give him sufficient scope he decided also to use the sixth lines counting up or down from the entrance or exit of a character or a stage direction, and also the sixth lines counting up or down from the beginning or end of a scene, and it will be found that this is the method that he adopted.[28]

Johnson has discovered at least twenty-two instances of Francis Bacon's name appearing in the First Folio. These examples along with many other coded messages are illustrated in his book, *Francis Bacon's Maze*. The following is one acrostic example of a sixth line cipher found in the first column of page 106 of the *Comedies (Much Ado About Nothing)* in the First Folio. This illustrates the use of lines to spell Bacon, his initial "f" and the word "pig."

```
Ba   6  BAssage to the PIGmies, rather than hould three words
con  5  CONference with this harpy, you have no employment
F    4  For me.
     3  None but to desire your company
     2  O good [sic. God] sir heeres a dish I love not I cannot in-
     1  dure this Lady tongue. EXIT[29]
```

In his book *The Second Cryptographic Shakespeare*, Penn Leary offers an extract from Bacon's *Advancement and Proficience of Learning*, Book VI:

> Wherefore let us come to CYPHARS. Their kinds are many as, *Cyphars* simple; *Cyphars intermixt with Nulloes*, or non-significant Characters; *Cyphars of double Letters under one Character; Wheele-Cyphars; Kay-Cyphars; Cyphars of words; Others.*[30]

Some of these cipher systems will be explained in chapter 3, as they relate very closely to the esoteric numerology method used in *Sacred Vessel of the Mysteries*.

MASTER R AND CURRENT LITERATURE

There is little known literature directly related to the Master R. The book noted earlier, *Master R: Lord of Our Civilization*, by Michael Taylor is an overview of the lives lived by Master R. According to Taylor, many of these lives were disclosed by various esoteric groups such as the Rosicrucians, Freemasons, and the Theosophical Society.[31] Taylor adds to the list by claiming that Carl Jung, Jr. and his grandfather Carl Jung, Sr. were both incarnations of Master R.

Master R: Lord of Our Civilization is worth reading just for the information provided about Francis Bacon alone. The other chapters of the book are very interesting as they give a panoramic view of the tremendous scope of experience garnered by the Master R during his lifetimes, to say nothing of the contribution he made to Western civilization and even the entire world. Each must judge the authenticity of this information for himself, but Taylor does a good job linking various clues and characteristics which form a chain of similarities from the life of St. Alban in 303 A.D. to Carl Jung, Jr. in the twentieth century. Michael Taylor describes these clues in the following paragraph:

> Proclus was exiled from Athens for a year for his "occult" and "pagan" beliefs. This echoed the Master R's past and foreshadowed his future. Saint Alban died standing up for his beliefs, while Roger Bacon was imprisoned for many years standing by his convictions. Proclus was a poet as well as a philosopher. He wrote hymns to the goddess of Poetic Inspiration, Pallas Athena for instance. Pallas Athena also known as the Spear-shaker, was Francis Bacon's muse in Elizabethan times. Bacon used the pen-name "Shakespeare"

because of his link to Pallas Athena. The philosophy of Proclus, untainted by partisan matters of doctrine, attempted to be a universal system to explain all phenomena, natural and spiritual. This work by Proclus foreshadowed attempts by Roger Bacon, Christian Rosencreutz and Francis Bacon to achieve exactly the same goal.[32]

Some of the source material upon which Michael Taylor bases his information comes from Peter Dawkins of Great Britain who has written on various esoteric subjects including Francis Bacon and the Master R. Of particular interest is his book in two parts entitled *The Master*. One of the primary sources of information for our study is a poem Dawkins wrote which he believes was directly inspired by the Master R. This poem is titled "A Word From the Master" and it is shown below exactly as it appears in *The Master*, Part 1:

> My name is a mask.
> I am one yet more than one.
> My name is a cipher: it is "1.9." and "9.3.".
> C.R.C. is an epigram.
> Saint-Germain is a pseudonym.
> My life is my own, yet my life is that of all souls,
> a parable of what is, what was and what may be.
> My life is my work and my love.
> I cannot name myself,
> as the intention of my work is that you should seek,
> and by seeking discover me,
> and by discovering me, know me.
> My essence is Silence, like the voiceless fragrance of a Rose.
> Who can name Silence?[33]

Mr. Dawkins shares many valuable insights into the mystery of the Master R, while at the same time providing corroborating quotes by Djwhal Khul such as the following, which he takes from *The Externalisation of the Hierarchy*, p. 274:

The work of the Master R has always been recognised as of a peculiar nature and as concerned with the problems of civilisation, just as the work of the Christ, the Master of all the Masters, is concerned with the spiritual development of humanity, and the work of the Manu is occupied with the science of divine government, with politics and law.[34]

Dawkins comments that:

The foundation for the Master R's work as Lord of Civilisation was laid chiefly during his incarnation as Francis Bacon—an incarnation which to some extent parallels that of Jesus of Nazareth, both of them anchoring an Avataric impulse in the world whilst undertaking the initiation of Crucifixion; hence the importance of that Baconian life and the extraordinary work accomplished then.[35]

Dawkins makes the point that the name "Francis" means "free" and thus refers to the Freemasons which Bacon headed in England during his time. Dawkins paraphrases Leadbeater as saying "that in Co-Freemasonry the Master R is referred to as 'the Head of All True Freemasons throughout the world.'" Dawkins quotes the following from Leadbeater's *The Hidden Side of Freemasonry*:

[The preservation of the ritual and symbols of Freemasonry] was always in the hands of the Chohan of the Seventh Ray, for that is the ray most especially connected with the ceremonial of all kinds, and its Head was always the supreme Hierophant of the Mysteries of ancient Egypt. The present holder of that office is the Master of Wisdom of whom we often speak as the Comte de St. Germain. He is also sometimes called Prince Rakoczi, as he is the last survivor of that royal house. Exactly when he was appointed to the Headship of the Ceremonial Ray I do not know, but he took a keen interest in Freemasonry as early as the third century AD. We find him at that period as Albanus, a man of noble Roman family, born at the town of Verulum in England.[36]

The latter part of this extract shows how this master soul we now call the Master R, when incarnated as Francis Bacon, somehow felt a connection to Albanus. Bacon expressed this outwardly by taking the title of baron Verulam in 1618 and creating the title viscount St. Alban in 1621.

In Part 1 of *The Master*, Peter Dawkins discusses the various lives of the Master R, but especially focuses on his life as Christian Rosicross (C.R.C.) and Saint Germain. (As you can see, these are the only two names revealed in the poem from Master R.) We will not go into great detail in regard to these two lives except as they relate to certain clues found in the Great Invocation. Of these two, C.R.C. is the most pertinent due to the symbolism associated with the rose and the cross. Both of these symbols emerged in the research associated with the Great Invocation and published in my earlier book.

As for St. Germain, he was one of the most mysterious and influential figures of the eighteenth century who suddenly "appeared in the diplomatic circles of Europe" according to Manly Hall. Hall describes him as "...the most baffling personality of history—a man whose life was so near a synonym of mystery that the enigma of his true identity was as insolvable to his contemporaries as it has been to later investigators."[37]

Comte St. Germain seems to have been an expert in almost every field of knowledge of his day. He was an artist, linguist, and historian (claiming memory of lives and events going back 2,000 years). He was a chemist and master politician. It is historically known that he traveled extensively, including Russia and Persia, and used many different names in order to protect his true identity. Many countries of Europe employed him as a secret agent and he carried credentials which allowed him free access to the highest political and royal circles of Europe. Beyond all this, it is said that he had an uncanny psychic ability and was a follower and practitioner of Eastern esotericism. He was a member of the Masons, and associated with the highest ranking and most respected Masons of his day, some of whom founded the United States of America.

St. Germain may have appeared in America as a mysterious professor who influenced both Washington and Franklin (both Masons and perhaps Rosicrucians) in the design of the American flag. The story of the old professor's influence on the design of the American flag appears in *Our Flag* (1890) by Robert Allen Campbell. In another incident, reported by Manly Hall in his book *The Secret Destiny of America*, a stranger (the old professor, St. Germain?) appeared in the balcony of Independence Hall in Philadelphia to rally the wavering colonial leaders to sign the Declaration of Independence. After a rousing speech which inspired the founding fathers to rush forward and sign the Declaration of Independence, the stranger is said to have mysteriously vanished[38]

Finally, in regard to St. Germain, Hall says the following: "The Comte de St. Germain and Sir Francis Bacon are the two greatest emissaries sent into the world by the Secret Brotherhood in the last thousand years."[39]

Apparently the Master R continues his work in various ways

including that of teaching the Ageless Wisdom. During the period from the late 1950's into the 60's, a woman named Lucille Cedarcrans was receiving and teaching a stream of the Ageless Wisdom which purportedly came mainly and directly from the Master R. These instructions formed a series of courses which were originally intended to form a curriculum of the Wisdom to be taught in a physical school setting. This never came about, although Cedarcrans traveled to various parts of the United States to spread this work of the Hierarchy.

The series of courses taught by Cedarcrans and her students were not put into book form and not commercially available until May of 1993 with the publication of *Nature of the Soul*, a forty lesson course in the Ageless Wisdom. This was made possible by the publisher, Wisdom Impressions, which according to the copyright page of *Nature of the Soul*, "is a loosely-organized group of students and teachers of The Wisdom."

According to these teachings, three Masters in the Hierarchy, namely Morya, Djwhal Khul, and Rakoczi formed a new Ashram at some point after World War II in order to take advantage of the cyclic return of the seventh ray and the beginning of the Aquarian Age. In 1997 Wisdom Impressions published a booklet entitled *The Synthetic Ashram*. We read the following:

> ...Three major ray energies...have been brought together into a synthesis in the creation of the Ashram....[This] Ashram is held in focus by the Master M., the Master D.K., and the Master R. with the aid of certain initiating disciples taken from the Ashram of each (that is, the First ray Ashram, the Second ray Ashram and the Seventh ray Ashram)...In its subjective reality within the field of Hierarchical activity it has been created, as you know, by the focused effort of the Masters D.K., M., and myself.[40]

It is obvious from the above wording that the Master R is conveying the information in this booklet. Further evidence of the creation of a new ashram from an entirely different source is found in the book, *The Externalisation of the Hierarchy*:

> April-May 1946
> I have delayed writing my usual Wesak message until this late date because of a certain event of the Hierarchy which was maturing and which necessitated my entire attention. This event was connected with

the Wesak Festival and involved among other matters the formation of a new Ashram in which the Wisdom aspect would be of particular importance and not the Love aspect....This Ashram, when duly formed and established, will enable the Members of the Hierarchy to respond to this aspect of the divine Purpose—the Purpose which as you know lies behind and implements the Plan; this Ashram, related to the Buddha, will be specifically under the close supervision of the Christ, and also of the Lord of Civilisation—at this time the Master R. They are the only two Members of the Hierarchy able to register the divine Purpose (in regard to its immediate objectives) in such a manner that the entire Hierarchy can be informed and can then work unitedly and intelligently at its implementation.[41]

This extract not only corroborates the statement by Master R in the Cedarcrans material, but also it makes clear the high spiritual attainment of Master R by pointing out that only he and the Christ are able to register the immediate objectives of the divine Purpose.

This completes what I have been able to gather about the cooperative work between the Master R and the Master DK in the twentieth century. It is a continuation of that Hierarchical plan initiated in 1400 A.D. which will extend into the future through the newly created Synthetic or Wisdom Ashram. The Master R states that the Synthetic Ashram "is now moving into the responsibilities which it will assume fully at the turn of the century and carry over a 2500 year period."[42]

Notes

1. Alice A. Bailey, *Initiation, Human and Solar*, 58-9.
2. Alice A. Bailey, *The Externalisation of the Hierarchy*, 507-8.
3. Alice A. Bailey, *Discipleship in the New Age*, vol. II, 383.
4. C. W. Leadbeater, *The Masters and the Path*, 269
5. Bailey, *Initiation, Human and Solar*, 58.
6. Ian Scott Kilvet, ed., *British Writers*, vol 1. Essay by Brian Vickers, "Francis Bacon."
7. Ibid., 264-5.
8. Ibid, 264.
9. Manly P. Hall, *The Secret Teaching of All Ages*, 166.
10. Vickers, 268.
11. Michael Taylor, *Master R: Lord of Our Civilization*, 77.
12. Hall, *The Secret Teaching of All Ages*, 165.
13. Ibid., 165.
14. Ibid., 166.
15. Ibid., 168.

16. Peter Dawkins, *Arcadia*, 89.
17. Ibid., 89
18. Ibid., 93, 94.
19. Ibid., 98. The term Areopagus was adopted by Bacon and others in his intellectual circle to signify the hill in ancient Greece where tribunals were held.
20. Bailey, *Discipleship in the New Age*, vol. II, 407.
21. Karl F. Hollenbach, *Francis Rosicross*, 75.
22. Ibid., 71.
23. Taylor, *Master R: Lord of Our Civilization*, 96.
24. This is a cipher system based on various combinations of the letters A and B.
25. Ibid., 99-100.
26. Ibid., 100.
27. Ibid., 100.
28. Edward D. Johnson, *Francis Bacon's Maze*, 1.
29. Ibid., 4.
30. Penn Leary, *The Second Cryptographic Shakespeare*, 123.
31. Taylor, *Master R: Lord of Our Civilization*, 9.
32. Ibid., 21-22.
33. Dawkins, *The Master*, part 1, 19.
34. Ibid., 10.
35. Ibid., 9-10.
36. Ibid., 8.
37. Hall, *The Secret Teaching of All Ages*, 199.
38. Hall, *The Secret Destiny of America*, 164-72.
39. Hall, *The Secret Teaching of All Ages*, 200.
40. Lucille Cedarcrans, *The Synthetic Ashram*, 1, 2.
41. Bailey, *The Externalisation of the Hierarchy*, 541.
42. Cedarcrans, *The Synthetic Ashram*, 1.

CIPHERS AND NUMBERS

The work of the Buddha is expressed in words all beginning with the fourth letter of the alphabet, the letter D....
The work of the Christ is expressed for us in words beginning with the ninth letter of the alphabet, the letter I...
These things happen not idly but all have their underlying purpose.

The *Externalisation of the Hierarchy*, 413.

The previous chapters have laid the groundwork for the theory that the soul known as Francis Bacon later evolved to become a member of the spiritual Hierarchy and is now known as the Master R. Taking this idea as a working hypothesis, we must ask what it is that links the life of Francis Bacon to the symbolic use of coding in the Great Invocation. The answer is cryptography, because it is a known historical fact that Francis Bacon studied cryptography and incorporated number codes, anagrams, and other literal devices in his writing. In fact, this is the basis of the Baconians' belief that he wrote the Shakespeare material, for in that massive body of literature are many anagrams and number codes spelling the names "Bacon" and "Francis," among other details related to Bacon's life. Therefore, if Bacon later became the Master R, it is reasonable to theorize that the talent and interest in cryptography, wordplay, and veiling techniques continue to play a part in the writing and teaching methods of Master R.

This premise is vitally important to our study because, if the

Master R aided in the design and wording of the Great Invocation in some way, then evidence of his style, unique methods of wordplay, and enciphering techniques might be detectable. These can be thought of collectively as Master R's particular "trademark."

A further twist to all this is the distinct possibility that the Tibetan may have known Master R in a previous lifetime in England. In her autobiography, Alice Bailey reports the following:

> The Tibetan's style has improved over the years. He dictated a cumbersome, poor English in the beginning, but between us we have managed to work out a style and presentation which is suited to the great truths which it is His function to reveal, and mine and my husband's to bring to the attention of the public.[1]

The reason DK was dictating such a cumbersome English is revealed in his own words in the following extract. It appears in a series of published letters to a group of students which are collected in two volumes entitled *Discipleship in the New Age*:

> To R. A. J.
> August 1940
>
> MY BROTHER AND MY FRIEND:
>
> For you, as for all disciples at this time of world crisis, life has been exceedingly difficult. This is not a platitudinous truism—in spite of A.A.B. remarking sub rosa that it was. She knows me so well that for years her comments have proved a source of amusement to me and sometimes have proved most helpful in aiding me to understand the occidental mind. I am an Oriental of the fourth root race and although I have had two European incarnations I still at times fail to grasp or understand the occidental reaction.[2]

It is altogether possible that at least one of these incarnations was in England during the Elizabethan era. There is some evidence in the Tibetan's own writing to suggest this. Although his English is based on the vocabulary available in Alice Bailey's memory (later nineteenth to middle twentieth century English), "strange" usages appear to slip through now and then through the use of such words as "anent," "e'en," and "oft" to name just three examples.

According to Webster's, "anent" means concerning or regarding. It is a Middle English word derived from Old English in the form of "onefn" and the present form "anent" is considered an obscure term.

The word "e'en" is the literary use of the word "even." It is normally found in poems and lyrics. The word "oft" is the original form of often and is traced to Middle English, *circa* 1100 to 1500. Now the interesting part: a search of the CD ROM of the entire collection of Djwhal Khul's dictated books and Alice Bailey's personally authored books reveals the following facts.

The word "anent" appears 543 times. Every use of this word is by the Tibetan. Alice Bailey never used it once. The word appears in *The Unfinished Autobiography* one time; not in the story Alice writes, but in the appendix in an article on page 256 written by Djwhal Khul entitled "My Work." The word "e'en" appears 57 times. Again, it is never used by Alice Bailey, only by the Tibetan. Finally, the word "oft" is used 359 times and again, never by Mrs. Bailey.

It is natural to surmise that these British words are simply coming from Alice Bailey's own brain and for some unknown reason she did not use these words in her own books. If this were the case, however, then why is the British word "whilst" used 638 times by *both* Alice Bailey and the Tibetan? A search of the CD ROM indicates that "whilst" was used 89 times in the books which Alice Bailey wrote (6) and 549 times in the Tibetan's books which Alice Bailey recorded for him (18). (Note that this total of 549 is very close to the 543 uses of "anent" as shown above.) If all these words in question were simply coming from Alice Bailey herself, then there should be no distinction between their use by either the Tibetan or Alice Bailey. One has to wonder why these obscure and outmoded English words are used strictly by DK and not Alice Bailey. Despite the fact that these are "cumbersome," old and poetic English words, the odds seem to favor AAB using them more than Djwhal Khul—*unless one (or both) of his European incarnations was in England.*

Perhaps the Tibetan was a student of Bacon's at that time and learned cryptographic techniques from him, or even from Dr. John Dee who taught Bacon and others in his circle. Perhaps Djwhal Khul was John Dee. This is all speculation of course, but the important point here is that there is more than anecdotal information connecting the Tibetan to the Elizabethan era—there is actually hard data to back up this idea. Most importantly, this data is provided by Djwhal Khul himself. Therefore, it is quite possible that the Master DK and the Master R worked together in England and that they both have a knowledge of ciphers. The important point to bear in mind is that DK has had only two experiences in the West, while the Master R has had many, most notably as Francis Bacon, perhaps the greatest mind of the Elizabethan era.

Based on the information provided in chapter 2 linking Bacon with cryptography and the clever use of wordplay and the fact that the Great Invocation is loaded with numeric symbolism, it is logical to conjecture that Master R may have been involved to some degree in designing and structuring the English translation of the Great Invocation. If so, are there any written documents available, either from Francis Bacon or the Master R, which can be used to test this theory? Yes, there are. That material will be offered in chapter 4.

As already explained, evidence of the claim that Master R was once Francis Bacon has been gathered from at least two sources. Additionally, information suggesting he was the actual author of the Shakespearean literature, a Rosicrucian, and a Freemason comes from several other sources. These latter sources test their theories by examining ciphers and codes placed in various writings. Many of those writings come directly from what is commonly referred to as the First Folio of Shakespeare, published in 1623, and others come from the *Sonnets*. (By good fortune I came across a newly published [1998] facsimile edition of the First Folio just prior to beginning the writing of this book, and I have been able to personally examine the coded passages cited by some of these authors.) Besides these literary writings by Bacon/Shakespeare, Peter Dawkins has published "A Word from the Master" (Master R) mentioned previously. I will compare the material related to Shakespeare and the poem published by Mr. Dawkins to the Great Invocation to determine if any ciphers, number clues, or word clues exist which mark the presence of the Master R's influence.

The Great Invocation will be used as the benchmark to test the Bacon, Shakespeare, and Master R writings (which may contain codes and other hidden messages) since it contains so many symbolic number codes and combinations suggesting deliberate design and enciphering. The comparative testing includes specific numbers, phrases, words, symbols, and methods reflecting similarity of conceptual style. Some examples are:

- Use of the midpoint of a particular writing (the middle word, for example) in order to convey an important idea.

- A pattern of recurring numbers.
- Any ciphers, numbers, or words in one writing which also appear in, or suggest a reference to another of the writings.

MODERN ENGLISH GEMATRIA

Gematria, which originated with the Hebrews and Greeks, is a method of converting letters to numbers and numbers to letters in order to code specific information into words. They did not have number symbols in their writing system, so they employed the letters of their respective alphabets to communicate numeric values. This created a unique situation in which the words of their languages innately represented numeric values. The theory of gematria is that these values are intimately connected with the meanings of the words themselves. Consequently, words of equal value were (and are) believed to have a close correspondence on a subjective level, even though the two words may have opposite or contradictory meanings in the literal sense. (Using English, rather than Hebrew or Greek, I applied this system of gematria to the Great Invocation in *Sacred Vessel*. In two of his books Djwhal Khul employs a similar process of letter/number evaluation which he terms "esoteric numerology."[3])

Modern languages use number symbols in addition to alphabets, so gematria today does not work in exactly the same manner as in the ancient Hebrew and Greek systems. However, there is some evidence suggesting that letters and the patterns they form in the production of language have some inner corresponding connection not apparent on the surface or in the literal sense. These patterns are based on the numeric value assigned to the letters of a particular alphabet.

Languages are based on specific patterns of speech. The letters comprising the alphabets of languages appear in a set order and therefore, the letter elements can be ranked, from 1 to n. In English this means that the letters are ranked from 1 to 26. Thus, when words are constructed and built into sentences, not only are there letter patterns present, but number patterns as well. Someone with the genius of Francis Bacon could very possibly create word patterns in both beautiful and logical sequences while simultaneously conveying hidden meanings based on the number patterns and totals formed from those very words or phrases.

At the level of consciousness and knowledge attained by Master

R or Master DK, it is altogether possible that they have access to special knowledge, as well as the mental capacity to structure word forms in such a way that particular messages, connections, correspondences, and layered meanings can be conveyed to those who have the keys to unlock the doors. I believe there are many keys and many doors of access. One particular sentence or phrase may possess several keys for unlocking doors to various levels. Access to these keys and their proper use depend on the spiritual development and *mental* dexterity of the one who approaches the door.

The Great Invocation represents several doors. Door one is made up of words conveying a world prayer of great potency and inspiration. Door two is made up of the meanings of those words as understood by esoteric students. Door three provides access to the inner teachings hidden within the words of the prayer. This is the door which has been opened in *Sacred Vessel of the Mysteries*. It was the key of numbers which unlocked it and we will use the same key in this book. A fourth door exists which leads to the mysteries of sound and rhythm. The key to this door remains hidden.

Table 3.1 contains the values assigned to the alphabet using the Alpha Number (AN) method, a term coined by William Eisen, author of various books on the use of gematria in English.

Table 3.1. Modern AN Values.

A	1	N	14
B	2	O	15
C	3	P	16
D	4	Q	17
E	5	R	18
F	6	S	19
G	7	T	20
H	8	U	21
I	9	V	22
J	10	W	23
K	11	X	24
L	12	Y	25
M	13	Z	26

To find the AN value for the word "NUMBER," look up each letter in table 3.1 and find the total by adding the values of letters together. The letter values are shown here as: 14 (N) + 21 (U) + 13 (M) + 2 (B) + 5 (E) + 18 (R) = 73. So, the word "NUMBER" has an AN value of 73.

Another conversion technique is called the RAN method, which means "reduced alpha numbers." This simply means that all the letters of the alphabet are reduced to single digits when used to find the value of a given word. Table 3.2 illustrates the RAN values of the alphabet.

Table 3.2. Modern RAN Values.

1	2	3	4	5	6	7	8	9
A	B	C	D	E	F	G	H	I
J	K	L	M	N	O	P	Q	R
S	T	U	V	W	X	Y	Z	

These values are the ones most often employed in numerology, but not so much in gematria. The difference is not in the values themselves, but in the process of reducing a number to its single digit value or root value. Gematria does not reduce words, phrases, etc. to root values because this process limits the results to only the digits 1 through 9 and therefore, eradicates the distinctive value of a given word or phrase. In other words, standard numerology's nine fundamental categories of meaning are too general to find significant correspondences between specific words and phrases. Thousands of words have the root value of 5, but far less have the value of 176, which reduces to a 5 (1 + 7 + 6 = 14, 1 + 4 = 5). In any event, table 3.2 shows the values of the alphabet using the RAN method.

As can be seen in table 3.2, the letter J now equals 1 instead of 10, as in table 3.1, because the 1 and 0 have been added together reducing the value of the letter J to 1. Using this method for the word "NUMBER" yields a different total: 5 (N) + 3 (U) + 4 (M) + 2 (B) + 5 (E) + 9 (R) = 28 (RAN).

In addition to the fact that the two methods result in different totals, 73 AN and 28 RAN respectively, both these totals can ultimately be reduced to their root value, which in this case is 1. This is done as follows: AN value 73, 7 + 3 = 10, 1 + 0 = 1 and RAN value 28, 2 + 8 = 10, 1 + 0 = 1. Even though the word "number" has a root value of 1, it also has a value of 73 and 28 depending on the method used to convert it.

An important point to remember is that although standard numerology reduces all words to their root values, in our analysis a word or phrase can be expressed and compared in its AN, RAN or root value form. The exception to this rule is when a word results in a total of 11 or 22. Then the number is not reduced any further. Therefore, 11 does not become 2 and 22 is not reduced to 4; they remain 11 and 22 and are called master numbers. A summary of these methods follows using several different words as examples:

Number—AN value 73.
Root value 1—7 + 3 = 10, 1 + 0 = 1.
Number—RAN value 28.
Root value 1—2 + 8 = 10, 1 + 0 = 1.

Christ—AN value 77.
Root value 5—7 + 7 = 14, 1 + 4 = 5.
Christ—RAN value 32.
Root value 5—3 + 2 = 5.

Will—AN value 56.
Root value 11—5 + 6 = 11.
Will—RAN value 20.
Root value 2—2 + 0 = 2.

ELIZABETHAN GEMATRIA METHODS

Three other gematria systems will also be applied in this investigation. These systems were the ones used by Francis Bacon and others during his lifetime. They were referred to as cipher systems and are identified in that way by the researchers who investigate these Elizabethan coding methods. (Although we will use the term cipher more than gematria when referring to these older techniques, they are all essentially gematria.) They are actually identical in concept to the AN and RAN methods except for the fact that the Elizabethan English alphabet was shorter than our modern one.

The system referred to most often in the material which forms the basis of this study is called the Elizabethan Simple Cipher (ESC) and is based on twenty-four letters. The English alphabet in Elizabethan times consisted of only twenty-four letters because there was no J and U. For example, the word JOSEPH as known today would have appeared as IOSEPH in Elizabethan English. Again, the word ADVENTURER as seen here actually appeared as ADVENTVRER in Bacon's time, the second V serving as our present day U. The letter V thus served double duty as both a "v" sound and "oo" or "yoo" sound. Confusing matters even more, the lower case letter "v" was printed as a "u," but it was still a "v." An example of this usage follows. It is taken from Ben Johnson's dedication to the author of the First Folio in which it appears.

Figure 3.1.Elizabethan Use of U and V.[4]

To the memory of my beloued,
The AVTHOR
Mr. William Shakespeare:

As this illustration shows, the letter "v" in "beloved" is printed as our modern day letter "u" in lower case. Yet in the word "author," typeset in upper case, the "u" is printed as our modern "V." The good news about this is that we do not need to use this instance very much in our examination of Elizabethan writings. It is mentioned here in order to alert the reader to the differences between modern and Elizabethan methods of using the English language.

It is also difficult to sort out the various uses of these two letters in the original facsimiles because in Elizabethan times, there were no universally accepted spelling rules as found in modern English. Despite this, it is obvious from various examples that the letters I and V were performing a dual role in particular words. Therefore, the number values assigned to the Elizabethan alphabet for the purposes of creating ciphers appear in the following four tables.

It should be noted that the modern and Elizabethan gematria methods illustrated in these two sections are referred to in cryptography as "substitution" ciphers; numbers are substituted for letters in order to derive word and phrase values.

Table 3.3. ESC AN Values.

A	1	N	13
B	2	O	14
C	3	P	15
D	4	Q	16
E	5	R	17
F	6	S	18
G	7	T	19
H	8	V	20
I	9	W	21
K	10	X	22
L	11	Y	23
M	12	Z	24

Table 3.3 contains the letters and values of the "Elizabethan Simple Cipher" (ESC). Take note of how similar this cipher is to that of the Alpha Number (AN) method shown in table 3.1. The only difference between the two is the addition of the letters J and U in their respective locations in the modern English alphabet and the consequent adjustment of the numbers assigned to the letters.

Just as modern English has an AN and RAN gematria scheme, it is possible to do the same with the Elizabethan alphabet. The ESC system employing RAN values appears in table 3.4

Table 3.4. ESC RAN Values.

1	2	3	4	5	6	7	8	9
A	B	C	D	E	F	G	H	I
K	L	M	N	O	P	Q	R	S
T	V	W	X	Y	Z			

Another cipher used by Francis Bacon (and others) is called the Elizabethan Reverse Cipher (ERC) as seen in table 3.5. This particular method plays a smaller role in our investigation than that of the ESC method.

Table 3.5. ERC Values.

A	24	N	12
B	23	O	11
C	22	P	10
D	21	Q	9
E	20	R	8
F	19	S	7
G	18	T	6
H	17	V	5
I	16	W	4
K	15	X	3
L	14	Y	2
M	13	Z	1

The final example of ciphers associated with Francis Bacon is called the Rosicrucian Kay Cipher (RKC). (Like the previous ERC, this system does not play as large a role as the ESC.) The origin of this name will become clear in the following explanation which comes from Hollenbach:

> Woodward stated that a Baconian friend, W.E. Clifton, discovered the Kay Cipher after noticing that the letter "K" was the first letter requiring two figures (10) in the Simple Cipher (where A=1, B=2, etc.) and realized the difficulty of using the Simple Cipher for continuous figures, as some letters would require one figure and others two. For example:
>
> 1223 might mean - A,B,B,C or 12, 23 meaning - M, Y.
>
> In The Repertorie of Records, published in 1631, Clifton discovered alphabetical listings of chests in which records had been placed. In accordance with the 24 letter Elizabethan alphabet, the 24th chest was under the letter "Z." The 25th was under "&," the 26th under "E," and the 27th, curiously, under a small "a." This suggested to Mr. Clifton that the letter "A" was to be numbered 27 in the Kay Cipher and the numbering (28, 29, etc.) continued through the 9th letter "I." Thus, all letters in the Kay Cipher are represented by a two digit number.[5]

Applying the cipher system which Clifton discovered, the Elizabethan alphabet corresponds to the number values shown in table 3.6 which became known as the Rosicrucian Kay Cipher.

Table 3.6. RKC Values.

K	10	X	22
L	11	Y	23
M	12	Z	24
N	13	A	27
O	14	B	28
P	15	C	29
Q	16	D	30
R	17	E	31
S	18	F	32
T	19	G	33
V	20	H	34
W	21	I	35

NOTE: AN and RAN labels applied to any words or phrases in the text always refer to the modern English values shown in tables 3.1 and 3.2 respectively.

Elizabethan English gematria is always labeled ESC. All ESC number results are based on the AN values shown in table 3.3. No AN label will appear with ESC results. ESC RAN values will be labeled as such.

All ERC and RKC methods are based on the values shown in their respective tables and are labeled either ERC or RKC.

OTHER CIPHER METHODS

In addition to the systems enumerated in this chapter, there are several other methods which Bacon employed to code information into his writing. They are straightforward and require little explanation. (Note that most of these techniques were not unique to Francis Bacon, and were used by various writers and government officials of that era.) The first method is the capitalization of particular words in order to alert those "in the know" that an important bit of information is being communicated. This is sometimes used in the form of acronyms, such as in Masonry, where T.G.A.O.T.U. stands for The Grand Architect of the Universe. If this item appeared in Elizabethan Simple Cipher (ESC) it would appear as the number line—19.7.1.14.19.20. Furthermore, because this number line equals 80 when added together, the number 80 might be inserted into certain writings as a code to other Masons. This is purely an example of possible coding techniques and not meant to be taken as actual.

Another technique involved placing particularly important words on page numbers or line numbers which equaled the value (or multiples of the value) of the important word, phrase, or sentence itself. This is a technique often cited in the works of Shakespeare and an example will be given here shortly.

The final two methods involve the use of hyphenation and italics. The following illustration demonstrates and also includes some of the other methods mentioned above. These come from a fascinating booklet by Edward D. Johnson entitled *Bacon-Shakespeare Coincidences.*

> In the first column of page 53 in the *Histories* (Henry IV, Part 1, end of Act 1, and beginning of Act 2) we find the word Bacon spelt with a capital B on the 48th line. If we count all the spoken words from the top until we come to this word Bacon we find that BACON is the 371st spoken word. In this column are seven italic words, and fifty-three (the page number) multiplied by seven is also 371. It will be found that on the 25th line are two words, "Heigh ho," but there is a hyphen between them to make them count as one word, and that on the 44th line are two words "Chamber lye," but there is a hyphen between them to make them count as one word. If there had been no hyphen between Heigh and Ho and between Chamber and lye, the word Bacon would not have been the 371st word and it would not have borne the same number as the page number multiplied by the italic words in the column.[6]

Using information about Bacon's possible authorship of the Shakespeare literature as a reference point, I have applied Bacon's numbers and techniques to the numbers and symbols found in the investigation of the Great Invocation. Additionally, I have analyzed the poem "A Word from the Master" which supposedly comes from the Master R and was recorded by Peter Dawkins. I have applied the numeric information from that poem to numeric information about the Great Invocation and to particular numbers important to Francis Bacon. In fact, I have compared various factors from all three sources (Bacon/Shakespeare literature, Peter Dawkins' poem, and the Great Invocation) to find out if there are any correspondences suggesting a common influence.

This is done in several ways, such as counting the numbers of words in various writings, looking for peculiar capitalizations, and examining the numeric order of a word in the literary work in question. Each location in the numeric order is called a word-position. In *Sacred Vessel* I used an analytical technique on the words and letters of the Great Invocation which involved counting the number of words and letters of the prayer. The result of this process revealed that there are 113 words and 443 letters comprising the Great Invocation.

Armed with this simple piece of information, I assigned a number to each word of the Great Invocation according to its order of appearance in the prayer. Thus, the first word "From" was assigned word-position 1, the second word "the" was assigned word-position 2 and so on to the end, with the last word "Earth" being assigned word-position 113. Whenever a *word-position* is mentioned in our study, it means the relative position of that particular word in the Great Invocation according to its position in the prayer. This technique is also applied to the writings attributed to Francis Bacon and Master R.

In addition to the word-position value, there is the actual gematria or numerological value of that word. For instance, using the word "From" in the example above, we know it is the first word of the Great Invocation. As a result it is assigned the word-position value of 1. In addition, it also has an alpha number (AN) value of 52. This is its gematria value. In the latter part of the book I will apply what I call the "Essence Value" to the investigation. The Essence Value is the word-position value plus the gematria value. Hence, the word "From" has an Essence Value of 53 because its word-position value is 1 and its AN value is 52 (1 + 52 = 53). The Essence Value can be based on the AN, RAN, or root value of any word plus its word-position value.

In analyzing the Great Invocation, I saw the words as a set of symbolic units which could be arranged or grouped in order to express metaphysical concepts. For instance, the middle aspect of the Christian trinity is the Son or Christ, the other two being the Father and the Holy Spirit. Using this principle, I divided the words of the Great Invocation into three parts. Symbolically, I wanted to find the middle word or heart of the Great Invocation. The middle word is found at word-position 57. That word is "is." (Statistically, this middle word-position is called the median.) This also means that there are 56 words before the middle word and 56 words after it. We can view this as 56 + 1 + 56 = 113.

One of the intriguing aspects of this word-position symbolism is that it was used in Psalm 46 of the King James Bible which some Baconians believe Bacon edited. Psalm 46 will be examined in detail later. The point is that I had no knowledge of the Psalm 46 phenomenon (and other coding forms) when I wrote *Sacred Vessel*.

Bringing the techniques illustrated in that book forward to the present investigation, I have searched for clues in particular samples such as Psalm 46, several passages from Shakespearean literature, and "A Word from the Master." In short, I have used the same methods with this material as I used when investigating the Great Invocation. The reasoning behind this is based on the simple idea that if Master R worked with the Great Invocation according to a style of his own, a style developed many years ago during the Francis Bacon incarnation, then those same techniques and identifying marks—that same style applicable to him alone—might very well be evident in the writing and ideas of Francis Bacon.

Recall the words of Master R's poem, "I cannot name myself, as the intention of my work is that you should seek, and by seeking discover me." Are there clues in Shakespeare, Psalm 46, "A Word From the Master," and the Great Invocation which contain traces of Rakoczi? Following the advice of his poem, let us now seek.

Notes

1. Alice A. Bailey, *The Unfinished Autobiography*, 167.
2. Bailey, *Discipleship in the New Age*, vol. II, 473.
3. For these examples of Djwhal Khul's use of estoeric numerology see, *Esoteric Psychology*, vol. I, 346-7 and *The Rays and the Initiations*, 79-81.
4. William Shakespeare, *Mr. William Shakespeare's Comedies, Histories, & Tragedies, A Facsimilie of the First Folio, 1623*, 9.
5. Hollenbach, *Francis Rosicross*, 118-21.
6. Edward D. Johnson, *Bacon-Shakespeare Coincidences*, 17.

TRACES OF THE
MASTER R

The intention of my work is that you should seek,
and by seeking discover me,
and by discovering me, know me.

"A Word from the Master" by Peter Dawkins

The primary factors which initiated this investigation and which also relate to the Great Invocation involve particular symbols associated with the Master R especially during his incarnation as Francis Bacon, prior to achieving mastery. This chapter will examine three primary symbols of significance—the rose, the goddess Athena, and the ship. I have identified these as traces of the Master R. There are others, but these three stand out because I discovered their connection to the Great Invocation prior to any idea that the Master R may have been involved with the mantram. In fact, Master R appears nowhere in *Sacred Vessel* and played no part in the premise of that book. I began my research in 1993, received the first copies of the book on October 1, 1997 and met Michael Taylor in New Zealand about one week later. Hence, it is important to realize that the information in this chapter represents a tangible bridge linking symbols coded into the words of the Great Invocation with symbols associated with Master R, especially in his lifetime as Francis Bacon. With this thought in mind, let's explore the details of this connection.

THE ROSE

There is evidence showing that Francis Bacon was related in some way to the Rosicrucian Fraternity in England, and in lesser degree to the Rosicrucian groups in continental Europe. The symbol of the Rosicrucians is a cross with a rose placed at the intersection of the vertical and horizontal arms. This rose symbolizes the unfoldment of the human soul and the consequent release of spiritual love and compassion into the world. At the same time, the rose symbolizes the presence of Christ in the world and the redemption of humanity through sacrifice. This theme of redemption applies to saviors of all religions in general.

Since Bacon was dedicated to the reformation of the arts and sciences, the establishment of a secret order (such as the Rosicrucians) dedicated to the enlightenment of society would naturally interest him. As a leading figure at the very center of the English intellectual establishment, he quite probably had more than a passing interest in the Rosicrucian Fraternity. The main point is that Francis Bacon had some association with the Rosicrucians and their philosophy, including the symbol of the rose cross. In addition, Dawkins and Hollenbach believe there was a connection between the Rosicrucians and Freemasonry, and that Bacon was very much involved in both organizations.

Recalling the Tibetan's commentary about the Hierarchical movement begun in the 16th century, the following remarks by Hollenbach are noteworthy:

> The Rosicrucian Order of the seventeenth century was an adaptation of the wisdom of the Mysteries for the needs of a new world. Originating in England, it was founded by Francis Bacon and a group of enlightened philosophers as part of Bacon's plan for the general reform of the states of Europe.[1]

If one follows the logic of this premise of Hierarchical planning, Bacon becomes a key player in the effort of the Hierarchy to reform civilization as part of a 500 year plan of globalization. Even the title of Bacon's unfinished work *The Great Instauration* exudes the spirit of human advance toward world unity and general enlightenment. In fact, Webster's defines "instauration" as an archaic word meaning *restoration*, and interestingly, the Great Invocation ends with

58 CHAPTER 4

the phrase "restore the Plan on Earth." In *A Treatise on White Magic*, DK discusses this Hierarchical effort of globalization and integration and states, "This period has been occultly called the 'age of *restoration* [emphasis, JB] of what has been broken by the fall.'"2 The Tibetan's use of the specific term "restoration" may be a subtle hint of Master R's influence on Djwhal Khul's description of this particular historical era. (It might even be a hint of DK's presence during that era.)

The symbol of the rose at the center of the cross in *Sacred Vessel of the Mysteries* evolved through an analysis of the number of words in the Great Invocation. By applying the fundamental esoteric idea of the triad to the number of words in the Great Invocation, I located the word at the exact center—the word "is" at word-position 57. I eventually realized there was a resonance between the three elements— the first fifty-six words, the last fifty-six words, and the middle word at position fifty-seven. After discovering that the middle word "is" has a numeric value of 28 (AN), I saw that the two sets of 56 words could be divided into two groups each, thus forming four sets of 28 words which equal the value of the middle word itself. From a symbolic standpoint, the words of the Great Invocation could be expressed as a cross with four equal arms, since the four sets of words all equal 28, leaving the middle word to be placed at the center. This symbolic depiction of the Great Invocation reminded me of the Rose Cross of the Rosicrucians; but the hidden bonus here is the fact that the word ROSE has a numerological value of 57 (AN) which equals the word-position of the middle word "is." The following diagram appears on page 307 of *Sacred Vessel of the Mysteries*. It depicts the word structure of the Great Invocation as a rosy cross. (We will return to this Rose Cross theme when we discuss the number 287.)

Figure 4.1. Rosy Cross of the Great Invocation.

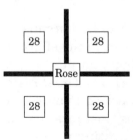

In summary, structural features of the Great Invocation can be graphically illustrated in the form of an equal-armed cross with the word "rose" at the center, thus demonstrating the primary symbol of the Rosicrucian Fraternity so closely connected to Francis Bacon. Might this be a way for Master R to communicate the timeless presence of the Ageless Wisdom Mysteries throughout history and simultaneously indicate his influential presence in history as well?

ATHENA

Dawkins discusses the Greek goddess Athena as the inspiring Muse of Francis Bacon.[3] In his book, *Arcadia*, Dawkins discusses this idea in a chapter entitled "Athena's Veil." Two illustrations depicting Pallas Athena are also reproduced in that book; one from Bacon's *The Wisdom of the Ancients* and another from *New Atlantis*.

Many of the scholar poets of Bacon's day appear to have a common "AA" symbol printed at the top of various publications. These authors or pseudonymous authors included "Edmund Spencer, Sir Philip Sydney, Thomas Lodge, Ben Jonson, Christopher Marlowe, William Shakespeare and Sir Francis Bacon."[4] (See page 77.)

> "ATHENA" is normally spelt with an "E" on the end of her name (viz. Athene), but the initiates spelt it with an "A", giving an "A" at the beginning and an "A" at the end—a Double "A" (AA)—and in many of the printed poetry, plays and writings produced by the Renaissance initiates, the call sign which they used was a "Double A" symbol as a headpiece on a page, with one of the 'A's shaded, the other left light.[5]

Dawkins' comment about the spelling of Athena is very significant in light of my early research on Athena. I knew very little about the goddess at the time and was slightly confused by the different spellings of her name (Athene and Athena). As recorded in my first book, the name Athena has a significant numerological relation to the Great Invocation, whereas the gematria of Athene does not.

Dawkins also suggests the two A's represent the first letters of the names Apollo (or Adonis) and Athena. He goes into great depth on the significance of this AA symbol[6] and names several books of Bacon's time in which the "AA" signature appears.

From these dates onward [1579, JB] many of the finest examples of English literature, of the Elizabethan-Jacobean period, carried the "AA" device in one form or another (usually as a headpiece), including Shakespeare's Sonnets (1609), the 1st folio edition of the Authorised Version of the Holy Bible (1611), the Genealogies in the 1st quarto edition of the Scriptures (1612) and Shakespeare's 1st folio edition of Comedies, Histories, and Tragedies (1623).[7]

Further associations between Athena and Francis Bacon are found in the description sometimes attributed to the goddess—that of spear-shaker. The allusion to Shakespeare is obvious. Dawkins points out that the title taken by Bacon in 1618, Lord *"Verulam*, has a close meaning to 'Spear-shaker' (*i.e.Veru*, Latin for 'javelin/spear' + *lam*, English for 'to beat/thrash')."[8]

Bacon and the other members of his secret circle of Rosicrucians and Freemasons adopted Athena as their Muse because she not only represented the synthesis of the arts, but also she protected the Ageless Wisdom, veiling it in secrecy until the student of Light was ready for its revelation. Dawkins puts it well with the following commentary:

> The association of anonymity or secrecy with Pallas Athena is well known. Athena is said to wear a helmet of light which renders her invisible. But those who discover how, can lift her vizor (or veil) of light and see her face....The Veil is *par excellence* her symbol; for the veil conceals in order to reveal. The Rose is also, *par excellence*, a symbol with the same meaning, and Athena and the Rose can be equated with each other.[9]

In *Sacred Vessel of the Mysteries,* the symbolic presence of the goddess Athena is well demonstrated by the structure of the Great Invocation. Of major significance is the fact that this symbolic presence of the goddess is veiled. In fact the word "veiled" equals 57 (AN) and it is through the relationship of the middle word at position 57 to the remaining words of the Great Invocation that the symbolism of Athena is unveiled. This all relates to the number 7.

The ancient Greeks associated the number 7 with the goddess Athena. Her full name as Pallas Athena Parthenos was created to demonstrate this relationship. Each of the three names expresses the number 7. In Greek gematria, "Pallas" (maiden) equals 343 which is the product of 7 x 7 x 7 and "Athena" equals 77.

(Interestingly, Athena in English equals 49 (AN) which is the result of 7 x 7.) Greek gematria for "Parthenos" (virgin) equals 515, which for the Greeks represented a circle divided into seven sections. The number of degrees of each arc of a circle divided into seven parts equals approximately a rounded 51.4. (The Greeks did not use the decimal point.) Thus, the creation of the Greek word "parthenos" (equaling 515) was as close as the Greeks could come to expressing the division of a circle into seven parts in the form of a word.

These numbers are present in the Great Invocation in several remarkable ways. First, the number of essential words needed to construct the Great Invocation (without repeated words, such as "the" or "from") amounts to 51 or the number of whole degrees represented by the word "Parthenos." Furthermore, these fifty-one words are composed of 226 letters. Using the English alphabet, the numerological value of Pallas Athena Parthenos equals 226. Second, the name Athena equals 49 or 7 x 7. When the Great Invocation is divided in such a way that the first forty-nine words (counting from the beginning) and the last forty-nine words (counting from the end) are set aside, the remaining fifteen words in the center have a numerological value of 777. Symbolically speaking, Athena (first forty-nine words), and Athena (last forty-nine words), encompass "Pallas Athena Parthenos" or 7 x 7 x 7 in the middle. This symbolic presence of Athena at the beginning and ending of the Great Invocation can be viewed as A and A, connecting it with the "AA" signature of the Rosicrucian Fraternity and Francis Bacon.

Finally, just as Dawkins equates Athena and the Rose, so too does the Great Invocation. In figure 4.1, the word "rose" represents the fifty-seventh position and central point of the Great Invocation. The word occupying that central location is "is" and this word equals 28 or *four* 7's. Additionally, there are four groups of twenty-eight words surrounding "is" and these groups can *also* be divided into four 7's. Thus, there is a conceptual link between the symbols of Athena and the rose in the Great Invocation. This connection is graphically depicted in figure 4.2 on the following page. This diagram appeared in my earlier book and is reproduced here in order to illustrate the two symbols embedded in the Great Invocation which were *also* close to the heart of Francis Bacon more than four centuries ago.

Figure 4.2. Septenary Cross of Athena.

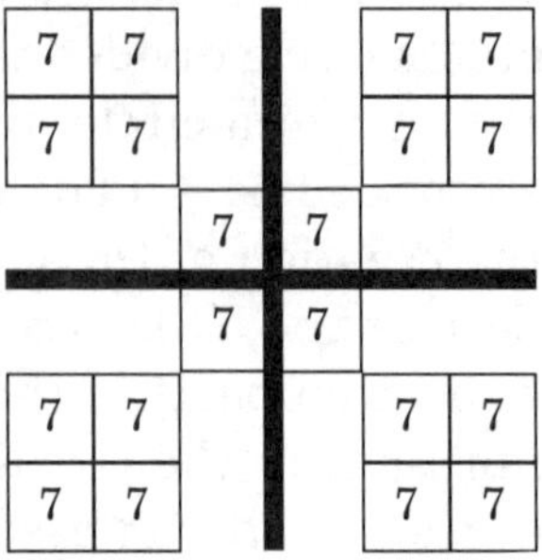

7	7		7	7
7	7		7	7

	7	7	
	7	7	

7	7		7	7
7	7		7	7

The presence of this distinct septenary theme in the Great Invocation cannot be denied. The sevenfold expression of the planes of consciousness, energies, and cycles is the foundation and superstructure of the entire Ageless Wisdom teachings, especially as presented by the Tibetan through Alice Bailey. The fact that the number 7 plays such a fundamental role in the structure of the Great Invocation is elegantly appropriate. The relationship between Athena, the Goddess of Wisdom, and the Ageless Wisdom is as natural as a fish in water. The deeper meanings of all this are explained in detail in *Sacred Vessel of the Mysteries*. The knowledge that Francis Bacon chose as his Muse a major symbol of the quest for wisdom—Athena—adds an additional layer of meaning as to why she is found in the Great Invocation in the first place. Her role as the protectress of the Wisdom is certainly enough of a reason, but the close ties to Bacon strengthen the theory that Master R, through his identification with Athena in the Bacon lifetime, carried that theme through to the Great Invocation.

THE SIGNATURE OF SIRIUS

The AA signature may have other meanings in relation to the Great Invocation beyond its connection to Athena. Although a bit more abstract, it may appear in the form of the "Signature of Sirius" which appears in figure 4.3. As explained in my first book, the numerological value of a word in the Great Invocation can be used as a reference number for finding the word-position of another word in the Great Invocation. Using this technique, one is able to move

Figure 4.3. Signature of Sirius.

1 From 52	2 the 33	3 point 74	4 of 21	5 Light 56	6 within 83	7 the 33
8 Mind 40	9 of 21	10 God 26	11 Let 37	12 light 56	13 stream 76	14 forth 67
15 into 58	16 the 33	17 minds 59	18 of 21	19 men 32	20 Let 37	21 Light 56
22 descend 54	23 on 29	24 Earth 52	25 From 52	26 the 33	27 point 74	28 of 21
29 Love 54	30 within 83	31 the 33	32 Heart 52	33 of 21	34 God 26	35 Let 37
36 love 54	37 stream 76	38 forth 67	39 into 58	40 the 33	41 hearts 71	42 of 21
43 men 32	44 May 39	45 Christ 77	46 return 96	47 to 35	48 Earth 52	49 From 52
50 the 33	51 centre 65	52 where 59	53 the 33	54 Will 56	55 of 21	56 God 26

| | | | 57 is 28 | | | |

58 known 77	59 Let 37	60 purpose 110	61 guide 46	62 the 33	63 little 78	64 wills 75
65 of 21	66 men 32	67 The 33	68 purpose 110	69 which 51	70 the 33	71 Masters 95
72 know 63	73 and 19	74 serve 69	75 From 52	76 the 33	77 centre 65	78 which 51
79 we 28	80 call 28	81 the 33	82 race 27	83 of 21	84 men 32	85 Let 37
86 the 21	87 Plan 43	88 of 21	89 Love 54	90 and 19	91 Light 56	92 work 67
93 out 56	94 And 19	95 may 39	96 it 29	97 seal 37	98 the 33	99 door 52
100 where 59	101 evil 48	102 dwells 75	103 Let 37	104 Light 56	105 and 19	106 Love 54
107 and 19	108 Power 77	109 restore 100	110 the 33	111 Plan 43	112 on 29	113 Earth 52

through the mantram from word to word. Eventually this process leads to a word loop which cannot be escaped. This loop is named the "Signature of Sirius" because the numerological value of the words in that loop are equal to the phrase "the Great White Lodge on Sirius."

Several things are interesting about this loop. First, the name "Signature of Sirius" is similar to Dawkins' name for the Athena/Apollo device of Bacon and the Rosicrucians—the "AA Signature of Light." I was surprised when I saw that name applied to it as it immediately reminded me of the name I had chosen to call the infinity word loop I found in the Great Invocation. Second, the loop in the Great Invocation forms two triangles connected at their points, which suggest two A's without the legs of the letter. Third, the four words which form this loop are "the Light of God" or "the God of Light." As we have just learned, Apollo was known as the God of Light since he represented the sun. In turn, Athena was known as the Goddess of spiritual Light which is wisdom. Recall that the newly formed Synthetic Ashram is a Wisdom Ashram.

At this point the possible relationship between the Signature of Sirius and the AA Signature of Light is tenuous at best and could easily be taken as a coincidence, except for the following information from an entirely new source.

BACON, NAPIER, AND ZEROS

The Signature of Sirius takes on a whole new meaning through a topic discussed in Penn Leary's *The Second Cryptographic Shakespeare* (briefly referred to in chapter 2). Through his own research on the authorship of Shakespeare, Leary unknowingly provides a crucial link between Francis Bacon and the Signature of Sirius.

Before continuing, I just want to say that I consider his book recommended reading for anyone interested in the Bacon/Shakespeare question. It is well researched and serious, but with just the right touch of humor to avoid dryness. In any event, I did not come across Leary's book until I was well into my research on this topic, but what he revealed in several areas caught my attention immediately.

Although there are many areas of Leary's work that could be mentioned, I am focussing my attention on one area which involves

Bacon's apparent admiration of the work of John Napier, the inventor of logarithms. When I first encountered Napier in Leary's book, I couldn't imagine how Bacon, Shakespeare, and Napier could be relevantly connected. Leary, however, convincingly demonstrates that they are connected in a fascinating way.

The connection involves the Dedication of Shakespeare's *Sonnets* and a cryptographic cipher embedded in it. A detailed explanation of how this was accomplished is impossible here, so I will simply give a synopsis of the story.

Shakespeare's *Sonnets* have been a mystery since their appearance because no one can explain to whom they were written. Furthermore, the Dedication (which is our focus) is even more mysterious in that it doesn't make much sense and is cryptic even on the surface; especially the strange periods inserted between the words (first three lines shown here). It is reproduced in figure 4.4.

Figure 4.4. Titlepage of Shakespeare's *Sonnets*.

[title page]

SHAKE-SPEARE**S**

SONNET**S**.

Neue**r** before Imprinte**d**.

———————————

———————————

A**T** LONDO**N**
By **G**. El**d** for **T.T**. and are
to be solde by Willia**m** Asple**y**.
1609

[Dedication, first 3 lines:]

TO.TH**E**.ONLI**E**.BEGETTE**R**.O**F**.

THES**E**.INSVIN**G**.SONNET**S**.

M**r**.W.H. ALL.HAPPINESSE.

As Penn Leary explains in his book, he spent many grueling hours trying to find the key to decoding the secret message hidden in the Dedication. It is well worth reading in its entirety, but for our purposes I am going to get right to the conclusion of the matter. Here is Leary's explanation and decipherment of the Dedication:

> The ciphertext letters are selected by using the last letter of each capitalized word (and a capitalized letter standing alone is to be recognized as the last letter of a capitalized word) beginning with SHAKE-SPEARES on the title page and ending with the lower case, super-scripted "r" in "Mr." in the Dedication. When you come to the date, "1609" enter the letters "A F I" because these numbers represent the elementary, numerically corresponding letters of the Elizabethan alphabet (there is no letter equivalent to the number zero).[10]

At this point in his explanation Leary creates a line of letters according to the instructions given above. He then proceeds to decipher this line using a common technique of cryptography in which the alphabet is shifted four positions starting from the letter A or from the letter Z. For example, when shifting the alphabet forward, the letter A is enciphered as E since the letter E is four positions from A in the alphabet. If the backward coding method is applied, then A would be enciphered as W since the letter W is four positions from Z in the alphabet.

In this case Bacon, according to Leary, shifted the alphabet backward by four positions. The other important factor here is that Bacon used a twenty-one letter alphabet for his cipher work. (This is intriguing since there are twenty-one key words in the Great Invocation. See chapter 7.) The final result of the entire process is duplicated below.

O O N Y P I R C Y P P H R S B E K A A N B A C O N

At first glance, much of this line looks like gibberish except for BACON at the far right. On close examination however, one can also read NYPIR (Napier) and CYPPHRS (ciphers) and BEKAAN (Beacon or Bacon). The odds of this occurring by chance are astronomical, to say the least. Also, of particular note are the two letter O's at the beginning of the line. These are actually ZEROS and are meant to show how important the zero is in logarithms.

It is known that Napier began working on logarithms in 1590 and that another mathematician named Henry Briggs was also doing similar work. These two men eventually corresponded and had two meetings in which they shared information resulting in a major advance in mathematics through the use of the zero (or cipher) in relation to logarithms. Leary offers an extract on the importance of the zero:

> In his *Descriptio* of 1614 Napier says, "It was indeed left at liber-tie in the beginning, to attribute nothing, or 0, to any sine or quanti-tie [for its logarithm]." And Briggs says, in the *Arithmetica Logarithmica* of 1624, "I myself...to my auditors in Gresham College, remarked that it would be much more convenient that 0 should be kept for the loga-rithm of the whole sine...And concerning that matter I wrote immedi-ately to the author himself [Napier]; and as soon as the season of the year...permitted I journeyed to Edinburgh, where...he said that he had for some time been of the same opinion...that the change should be...that 0 be the logarithm of unity..."[11]

Leary follows this up with a very interesting point:

> There is no reason to believe that all of this mathematical activity was a deep secret within the London philosophical (scientific) com-munity, or to Francis Bacon who lived among them and showed great respect for mathematics in his published works. It should not be sur-prising that Bacon in 1609...made, as we shall see, a hidden notation that the expression 00 represented Napier's ciphers....The fact that he did so *in a concealed cipher*, and called attention to it with thirty anom-alous decimal points, demonstrates the peculiarity and strangeness of his imagination.[12]

Later in his book, Leary shows that the person who wrote the *Sonnets* knew something about logarithms and had to know about them before 1609, the date when the *Sonnets* were first published. This is highlighted in sonnet 136. Leary offers the pertinent lines (using the Elizabethan style) and then explains:

In things of great receit with ease we prooue
Among a number one is reckon'd none
Then in the number let me passe vntold,
Though in thy stores account I one must be.

> Only in a table of logarithms does 1 = 0. The log of 1 is zero, the log of 10 is one, the log of 100 is two, etc. Logarithms are used most-ly "in things of great receipt," that is, with large numbers to simplify

multiplication and division and in calculating powers and roots. But
in "thy stores account" (a simple inventory) one still equals one and
must be counted in the conventional manner.[13]

Thus, Leary contends that the deciphered message from the
Dedication of the *Sonnets* is praise for Napier in his use of zeros as
integral to his discovery and development of logarithms. This
praise is delivered via the message OO (two zeros), NYPIR
(Napier), CYPPHRS (ciphers or zeros), BEKAAN (beacon or light),
and BACON (Francis Bacon, the suggested author of the *Sonnets*).
This discovery is remarkable in its own right, but it has an equally
remarkable counterpart in the Great Invocation and its connection
to the Master R.

It is here that the Signature of Sirius takes on a much more
compelling role as a major item of evidence linking Francis
Bacon/Shakespeare, Master R, and the Great Invocation. As indicated in figure 4.3, four words in the Great Invocation form an
infinity loop made up of the words "the Light of God" or "the God of
Light." The loop formed by these four words appears as two inter-
laced triangles, but these two triangles can just as easily be viewed
as TWO ZEROS. Additionally, since they form an endless loop, they
trace an infinity sign, which conceptually represents zero.
Furthermore, the value of the four words which make up this infinity sign equals 136—the *number of the sonnet* in which Leary identifies the reference to logarithms! This additional information surely places the Signature of Sirius in a class of evidence linking the
Master R to the Great Invocation beyond that of pure coincidence.

Before leaving this topic, a fellow student discovered another
subtle clue connecting the writing of Shakespeare with the Great
Invocation, namely, its poetic meter. Scanning its rhythm and meter
reveals that the entire mantram is generally laid out in iambic pentameter, the same as many of Shakespeare's plays. The lines of stanzas one and two are 5, 5, 3 respectively. The lines of stanzas three
and four are 5, 5, 5, and the last line comprising stanza five is iambic
hexameter. Hence, ten lines out of the thirteen, or more than sev-
enty-five per cent of the Great Invocation is written in iambic pentameter, the general poetic rhythm and meter found in the writing
of Shakespeare. It should be noted that neither of the earlier stanzas of the Great Invocation given by Djwhal Khul in 1935 or 1940 are
written in this poetic style. (See appendix C, Stanzas One and Two.)

THE SHIP METAPHOR

The title of the book, *Sacred Vessel of the Mysteries*, refers to a vessel carrying the Mysteries connected with the fundamental questions of life on our planet, such as our purpose, origin, and destiny as a race. Obviously this is a sacred vessel because the Mysteries contained within its protective walls are profoundly important to humanity. The idea for the vessel was born from the phrase "the celestial ship." This phrase has an AN value of 171, which represents the sum of the three word-position numbers at the center of the Great Invocation—positions 56, 57, and 58. The words in these three locations are "God is known." Due to its central location in the invocation, this phrase depicts God as the Center of all life. Beyond this, the number 171 carries enormous symbolic meaning in relation to the ship metaphor.[14]

Among other things, the celestial ship refers to the Greek ship, Argo, which carried Jason and the Argonauts on their search for the golden fleece. The Argo was inspired by Athena and it was she who protected Jason and his men in their quest. At the end of the journey, Athena placed the Argo in the heavens where it became known as the celestial ship.

The ship metaphor goes much deeper than this and is found in many ancient religions of the past. An extract from Higgins' study of the mystery religions of the ancient world points this out:

> Every one has heard of the celebrated boat of Isis among the Egyptians, Greeks, and Romans. But the Northern nations also worshipped her in the form of a ship. This ship was placed in the constellations and called the Argo. In Egypt this was called Sothis or the Star of Isis. This very well connects the Arga and Isis and Saviour—the ship in which the seed of nature was preserved. The Egyptians, Greeks, and Romans, all had festivals in the spring season to the ship of Isis.[15]

In Helena P. Blavatsky's *The Secret Doctrine*, the ship or vessel metaphor is expanded to describe the feminine principle:

> Its form and shape changed with every country, provided it remained a vessel, a symbolic "navis" or boat-shaped vehicle and a *container*, symbolically of germs or the germ of life.[16]

Isis and Athena shared many of the same qualities and both represented the divine feminine principle. Consequently, the ship of Isis reappears later in the Greek story of Athena as the mythical/mystical ship Argo, which later becomes the celestial ship after it is placed in the heavens by Athena. The fascinating numerological factor here is that "the celestial ship" (171) equals a term which can be applied to Athena, namely "the Queen of Heaven." Although this term is given to Isis, and in the Greek pantheon might more accurately apply to Hera, wife of Zeus, it can be attributed to Athena as leader of the Muses and guardian of the Mysteries.[17]

Argo, the celestial ship, and the Great Invocation are tied to Francis Bacon through one obvious factor, which is the goddess Athena. There is another factor, however, which is not so obvious. This involves the titlepage illustration in Bacon's book, *Advancement and Proficience of Learning*, published in 1640 (fig. 4.5). Quoting Peter Dawkins, "This titlepage illustration is an example of cabalistic design and symbology, and contains a wealth of data to unlock the doors of the Baconian-Rosicrucian treasure-house of knowledge."[18]

The illustration contains two pillars in the foreground, one of science and one of philosophy. As stated by Dawkins, the illustration contains various symbols such as the twin pillars (the left light and the right dark), the sun, moon, and two arms with outstretched hands clasping one another at the top. At the bottom in the foreground are two owls holding torches (symbolic of the light of wisdom and Athena). The bases of the pillars each depict two equilateral triangles with various Latin words written within them referring to philosophy, history, nature, and ratio, among other subjects. Three books placed atop each other are "sandwiched" between the base and the middle section of each pillar. These six books bear titles to the various volumes of the *Advancement and Proficience of Learning*. *Novum Organum* is the most recognizable. (Curiously, stretched between the two pillars is a banner declaring the title of the book itself followed by "IX Bookes." This "IX" appears to be the Roman numeral for 9. The illustration, however, shows three books placed on each pillar. Perhaps the phrase "IX books" is meant to indicate S[IX] with the "S" left out.) Finally, the tops of the pillars are in the form of elongated pyramids. There are other features, but these are sufficient to indicate some of the detailed symbolism.

For our purposes, the most important feature of the illustration is the full sailed ship moving through the sea from right to left in the background between the two pillars. The direction is symbolic in

Figure 4.5. Bacon's Titlepage from *The Advancement of Learning*.

that the moon and dark pillar are on the right, while the sun and light pillar are on the left—the direction toward which the ship is sailing. The allusion to the ship Argo and the vessel theme of *Sacred Vessel of the Mysteries* is obvious.

There is more, however. Just beneath the ship and placed between the two pillars are the words in Latin, *Multi pertransibunt & augebitur Scientia*. Dawkins translates this phrase as "Many shall pass through and learning shall be increased."[19] The numerological value of the Latin phrase is of particular interest because it appears immediately beneath the ship. The gematria value of this Latin phrase equals 416 (AN) and 155 (RAN) using the ESC system. These number values are of no particular significance in relation to our study; however, when we apply the modern English alphabet values to the same phrase the result is worth examining.

The modern English gematria value of this phrase equals 436 (AN) and 157 (RAN). The RAN value is of major significance in relation to the Great Invocation since 157 equates numerologically to the title "the Invocation for Power and Light," which according to the Tibetan is the official name of the Great Invocation.[20] Just as important perhaps is the fact that the phrase "the celestial boat" has a RAN value 157 thus further linking the boat or ship metaphor with the ship depicted in Bacon's titlepage.

The AN value of the Latin phrase is also of significance. In *Sacred Vessel* the celestial ship is related to a mysterious phrase given by Djwhal Khul and which concerns initiation. That phrase is "the Boat of Mystery which Ploughs the Ocean." This phrase equals 437, therefore indicating a difference of 1 between Bacon's Latin phrase and DK's phrase pertaining to initiation.

According to a cabalistic technique called "colel," this is perfectly acceptable and represents a direct numerological correspondence. Nigel Pennick states that, "In gematria there is also the convention of 'colel' which allows a discrepancy of one between any two word totals, allowing a little leeway in interpretation."[21] In all the gematria calculations in my previous and present work, I have used this technique twice; one time here and once in my first book. Although it is an acceptable technique, I prefer to use exact correlations.

Nevertheless, these circumstantial bits of evidence indicate an unusual coincidence, at the least, and distinct traces of a possible esoteric trail connecting Bacon, Master R and Master DK, at most.

Although these results contain some interesting correspondences, I don't consider them primary numeric codes because their gematria values in Elizabethan English do not link with any equivalent modern English terms. Yet there are enough marginal correlations to include them as part of the overall evidence for consideration.

In fact, most of the correspondences may actually concern the meaning of the phrase rather than its numeric value. The translation of the Latin phrase is, "Many shall pass through and learning shall be increased." This statement suggests a time when initiation into higher knowledge will be available to many people. This idea of initiation into greater knowledge and wisdom forms the basis of the mystical phrase, "the Boat of Mystery which Ploughs the Ocean." This is one of several phrases given by the Tibetan which relate to the third initiation.[22] The revelation of the meaning of this phrase (and the others) to the initiate is literally an increase of knowledge through the process of symbolically passing through the door of initiation. The phrase "the door of Initiation" is employed by the Tibetan in many of his books[23] and equals 109 (RAN). This value (109) when multiplied by 4 equals 436, the modern value of Bacon's phrase "*Multi pertransibunt & augebitur Scientia.*"[24] The meaning of this product (436) and its factors (4 x 109) is significant because it relates to symbolism found in a book by John Dee.

John Dee has already been discussed as a possible mentor to Francis Bacon and other members of the Elizabethan circle of scholars and artists, a group which may well have been the first Rosicrucians and Freemasons of Britain. In 1577, Dee published a book entitled *GENERAL AND RARE MEMORIALS pertayning to the Perfect Arte of NAVIGATION*. This work by John Dee also contains a titlepage with a ship theme, although it was published sixty-four years before Bacon's *Advancement and Proficience of Learning*.

Peter Dawkins provides a lengthy interpretation of Dee's titlepage in the appendix to *Arcadia*. However, we will only consider several features which relate directly to our subject. The illustration contains an armada of five Spanish ships, a row boat, and a large ship carrying Queen Elizabeth I. Despite these historical features, Dawkins interprets the primary theme of this illustration as Masonic. He describes various Masonic emblems appearing in the illustration which signify initiations into the degrees of Masonry. The first degree is symbolized by a gateway leading into a town with

a rocky hill beyond. This obviously refers to the passing of the
Entered Apprentice (First Degree) into the community of the
Masonic Lodge. The symbol of the second degree is an ear of corn,
signifying the mental growth and ripening process of the Fellow
Craft degree. The third symbol related to the third degree (Master
Mason) is a skull which is symbolic of death and burial in the tomb.
Dawkins next describes the fourth degree:

> This Arch Degree (known as the Royal Arch) is depicted by the great
> ship in which sails the Sovereign, Queen Elizabeth, and her three
> Principals of the Royal Arch.

This is significant because as we have just seen, when 109 (the
door of initiation) is multiplied by 4, it equals the Latin phrase on
Bacon's titlepage. This might therefore symbolize the fourth door of
initiation or the Arch Degree represented by Elizabeth's ship.
Continuing with the same extract, Dawkins states:

> Another word for ship is "ark", a word associated with the Greek
> word *arche* from which we have our English word "arch". Arche means
> "the Beginning without End", and refers to the Circle of Existence
> which contains all life. It is the womb or vessel of life, in which all life
> processes take place....By analogy, all pure and complete life forms
> are microcosmic vessels of life...In terms of the human being, it refers
> particularly to man's soul, which is, when perfected, an immaculate
> vessel...Thus, it is depicted as an actual ship or vessel—the Royal
> Ark—sailing the seas of time and matter, and bathed in the Light from
> on high that descends into matter from the heavenly Mind of God.[25]

These words by Peter Dawkins are really quite amazing in terms of
similarity to descriptions and conclusions regarding the Great
Invocation published in *Sacred Vessel of the Mysteries*. This is especially true when Dawkins describes the ship or vessel "sailing the
seas of time and matter." His description invokes an image of "the
Boat of Mystery which Ploughs the Ocean."
     There are other instances of shared concepts. In *Sacred Vessel*
we read:

> Might not "the Queen of Heaven," the Argha or Argo—the celestial
> ship—at the exact center of the Great Invocation represent the divine
> vessel that carries the mantram of salvation to humanity?...This con-
> tainer is sacred because it carries the seeds of Life.[26]

> In a sense we can say the universal Argo represents the vessel of wisdom...The Argo, also symbolizes the vehicle for the ageless wisdom....At the individual level, the Argo or Argha is the causal body of the soul, the sacred vessel which holds the accumulated experiences and wisdom of the incarnating soul through many lifetimes.[27]

Another extract from Dawkins regarding the vessel metaphor follows:

> The perfect, immaculate vessel in which shines the Light of God is the Christ soul—the Virgin Mary who has given birth to (i.e. become) the Christ manifestation. The immaculate aspect of the ship that is depicted in Dee's picture is represented by the Queen, who is symbolically known as the Virgin Queen and given the title of the Virgin Mary.[28]

A reference to the zodiacal sign Virgo in *Sacred Vessel* states:

> As the guardian of the Wisdom she [Virgo] symbolizes the Great Mother Who carries the Christ Light within her body. In fact, Djwhal Khul relates Virgo to "The Hidden Light of God." Thus, the Great Invocation, like Virgo, is a sacred vessel carrying "the Light of God" or "the God of Light" hidden within its womb.[29]

Note Dawkins' earlier reference to the womb or vessel of life and the correspondence in the extract above. Of even greater significance is the citation regarding the "the Light of God" in *Sacred Vessel of the Mysteries* and Dawkins' reference to the Virgin Mary containing the "Light of God." Especially interesting is the fact that Athena, like the Virgin Mary, was a virgin mother, as was Elizabeth I, if the story of Francis Bacon's birth is correct. "The God of Light" or "the Light of God" hidden in the Great Invocation refers to the "Signature of Sirius" noted earlier in this chapter. Just as "the Light of God" is hidden in the Virgin Mary and all the archetypal virgins of the past, we see that this phrase also lies hidden within the womb of the Great Invocation, only to be revealed through the decoding of its words.

In the final comments about Dee's illustration from the *Perfect Arte of NAVIGATION*, Dawkins notes that the orientation of the objects are such that East lies at the top of the scene and West at the bottom. This orientation is further evidence of Masonic symbolism because this East/West alignment matches the orientation of Masonic lodges. He states that, "Since Light symbolically comes from (or rises in) the East, Dee has rightly shown the East as being the place of the heavens, from which the light shines down upon the rest of the landscape."[30] Interestingly, the cover illustration of *Sacred Vessel of the Mysteries* is quite similar in design. A ship with two torches is flooded by a powerful light emanating from the sun Sirius which is placed in the upper right corner of the scene. The light streams forth from upper right to lower left.

Dawkins' description of this Light from the East sounds very much like a phrase referred to by the Tibetan and included in *Sacred Vessel of the Mysteries*: "the light which ever shineth in the East." Djwhal Khul links this phrase to the term *Shekinah*. This is a Hebrew word related to the holy spirit, the third aspect of divinity, which is the form side of manifestation, the feminine archetype. *Shekinah* corresponds to Dawkins' description of the Virgin Mary, Athena, and Queen Elizabeth I riding in the ship in John Dee's illustration. Furthermore, "the light which ever shineth in the East" and "the Boat of Mystery which Ploughs the Ocean" both have the identical numerological value of 176 (RAN). This number is significant because it equals the total root value of the twenty-one key words of the Great Invocation (see chapter 7). This numeric fact ties Dee's and Bacon's symbolic titlepages together with the Great Invocation in two ways: from the symbolic metaphor of the celestial ship or vessel, and by way of the symbolic depiction of the Masonic and mystical reference to the light in the East. Additionally, "the Boat of Mystery which Ploughs the Ocean" is a phrase which DK relates directly to "the Brahma or third aspect"[31] (of divinity), thus linking it also to *Shekinah*, the pure feminine archetype related to Athena and Elizabeth I.

The clue which triggered this cascade of correspondences was found at the middle of the Great Invocation where the three word-positions 56, 57, and 58 (totaling 171) are located. Francis Bacon's inherited family motto adds further food for thought concerning the central symbolism of 171. That motto is *Mediocria Firma* which translates as "The middle position is the sound one."[32] This Latin motto is a clear description of the method I used in my earlier research to find much of the esoteric information hidden in the Great Invocation. Identifying the *middle* phrase, the *middle* word, and *middle* letter lifted the veil of mystery which shrouded the symbolic message hidden within the Great Invocation.

Notes

1. Hollenbach, *Francis Rosicross*, 18.
2. Bailey, *A Treatise on White Magic*, 409.
3. Dawkins, *Arcadia*, 159.
4. Dawkins, *The Master*, part 2, 34. Example of AA symbol.

5. Dawkins, *The Virgin Ideal*, 21.
6. See Dawkins, *The Master*, part 2.
7. Dawkins, *Arcadia*, 198.
8. Ibid., 169.
9. Ibid., 162.
10. Leary, *The Second Cryptographic Shakespeare*, 148.
11. Ibid., 72.
12. Ibid., 73.
13. Ibid., 161.
14. The number 171 has other profound meanings beyond the celestial ship. Space does not allow their discussion here. Readers are directed to *Sacred Vessel of the Mysteries* for further information.
15. Godfrey Higgins, Esq., *Anacalypsis*, vol. 1, 798.
16. Helena, P. Blavatsky, *The Secret Doctrine*, vol. 4, 30.
17. It should be noted that Elizabeth I was considered a personification of Athena amongst those in the inner circles of her court. See Dawkins, *The Virgin Ideal*, 20-1.
18. Dawkins, *The Master*, part 2, 9.
19. Ibid., 8.
20. Bailey, *Discipleship in the New Age*, vol. II, 157. Interestingly, the page number corresponds to the numeric value of the title of the mantram. Note that "the" must be included as part of the title for it to equal 157.
21. Nigel Pennick, *Magical Alphabets*, 22. It should be noted here that colel was not used in *Sacred Vessel of the Mysteries*, although it could have been invoked in the case of the numbers 861 and 862. See *Sacred Vessel of the Mysteries* pp. 154, 155, 288.
22. Bailey, *Initiation, Human and Solar*, 168, 171.
23. The term "the door of initiation" appears fifty-one times in twelve books written by Djwhal Khul.

24. The ampersand has no numeric value in gematria, however if it is counted as one character, it increases the value of the phrase to 437, the equivalent of "the Boat of Mystery which Ploughs the Ocean."

25. Dawkins, Arcadia, 254. Note: The Royal Arch Degree is the fourth in order according to the Capitular Rite of Masonry. Earliest evidence of the conferring of this degree exists in two instances 1753 in America and 1758 in England. Modern Scottish Rite Masonry places this degree much later (26 of 33 degrees).

26. John Berges, *Sacred Vessel of the Mysteries*, 158.

27. Ibid., 272-3.

28. Dawkins, *Arcadia*, 254.

29. Berges, *Sacred Vessel of the Mysteries*, 293-4.

30. Dawkins, *Arcadia*, 255.

31. Bailey, *Initiation, Human and Solar*, 171.

32. Kevin Guinagh, *Dictionary of Foreign Phrases and Abbreviations*, s.v. mediocria firma.

MEDIOCRIA FIRMA

Find thou that narrow, middle way. It leads you to your goal.

Esoteric Psychology, vol. II, 38.

The technique of using the middle word, phrase, or letter of the Great Invocation as an indicator of information symbolically coded into the mantram is extensively explored in *Sacred Vessel of the Mysteries*. The paramount importance of the middle of the Great Invocation in terms of the middle phrase—"God is known," the middle word—"is," and the middle letter—"s" cannot be too strongly emphasized. The midpoint or central core of the Great Invocation is the touchstone of revelation for its inner mysteries.

So it was a great shock when I learned that Francis Bacon's family motto was *Mediocria Firma—the middle position is the sound one*, or to paraphrase, *the middle way is sure*. This motto is found on Bacon's Heraldic Achievement emblem in figure 5.1.

My first thought was, "My God, this is the primary basis of the Great Invocation's esoteric coding." This fact alone supports the theory that Master R helped compose the Great Invocation. Beyond this fact, however, I wondered if Bacon might have used this motto literally by placing clues in the middle of any writings.

Figure 5.1. Bacon Family Motto, *Mediocria Firma*.

I have not had the time to extensively explore Bacon's writing in this regard, but I believe this veiling technique appears in at least one instance related to the Bacon/Shakespeare question. This subtle coding technique occurs in Psalm 46 of the 1611 translation of the King James Bible, of which (Baconians believe) Francis Bacon was the final editor. Despite this belief, no hard evidence is readily available to back up this claim.

When King James I took the throne in 1603, the most popular English Bible was the Geneva Bible. Through the years many political commentaries had been added to the margin notes of this Bible and this may have been one of the motivating factors in King James' decision to commission a new translation. King James assigned approximately fifty theologians and church officials to the task. Committees were assigned sections of the Bible to translate. When they had completed their tasks, a small group consisting of several lead theologians performed the final editing. This final document was presented to King James for his approval before it was to go to the printer.

It is at this crucial stage that some Baconian researchers believe Francis Bacon exerted his influence. He was already close to King James and very influential at court. Bacon was knighted by King James in 1603, was solicitor general in 1611, and became the attorney general in 1613. Not only did Bacon have the opportunity and literary skills to examine the new Bible translation, but also he had the trust of the king. Thus, we come to Psalm 46.

As explained earlier, the entire Bacon/Shakespeare question was new to me in 1997. When I read that Bacon may have deliberately arranged the words of this psalm in particular positions in order to bring attention to a message in the message, I immediately recognized this as the same technique used in the Great Invocation. It was this that set me to analyzing the Psalm.

The 1611 edition of Psalm 46 with the original spelling of Bacon's day reads:

God is our refuge and strength, a very present helpe in trouble.
Therfore will not we feare, though the earth be remoued, and though the mountaines be caried into the midst of the sea;
Though the waters thereof roare, and be troubled, though the mountaines shake with the swelling thereof. [Selah.]
There is a riuer, the streames wherof shall make glad the citie of God: the holy place of the Tabernacles of the most High.
God is in the midst of her; she shal not be moued; God shall helpe her, and that right early.
The heathen raged, the kingdomes were mooued: he vttered his voyce, the earth melted.
The Lord of hosts is with vs; the God of Iacob is our refuge. [Selah.]
Come, behold the workes of the Lord, what desolations hee hath made in the earth.
He maketh warres to cease vnto the end of the earth: hee breaketh the bow, and cutteth the speare in sunder, he burneth the chariot in the fire.
Be stil, and know that I am God: I will bee exalted among the heathen, I will be exalted in the earth.
The Lord of hosts is with vs; the God of Iacob is our refuge. [Selah.][1]

Of particular interest here is the fact that the word "shake" is the 46th word from the beginning and the word "speare" is the 46th word from the end, not counting "Selah." Obviously, when joined these two words spell "shakespeare." This technique may have been used in other parts of the Psalms or the Bible, but this example suggests that Francis Bacon, as the possible final editor of the King James edition of the Bible, saw an opportunity to arrange the words "shake" and "speare" into the 46th positions (counting from beginning and end) in the 46th Psalm. Baconians use this example to fortify the theory that Bacon wrote the Shakespearean plays. It is important to mention that the words "shake" and "speare" do not hold these same positions in Psalm 46 as it appears in the Geneva Bible. In the Geneva Bible "shake" occupies the 47th position from the beginning and "speare" is 45 positions from the end of the psalm. The editing process of the King James Bible reduced Psalm 46 from 203 words to 201 words, and repositioned shake and speare to locations which might attract notice.

This wordplay exhibits a technique of using particular word-positions to draw attention to a deeper message within the outer message. This technique is used in the Great Invocation, for instance, when we identify the middle phrase (God is known) by counting 55 words from the beginning and 55 words from the end.

An interesting side note to the word Selah that bears directly on our investigation is that this word appears in Lesson 35 of the book *Nature of the Soul*. Recall that this is one book in a series dictated to Lucille Cedarcrans by the Master R as part of the work of the Synthetic Ashram (See section on Master R in chapter 2.) The word Selah as used in *Nature of the Soul* is the name of the deva (angelic being) who is the vehicle for mass human personality consciousness. The point of mentioning it here is that if the Master R was indeed Francis Bacon and helped edit the King James Bible, then he would have been somewhat familiar with the Hebrew word Selah which appears in various Psalms. *The Nature of the Soul* material uses terminology which is almost identical to that used by DK in the Alice Bailey books, yet nowhere in those books is the word Selah used. It is, therefore, rather provocative that this word should suddenly turn up in material dictated by Master R.

Chapter 2 describes the work of Dr. John Dee and his influence on Bacon and other students of the Mysteries during the Elizabethan Age. One of those students may have been George Wither, a less known writer and poet who was a contemporary of Bacon's. It is interesting that in *The Master*, part 1, Dawkins provides several illustrations from George Wither's *Collection of*

Emblemes, Ancient and Moderne published in 1635. One of the illustrations depicts the two-faced Roman god Janus. At the top of the illustration are the words *"He, that concealed things will finde, Must looke* before *him and* behinde."[2] Might this be a hint for a technique of concealing information in a writing by placing a particular number of words "before" and "behinde" the key word, letter, or phrase which holds special meaning not otherwise obvious? This may seem a bit of a stretch when applied to Bacon's "editing" of Psalm 46, but the Janus illustration appears on page 138 of Wither's book. This is an interesting fact since 138 is the product of 46 x 3 and the wordplay in Psalm 46 uses the 46th word from the beginning and the 46th word from the end, thus amounting to the use of 46 three times in order to identify Shakespeare. Is this a coincidence or a clever clue to looking before and behind in order to discover a message not obvious to the casual observer?

Figure 5.2. George Wither's Janus Epigram.

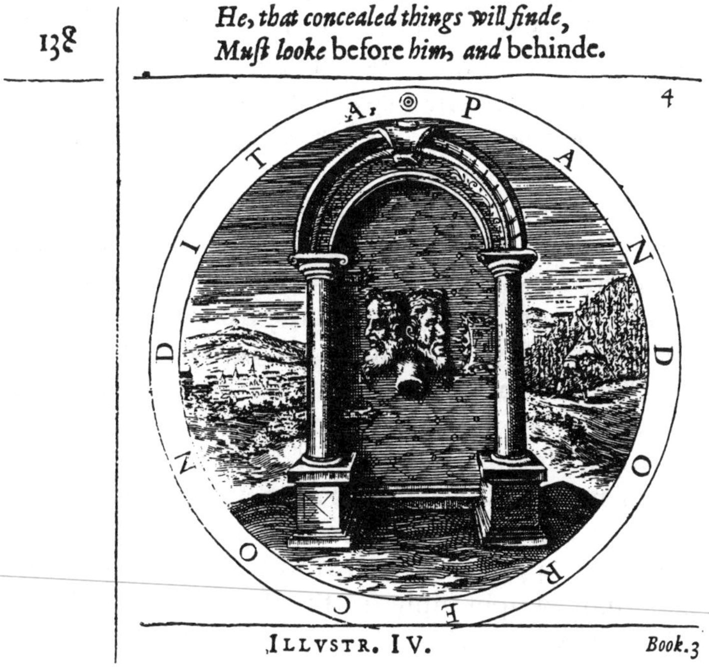

138

He, that concealed things will finde,
Must looke before him, and behinde.

ILLVSTR. IV.   Book.3

Psalm 46 and the "shakespeare" coincidence is rather fascinating, but there is more to Psalm 46 than meets the eye of those who are only searching for clues to Shakespeare's identity. If the Janus idea is not enough to tweak the curiosity, a more direct key lies in Bacon's own family motto—*Mediocria Firma—the middle way is sound*. It is obvious that the number 46 is a clue to finding the words "shake" and "speare" based on the count of 46 from the beginning and the ending of the Psalm. However, if we are assuming that Bacon is responsible for this play on words, he might have gone further by using the device of his family motto, *Mediocria Firma*, to conceal information about himself.

Using figure 5.3 (or appendix A1) as a guide, note that Psalm 46 can be divided into three equal parts of sixty-seven words each (201/3 = 67). It is interesting to note, therefore, that the name "Francis" has an ESC value of 67. Hence, not only is the number 46 referenced three times, in order to identify Shakespeare, but the 201 words of the Psalm identify the "editor" three times by the division of its words by 3. Additionally, notice that the middle word at position 101 bisects the middle column, dividing it into an upper and a lower section of thirty-three words each. Once more this reveals a startling bit of information. The ESC value of the name "Bacon" equals 33. Consequently, the left column corresponds numerically to "Francis" and the *upper portion* of the middle column corresponds to "Bacon," ending at the middle word. Conversely, the right column corresponds numerically to "Francis" and the *lower portion* of the middle column corresponds to "Bacon," up to the middle word. Consequently, just as Shakespeare is found in Psalm 46 by counting forty-six words toward the middle from the beginning and end of the psalm, Francis Bacon is found by approaching the middle from the beginning and the end of the psalm. This is indicated by the directions of the arrows in figure 5.3. This elegant arrangement of Psalm 46 clearly demonstrates that Francis Bacon encompasses this entire Psalm based on the middle word as the working agent of *Mediocria Firma*.

Using the principles of *Mediocria Firma* and Janus, we have discovered that the middle word located at the 101st position is "mooved" (moved). Appropriately, a shaken spear is *moved*. Also, using Elizabethan simple ciphers (the ESC method), "mooved" equals 69. Following the advice of George Wither from his Janus epigram, let's look before and behind "mooved" to see what, if anything, is concealed. Since the ESC value of mooved is 69, we will use that number as a key to locate possible clues. As shown in figure 5.3, the

Figure 5.3. Gematria List of Psalm 46.

#	word	value	#	word	value	#	word	value
1	God	25	68	of	20	135	in	22
2	is	27	69	the	32	136	the	32
3	our	51	70	Tabernacles	95	137	earth	50
4	refuge	60	71	of	20	138	He	13
5	and	18	72	the	32	139	maketh	55
6	strength	106	73	most	62	140	warres	79
7	a	1	74	High	32	141	to	33
8	very	65	75	God	25	142	cease	32
9	present	92	76	is	27	143	vnto	66
10	helpe	44	77	in	22	144	the	32
11	in	22	78	the	32	145	end	22
12	trouble	88	79	midst	62	146	of	20
13	Therfore	96	80	of	20	147	the	32
14	will	52	81	her	30	148	earth	50
15	not	46	82	she	31	149	hee	18
16	we	26	83	shal	49	150	breaketh	67
17	feare	34	84	not	46	151	the	32
18	though	76	85	be	7	152	bow	37
19	the	32	86	moued	55	153	and	18
20	earth	50	87	God	25	154	cutteth	93
21	be	7	88	shall	49	155	the	32
22	remoued	77	89	helpe	39	156	speare	61
23	and	18	90	her	30	157	in	22
24	though	76	91	and	18	158	sunder	77
25	the	32	92	that	47	159	he	13
26	mountaines	124	93	right	60	160	burneth	84
27	be	7	94	early	57	161	the	32
28	caried	39	95	The	32	162	chariot	71
29	into	55	96	heathen	59	163	in	22
30	the	32	97	raged	34	164	the	32
31	midst	62	98	the	32	165	fire	37
32	of	20	99	kingdomes	92	166	Be	7
33	the	32	100	were	48	167	stil	57
34	sea	24	101	mooued	69	168	and	18
35	Though	76	102	he	13	169	know	58
36	the	32	103	vttered	89	170	that	47
37	waters	81	104	his	35	171	I	9
38	thereof	74	105	voyce	65	172	am	13
39	roare	54	106	the	32	173	God	25
40	and	18	107	earth	50	174	I	9
41	be	7	108	melted	56	175	will	52
42	troubled	92	109	The	32	176	bee	12
43	though	76	110	Lord	46	177	exalted	67
44	the	32	111	of	20	178	among	47
45	mountaines	124	112	hosts	59	179	the	32
46	shake	42	113	is	27	180	heathen	59
47	with	57	114	with	57	181	I	9
48	the	32	115	vs	38	182	will	52
49	swelling	95	116	the	32	183	be	7
50	thereof	74	117	God	25	184	exalted	67
51	There	54	118	of	20	185	in	22
52	is	27	119	Iacob	29	186	the	32
53	a	1	120	is	27	187	earth	50
54	riuer	6	121	our	51	188	The	32
55	the	32	122	refuge	60	189	Lord	46
56	streames	90	123	Come	34	190	of	20
57	wherof	76	124	behold	44	191	hosts	59
58	shall	49	125	the	32	192	is	27
59	make	28	126	workes	85	193	with	57
60	glad	23	127	of	20	194	vs	38
61	the	32	128	the	32	195	the	32
62	citie	45	129	Lord	46	196	God	25
63	of	20	130	what	49	197	of	20
64	God	25	131	desolations	126	198	Iacob	29
65	the	32	132	hee	18	199	is	27
66	holy	56	133	hath	36	200	our	51
67	place	35	134	made	22	201	refuge	60

The words of Psalm 46 are divided into groups of ten for ease of counting.

word "of" is sixty-nine positions before "mooved" in position 32, and
the word "that" is sixty-nine positions after "mooved" in position 170.
Recall that St. Alban was said to have been martyred in the year
303 A.D. Dawkins points out, however, that this year is not to be
taken literally. Actually, it is a Freemasonic code for 33 because the
zero acts as a filler or null character between the threes.[3] Here too,
Psalm 46 stands out as special since the sum of the three word-positions resulting from Janus' advice (32, 101, and 170) equals 303 as
indicated in table 5.1. Removing the zero from 303 leaves 33—the
ESC value of Bacon. Another curious feature about this number 303
relates to the Janus epigram by Wither. When the word-positions of
the two words *immediately* before and behind "mooved" are added to
it, they also equal 303 (100 + 101 + 102).

We have determined the total value of the three word-positions
of Psalm 46 (303), but what about the actual values of the two words
which "mooved" is referencing? The word "of" at position 32 equals
20 and the word "that," at position 170 equals 47. 20 + 47 = 67 which
is the ESC value of "Francis." In effect, the two totals in the table
below are the number ciphers for Francis Bacon—67 and 3(0)3.

Table 5.1. Middle Word of Psalm 46.

Words	Position in Psalm	ESC Values
of	32	20
mooved	101	NA
that	170	47
Totals	303	67

It appears that Francis Bacon may have left another clue relating him to Shakespeare in Psalm 46. Calculating the name Francis
Bacon using RAN values in the ESC system results in 55 (see table
3.4). Following the same procedure as before, refer to figure 5.3 and
count 55 word-positions backward and forward from the middle
word "mooved." If you have counted correctly, you have arrived at
the words "shake" and "speare." These results strongly suggest that
the family motto *Mediocria Firma* is a formula Bacon may have
applied to this psalm along with the Janus hint left by George

Wither and supplied by Peter Dawkins.

Dawkins points out that the two Roman Centurions which appear on Francis Bacon's Heraldic Achievement (fig. 5.1) as baron Verulam, viscount of St. Alban, relate to Bacon's previous life as St. Alban. He was a Roman Centurion who was the supposed founder and first Grand Master of Freemasonry in Britain.

Furthermore, the Roman numeral for 100 is the letter C. Since the letter C is the third letter of the alphabet, the double C (two Centurions) signifies 33 which is the ESC equivalent for Bacon, and also the 33rd Degree of Masonry.[4] The ESC value for Francis Bacon equals 100 (67 and 33 respectively).

Applying this symbolism to Psalm 46, the two Centurions correspond to the entire group of 100 words before and after the middle word "mooved." Because the name "Francis Bacon" equals 100, the group of words before and behind "mooved" indicates the symbolic presence of Francis Bacon in Psalm 46—*along with Shakespeare.*

Acting on the premise that Master R influenced the composition of the Great Invocation, let's see if it yields similar results by applying the same technique to it as we did to Psalm 46. The middle word of the Great Invocation is the word "is." (See appendix A2.) Its value is 28 (AN). We locate the twenty-eighth word before "is" ("Love" in word-position 29) and the twenty-eighth word after "is" ("Let" in word-position 85). As indicated in table 5.2, the words "Love" and "Let" equal 91 when their AN values are combined. The number 91 is very much related to the Great Invocation since it corresponds with "The Star." This name refers to the seventeenth major Tarot card and also to the star Sirius. Additionally, the two digits 9 and 1 correspond to I and S which spell "is;" this refers back to the middle word.

As table 5.2 also shows, when we add these three word-positions together they yield 171 (29 + 57 + 85). Recall that 171 is the sum of the three middle word-positions of the Great Invocation and it corresponds to "the celestial ship," "the Queen of Heaven," and "Hermes-Mercury." (Hermes is a key factor in this study and we will have much to say about this important archetypal being later.)

The total AN value of "Love" and "Let" (91) is also quite significant. This value came to light in my earlier book as follows:

> The word "is" has an AN value of 28 which corresponds to "The Star" card in the Tarot using the RAN method. Through its AN value

of 91, "The Star" still corresponds to the word "is" since it can also be depicted as 91 by substituting 9 for "i" and 1 for "s" using the RAN method. Thus, "is" equals "The Star" using both numerological methods. Thus, "The Star"—91, is hidden at the center of the Great Invocation in the word "is;" it is "veiled" (57) in the 57th position of the Great Invocation.[5]

Table 5.2. Middle Word of Great Invocation.

Words	Position	AN Value
Love	29	54
is	57	na
Let	85	37
Total	171	91

The star hidden at the center of the Great Invocation is Sirius. We will discuss this in the next section.

At this point, it is important to remember that the word-positions 29 and 85 have been predetermined *because* the numerological value of the word "is" at the center of the Great Invocation dictated the quantity of word-positions necessary to arrive at the location of each word. The same holds true for Psalm 46; the ESC value of "mooved" *predetermined* the word-positions located before and after it.

This is significant because it indicates the application of the *same technique* to two different writings which produces similar results in each.[6] Figures 5.4 and 5.5 clearly illustrate the point. Just as the number 303 applies meaningfully to Psalm 46, the number 171 is of major importance to the Great Invocation as discussed earlier in relation to the Argo and ship metaphor. The formula, *Mediocria Firma* is the common denominator, isolating the middle word and phrase of the two works and producing these two numbers.

The numbers related to the middle phrase (171), middle word (57), and middle letter (19) of the Great Invocation play a large role in uncovering information related to various esoteric topics. We will soon see that numbers 57 and 19 play a role in the Bacon theme as well.

One final point of interest: The middle phrase of the Great Invocation begins with "God is," which is exactly how the 46th Psalm begins. Note that no other psalm in the Book of Psalms begins with these two words.

Figure 5.4. The Three Middle Words of Psalm 46.

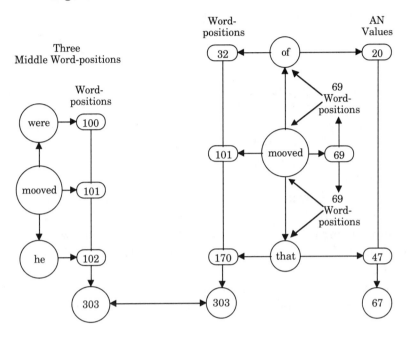

Figure 5.5. The Three Middle Words of the Great Invocation.

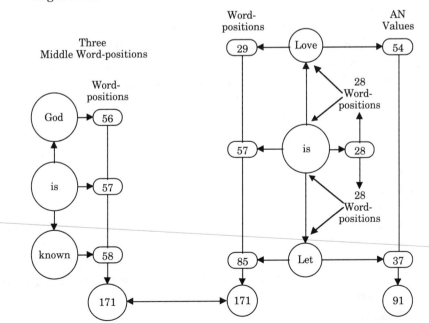

The following summary of the major clues found in Psalm 46 reveals evidence of continuity between it and the Great Invocation in terms of technique and methodology related to the physical center of each prayer:

1. Psalm 46 reveals the name of two personages: A) Shakespeare, via the words "shake" and "spear," located forty-six positions from the beginning and ending. B) Francis Bacon, via the fact that there are exactly 100 words before the middle word of the psalm and 100 words after the middle word. The number 100 is the ESC value of Francis Bacon.

2. Using a similar technique involving the midpoint (*Mediocria Firma*), the Great Invocation reveals hidden symbolic information. Its middle phrase "God is known" begins the same way as Psalm 46—"God is." No other psalm in the King James Bible opens with these words.

3. The middle word of Psalm 46 is "mooved" and equals 69 (ESC). Counting forward and backward 69 positions from the middle word locates the words "of" and "that," respectively. The total ESC value of these two words equals 67 which is the ESC value of "Francis." The total value of these two word-positions plus the position of the middle word equal 303 (32 + 101 + 170). The number 303 relates directly to the symbolic year of St. Alban's martyrdom.

4. The middle word of the Great Invocation, "is," equals 28 (AN). Using the same technique as in item 3, by counting 28 positions backward and 28 positions forward, locates the words "Love" and "let," respectively. The combined AN value of these two words equals 91. Number 91 is the AN value of "the star" (Sirius) and its RAN value is 28 which is the same value as the middle word itself. The total value of these two word-positions plus the position of the middle word equals 171 (29 + 57 + 85). This is also the value of the three middle word-positions.

5. The sum of the three word-positions (100 + 101 + 102) in the middle of Psalm 46 equals 303 and relates directly to Freemasonry, St. Alban, and Bacon's cipher signature. Likewise, the sum of the three word-positions in the middle of the Great Invocation equals 171 (56 + 57 + 58) and relates directly to the celestial ship, the Queen of Heaven, and Hermes-Mercury.

Thus, the middle way is sure—*Mediocria Firma*.

THE MIDDLE LETTER OF THE GREAT INVOCATION

As a direct result of the symbolic placement of the letter "s" at the midpoint of the Great Invocation, the number 19 and its multiples produce over forty terms related to significant esoteric information in the philosophy of the Ageless Wisdom. As an example of the importance of 19, *Sacred Vessel* examines the words located at multiples of nineteen word-positions. The results of that process appear in table 5.3.

Table 5.3. Multiples of 19.

Multiples of 19	Word-position	Word	AN	RAN
1 x 19	19	men	32	14
2 x 19	38	forth	67	31
3 x 19	57	is	28	10
4 x 19	76	the	33	15
5 x 19	95	may	39	12
	285	Totals	199	82

The total value of the word-positions that these five words occupy equals 285, which corresponds to "the central spiritual Sun," a term used by Djwhal Khul to represent the source of all life in our solar system including physical, psychological, and spiritual aspects. The term also suggests the rulership of the star Sirius over our solar system. This rulership is symbolized by the numbers 28 and 91 at the center of the Great Invocation in the form of the word "is." (See point 4 in last section.) The AN value of the five words equals 199 which corresponds to the phrase "star of initiation;" the RAN value equals 82 and also corresponds to "star of initiation."

The star of initiation being referred to is Sirius which has a value of 95 (AN) or 5 x 19. Although the star is a symbol of initiation in the general sense, ultimately the entire process of initiation originates in Sirius. Even though the first degree of initiation, the Birth, is far removed from the spiritual heights of the highest initiations, the star of initiation still stands as an eternal symbol of those profound expansions of consciousness called initiations.

Peter Dawkins also illustrates the importance of 19 via the letter "T" which was the nineteenth letter of the alphabet in the ESC system of gematria. From Dawkins we learn the following:

> In Baconian-Elizabethan simple cipher, T equals 19, T.T. equals 38, and T.T.T. equals 57.
> 1.9 transcribes as A.I., one of the ways of writing (and sounding) the Secret Name of God.
> 3.8 interprets as C.H., the synonym for Christ.
> 5.7 transcribes as E.G., not in itself of such great import, but as the simple cipher signature (57) of "FRA. BACON" it does carry significance.[7]

In addition to the multiples of 19 displayed in the previous table, *Sacred Vessel of the Mysteries* contains another table of esoteric terms (most of them related to Sirius) whose numerological values are multiples of 19. It should be pointed out that Dawkins' comment above regarding "sounding the Secret Name of God," relates to the secret mystic phrase revealed at the third initiation and discussed in the last chapter. This phrase is "the Boat of Mystery which Plows the Ocean" and its value is a multiple of 19 ($23 \times 19 = 437$). Curiously, it appears on page 171 of the Tibetan's book entitled *Initiation, Human and Solar*. Recall that the number 171 corresponds to the phrase "the celestial ship." Just as significant, it is also a number representing a multiple of 19 ($9 \times 19 = 171$).

THE MIDDLE WORD OF THE GREAT INVOCATION

Of further significance is the fact that the middle word of the Great Invocation is in the fifty-seventh position and Dawkins states (in the previous extract) that the number 57 is the ESC equivalent of "FRA. BACON" (meaning Frater or Brother). Besides being the AN equivalent of "rose," the word "veiled" also equals 57. We have established a relationship between Francis Bacon, the rose cross, and the Rosicrucians. The word "veiled" carries the story further by describing the *modus operandi* of not only Bacon, but also more significantly, the Master R. Dawkins describes the Master R in the following way: "he is the master of veiling," he is "a master of wit, allusion, metaphor, symbolism, ambiguity, paradox, enigma and poetic imagination."[8] Certainly these qualities—especially veiling—lie at the heart of this examination of the "veiled" clues scattered through Bacon's writings; and the symbolic structure of the Great Invocation definitely demonstrates "poetic imagination." Are these signs of the Master R's influence? The fact that the word "veiled" equals 57 and that the 57th word-position lies at the middle of the Great Invocation is suggestive in and of itself. The additional knowledge that 57 also equals "Fra. Bacon" suggests his veiled presence at the middle of the Great Invocation and naturally draws our attention to the possibility that there is a larger design at work here.

Peter Dawkins also mentions the number 3.8 or 38 in the above extract. Earlier it was mentioned that the Great Invocation can be divided into four sections of twenty-eight words each, excluding the middle word "is," thus symbolizing an equal-armed cross. The Tibetan states that the equal-armed cross is a symbol of the Path to Sirius. Since the premise of my first book is that the Great Invocation may be Sirian in origin, this theory was tested by dividing the Great Invocation into four twenty-eight word sections (fig. 4.1). The words in each of these quadrants were totaled and the numerological results interpreted. This was a three stage process. The results are illustrated in figure 5.6.

Figure 5.6. Gematria Crosses of the Great Invocation.

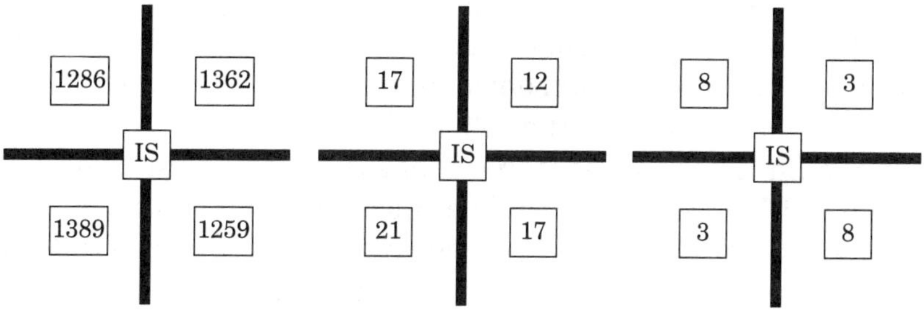

The numbers in these three crosses indicate the values of the twenty-eight words of the Great Invocation placed in each quadrant. The cross at the left contains the original word totals. The middle cross represents the numerological reduction of the corresponding totals, and the cross on the right contains the final reductions of those word totals to their root values.

As you can see, the numbers in the cross on the right equal 8, 3, 3, and 8 respectively. These are the same numbers mentioned by Dawkins (3.8) which he says represent C and H for CHrist (see table 3.4). These numbers take on even greater significance, however, by the fact that they are the AN (83) and RAN (38) values of the name, "RAKOCZI." Recalling that word-position 57 corresponds to the value of the word "veiled," we remove another veil of the cross motif: RAKOCZI "IS" VEILED within the Great Invocation.

Figure 5.7. Gematria Cross of Rakoczi.

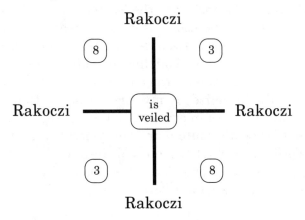

This fact is outstanding in terms of the theory that the Master R has influenced the English rendering of the Great Invocation in some way. Whether read up, down, left, or right, the numbers in figure 5.7 combine to form either 83 or 38.

It should not go unmentioned that these same numbers equal the name "Blue Lodge" which is a Masonic term for the three primary degrees of Masonry: Entered Apprentice, Fellow Craft, and Master Mason. Coincidently, we find a triple meaning here:

1. The Great Invocation depicted as the rose cross (figure 4.1), thus corresponding to the Rosicrucians and Bacon.
2. The Great Invocation depicted to reveal the numbers corresponding to the "Blue Lodge" of Masonry—a fraternity overseen and led by the Master R. Additionally, various researchers believe Francis Bacon had at least some influence on Masonry's birth in England.

3. The Great Invocation depicted with "Rakoczi" veiled at its heart.

NAMES OF THE MASTERS

Although Manly Hall spells Rakoczi as Ragoczy and Dawkins spells it Rakoczy, the spelling which corresponds to the 83 38 pattern is that given by the Master DK in the book *Initiation, Human and Solar* which was quoted in chapter 1. This certainly suggests that the particular spelling chosen by Djwhal Khul matches the numbers found in the quadrants of the Great Invocation. This spelling can also be found in Helena Blavatsky's writing as well as that of Leadbeater.

This 83 38 number code brings up another interesting possibility: that *both* Masters Rakoczi and Djwhal Khul coded their identifications into the Great Invocation because the name "Djwhal Khul" *also* equals 38 using the RAN system. However, unlike the name Rakoczi, the name Djwhal Khul only equals 38 using the RAN method and cannot equal 83 by the AN method. When the AN method is applied to it, the result is 110, thus negating a double match as in the case of Rakoczi.

There are at least two other instances of Djwhal Khul's influence within the Great Invocation. One of these will be discussed later, but the other one can be mentioned now. The name "Master DK" has an AN value of 91 and a RAN value of 28. These are the same numbers discussed earlier and related to "is," the middle word of the Great Invocation. In this case, "Master DK" corresponds to the value of the middle word through the number 28. Based on our earlier remarks about the AN value of "veiled" (57), we can also interpret this to mean that "Master DK" is veiled in the center of the Great Invocation—at position 57.

This numeric correspondence should not be dismissed too lightly, as I believe it signals that Djwhal Khul had some part to play in the design of the Great Invocation. We will, however, find that correlations and numerical correspondences to Master R are overwhelmingly prevalent compared to Djwhal Khul. This adds to the credibility factor in terms of the Great Invocation's English translation because it hints at a cooperative endeavor between at least two masters of the Hierarchy.

The Great Invocation is a world prayer of a very high order which is meant to invoke the spiritual energies of Light, Love, and Power to restore the Plan on Earth. An integral part of the Plan's restoration is the reappearance of the World Teacher. According to DK, there are five masters working specifically on this project:

> There are five Masters and five Ashrams involved in this prepara-
> tory work. First of all, there is the Ashram of the Master K.H.; this is
> the presiding Ashram in this work owing to the fact that it is a second
> ray Ashram and, therefore, upon the same line of energy as that of the
> Christ Himself; another reason is that the Master K.H. will assume the
> role of World Teacher in the distant future when the Christ moves on
> to higher and more important work. Next comes the Ashram of the
> Master Morya; the reason for this is that the whole procedure is pro-
> jected from Shamballa and the Ashram of the Master Morya is ever in
> close touch with that dynamic centre. The Master R.—as the Lord of
> Civilisation—is also closely involved; He is also—and this is of major
> importance—Regent of Europe.
>
> I have also at times referred to the Master Who is responsible for
> the reorganisation of Labour...I myself am the fifth Master concerned
> in this work and am—as it were—the liaison officer between those dis-
> ciples who are working in the field of the world and Those Masters
> Who are directly responsible to the Christ for the needed work of
> preparation.[9]

This extract clearly shows that there are five Masters of the Hierarchy involved in the preparation work for the reappearance of the World Teacher. I will only point out that the Tibetan is the "liaison officer" between the Masters behind the scenes and the disciples working in the outer world. This is another reason to suggest that DK may have only been passing the Great Invocation along to Alice Bailey. In effect, he had the responsibility of making sure that the English composition of the Great Invocation was not changed in any way by Alice Bailey. It was to be taken down by her word for word, just as Djwhal Khul had received it.

Whatever the possibilities are, there is no denying the fact that whoever composed the Great Invocation, it is a work of creative genius—a crowning achievement which ties together the golden strands of the Mysteries in one beautifully synthetic Sound Form.

Notes

1. *The Holy Bible,* 1611, King James Version, Psalm 46.
   The word "Selah," according to Webster's, is an unknown Hebrew word which is believed to mean a rest or pause between various verses in the Psalms.
2. Dawkins, *The Master*, part 1, 18.
3. Ibid., 31.
4. Ibid., 31
5. Berges, *Sacred Vessel of the Mysteries*, 207-8.
6. This is new information not found in *Sacred Vessel of the Mysteries*. Its detection was prompted by the similar discovery in Psalm 46.
7. Dawkins, *The Master*, part 1, 26-7.
8. Ibid., 16.
9. Bailey, *Discipleship in the New Age*, vol. II, 596-7.

FROM SHAKESPEARE
TO EGYPT

*A rosy cross is seen, and at the centre of the cross,
where four arms meet, a rose.*

Discipleship in the New Age, vol. I, 675-6.

During research on the Great Invocation, much evidence emerged suggesting an overriding theme related to the star Sirius. In the writings of Djwhal Khul, Sirius plays a major part in the evolution of human life on Earth.

One of the clues involving Sirius and its connection to the Great Invocation comes from *A Treatise on Cosmic Fire* by Alice Bailey.[1] The particular clue of interest involves what DK calls the Path to Sirius. This path is a method of specialized training offered to the Masters of the Hierarchy at a certain stage in their spiritual unfoldment. In a description of that path, the Tibetan notes that the numbers 14 and 17 provide clues to the identities of the groups of cosmic lives connected with it. These lives are called Creative Hierarchies. They are not pertinent to this discussion, but the numbers 14 and 17 are.

In the same section containing the numbers 14 and 17, DK states that this Path to Sirius involves "duplex rotary motion."[2] In order to follow the hints given by DK, the numbers 14 and 17 were treated as anagrams and rotated to form the following numbers: 1, 4, 7, 11, 14, 17, 41, 47, 71, and 74. These are the numbers which can be created from 14 and 17. The sum of these ten numbers equals 287. This value equals the phrase "Sirius the Great White Lodge" (AN). Thus, duplex rotary motion indeed yields information related to Sirius; especially since, according to DK, the Great White Lodge originates on Sirius. In other words, the spiritual Hierarchy of Earth is a branch Lodge of the original Lodge on Sirius. This concept is obviously applicable to the Masonic tradition of the Grand Lodge which establishes satellite lodges around the world.

Following up on this Masonic theme is the curious fact that these two numbers—14 and 17—correspond to the last names of (John) Dee (14) and (Francis) Bacon (17) using RAN values. By giving these two particular numbers, is Djwhal Khul hinting that Dee and Bacon were members of the Great White Lodge on Earth?

After the publication of *Sacred Vessel of the Mysteries* and my visit to New Zealand, I began to read books about the Bacon/Shakespeare connection. In that literature, the number 287 appears in Hollenbach's *Francis Rosicross*. Although Hollenbach does not make clear who discovered it, the number 287 surfaces in at least three places in the First Folio of Shakespeare's plays published in 1623.

The first instance involves an introductory message by Ben Jonson, an English poet and dramatist of the day. His short introduction, entitled "To the Reader," contains 287 letters as shown below.

Figure 6.1. To the Reader and Number 287.

To the Reader	11
This Figure, that thou here seest put,	30
It was for gentle Shakespeare cut;	28
Wherein the Graver had a strife	26
with Nature, to out-doo the life:	25
O, could he but have drawne his wit	27
As well in brasse, as he hath hit	25
His face, the Print would then surpasse	32
All, that vvas ever vvrit in brasse.	28
But, since he cannot, Reader, looke	27
Not on his Picture, but his Booke.	26
B.I.[3]	2
	287

It should be reiterated that in Elizabethan times, exact English spelling did not exist and some words appeared spelled with a "w" while others were spelled with a double "v." This inconsistency appears in Ben Jonson's introduction to Shakespeare. For example, "was" in line two is spelled with a "w," while "was" in line eight is spelled with a double "v;" thus adding an extra letter to the count.

The second instance where the number 287 is found appears in the list of principal actors in the plays of the First Folio. When all the letters of the actors' names, along with the statement "The Names of the Principall Actors in all these Playes" are summed up, they total 287.[4]

The third example comes from a strange word appearing in the play *Love's Labor's Lost*, Act V. The word is "honorificabilitudinitatibus" which has an ESC value of 287. Quoting Hollenbach:

> According to Edwin Durning-Lawrence in <u>Bacon is Shakespeare</u>, this word first appeared in the Latin Dictionary called <u>Magnae Derivations</u>, written in the latter half of the twelfth century...
> Durning-Lawrence points out that the word, which has 27 letters, appears on the 27th line of page 136 of the Comedies in the 1623 First Folio as well as being the 151st word in ordinary type.[5]

According to Hollenbach this word also appears as a diagram in the papers of Francis Bacon in a collection at the British Museum.[6] Before continuing, there are two important details to note. First, the numbers 151 and 136 when added together equal 287. Obviously this word was specifically placed in order to draw attention to the significance of the number 287. Second, the technique of placing a word of 27 letters on the 27th line and placing that word in the 151st position on page 136 is similar to the specific placement of words in the Great Invocation for numeric and symbolic reasons. As we will soon see, one of those reasons appears to be directly related to the number in question.

Continuing with Hollenbach:

> These numerical arrangements, according to Durning-Lawrence, indicate the meaning of the word is found in the acrostic Latin hexameter, which is formed from the letters of this word: HI LUDI F. BACONIS NATI TUITI ORBI which are translated: These plays F. Bacon's offspring are preserved for the world.[7]

Taylor (author of *Master R: Lord of Our Civilization*) cautions that others have arranged the same letters to yield opposite meanings, although he does not indicate who the other researchers are, or what other phrases were derived from the 27 letters.[8] Taylor makes a good point, however, which is that although other words or phrases can be derived from this "nonsense" word, it is the fact that it has a value of 287 which is significant. This point is well taken because further investigation shows that the number 287 is also the value of the cipher signature of the Rosicrucians, "Fra. Rosi Crosse," (Fraternity or Brotherhood of the Rosi Crosse) using RKC (Rosicrucian Kay Cipher. See table 3.6). In addition, Dawkins points out that "Freemasonic legend states that St. Alban founded Freemasonry in Britain in the year 287 AD."[9]

The fact that the number 287 plays a role in both the Bacon/Shakespeare issue and in the Great Invocation does not mean the two subjects are necessarily related. If this number were the only point of correspondence between the two, it could be ascribed to mere coincidence, but there is more. When we calculate "Fra. Rosi Crosse" using the ESC system, it equals 157. This number equates to the following phrases (all AN values): "the human soul," "the celestial boat," "the great goddess," "throne of Isis," and "the Great Sacrifice." These phrases are related to one another through numerological correspondence and the Ageless Wisdom philosophy. The Great Sacrifice refers to Sanat Kumara, the cosmic Entity Who incarnated in Lemurian times and thus created the human kingdom or "the human soul." The throne of Isis is a descriptive term for the ruling power of "the great goddess" Isis. *Sacred Vessel* discusses the archetypal relationship between Isis and Athena in some detail. The celestial boat is a powerful image, especially in light of the previous discussion of the ship metaphor in chapter 4. Athena is, of course, associated with the Argo, but in ancient Egyptian illustrations Isis is sometimes depicted traveling in her celestial boat as one of the Egyptian deities who lives among the stars and is associated with powers beyond the lower world of Earth. This same imagery appears in the Elizabethan era in John Dee's titlepage from *GENERAL AND RARE MEMORIALS pertayning to the Perfect Arte of NAVIGATION*, depicting Elizabeth I seated in her ship facing the Spanish armada.

Finally, referring to the Triangular-armed Cross of the Great Invocation in figure 6.2, note that the four words surrounding the middle word "is" form a small cross as they cut through the word "is" at right angles to each other. The AN value of these four words equals 157. These four words are "of," "God," "known," and "the"   (21 + 26 + 77 + 33 = 157). If symbolism means anything, the fact that the four words surrounding the middle word (whose fifty-seventh position corresponds to the word "rose") have a numerological value which can be equated with "Fra. Rosi Crosse" is profound indeed and signals the possibility of deliberate planning on the part of either the Master DK, Master R, or both. Furthermore, the RAN value of these same four words totals 67, which is *also* the ESC value of "Francis."

Figure 6.2. Heart of the Cross—Number 157.

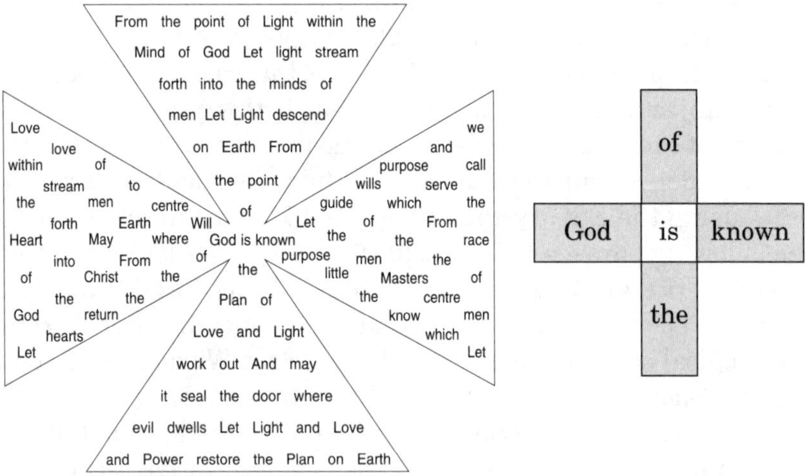

The fact that "honorificabilitudinitatibus" has a value of 287 which relates it to so many pertinent topics is remarkable, but another aspect of this number involves the *placement* of "honorificabilitudinitatibus" in *Love's Labor's Lost.* As previously stated, this strange word appears on page 136, line 27, word 151 (not counting italicized words) of that comedy. These numbers are significant in relation to the Great Invocation. Let's take them one at a time.

151. This number has an indirect relationship to the Great Invocation through words and phrases associated with the overall theme of redemption, which the Great Invocation itself invokes. This number correlates to the following terms, which all equal 151 (AN): "the Plan of Love," "Sophia Wisdom," "Jesus Christ," "the Great

Work," and "Rosy Cross." These last three items are especially significant since they relate directly to the Rosicrucians; and certainly
Sophia Wisdom plays an important role in this as the divine
Feminine expression of God. Finally, the Plan of Love is obviously
central to all of these elements.

136. This is the number derived from the Signature of Sirius (see
Bacon, Napier, and Zeros, chapter 4). The words "the Light of God"
or "the God of Light" have the AN value of 136, but more importantly, their RAN value equals "the Great White Lodge on Sirius."

27. The number 27 appears in my earlier book in relation to
Horus, the son of Osiris and Isis. The RAN value of Horus is 27 and
this is the only obvious correspondence to the placement of "honorificabilitudinitatibus" on line 27 of *Love's Labor's Lost*. This isn't too
noteworthy except for one important fact—this 27 letter word is not
all on line 27. Only the *first 16 letters* appear on line 27—the remaining 11 letters appear on line 28. Whether by accident or design this
hyphenation of "honorificabilitudinitatibus" into two parts, strad-
dling lines 27 and 28, is intriguing because of my previous findings.[10]

These three Egyptian deities represent the fundamental trinity of the ancient Egyptian religion. Osiris equates with the Christian
Father, Isis with the Holy Spirit, and Horus with the Son. Since
Horus is the product of the union between Osiris and Isis, numbers
can be applied to the values of these names to derive their symbolic meaning. Using all RAN values, Osiris equals 35, Isis equals 20,
and Horus equals 27. However, if we symbolically join Osiris and
Isis numerically, they equal 55 (35 + 20). Horus can be represented
as the average between the two parents, or 27.5. Using the words of
the Great Invocation as an index, it is obvious that 27.5 is neither
word-position 27 nor position 28, but inclusive of both. Symbolically
speaking, Horus represents word-positions 27 and 28 in the Great
Invocation. The words "point" (74 AN) and "of" (21 AN) occupy those
two positions. When combined, they total 95 which is the value of
Sirius. The strange coincidence here is not so much with Sirius as it
is with the curious fact that the numbers 27 and 28 are involved in
the Horus example from *Sacred Vessel of the Mysteries* AND in the
placement of "honorificabilitudinitatibus" in *Love's Labor's Lost*.

Another curiosity surfaces when the 16 letters on line twenty-
seven and the 11 letters on line twenty-eight are multiplied. The
product of 16 x 11 equals 176. This is the value of "the light which

ever shineth in the East" and "the Boat of Mystery which Ploughs the Ocean," two phrases discussed earlier in the Ship Metaphor section of chapter 4.

The numbers in question, which designate the location of the word "honorificabilitudinitatibus" in *Love's Labor's Lost* are 136 (the page), 27 and 28 (the lines), and 151 (the word). These numbers combine to equal 342 (136 + 27 + 28 + 151). This number is very relevant to the Great Invocation for two reasons. First, it is 2 x 171. As already discussed in some detail, 171 represents the sum of the three middle word-positions of the Great Invocation. At least two phrases equaling 171 relate to both the Great Invocation and the Bacon/Rosicrucian theme, which are "the Queen of Heaven" and "the celestial ship." By another apparent coincidence, the 16 letters of "honorificabilitudinitatibus" which appear on line twenty-seven of *Love's Labor's Lost* equal 171 (AN).

Second, the number 342 is also the product of 18 x 19. The number 19 and its multiples play a key role in the symbolic coding of the Great Invocation. In light of the discussion of Horus, it is interesting that the number 19 was also important to the ancient Egyptians.

THE NUMBER OF THE HUMAN SOUL

This 19 theme continues to appear here just as it does in the previous chapter in relation to the Great Invocation and the star Sirius. The difficulty here is that we have found a mysterious relationship (perhaps purely coincidental) between the location of the word "honorificabilitudinitatibus" and the Egyptian god Horus and consequently Osiris and Isis. It appears that the number 19 is the common denominator between Horus and "honorificabilitudinitatibus." The source of this common denominator comes from ancient Egypt. According to philosopher and Egyptologist R. A. Schwaller de Lubicz, the number 19 was very important to the ancient Egyptians. Through years of tireless research Schwaller de Lubicz, his wife, and several others meticulously measured every part of the Temple of Luxor in Egypt. He calls this the Temple of Man because the layout of the entire temple is consistent with the ratios and proportions of the human body. It is impossible to go into the details of this enormous discovery here except for one important aspect which directly impinges on our topic. His team discovered that the Egyptian art and architecture found in the temple of Luxor was laid out on grids of nineteen squares. This scheme is present on other monuments as well and has even been traced to some Mayan temple art.

According to Schwaller de Lubicz, the key to understanding the full import of this practice involves the relationship between the numbers 18 and 19. In the many depictions of gods, pharaohs, and ordinary humans on the walls of the temples, a boundary distinguishes the part of the human head immediately above the eyes from the rest of the body. This boundary separates the lower eighteen units of the grid and the topmost nineteenth unit. It should be noted that the human figure most often is placed in a scene which might be larger or taller than nineteen units, but the human figure itself is placed in such a way that the nineteenth unit of a grid placed over the scene still falls between the eyes and the top of the head.

Schwaller de Lubicz calls this unique measure the "human canon." The mathematics involved in his analysis of this discovery are much too complicated to go into here, but these are presented in exhaustive detail in his monumental work *The Temple of Man*. The human canon of the ancient Egyptians (based on 19) is the law governing the divine proportions built into the human form. The placement of the nineteenth level at the upper portion of the human head signifies the use of the intellect and mind as distinct from the lower kingdoms of nature, which lack the degree of intellect, reason, and self-awareness of a human being.

The Ageless Wisdom teaches that humanity was given mind by Beings of cosmic origin—specifically, Sanat Kumara and His Assistants. Ultimately, the creation of humanity was aided by an even higher order of Lives on Sirius. Much more about this later, but for now let it be noted that the numeric value of Sirius (95) is the result of 5 x 19. Schwaller de Lubicz states that:

> Cosmic Man is equivalent to 5. When he allows himself to be sexual, to be dual, he is chased out of Paradise, that is, he falls into the terrestrial world and its vicissitudes. Then he becomes 6.[11]

I would point out that the numbers associated with the name "Sanat Kumara" contain three 5s and one 6 (55, 65). The planetary Logos is the Cosmic Man, Who in the incarnated form of Sanat Kumara, becomes the terrestrial man symbolized in His name containing the fives and six.

The Ageless Wisdom teaching given by DK (and that presented by H.P. Blavatsky) asserts that the soul or causal body of a human being resides on the nineteenth sub-plane or dimension of our solar system. The lower eighteen sub-planes are called the planes of human form or personality. The boundary between the eighteenth and nineteenth levels is the major dividing line between the human world of illusion and the higher worlds of spiritual awareness. This may explain why some depictions show a god, royal personage, or priest standing next to an "ordinary person" whose stature falls one unit short of the nineteenth level. The more evolved individual stands one level higher, encompassing all nineteen levels. The human of full stature (nineteen levels) thus indicates those who have been initiated into the spiritual life of the soul. They have integrated the lower eighteen divisions of the personality form world with the nineteenth level of the soul. They are not necessarily perfected humans, but they are definitely on the spiritual path.

Apparently, the ancient Egyptian priests and initiates knew this and built it into their temples and monuments. This ageless teaching is thus presented in various forms from the ancients to the modern era. In Bacon's time, such matters were veiled in secrecy and ciphers and were only taught to those committed to the improvement of the human condition through such groups as the Rosicrucians and Freemasons.

There is obviously much more here which warrants further study, but the important point is the fact that this number 19 appears through the specific placement of "honorificabilitudinitatibus" in *Love's Labor's Lost*, a play which Bacon may have written under the name of Shakespeare; and in turn it plays an important part in the symbolism related to the Great Invocation and to Sirius—95 or 5 x 19.

All these examples display a corresponding link between topics covered in *Sacred Vessel of the Mysteries* and a coding technique present in the works of Bacon/Shakespeare, centered around the numbers 287 and multiples of 19 such as 171 and 342. As interesting as these number correlations are, the coming chapters will demonstrate more number correspondences which are even more compelling in their function as links between Francis Bacon, the Great Invocation, and the Master R.

THREE LETTERS

I am ending this chapter with one more small, but fascinating interplay between *Love's Labor's Lost*, the number 287, and the Great Invocation. Using the ESC system, the letter L equals 11. This strange word, "honorificabilitudinitatibus," which equals 287 is located in a play whose title contains words which all begin with the letter "L" (Love's Labor's Lost). Thus, Bacon's cipher number—33— appears via the acronym for the play's title, LLL—11 + 11 + 11 = 33.

By alphabetizing all 443 letters comprising the Great Invocation, we discover that it contains precisely three letter K's. In modern English, the AN value of "K" equals 11. Simple calculation shows that the number 33 is present in the Great Invocation via the three letter K's (3 x 11 = 33). This information is certainly meaningful, but the really intriguing aspect of this is that the middle K of the three is the *287th letter* of the 443 letters composing the Great Invocation!

Notes

1. Alice A. Bailey, *A Treatise on Cosmic Fire*, 1258-61.
2. Ibid. 1260.
3. Shakespeare, *Mr. William Shakespeare's Comedies, Histories, & Tragedies, A Facsimilie of the First Folio, 1623*, 2.
4. Ibid., 15.
5. Hollenbach, *Francis Rosicross*, 125.
6. Ibid., 122.
7. Ibid., 125.
8. Taylor, *Master R: Lord of Our Civilization*, 108.
9. Dawkins, *The Master*, part 1, 31.
10. Berges, *Sacred Vessel of the Mysteries*, 332-6.
11. R. A. Schwaller de Lubicz, *The Temple of Man*, 316.

SEEKING

FRANCIS BACON

Any apparent simplicity is the veil of deeply hidden truth,
and it is for this that the disciple must search.

Discipleship in the New Age, vol. II, 411.

In this chapter we will explore the name "Francis Bacon" in greater detail by examining its presence in Shakespeare and as a numeric code in the Great Invocation. Several years of research have brought to my attention an abundance of information indicating that Bacon used cryptography in various ways. As reported in chapter 4, Penn Leary has uncovered a mass of data which reveals the presence of the name Bacon in various forms throughout the plays and the *Sonnets* of Shakespeare. If indeed the Master R was once incarnated as Francis Bacon, it is possible that his style of embedding hidden information continues in his communications with esoteric students to the present era.

As already discussed, the cipher number for Bacon using the ESC system equals 33. The complete name of Francis Bacon equals 100—Francis equals 67 and Bacon equals 33. If we examine the illustrated cross pattern related to Rakoczi (83 38) (figs. 5.6 and 5.7), we find that the name Francis Bacon is also present. The intermediate values of the 28 words in the four quadrants are 17, 12, 21, and 17 (see fig. 7.1). Using RAN values reveals that Bacon equals 17. Numbers 21 and 12 combine to equal 33, Bacon in the ESC system. Furthermore, numbers 17 and 17 combine to equal 34, which when added to 33, equals 67 or Francis (ESC). Consequently, the numbers arrayed around the cross in figure 7.1 contain the name Francis Bacon in *both* the modern and Elizabethan gematria systems. (These same numbers—17, 12, 21, and 17 are finally reduced to their root values of 8, 3, 3, and 8 which, of course, correspond to Rakoczi as earlier illustrated.)

Figure 7.1. Bacon's Cross.

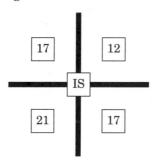

Therefore, by creating a Rosicrucian/Sirian Cross and arranging an equal number of words from the Great Invocation around its arms, the names of Francis Bacon as well as Rakoczi (and Djwhal Khul, 38 RAN) are present within the word structure and gematria of the Great Invocation.

Another interesting aspect to Bacon's name in ESC is that it reduces to 4 (Francis = 67, 6 + 7 = 13, 1 + 3 = 4) and 6 (Bacon = 33, 3 + 3 = 6). The numbers 4 and 6 can be placed side by side to form the number 46, thus matching Psalm number 46 and the two words, "shake" and "speare," which are also keyed to the number 46 by their position in the psalm.[1]

In the First Folio edition of *The First Part of King Henry the Fourth* (referred to as *King Henry IV* from here on), there is a passage on page 56 in which the name "Francis" is repeated thirty-three times. Also, the word "Bacon" appears three times in Act 2, scenes 1 and 2 of the same play—once on page 53 and twice on page 54. It is interesting to note that when the digits of page 56 are multiplied they equal 30 (5 x 6). When 30 is multiplied by the number of times

Francis appears on page 56 (33 times), the result is 990 (5 x 6 x 33). When the three appearances of Bacon are added to 990, the resultant sum is 993. This number is the last page of the First Folio as shown in figure 7.2.

This exercise may seem a bit contrived until we realize that this final page number has been typeset backwards. Since the left facing page is 398, the next page should be 399 except that it has been reversed to read as 993.[2] This page anomaly is connected to the name Francis Bacon.

Figure 7.2. Final Left and Right Pages of the First Folio.

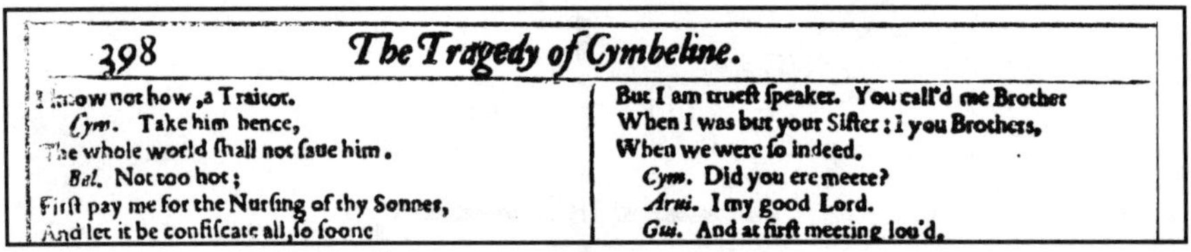

398 *The Tragedy of Cymbeline.*

I know not how, a Traitor.
Cym. Take him hence,
The whole world ſhall not ſaue him.
Bel. Not too hot;
Firſt pay me for the Nurſing of thy Sonnes,
And let it be confiſcate all, ſo ſoone

But I am trueſt ſpeaker. You call'd me Brother
When I was but your Siſter: I you Brothers,
When we were ſo indeed.
Cym. Did you ere meete?
Arui. I my good Lord.
Gui. And at firſt meeting lou'd,

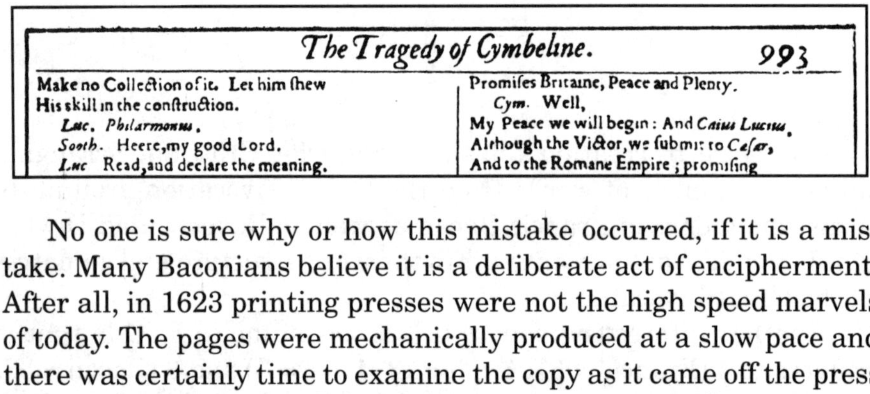

The Tragedy of Cymbeline. 993

Make no Collection of it. Let him ſhew
His skill in the conſtruction.
Luc. *Philarmonus.*
Sooth. Heere, my good Lord.
Luc Read, and declare the meaning.

Promiſes Britaine, Peace and Plenty.
Cym. Well,
My Peace we will begin: And *Caius Lucius*,
Although the Victor, we ſubmit to *Cæſar*,
And to the Romane Empire; promiſing

No one is sure why or how this mistake occurred, if it is a mistake. Many Baconians believe it is a deliberate act of encipherment. After all, in 1623 printing presses were not the high speed marvels of today. The pages were mechanically produced at a slow pace and there was certainly time to examine the copy as it came off the press before proceeding with the entire run.

One attempt at an explanation for this number reversal comes from Penn Leary who notes that the three digits can be combined to equal 21 (9 + 9 + 3 = 21)—the number of letters in the alphabet used to encode many passages of Shakespearean literature. In Leary's book, this is borne out by the many decoded Shakespearean passages which contain the names "Francis" or "Bacon" with various spellings as shown earlier.

The strange occurrence of the name "Francis" thirty-three times on page 56 and "Bacon" three times on two other pages of *King Henry IV* does serve to draw attention to Francis Bacon as the source of the reversal of the final page of the First Folio. Performing several arithmetic operations on the digits contained in the page number 993 yields meaningful information by using one digit as the divisor and the remaining digits as the dividend. This can be accomplished in three ways. These are—99 divided by 3, 93 divided by 9, and 39 divided by 9. As figure 7.3 illustrates, the first operation yields 33 "Bacon." The second operation, 93 divided by 9 yields 10.33333 (to infinity). Removing the decimal point results in the number 103 "Shakespeare" followed by "Bacon" (33) to infinity. The third operation, 39 divided by 9 yields 4.333333 (to infinity). This last result is interesting because it is associated with Psalm 46.

Figure 7.3. Arithmetic of 993.

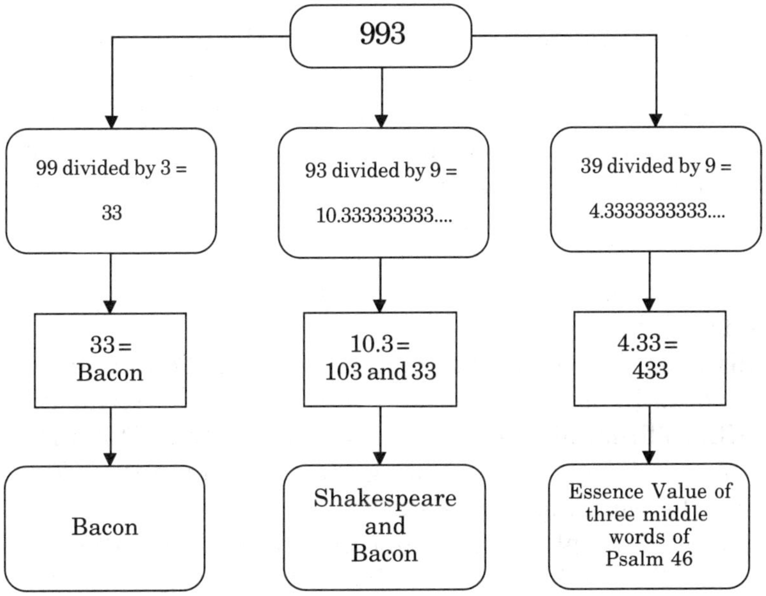

Recalling Bacon's family motto *Mediocria Firma*, we identify the *middle* word of Psalm 46 as "mooved" in word-position 101. Taking the cue from Wither's Janus epigram, we symbolically look before and behind prior to "burying" the clue at our feet. Therefore, the word immediately *before* mooved is "were" in position 100 and the word immediately *behind* mooved is "he" in position 102. Now that we have located the three middle words, we need to obtain the values in ESC. As table 7.1 shows, the final total of 433 matches the third operation—39 divided by 9 (after removing the decimal point). Again we have a reference to the middle of Psalm 46 followed by 33 (Bacon) to infinity. Note that the combining of a word-position and the gematria value of the word in that position is termed the "Essence Value."

Table 7.1. Three Middle Words of Psalm 46.

Words	Word Position	ESC	Essence Value
were	100	48	148
mooved	101	69	170
he	102	13	115
Totals	303	130	433

All three examples plainly show that the numbers 9, 9, and 3 can be mathematically manipulated to produce the ESC numbers which correspond to the names of Bacon and Shakespeare. The third example (433) refers us to Psalm 46 in which the words "shake" and "speare" have been cleverly positioned in order to draw attention to them, just as the reversal of the page number from 399 to 993 draws attention to it. This is an important point because whether or not the page number is reversed does not change the mathematics since the digits are still the same.

This is not the first time we have seen this deliberate positioning of words in order to communicate a number. Recall the word "honorificabilitudinitatibus" which is placed on the 151st line of page 136 of *Love's Labor's Lost* yielding the cipher number 287 and the fact that the word itself equals 287.

Another example of this phenomenon includes the very first word of the First Folio—"Boteswaine" (an old English term for ship's officer). Penn Leary clearly demonstrates Bacon's influence in Shakespeare when he deciphers this word as "FSBIACCEN" in which FS is the signature abbreviation for Francis followed by the phonetic spelling of Bacon. The letters "fsbiaccen" equal 60 in ESC and have no obvious meaning, but the word "Boteswaine" does. The ESC value of Boteswaine equals 126. In the First Folio we find Boteswaine located on page 1, line 26 of *The Tempest*. By placing a 1 (for page one) adjacent to 26 (for line twenty-six), we obtain the number 126—the ESC value of Boteswaine. Again, for those who know the use of ciphers, attention is being drawn to a specific word; a word which just happens to refer to Francis Bacon. We see then that the First Folio begins and ends by referring to Francis Bacon through the use of ciphers and gematria.

Perhaps one of the most dramatic clues to a possible connection between Francis Bacon/Master R and codes in the Great Invocation appears on pages 53, 54, and 56 of *King Henry IV*. The specific connection involves the value derived from the total number of times the name Francis Bacon appears in *King Henry IV*.

The name "Francis" has an ESC value of 67 and because it appears 33 times we multiply its value by its number of appearances to derive its total value in the play. Hence, 33 x 67 = 2211. The word "Bacon" appears 3 times. Therefore, if Bacon equals 33 (ESC), its total value in the play equals 99. Consequently, the total value of the words "Francis Bacon" in *King Henry IV* equals 2310 (99 + 2211). The number 2310 is a possible number-bridge spanning the 350 or so years between the author of *King Henry IV* and the English translator of the Great Invocation.

Here is the rest of the story. In 1993, I identified twenty-one capitalized words in the Great Invocation which I named "key words" because they are numerologically significant as a group within the context of the entire Great Invocation. When examining the Great Invocation, take note that twenty-one words are capitalized (boldface type), excluding leading verse line words.

From the point of **Light** within the **Mind** of **God**
Let light stream forth into the minds of men.
Let **Light** descend on **Earth**.
From the point of **Love** within the **Heart** of **God**
Let love stream forth into the hearts of men.
May **Christ** return to **Earth**.
From the centre where the **Will** of **God** is known
Let purpose guide the little wills of men—
The purpose which the **Masters** know and serve.
From the centre which we call the race of men
Let the **Plan** of **Love** and **Light** work out
And may it seal the door where evil dwells.
Let **Light** and **Love** and **Power** restore the **Plan** on **Earth**.

For the sake of clarity, extracts about the key words from *Sacred Vessel* are reproduced here:

An interesting aspect of these capitalized words is an inconsistency involving two words—light and love. Note the differences in their capitalization in the first two stanzas of the Great Invocation.

This distinction may indicate that the Light of God and the Love of God are to be distinguished from the light that streams into the minds of men or the love that enters the hearts of men. Perhaps the entry of divine Light and Love into the human world of form is symbolized by the lower-case spelling of light and love in stanzas one and two. Symbolically speaking, the Light and Love of God lose their pure divinity as they enter the denser parts of the created world and are therefore shown as lower-case. Alternatively, one might argue that since "Light" is diminished to "light" when it enters the minds of men then why is the word Light capitalized in the third line, when it has descended on Earth?

After examining the Great Invocation in detail it is obvious to me these twenty-one capitalized words have a deep symbolic meaning not easily recognized. There is a basis for the location of these key words in specific stanzas, for the number of letters in these key words and for their numerological value....The evidence suggests "light" and "love" were purposely written in lower-case to create and maintain specific numerological consistency on a theme woven throughout this mantram. All these "threads of symbolic meaning" are necessary to hold this "fabric of words" together. This Great Invocation appears to be a tapestry of words intentionally woven into an intricate hidden pattern of deep significance.[3]

When the above information was written, an effort had been made to rationalize the reasons why the words "light" and "love" were presented in lower case, but as revealed in the last paragraph of the extract above, I already had suspected some deeper, less obvious reason for this strange and seemingly illogical capitalization method.

The specific capitalization of only twenty-one words may have a direct bearing on the Master R and his prior incarnation as Francis Bacon, a *master* of ciphers and codes who only used *twenty-one* letters to encipher his messages. Although these key words have other meanings as I explain in my first book, we will focus on their possible relationship to Master R. In order to do this we must view these key words according to their symbolic meaning based on their appearance in the Great Invocation. Let me explain what this means.

As already discussed, the Great Invocation contains twenty-one key words. From an exoteric standpoint these words consist of two groups—those words which appear one time and those which appear more than one time. From an esoteric standpoint, however, these key words are categorized into three groups. The first group consists of those key words which appear only one time. The second group is composed of those key words which *generate more of their own kind.* The third group is comprised of the offspring of the second group. Thus, these three groups are termed celibate, non-celibate, and offspring. They are depicted in figure 7.4. Notice that the five non-celibate keywords have reproduced ten additional words. This fact will be important as we proceed.

Figure 7.4. Key Word Lineage.

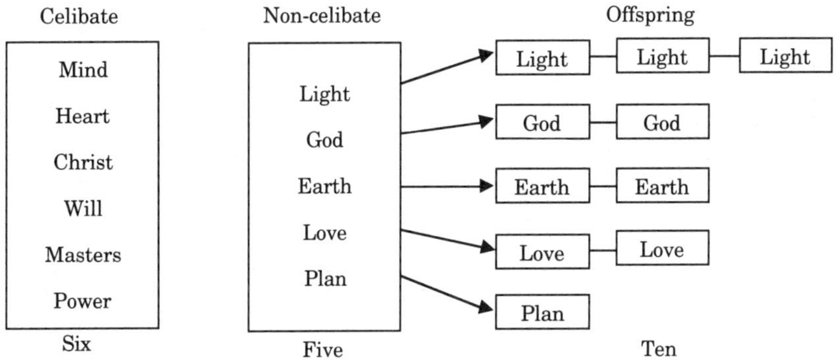

The following table shows the letter count and AN gematria values of each group of key words. The total values for the Celibate group on the left side of the table show no real importance to our study. The Non-celibate group, however, contains two quite interesting numbers in the bottom "Totals" row. The first number to note is 21. This is the total number of letters comprising the five words in the Non-celibate group. Recall that Bacon used a twenty-one letter alphabet for his cipher work. The other important number in this group is 231—the AN value of the five Non-celibate words. Multiplying the ten Offspring key words by the total AN value of these Non-celibate key words which gave them birth results in 2310, the exact gematria value of "Francis Bacon" in *King Henry IV.*

The key to understanding this number bridge of 2310 is not the number itself, but the fact that this number connects two completely different types of writing separated by more than 300 years. The number 2310 is the energy equivalent of Francis Bacon as that name appears in *King Henry IV.* Following the theory, Francis Bacon is telling us that he gave birth to the play *King Henry IV* (and other

Shakespearean works) just as the Non-celibate key words gave birth to the Offspring group.

Table 7.2. Key Word Lineage Gematria.

Celibate	Letter Count	AN	Non-celibate	Letter Count	AN	Off-spring	Letter Count	AN
			Light	5	56	Light	5	56
Mind	4	40				Light	5	56
			God	3	26	Light	5	56
			Earth	5	52	God	3	26
			Love	4	54	God	3	26
Heart	5	52				Earth	5	52
Christ	6	77				Earth	5	52
Will	4	56				Love	4	54
Masters	7	95				Love	4	54
			Plan	4	43	Plan	4	43
Power	5	77						
Totals 6	31	397	5	21	231	10	43	475

It is obvious that the Non-celibate group is connected to Bacon. Why? Because this is the group of key words which is the creator of *additional words*, just as Francis Bacon was the creator of the words comprising the Shakespearean literature. Within the context of the Great Invocation, this tells us that he is also the creator of these words. His cipher alphabet number is present in the form of the twenty-one letters and furthermore, the number 231 is the sum of the addition of the first *twenty-one* integers (1 + 2 + 3.....+ 21).

Aside from pure coincidence, one logical conclusion for this numeric correlation suggests that the Master R was, at the very least, influential in determining the capitalization of particular words within the Great Invocation in order to show a relationship (and continuity) to his prior work as Francis Bacon. Also, keep in mind that this matching number correspondence would not exist if the words "light" and "love" had been capitalized (to match their counterparts) as logic would seem to dictate.

The symbolism of these Non-celibate key words indicates that they are creators and that they indeed have Offspring. The number 2310 links these Non-celibate and Offspring words to the words "Francis" and "Bacon" in *King Henry IV*. This suggests that Francis Bacon was the creator of Shakespeare, or at the very least, played some role in that body of literature.

A clue to the identity of the creator/composer of the English version of the Great Invocation is found in the Non-celibate key words themselves. As already noted, these five key words are composed of twenty-one letters. That feature, plus the fact that there are twenty-one key words in total suggest a direct link to Francis Bacon. The next clue completes the puzzle by strongly suggesting a direct link to Master R because, when these twenty-one letters are placed in a line, the middle letter of the group is "R." Furthermore, "R" is in the *eleventh* position which corresponds to the root value of "Rakoczi." Is this merely a coincidence or has the Master Rakoczi left his imprint buried in the middle of a group of words in the Great Invocation; not just any words, but *specific words which have been capitalized*, are distinctive within the larger group as *creators of other words*, and are numerologically linked with the placement of "Francis" and "Bacon" in *King Henry IV*? Francis Bacon was a creator of words and the name is hidden within the larger body of a play. The twenty-one key words and the sub-group of Non-celibate words are hidden within the Great Invocation. Furthermore, Bacon's own family motto *Mediocria Firma* is utilized as a device to show that at the middle of all these correlations, hidden within a specific group of twenty-one letters is the initial of the author of both these works—the Master R.

Table 7.3 R at the Middle.

L	I	G	H	T	G	O	D	E	A	R	T	H	L	O	V	E	P	L	A	N
1	2	3	4	5	6	7	8	9	10	11	12	13	14	15	16	17	18	19	20	21

Take a deep breath and prepare for more, because we are not quite finished with *King Henry IV*. As we have already seen in the case of "Boteswaine" and "honorificabilitudinitatibus," there is often a reason why certain words appear on specific pages and sometimes even on particular lines. This seems to be the case with the name of Francis Bacon in *King Henry IV*.

The name "Bacon" appears one time on page 53 and two times on page 54, and the name "Francis" appears thirty-three times on page 56. These numbers are linked with the Celibate and Non-celibate key words in table 7.2. As that table illustrates, these eleven words are composed of 52 letters. (This value is found by combining the letter count from both groups.) This number plays a key role demonstrating the hidden connection between *King Henry IV* and the Great Invocation. (We will see this occur again in chapter 9.)

Treating each page number and the quantity of names found on each page as two distinct elements, let's calculate a value for each name's appearance on a page. Figure 7.5 illustrates this procedure.

Figure 7.5. Bacon in King Henry the Fourth.

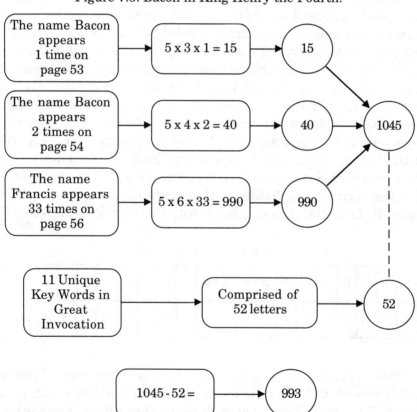

As figure 7.5 illustrates, when 52 is subtracted from 1045 the result is 993—the mysteriously reversed final page number of the First Folio. Generally speaking, these numbers tell us that eleven specific words found in the Great Invocation are connected to the First Folio of Shakespeare. More specifically, the fifty-two letters comprising these eleven words, when added to the final page of the First Folio (the page number printed in reverse), equal the exact value of the words "Francis" and "Bacon" appearing on specific pages in *King Henry IV*. This implies that the Great Invocation and the First Folio are connected to Francis Bacon.

This result may be coincidental, so let's look at one more example which does not include *King Henry IV*, but instead involves the key words of the Great Invocation and the Master R. These twenty-one key words are distributed through the five stanzas as follows:

Stanza one	5 key words
Stanza two	5 key words
Stanza three	3 key words
Stanza four	3 key words
Stanza five	5 key words

Naturally, the total key words in this list equal twenty-one; but when each number is treated as a factor and multiplied, the result is quite different—1125. Again, what meaningful number can be derived from 1125 through an interaction with another number pertinent to our study? The number 993 is an obvious choice since, from our last example, we already know it is related to the key words. Subtracting 993 from 1125 yields 132. This number appears rather innocuous until we realize it is the sum of 83 + 38 + 11. These are the three numbers corresponding to RAKOCZI—the AN value, RAN value, and root value respectively. Symbolically speaking, the factored product of the twenty-one specifically placed key words of the Great Invocation expresses a value which contains the "993" pages of the First Folio of Shakespeare along with the name Rakoczi in its three numeric forms.

The number 132 plays a large role later in the book. For now I will say that the number is derived from the word-positions five, six, fifty-six, and sixty-five in the Great Invocation (5 + 6 + 56 + 65 = 132). Note in table 7.2 that the two groups of original key words, *excluding* the Offspring duplicates, are composed of five and six words; each thus further reinforcing the role of the key words as a cipher bridge connecting Francis Bacon to Master R and identifying R as the hidden English composer of the Great Invocation.

These three exercises in esoteric gematria provide very suggestive evidence linking Master R to Francis Bacon, Shakespeare, and the Great Invocation. Without the capitalization of these specific words and their strategic placement in the Great Invocation, they cannot link with the specifically placed names, "Francis" and "Bacon" in *King Henry IV*.

FRANCIS BACON WORD SEARCH

Since there is some evidence of a complex relationship between the key words of the Great Invocation, *King Henry IV*, and the last page number of the First Folio, it is worthwhile to pursue other possible relationships between the numeric values of "Francis" (67), "Bacon" (33) and "Francis Bacon" (100) and these same values within the Great Invocation.

One method of searching for clues in the Great Invocation is to examine the letters of which it is composed. It contains 443 letters. The letter O is located at position 33, the letter D is located at position 67, and the letter T is found at position 100. These letters and their values do not exhibit any meaning in relation to our investigation. This does not necessarily mean the letters provide no clues to seeking the name "Francis Bacon" in the Great Invocation. For as we learned in the last chapter, when all 443 letters are sorted in alphabetical order we discover exactly three letter K's. And since the letter K has a numerological value of 11, this means that the total value of the these three K's equals 33—the cipher number for "Bacon." Also, recall that the middle K of the three is located at position 287—a number of significance to Francis Bacon, as discussed in the last chapter.

We have examined the letters, let's now examine the words located in these same numeric positions. To do this exercise, please refer to figure 4.3. Each block in the diagram contains two numbers and a word. The top number is the position of the word in the Great Invocation. The bottom number is the AN value of the word in the block. The theory is that a word-position relevant to the cipher number for "Bacon" (33) may yield details about Master R.

Locate the word in position thirty-three. The thirty-third word is "of." Note that the bottom number is 21. This is its AN value. The significance of the twenty-one key words qualifies this as being of some importance. Now we will use the AN value of 21 to locate the twenty-first word in the invocation. If you have followed the directions correctly, that word should be "Light" with a value of 56. This is of interest since the thirty-three appearances of "Francis" are on page 56 of *King Henry IV*. More intriguing, however, is the fact that the Essence Value of the thirty-third word-position is 54 (33 + 21) and the fifty-fourth word of the Great Invocation is "Will." Even though this refers to the Will of God, with all due respect, might it also refer to "Will" Shakespeare?

The following example demonstrates that such forms of coding are not that unusual. Using the ESC system, the entire name "Francis Bacon" equals 100. Because the letter C is the Roman numeral for 100, at least two researchers (Dawkins and Johnson) point out the presence of that letter in particular writings or illustrations as a symbolic code for Francis Bacon. The earlier reference to Dawkins' description of Bacon's emblem containing the two Roman Centurions is an example of this practice. Edward Johnson gives another example:

> In Marston's *Scourge of Villanie*, Satire IV, reference is made to some unnamed author as follows: "Whose silent name one letter bounds."
> So far as we know there is only one letter in the alphabet that applies to this description, and that is the letter C, because C is the Roman numeral for 100, which is the numerical count of the name Francis Bacon....
> In a little book entitled "*Mercury: or The Secret and Swift Messenger*," title paged to John Wilkins, on the first page of the Address "To the Reader" it will be seen that the first letter on the middle line (which is the ninth line counting either up or down) is a capital C, and in the middle of this same line are the words A HUNDRED.[4]

This example is included here not only to illustrate the use of the letter C as a cipher for Francis Bacon, but also to demonstrate once again how the deliberate placement and capitalization of words and letters have been used as coding techniques in apparently ordinary writings of the past. Especially note that the *middle line* was utilized to place the capital "C" thus reinforcing the cipher technique

based on *Mediocria Firma*. We now know that similar instances of
this practice are present in the Great Invocation by the placement
of words and phrases and by the capitalization of certain words.
(Note that there are 8 letter C's in the Great Invocation and nothing
of significance was found in relation to our study.)

Hollenbach offers this interesting commentary on the name
Francis:

> The last word in <u>The Tempest</u> in the First Folio is the word "FREE."
> (The name "Francis" derives from a Teutonic word meaning "free.") The
> simple count of this word is 33, Bacon's name in the simple count
> [ESC, JB]: F + R + E + E = 6 + 17 + 5 + 5 = 33 = BACON.
>
> In the reverse of this code [ERC, JB] A=24, B=23 etc. the word
> "FREE" is 67 F + R + E + E = 19 + 8 + 20 + 20 = 67 = FRANCIS.
>
> Thus, Bacon's name is concealed twice in the last word of <u>The
> Tempest</u>.[5]

Adding this information to Leary's "Boteswaine" discovery indicates
that Francis Bacon has apparently begun and ended *The Tempest*
with his own name!

Taylor also makes the point that the name "Francis" is derived
from a Teutonic word meaning "free." Taylor calculates the numeric value of "free" using the RKC system, showing that "free" and
"Bacon" both equal 105.[6] Curiously, "Francis Bacon" equals 105
using the AN system in modern English. Referring once more to figure 4.3, we find that the 105th word in the Great Invocation is "and"
which has a value of 19. Not only is 19 of enormous significance to
the Great Invocation and related esoteric themes already discussed,
but when 105 and 19 are combined they equal 124, which is the ESC
value of "Rosicrucian" and "W. Shakespeare." Just as significant, 124
is the AN value of the Bacon family motto *Mediocria Firma*.

Let's return to our main task of locating words corresponding to
the ciphers Bacon used in Elizabethan times. The next cipher is
based on the name "Francis" with an ESC value of 67. The sixty-
seventh word is "the" with a value of 33, which in effect can be translated as Francis (word-position 67) Bacon (word "the" = 33).
Following this logic, one might assume that word-position 100
should be of some significance since it is the value of "Francis
Bacon," but it contains the word "where" (59) which does not fit into
the numbers applying to Francis Bacon. As sometimes happens with

this type of investigation, however, surprises appear when they are least expected. Instead of this word-position yielding information about Francis Bacon, it contains information about the *Master R*, for we find that the Essence Value of word-position 100 totals 159 which is the AN value of "Master Rakoczi."

Figure 7.6 is a diagram summarizing the various reference points in the Great Invocation which result in the number values we have just discussed.

Figure 7.6. Francis Bacon Word Search.

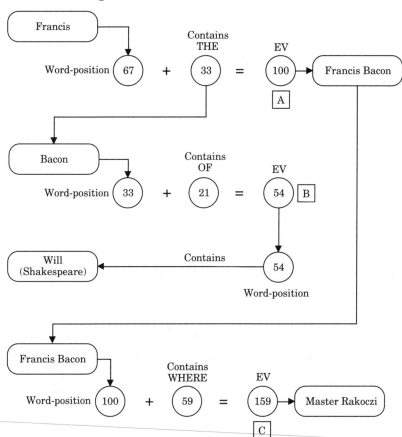

EV refers to Essence Value—word-position number + value of word.

If we suspend our natural tendency to question this as proof of the Master R's influence, this is really a rather clever device by the

Master. Apparently we are being led along by number clues associated with Francis Bacon's number ciphers in the Great Invocation. In the location where Francis Bacon should be—word-position 100 corresponding to his cipher number—we find the number 59 which leads apparently nowhere, but when combined with 100 equals the value of the full name of Master R—"Master Rakoczi." Naturally, the trail ends there because that is the name by which he is now known.

As remarkable as the results of our "esoteric word search" have been, there is one final calculation which completes the experiment and brings it to a very satisfactory conclusion. Note the boxes marked A, B, and C in figures 7.6 and 7.7. The numbers in these boxes are the Essence Values corresponding to Francis Bacon, Will (Shakespeare), and Master Rakoczi.

The total Essence Value of these three names equals 313, corresponding to "Invocation for Power and Light" (AN). More outstanding is the fact that 313 also corresponds to *Rakoczi's current title in the Hierarchy*—"Master R, Lord of Civilization" (see chapter 2). The details of these results are shown in figure 7.7 and table 7.4

Figure 7.7. Master R, Lord of Civilization.

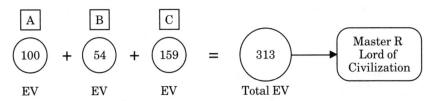

Table 7.4. Summary of Francis Bacon Word Search.

Name	Word-position	Contains	AN Value	Essence Value	Results
Francis	67	the	33	100	Francis Bacon
Bacon	33	of	21	54	Will (Shakespeare)
Francis Bacon	100	where	59	159	Master Rakoczi
Master R Lord of Civilization ◄——— 313					

Table 7.4 and figures 7.6 and 7.7 clearly demonstrate that by using the Essence Value of the word-positions, we have identified (in the Great Invocation) all the pertinent names associated with Master R—Francis Bacon, Will (Shakespeare), Master Rakoczi, and Master R, Lord of Civilization. There is no denying the numeric clues which persistently lead us to the names associated with Master R. These number clues are embedded in Shakespeare as well as in the Great Invocation. Maybe these correspondences are simply a series of coincidences or maybe they are a playful means of communication informing us that the authors of *King Henry IV* and the Great Invocation are actually one individual—the Master R. We may never know for sure. Only the Master R Himself can reveal whether these findings are a quirk of nature or continued evidence of His ingenious ability to conceal Himself from those who do not understand the nature of the Quest, while revealing enough of Himself to those who do.

Notes

1. This reduction to the root value was discovered by a fellow student.
2. There are many mispaginations in the First Folio. There are so many that Baconians believe they are deliberate and cannot be explained simply by typesetting errors.
3. Berges, *Sacred Vessel of the Mysteries*, 63.
4. Johnson, *Bacon-Shakespeare Coincidences*, 43.
5. Hollenbach, *Francis Rosicross*, 112-13.
6. Taylor, *Master R: Lord of Our Civilization*, 107.

A CRYPTIC MESSAGE

I have frequently hinted in my various books that the Sun, Sirius, is closely related to our planetary Life.

The Rays and the Initiations, 413.

"A WORD FROM THE MASTER"

This chapter investigates what is purported to be an actual communication from the Master R. As I explained in chapter 2, Peter Dawkins recorded this poem in 1993:

> My name is a mask.
> I am one yet more than one.
> My name is a cipher: it is '1.9.' and '9.3.'.
> C.R.C. is an epigram.
> Saint-Germain is a pseudonym.
> My life is my own, yet my life is that of all souls,
> a parable of what is, what was and what may be.
> My life is my work and my love.
> I cannot name myself,
> as the intention of my work is that you should seek,
> and by seeking discover me,
> and by discovering me, know me.
> My essence is Silence, like the voiceless fragrance of a Rose.
> Who can name Silence?

The two number elements, 1.9. and 9.3, are one of the most interesting aspects of this poem. These numbers represent a cipher or code of some kind. Dawkins suggests that 1.9. corresponds to the letters A and I, since A is the first letter of the alphabet and I is the ninth. This is shown in table 8.1. According to his explanation, AI is another way of referring to AA which, as explained earlier, was a symbol for a secret society or fraternity. This may have been connected to those who later formed the Rosicrucians.

Table 8.1 RAN Method.

1	2	3	4	5	6	7	8	9
A	B	C	D	E	F	G	H	I
J	K	L	M	N	O	P	Q	R
S	T	U	V	W	X	Y	Z	

Following the logic that 1.9. corresponds to AI, then 9.3. corresponds to IC. As indicated by the above table, this procedure follows the RAN method of assigning numbers to letters. What this also means, however is that the number 1 corresponds to A, J, and S; 3 to C, L, and U; and 9 to I and R. Therefore, 1.9. 9.3. can correspond to AIIC, or JRRL, or ARIC, or JRIU. In fact, many combinations are possible including SIRU. This last combination is of special interest since it contains all the letters necessary to form the word SIRIUS.

Because the Great Invocation contains so many clues relating to the star Sirius, the possibility that the cipher 1.9. and 9.3. has some relationship to Sirius cannot be overlooked. It is very possible that the AI and AA meanings ascribed by Dawkins are totally correct, but it is not beyond reason to suggest that there is another meaning to these number ciphers.

In order to demonstrate this we will decipher line three in Master R's poem. It reads: "My name is a cipher: it is '1.9.' and '9.3.'." Using AN values and replacing each element in line three with its number, we obtain the following numbers which appear in table 8.2.

Table 8.2. "My name is a cipher."

My	name	is	a	cipher	it	is	1.9 S.I.	and	9.3 R.U.
38	33	28	1	59	29	28	28	19	39

By theorizing that 1.9. equals SI, we obtain the total 28 (S = 19, I = 9, 19 + 9 = 28). In turn, by correlating 9.3. to RU, we obtain the total 39 (R = 18, U = 21, 18 + 21 = 39). By performing this conversion based on the letters SIRU, the message now reads "My name is a cipher: it is 28 and 39." The instructions cannot be much clearer, for 28 + 39 = 67. Hence, the decrypted message states "My name is a cipher: it is FRANCIS." Also note that the first four words in the line equal 100 which correlates with "Francis Bacon"in ESC. The AN method of gematria is the key to deciphering this poem. Using the RAN method as shown in table 8.1 (and in chapter 3) yields no results pertaining to Francis Bacon or Master R. I leave it to the reader to determine this for themselves by performing their own calculations. The next example will reinforce my assertion.

As we are discovering, these ciphers often have more than one level of interpretation and this example is no exception, for there is another message here. Based on AN values, the first five words in table 8.2 are combined: 38 + 33 + 28 + 1 + 59 = 159. This total equals "Master Rakoczi." Recall that number 159 is the Essence Value of word-position 100 in the Great Invocation.

This is only half of the message, however. The final five numbers in table 8.2 pertain to the Great Invocation just as 159 does. After the words "My name is a cipher" come the words "it is." In order to decipher the second part of this message, these two elements must be combined. Combining the AN values of these two words results in a total of 57 (29 + 28). This refers to the *fifty-seventh word* of the Great Invocation which is "IS." The next number is meant to confirm this— it is 28—the AN value of "IS." The final two numbers in the series are 19 and 39. The combined value of these two numbers equals 58. This refers to the *fifty-eighth word* of the Great Invocation which is "KNOWN." Putting the entire series together, using all ten elements of the line, yields the statement: "Master Rakoczi is known." This final message is illustrated in the following diagram, figure 8.1.

Figure 8.1. Master Rakoczi is Known.

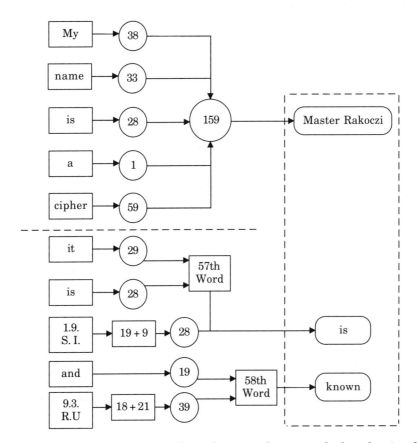

It must be pointed out that this result can only be obtained by using the values of SI and RU in place of the cipher numbers 1.9. and 9.3. Not only does this establish a connection with Sirius, but also it demonstrates quite remarkably that the Great Invocation can be used as a decoding device for obtaining the name of Master Rakoczi from his own poem, "A Word from the Master." A further clue to the possible connection between the Master R and the Great Invocation is found in the value of the title of the poem itself. "A Word from the Master" equals 222 (AN) which corresponds to the middle letter-position of the Great Invocation occupied by the all-important letter "s"—one more reminder of *Mediocria Firma*.

Line four of the poem contains the words "C.R.C. is an epigram." The AN value of this phrase equals 136. (The letters C, R, C have been added together—3 + 18 + 3 = 24.) The number 136 corresponds to Sonnet 136 and to the page number in *Love's Labor's Lost* which contains the word "honorificabilitudinitatibus." It is also the number which forms the "Signature of Sirius" (Fig. 4.3) in the Great Invocation from the four words "the Light of God" or "the God of Light." Furthermore, the number 136 also equals "the Great White Lodge on Sirius." Once again Sirius comes into the picture. These are two examples of coding in "A Word from the Master" which find correspondence within the Great Invocation. There may be others, but these suffice to make the point in terms of specific phrases.

SIRIUS

Before examining the rest of Master R's poem, we must give some further background on the place which Sirius holds in the teaching presented by the Master Djwhal Khul. According to his description of the cosmic influences affecting our planet, the star Sirius is of paramount importance. A tremendous amount of information is contained in my earlier book, but it is impossible to include that in detail here. Instead we will confine ourselves to general information and, more specifically, to that which is directly relevant to the Master R. It should be noted that when discussing Sirius, we are referring to the advanced Lives Who govern or oversee evolution in that solar system and our own. Here are a few facts from the esoteric standpoint:

- Sirius is the parent solar system to our own system
- Sirius governs all karma within our solar system.[1]
- Only through the direct intervention of Sirius was Sanat Kumara able to incarnate directly onto our planet and, as a consequence, created the human soul or fourth kingdom. This episode is called individualization.[2]
- Sirius is the originating source of the process of initiation on Earth. Initiation has always been the foundation and core of the mystery schools going back at least as far as the Egyptians.[3]
- Sirius is the source of Masonry. DK states that the true Blue

Lodge is found on Sirius.[4]
- The symbol of the cross is part of the consciousness of the Lives on Sirius.[5]

These few points demonstrate the enormous influence of Sirius on our planet, especially in the establishment of spiritual Light in humanity through the process of initiation. According to the Tibetan, the ancient Mystery Schools are Sirian in origin. Their teachings and philosophies are reflected later in the Rosicrucian and Masonic movements of the seventeenth century in Europe and Britain. This does not necessarily mean that the rituals and objects used in those rituals are replicas of those used in the Sirian system. It means that the original Mystery Schools established on Earth by the Hierarchy taught spiritual truths inspired by the knowledge passed down from Sirius—knowledge concerning the nature of life, death, and the purpose of human existence. DK states that this knowledge has been in the possession of the Hierarchy since its inception on Earth and it is revealed to the initiate in stages or degrees called initiations.

Since the spiritual Hierarchy represents the middle Christ aspect of the trinity on our planet, it is under the governing arm of Sirius. This is because Sirius represents the middle principle of the soul or Christ quality in relation to the universal trinity of the cosmos. Sirius is mysteriously connected to the Cosmic Christ and in a very real sense is the Cosmic Christ since it does represent the middle aspect on the cosmic scale.[6] (Generally speaking, the Ageless Wisdom philosophy describes these levels or scales of being as planetary, solar, and cosmic; although there are likely many other levels beyond the human range which are not distinguishable at this time.)

1993

The numbers given in the poem—1.9. and 9.3.—have been equated to SIRU and strongly suggest a relationship to Sirius. Beyond this however, these numbers can also be viewed as the year 1993. This may appear outlandish, but there is something meaningful about the year 1993 because that was the last year in which Sirius B reached its closest orbital approach to Sirius A. (This is known as periastron.)

The Sirian star system consists of two known stars. (Recent studies indicate the possible presence of a third star, but have not been officially confirmed to date.) Sirius A is the main star, the one we see at night. Sirius B is known as a white dwarf. It is a star which collapsed on itself at some point in the distant past. Sirius B is so tightly compressed that it cannot be seen with the human eye and a teaspoonful of its matter weighs several thousand pounds. As far as periastron occurring in 1993, this year is confirmed by the data shown below which comes directly from the Fourth Catalog of Orbits of Visual Binary Stars by C.E. Worley and W.D. Heintz.

Table 8.3 Separation of Sirius A and B.

Year	Degree of Separation
1990	4.536
1991	3.664
1992	2.907
1993	**2.532**
1994	2.713
1995	3.138
1996	3.485
1997	3.737
1998	3.978
1999	4.260
2000	4.597

In table 8.3, the column of numbers to the right of the years indicates the degrees of separation between the two stars. As you can see, the smallest degree of separation (periastron) was 2.532 degrees which occurred in 1993. This number indicates the smallest degree of separation and therefore, the closest distance between the two stars for that 50 year period.

According to the Worley and Heintz catalog, Sirius B completes one orbit around the larger Sirius A every 50.09 years (fifty years and roughly thirty-three days). For example, using hypothetical dates, if on December 31, 1492 Sirius B was at its closest position to Sirius A, it would return to its closest position fifty years later

(1543), but about thirty-three days further into 1543 due to the additional days of its orbital cycle (including leap years). This would place its closest approach on or about February 2nd, 1543. Each periastron of Sirius B to A would occur on a year ending in 43 or 93 (1543, 1593, 1643, 1693, etc.). Due to the extra 33 days, by the completion of the twelfth orbital period the date advances into a year ending in 44 (approximately January 24th, 2044). This means that 11 orbits of Sirius B around A comprise a 550 year cycle of years ending with the same digit. I have used these hypothetical dates because I have been unable to locate information indicating the exact date during the year when periastron occurs. As table 8.3 shows, the degrees of separation are definitely known for each year, but the month and day are not given or are not measured to that exactitude.

The significance of all this may be minor, but it was in the early months of 1993 when I received the first impulse to work with the Great Invocation which, as it turned out, had much to do with Sirius. The copyright year for Peter Dawkins' book about the Master R is 1993. Also, 1993 was the year in which the teachings from the Wisdom ashram (formed in 1946 and of which Master R and Master DK are leading members) were first made publicly available by Wisdom Impressions via the book *The Nature of the Soul*.

A small book entitled *Discourses*, purportedly containing teachings from the Master KH, appeared in its second edition in 1993. The book has a distinct Hierarchical tone, and speaks about topics such as the Rose Cross and the Order of the Star. It emphasizes working in groups of twelve and introduces a new invocation called the "Disciples [*sic*] Invocation," which is to be used along with the Great Invocation, but is not meant to replace it. Although the material in this book was received in the 1980s, the group which initially received this information fell apart for a time, reorganized in 1991 and published a new edition of the material in 1993 as *Discourses*.

The last example of a correlation between 1993 and the reception or appearance of esoteric material concerns a large book entitled *The Knowledge Book*. The material contained in *The Knowledge Book* originated in Turkey and is now available in English. This book contains more than a thousand pages of inspired information from a variety of cosmic sources. The human channel for this material is Vedia Bülent (Önsü) Çorak. The material contained within its pages is quite fascinating and sometimes difficult to comprehend. Despite this, there is an underlying consistency and continuity to the messages which cannot be ignored. The point of interest for us lies in several areas.

First, the messages in *The Knowledge Book* were dictated between 1981 and 1993. The book contains a letter dated, March 2, 1993, directing that the material contained in the book be ready for publication by November 6, 1993. Second, the book contains information about Sirius which it describes as the Focal Point of the Plan for our Earth. Third, the number 19 plays an important part in the cosmology of the presented material. In fact, the numbers 18 and 19 represent major themes of the overall cosmology of *The Knowledge Book*. These numbers refer to dimensions. The first eighteen dimensions develop human beings to a relatively perfect state of consciousness. At this point they enter the cosmic nineteenth dimension, termed the Omega Gate, leaving terrestrial evolution behind.

Understand that I have oversimplified a complex series of spiritual teachings in order to make a point which relates directly to our topic. Hence, no judgements about *The Knowledge Book* should be made based on the small amount of information I have gathered here.

Nevertheless, as we have already seen in chapter 6, the Egyptians also placed an important emphasis on the numbers 18 and 19. They also held the star Sirius in great respect. Furthermore, it goes without saying that the Ageless Wisdom presentation also follows the same pattern.

In summary, the meaning of the year 1993 and the 550 year cycle of Sirius may or may not be significant. The effect of this cycle (and others given by DK) on specific human events cannot easily be pinpointed. It is quite possible that these Sirian cycles affect the Hierarchy more than humanity.

The Tibetan tells us that the second ray of Love-Wisdom operates on a 500 year cycle. This may be linked to the Sirian cycle in some way since ray two represents the second aspect which is the same aspect of Sirius at the cosmic level. Thus, this Sirian cycle may only affect humanity indirectly via the Hierarchy. Nonetheless, the possibility of such a cycle adds another piece to a complex puzzle concerning the great initiative of the Hierarchy in the sixteenth century, namely, to create a global civilization of cooperative human beings. If there is such a 500 year cycle we may be near its completion.

CAPITALIZED WORDS

With this information in place regarding Sirius, we can proceed with another aspect of "A Word from the Master" which concerns its reproduction in Michael Taylor's book *Master R: Lord of Our Civilization*. The poem first came to my notice in Taylor's book. Because of my research with capitalized words in the Great Invocation, the first point which drew my attention was the capitalization of particular words. I performed numerological calculations on these words and arrived at some rather startling numbers. The phrases capitalized by Taylor are shown here as they appear within the poem and their values appear in table 8.4:

MY NAME is a mask.
I am one yet more than one.
My name is a cipher: it is '1.9.' and '9.3.'
C.R.C. is an epigram.
SAINT-GERMAIN is a pseudonym.
My life is my own, yet my life is that of all souls,
a parable of what is, what was and what may be.
My life is my work and my love.
I CANNOT NAME MYSELF,
as the intention of my work is that you should seek,
and by seeking discover me,
and by discovering me, know me.
MY ESSENCE IS SILENCE, like the voiceless fragrance of a Rose.
Who can name Silence?

Table 8.4. Capitalized Words in "A Word from the Master."

Phrase	AN	RAN	Root Total	Letters
MY NAME	71	26	17	6
CRC	24	15	6	3
SAINT-GERMAIN	130	58	4	12
I CANNOT NAME MYSELF	189	72	45	17
MY ESSENCE IS SILENCE	203	77	23	18
TOTALS	617	248	95	56

Due to space limitations, I have placed the phrases which apply to the AN and RAN columns in table 8.4 in the following table (8.5). The final totals for the root values and quantity of letters appear at the bottom of the table along with their corresponding words and phrases.

Table 8.5. Gematria of Capitalized Words.

Phrase	AN Correspondence	RAN Correspondence
MY NAME	71 Thoth	26
CRC	24	15
SAINT-GERMAIN	130	58 Thoth-Hermes
I CANNOT NAME MYSELF	189 The Heart of the Lion (Regulus in Leo)	72 Hermes-Mercury
MY ESSENCE IS SILENCE	203 Light from Sirius	77 The Dog Star Sirius
Totals	617 = Sirius, the Star of Sensitivity governing the Hierarchy	248 = The Great White Lodge on Sirius, the Eastern Christ Star
	Root Total 95 = Sirius	Total letters 56 = The sun Sirius

Table 8.5 contains five AN elements, five RAN elements, and four total elements. Of these fourteen elements:

- Six are directly connected to Sirius. I believe this is mean- ingful in light of all we have uncovered to this point about Sirius with its relation to the Great Invocation and to the numbers 1.9., 9.3., and 1993.
- One is related to the star Regulus, "the heart of the Lion" located in the constellation Leo. The Tibetan states that Leo is governed by Sirius;[7] therefore this is another connection to Sirius.
- Three are related to Thoth-Hermes-Mercury. Thoth is the Egyptian god of numbers, alphabets, and magical words of power. Thoth plays a large part in the symbolism of the

Great Invocation and an entire chapter of *Sacred Vessel of the Mysteries* is dedicated to Hermes Trismegistus. As the god of alphabets and words of power, Thoth-Hermes is connected to ray Seven and this fact alone connects Thoth or Hermes-Mercury to the Master R who is the Master of ray Seven in the Hierarchy, even though he is now the Lord of Civilization under ray Three.

- Four cells contain only numbers because there are no apparent corresponding words or phrases which relate to the Great Invocation or Sirius. However, when the values of these items are combined they total 195 (26 + 24 + 15 + 130). This number is relevant because it corresponds to the name "The High Priestess," the second major trump card of the Tarot. The following material is from my earlier research into the importance of The High Priestess in relation to Sirius and the Mysteries of Initiation:

The High Priestess—Arcanum II—is of specific interest to our study because she is the veiled Isis. In his classic work *The Pictorial Key to the Tarot*, A. E. Waite has this to say about The High Priestess:

"It is sometimes held to represent the Divine Law and the Gnosis, in which case the Priestess corresponds to the idea of the Shekinah. She is the Secret Tradition and the higher sense of the instituted Mysteries."

Waite's reference to the Mysteries concerns spiritual initiation and revelations about the nature and origin of human existence, the nature of God, and the world. According to DK, initiation is of the greatest importance in relation to Sirius, thus revealing a connection between The High Priestess (the veiled Isis), Sirius, and initiation.

The term Shekinah is also significant, meaning a Hebrew goddess or feminine archetype relating to the Holy Spirit. This is the third, or Mother aspect which is one of the three aspects expressed by Sirius. The Tibetan says the Shekinah is "the light which 'ever shineth in the East.'" Waite continues:

"She has been called Occult Science on the threshold of the Sanctuary of Isis but she is really the Secret Church, the House which is of God and man....she is the spiritual Bride and Mother, the daughter of the stars and the Higher Garden of Eden. She is, in fine, the Queen of the borrowed light, but this is the light of all. She is the Moon nourished by the milk of the Supernal Mother.

In a manner, she is also the Supernal Mother herself—that is to say, she is the bright reflection. It is in this sense of reflection that her truest and highest name in [sym]bolism[sic.] is Shekinah—the co-habiting glory....There are some respects in which this card is the high est and holiest of the Greater Arcana."

When Waite describes The High Priestess, Isis, as the "Secret Church," he is describing the spiritual Hierarchy, agent of the second aspect of the divine trinity on our planet. When he calls The High Priestess the "House which is of God" we may interpret this to mean Shamballa, the first aspect of the trinity. When Waite tells us The High Priestess is Shekinah, she then represents the Great Mother, the third aspect of the trinity, divine Intelligence, Sophia-Wisdom.

Sirius represents each one of these aspects in relation to our planet. Sirius is the origin of our planetary Hierarchy and of the process of initiation. The sun Sirius administers the Law of Karma throughout our solar system and therefore governs the activities of Shamballa. Sanat Kumara was only able to incarnate on Earth through the aid of the Sirian Law of Freedom. And finally, Sirius is the origin of the divine Intelligence of manas that flows into our solar system.[8]

This extract adds to what has already been given about Sirius and its prime importance in relation to our planet. The veiled Isis is in many ways symbolic of the Rosicrucian and Freemasonic societies formed by Bacon and others during the Elizabethan era. Their efforts were directly related to restoring the Mysteries while keeping them veiled from those who would destroy them out of ignorance and fear—hence, the use of symbols, ciphers, obscure statements, and coded texts. There will be more concerning Sirius later, but there is one more item to analyze before moving to the next topic.

The CRC element is the only item in table 8.5 which has no obvious correspondence to Sirius in both its AN and RAN expressions. However, the addition of CRC (24) to Thoth (71) equals 95 which is the value of Sirius. This should not be dismissed as a mere contrivance; it does have profound meaning and does represent an esoteric relationship as explained by Dawkins:

> *Jesus Christ*, as a title, is known through Cabala as being "our Father, brother C.R.C.", the true Founder and Head of the Rosicrucian Order....
>
> These things are not so well known nowadays, for it has been forgotten that the name *Christ* is derived from the Greek word, *Cristos* (Latin *Christus*), which itself is derived from the Egyptian word, *Kheru*, meaning "The Word"....
>
> The Egyptian god *Tat*, or *Tachut* (Greek *Thoth*, Hebrew *Tachath*), was known as the Lord of Maat, Lord of Truth, for *tat* (Thoth) is *Kheru*, the Word of Truth, the Creative Sound or Vibration of Love. In order to distinguish that which is incarnate or imminent [sic] from that which is transcendent, Thoth, when incarnate and properly expressed through the human personality, was commonly known as *Hermes Trismegistus*.[9]

In other words, there is a traceable relationship between the ancient god Thoth and the Christ—*the Word (Logos) made flesh* through Jesus. As Dawkins points out, there is a parallel between the two, since Thoth was personified through Hermes Trismegistus and Christ was later personified through Jesus. This historical progression of spiritual Light brought to the world by Thoth-Hermes and Christ-Jesus is noted by Djwhal Khul when he states that it was "Hermes, Who initiated the process of enlightenment for our race, the Aryan [fifth root-race, JB]."[10] Why, therefore, is it significant that these two terms (Thoth and CRC) combine to form a numeric correspondence to Sirius (24 + 71 = 95)? It is because Sirius is the originating source of the spiritual Light which Thoth and Christ represent on Earth.

This spiritual Light is symbolized by the AN value of the phrase "MY ESSENCE IS SILENCE" which equals 203 (table 8.5). If we set aside the meaning of these words, this number corresponds to the phrase "Light from Sirius" which is discussed at length in my first book. Both Thoth and Christ represent Light from Sirius.[11] The poem's phrase appears to serve a dual purpose. It provides a clue to the author of the poem and at the same time conveys information about Sirius through the value of its words. Generally speaking, the word "Silence" often relates to the Mysteries of Initiation of which all Initiates are forbidden to speak. And as we have seen, the Mysteries of Initiation are directly related to Sirius.

Although this completes the analysis of the capitalized words provided in Taylor's book, there is a bit more to the story. After obtaining Dawkins' two part book *The Master* in which the poem "A Word from the Master" appears in its original form, I immediately noticed that the capitalized words from Taylor's version were not present, although the poem was accurate in every other way. After putting great effort into proving the necessity of preserving the accuracy of the Great Invocation, I was surprised that Taylor capitalized so many phrases. I contacted him via e-mail and asked why he had taken the liberty to change the form of the poem. He explained that, "I did this to highlight what I thought was important in the passage. Amazingly, I did not have any other empirical basis for capping those words."[12] Thus, we are presented with another mystery involving the work of Master R! It goes without saying that so many references to Sirius and Thoth-Hermes are significant. The fact that Taylor highlighted them is interesting since he actually did not change the words, but simply brought those particular words to his readers' attention.

THE FINAL FIVE WORDS

The final part of the analysis of "A Word from the Master" encompasses the last five words of the poem. Initially, I saw nothing special about the last five words, but after working with the cipher numbers of Francis Bacon, I noticed something very interesting about the last two words of the poem—"name" and "Silence." Their AN values are 33 and 67 which correspond to "Bacon" and "Francis" using the ESC system. I then found the word "Rose" (with a value of 57) positioned very near to the two final words. Recalling that fifty-seven is the middle word-position of the Great Invocation, I decided to take a closer look. Since the last five words of the Great Invocation are very symbolic, I thought there might be the same importance here. After all, if the Master R was involved in the design and translation of the Great Invocation into English, maybe he left a similar trail of numbers in the final five words of the poem received by Mr. Dawkins.

By applying AN values to these final five words, we discover that there is definitely a message here that is undeniable in its clarity. In effect, it states that "Francis Bacon is Shakespeare!" Let's examine this more closely to find out how this is possible.

Table 8.6 displays these last five words with their AN values. The truly remarkable feature of these five words is that their AN values in modern English correlate exactly to "Francis Bacon" and "Shakespeare" in Elizabethan gematria. The gematria values of the first three words of the group do not appear relevant. The final two words are immediately recognizable, however, because they are the identical cipher numbers of Bacon (33) and Francis (67). If these last two words are read in reverse order, they read as "Silence name" or "Francis Bacon." This discovery naturally leads to the idea that all five words are meant to be read and interpreted in reverse order. Continuing backwards through the poem, the next word is "can" (18) located at position 101. Applying the ESC system to the value 18 produces the letter "s." This appears meaningless until the two words, "Who" and "Rose" are examined more closely. The key is to combine the AN values of these two words. When this is done the result equals 103. This is the ESC value of "Shakespeare." Hence, the deciphered words appear as "Francis Bacon s Shakespeare." Obviously, the letter "s" is meant to be read in two ways. The letter "s" can be interpreted as either a possessive, a contraction, or both. Thus, the message can be read in two ways: Francis *Bacon's* Shakespeare or Francis Bacon *is* Shakespeare.

Table 8.6. Cipher Message of Final Five Words.

Word-position	99	100	101	102	103
Word	Rose	Who	can	name	Silence
AN Value	57	46	18	33	67
Reversed Position	103	102	101	100	99
Word	Silence	name	can	Who	Rose
AN Value	67	33	18	46	57
Elizabethan Equivalent	FRANCIS	BACON	S	SHAKESPEARE	

Since the names Francis Bacon and Shakespeare appear in the final five words of Master R's poem and since *Mediocria Firma* appears to be a clue to revealing hidden information about the Master R, it does seem appropriate and logical that the word in the middle of the group—can—should have some significance beyond that of the letter "s." In this case perhaps the simple approach yields the correct result. "Can" equals 18. It could be that the number 18 simply refers to the eighteenth letter of our modern alphabet—the letter R, which we know identifies the Master R. In effect, the Master Rakoczi has placed three identities here—Francis Bacon, R, and Shakespeare. This is very clever indeed. The AN value of all five words in modern English equals 221. By extracting the middle word "can" from the midst of the other four words, we end up with the result shown on the following page.

Figure 8.2. My Essence is Silence.

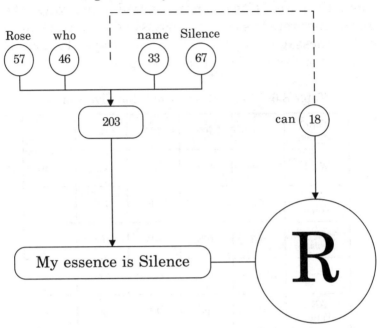

It just so happens that the result of subtracting 18 from 221 equals 203 which is the value of the phrase shown above. In effect, a statement has been made, "My essence is Silence" and it is sealed with the monogram of the Master Rakoczi—R!

This part of our examination of the last five words of the Master's poem reveals much about the past identity of Master R. As we will soon see, much more is revealed when these final five words of the poem are combined with the final five words of the Great Invocation. The outcome of their synthesis transcends their individual meanings by exposing the dim outlines of a cosmic Plan—a Plan in which our Earth and its humanity play a vital role as we enter the twenty-first century.

Let's examine the last five words of the Great Invocation. The phrase "restore the Plan on Earth" contains five words consisting of twenty-one letters. Again, the symbolism is consistent (and persistent) in that it points directly to the twenty-one key words and their relation to Francis Bacon's twenty-one letter alphabet.

The numerology of this five word phrase demonstrates beyond doubt the consummating beauty of this entire Word of Power. Here is an extract from *Sacred Vessel* which illustrates this point:

> "Restore the Plan on Earth" equals
>
>   257 (AN) or 2 + 5 + 7 = 14, 1 + 4 = FIVE
>
>   104 (RAN) 1 + 0 + 4 = FIVE...
>
> Let's examine these numbers a bit more closely. The RAN value of the five word phrase is 104. This number corresponds to the phrase "the lifting of the veil".... When the Plan is restored on Earth (thus activating the next phase of the greater Plan), "the lifting of the veil" will occur.
>
> The edict from on High, "restore the Plan on Earth" (104), thus equates and coincides with "the lifting of the veil" (104).
>
> The AN value of "restore the Plan on Earth" equals 257. There is only one other phrase in the Esoteric Numerology Lists... which corresponds to 257; however, it is not an AN value, but a RAN value. Esoterically present in the final five words of the Great Invocation...is the phrase "Sirius—the Star of Sensitivity—governing the Hierarchy" (257 RAN). This phrase consists of 47 letters. The two phrases in the Esoteric Numerology Lists with RAN values of 47 are "Isis-Sothis" and "The Christ." Indeed, Sirius (Isis-Sothis) is the Christ—it is the Cosmic Christ, the Second Aspect of the One About Whom Naught May Be Said.[13]

This passage demonstrates the direct and dramatic symbolism contained in the last five words of the Great Invocation. What was not mentioned at the time of that writing was a later discovery that the last five word-positions (109-113) add up to 555. This fact lays even more emphasis on the importance of the number 5. Beyond this, it demonstrates the power and beauty of symbolic numerology or gematria. The following two tables (8.7 and 8.8) contain the numerological data of the final five words of the Great Invocation and the poem "A Word from the Master."

The numeric similarity of these two tables is quite remarkable. The total word-positions in the Great Invocation equal 555 and the word-positions in "A Word from the Master" equal 505. Because the zero has no value, there are essentially all fives in both works. Additionally, the numerological totals equal 5, and the five words involved in both samples contain twenty-one letters, thus corresponding to the twenty-one key words in the Great Invocation and the twenty-one letters of the alphabet which Bacon used in his cipher work. Referring to table 8.8, notice that the RAN value of the five words equals 95. The key words of the Great Invocation consist of ninety-five letters and recall that 95 corresponds to Sirius.

Table 8.7. Final Five Words of the Great Invocation.

Word-position	Word	AN	RAN	Root	Letters
109	restore	100	37	1	7
110	the	33	15	6	3
111	Plan	43	16	7	4
112	on	29	11	11	2
113	Earth	52	25	7	5
Total 555	5	257	104	32	21
Root value of words		5	5	5	na

Table 8.8. Final Five Words of "A Word from the Master."

Word-position	Word	AN	RAN	Root	Letters
99	Rose	57	21	3	4
100	Who	46	19	1	3
101	can	18	9	9	3
102	name	33	15	6	4
103	Silence	67	31	4	7
Total 505	5	221	95	23	21
Root value of words		5	5	5	na

Lost in all this is one very subtle, but immensely important factor. It involves Bacon's technique of hyphenating words in order to gain control over the word count of a particular passage or series of words. An example of this practice is given in chapter 3 from Edward Johnson's book *Bacon-Shakespeare Coincidences*. In our case the hyphenated word in question is "Saint-Germain." This name does not necessarily have to be hyphenated. Yet it serves a very useful purpose in "A Word from the Master" because it makes the word count of that poem equal 103 words instead of 104! If this poem had

104 words it would not have a middle word and the results obtained in table 8.8 would not have been possible. In fact, the results obtained for the last five words of the poem would be different because the last five words would appear in positions 100, 101, 102, 103, and 104—totaling 510 not 505. Thus, the presence of 5s in the last five words would not result. This hyphenation subtlety is very suggestive of commonality between the cipher work of Francis Bacon and the Master R. Now it is clear why the statement in the poem reads "Saint-Germain is a pseudonym;" it is because the hyphen is being used to make one word out of what could just as easily be two.

Returning to our main point, the presence of so many numbers in the last five words of "A Word from the Master" which are consistent with the last five words of the Great Invocation suggests a deliberate effort to highlight a connection between the Great Invocation and this poem by the Master R.

Because there is such a similarity between the final five words of both works, it is quite possible that combining the various categories in tables 8.7 and 8.8 will reveal some deeper meaning. We do this by adding together four elements from each—the totals for the word-positions, the quantity of words, the root value of those words, and the total letters. I have done this for each of the two writings. The results appear in table 8.9.

Table 8.9. Total Value of Two Sets of Final Five Words.

Word Position	Words	Root Values	Letters	Totals
555	5	5	21	586
505	5	5	21	536
Combined Total				1122

As you can see, this synthesizing operation results in the number 1122. This number is pertinent for several reasons. First, by viewing this four-digit number as two sets of double digit numbers (a technique employed in my earlier research), we obtain the numbers 11 and 22. Combining these two totals results in 33, the ESC value of Bacon and the all-important Masonic number of the 33rd Degree signifying completion.

The second operation involves multiplying 11 and 22, resulting in 242. This number is significant because it is the AN value of "Thoth-Hermes-Mercury." This is important since both the energy and theme of Hermes as the Master of alphabets and words of power lie at the root of this entire study and its thesis. And as we have already seen, both these works are loaded with consistent numeric themes related to the Rosicrucians, Masons, Hermes, and Sirius as the source of the Mysteries. The persistence of this Hermetic archetype is not new. In my earlier work I elaborated on the connection between 11, 22, and Hermes:

> First, if we take the value of all three names of the Thrice Greatest, we have "Thoth Hermes Mercury" equaling 242 (AN). This number is remarkable in the sense that two of its factors are 11 and 22. We already know, according to the Tibetan, the number 11 symbolizes the adept using energy. In *Esoteric Psychology*, vol. I, while discussing the seven rays and the twelve creative Hierarchies DK states:
> "The 7 + 12 = 19, and if you add to these 19 expressions of the Life [One About Whom Naught May Be Said, JB] the 3 major aspects of Deity, which we call the life of God, the Father, the love of God the Son, and the active intelligence of God the Holy Ghost, you arrive at the mystic number 22, which is called (in esotericism) the number of the adept."
> So we see that 11 is the number of the adept using energy, and the number 22 is the adept himself. Therefore, when we multiply 11 x 22, we get the product 242 or Thoth Hermes Mercury. Therefore, the Thrice Greatest Hermes is the prototypal "adept using energy."[14]

The striking aspect of all this is that the number clues embedded in "A Word From the Master" confirm and add to what has already been uncovered in *Sacred Vessel of the Mysteries*. The fact that the Tibetan mentions the numbers 11 and 22 also adds to the mystery to some degree since these are the two numbers which produce 33 and 242. This suggests an underlying knowledge and single source of information gradually released into the public consciousness over time and in a very subtle way. This, too, is nothing new since we see evidence of this practice going back at least 500 years in European civilization and even further back in the esoteric philosophies of the Islamic, Christian, Greek, Hebrew and Egyptian cultures. What *is* new is the release of esoteric knowledge in uncoded form such as in Helena Blavatsky's *The Secret Doctrine* and the many books written by Djwhal Khul through Alice Bailey. Yet even in the information given out by the Tibetan, we see evidence of subtle forms of encipherment still employed by the Hierarchy. Some of this may be deliberate and some may be a natural phenomenon resulting from the interaction of alphabet patterns and numbers.

Returning to our analysis of 1122, we come to the final and most intriguing point. Recall in the beginning of chapter 7 we combined the numbers of the Rosicrucian/Sirian Cross to decode the name "Francis Bacon." First we added 21 to 12, resulting in 33, the ESC value of "Bacon." Next, we added 17 and 17 resulting in 34. Finally we added 33 and 34 resulting in 67, the ESC value of "Francis."

Figure 8.3. Bacon's Cross.

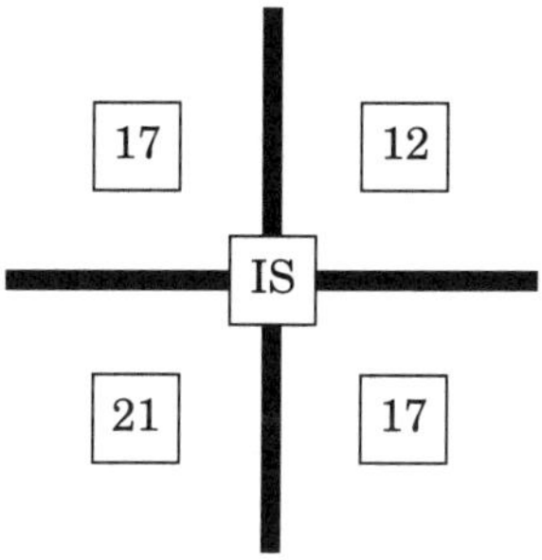

What we did not do in that exercise was *multiply* 33 by 34. Performing that calculation now produces the number 1122! In other words, when the positions, numeric values, and quantity of letters of the final five words of both writings are combined, they equal the numeric values of the words of the Great Invocation arrayed in the form of an equal-armed cross; a cross symbolically containing a rose at its center, and a cross which can be depicted exactly like the cross worn by the Master R as shown in chapter 1, and a cross similar to that described by DK which is related to the Beings living in the Sirian star system.

To complete our analysis of these final five words, I have reduced all the elements to a root value. For instance, the total word-positions 555 are reduced to 6 (5 + 5 + 5 = 15, 1 + 5 = 6). The total word-positions 505 reduce to 1 (5 + 0 + 5 = 10, 1 + 0 = 1). The total letters—21 each—reduce to 3 (2 + 1 = 3). When the final totals of the elements in each table are combined, they equal 19 and 14 respectively. This synthesis is shown in table 8.10. Adding these two numbers together yields 33, a number now familiar to us. If we reduce

them to their root values, they equal 1 (1 + 9 = 10, 1 + 0 = 1) and 5
(1 + 4 = 5). If they are combined by addition, they equal 6. If they are
multiplied, they equal 5. Thus, both operations yield the numbers 6
and 5 respectively, reflecting the Celibate and Non-celibate key
words discussed in chapter 7. This 6/5 theme will appear again in
later chapters indicating that it is a hidden foundational theme of
this coded material.

Table 8.10. Synthesis of Two Sets of Final Five Words.

Total Root Values	Word-positions	Words	Gematria Values	Letters	Totals
Great Invocation	6	5	5	3	19
A Word from the Master	1	5	5	3	14

EMERGENCE OF RAY FIVE

When these two numbers are multiplied in their unreduced final
stage as shown in table 8.10, we get an even more intriguing result,
19 x 14 = 266. The number 266 corresponds to one of the names of
the Lord of the *fifth* ray. That name is "The Brother From Sirius!"
This is quite remarkable in light of the fact that we have been examining two writings of Hierarchical origin with the sole purpose of
comparing the last *five* words of each. The sum of their word-positions is based in 5 (555 and 505) and the total gematria value of the
five words of each writing equals 5. In effect, table 8.9 contains the
composite numeric energy value of each set of five words. Ray five is
particularly relevant to our study because it is closely related to what
the Ageless Wisdom calls our current *fifth* root-race. We will explain
this in later chapters, but simply put, the fifth root-race represents
the modern global state of mind and consciousness which transcends
physical races and ethnic backgrounds. This is exemplified by the
rapidly forming borderless global community of the Internet.

The emergence of ray five in connection with the final five words
of these two writings is especially brought into focus by two other
names for the fifth ray Lord given by Djwhal Khul. The first is "The
Precipitator of the Cross" and the second is "The Rose of God." Our

study is filled with crosses and roses. Through the synthesized numbers of these two writings a pattern of relationship continues to manifest. This pattern includes Sirius, Hermes, Master R, Francis Bacon, the Rosicrucians, Masonry, and the modern esoteric movement including Blavatsky's Theosophical Society and Alice Bailey's work with the Tibetan. Here is some of what the Tibetan has to say about the Lord of the fifth ray:

> This fifth ray has so many names, owing to His close connection with man (since man was originally created), that it has not been easy to choose those which are of the most use in enabling the student to form an idea of the fifth ray characteristics and mission...six aphorisms were chanted by His six Brothers at that momentous crisis wherein the human family came into existence and the solar Angels sacrificed themselves. Esoterically speaking, they "went down into hell, and found their place in prison." On that day souls were born. A new kingdom of expression came into being, and the three highest planes and the three lower were brought into a scintillating interchange.[15]

As this extract explains, the fifth ray was very much involved with the creation of the human family, when the "solar Angels sacrificed themselves." The Brother from Sirius, the Precipitator of the Cross, the Rose of God—the Lord of the fifth ray—is mysteriously intertwined with the coming of Man to this planet. As our study continues to unfold, it is becoming obvious that no matter what symbols, numbers, events, deities, writers, masters or esoteric organizations occupy center stage, Sirius looms large behind the scenes directing the cosmic drama playing out on Earth.

The process of synthesizing the numeric energies of these two writings has borne much fruit. Through this procedure we see a definite pattern forming before our eyes. It points to some common source of knowledge which may provide answers to some fundamental questions underlying all our efforts. Is there a Plan of God which is so inclusive that it extends beyond the boundaries of our own small planet? Have the Masters R and Djwhal Khul concealed information about the nature of this Plan and our planet's role in it within their writings, and if so, why? The following chapters may provide some answers to these questions.

We have compared the Great Invocation to "A Word from the Master" in this chapter. In chapter 5, we explored the relationship between the Great Invocation and Psalm 46. In the next two chapters, we will bring all three together and see how their words are interwoven to form a pattern of numeric symbolism transcending their individual meanings.

Notes

1. Berges, *Sacred Vessel of the Mysteries*, 357-8.
2. Ibid., 322.
3. Ibid., 268.
4. Ibid., 206.
5. Ibid., 193.
6. Ibid., 312.
7. Alice A. Bailey, *Esoteric Astrology*, 299.
8. Berges, *Sacred Vessel of the Mysteries*, 133-5.
9. Dawkins, *The Master*, part 1, 25-6.
10. Bailey, *The Externalisation of the Hierarchy*, 39.
11. There is much more about the relationship between Thoth-Hermes and Sirius in *Sacred Vessel of the Mysteries*.
12. E-mail source.
13. Berges, *Sacred Vessel of the Mysteries*, 365-7.
14. Ibid., 292.
15. Alice A. Bailey, *Esoteric Psychology*, vol. I, 77-8.

WORD WEAVING

Behind the forms, the Weaver stands and silently he weaves.

Esoteric Psychology, vol. II, 360.

We have just described numeric coding in "A Word from the Master" which reveals the names of Francis Bacon, Shakespeare, and Master R. We also found coding related to Sirius and Hermes. Additionally, we explored the final five words of "A Word from the Master" which revealed the following coded message—"Francis Bacon's Shakespeare" and "My essence is Silence, R." We then compared these final five words with the last five words of the Great Invocation. This exercise revealed startling parallels suggesting deliberate design between the two works.

Earlier in chapter 5, we demonstrated the importance of the middle words of the Great Invocation and Psalm 46. There we employed a procedure based on a combination of the Janus epigram of George Wither and the Bacon motto *Mediocria Firma.* These exercises revealed meaningful numbers based on counting forward and backward through these two writings. (Refer to appendix A for the examples given in this chapter.) The "distance" we counted was determined by the numeric value of the middle word. For example, the middle word of Psalm 46 is "mooved" and its ESC value is 69. Therefore, we counted forward and backward 69 positions. We did the same with the Great Invocation based on the AN value of the middle word "is"—we counted forward and backward 28 positions. It is logical to perform the same exercise on "A Word from the Master" for this work also shows evidence of symbolic coding.

We can apply the same procedure to this poem as was done in the other two writings because it too contains an odd number of words—103. In order to find the median or middle word-position we divide 103 by 2 which yields 51.5. This means that word-position 52 is the midpoint of Master R's poem—there are fifty-one word-positions before and after this middle position. The word in the fifty-second position is "what" and its AN value is 52. Its position and value are identical. Here are two interesting items related to the number 52:

- word-position fifty-two in Psalm 46 contains the word "is," which as we now know is the middle word of the Great Invocation.
- word-position fifty-two in the Great Invocation contains the word "where." In actuality, the Great Invocation only contains fifty-one different words. The remaining words (sixty-two) are simply duplicates of the original or essential fifty-one words of which it is composed. Of these essential fifty-one words, "where" occupies the middle position.

This short exercise demonstrates that the middle word of "A Word from the Master" is key to fulfilling the motto *Mediocria Firma* by referring us to the middle words of the Great Invocation ("is" and "where") as explained above. This is illustrated further in the following examples.

When we perform the identical exercise on "A Word from the Master" as we did with Psalm 46 and the Great Invocation, we are immediately faced with a major problem. There are only fifty-one words before and after the middle word "what" because the poem only contains 103 words. Since "what" has a value of 52, our forward and backward count carries us beyond the limits of the number of words in each direction. This could be a clue indicating that we must go beyond the poem to the two other writings containing evidence of the Master R's influence.

Figure 9.1. Number 52 Links Three Works.

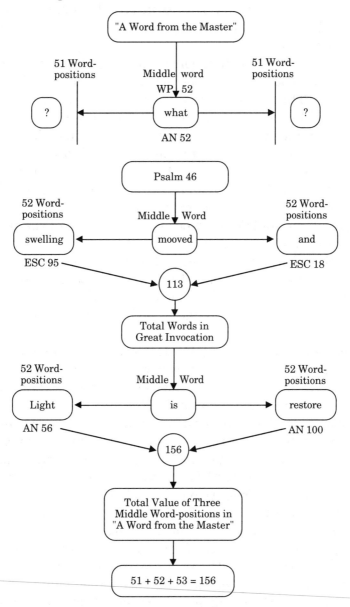

Beginning with Psalm 46, we count forward and backward from the middle word-position (101) 52 places. This results in locating the word "and" in position 153 and "swelling" in position 49. The

ESC values of "swelling" and "and" are 95 and 18 respectively. Combining these two values results in 113, the number of words in the Great Invocation. Apparently, we are being directed to it as shown in figure 9.1.

We perform the same function on the Great Invocation by counting forward and backward 52 positions, starting at the middle word-position (57). This results in locating the word "restore" in position 109 and "Light" in position 5. The AN values of "Light" and "restore" are 56 and 100 respectively, which combine to equal 156.

At first glance, this number appears to be of no significance; but looking a bit closer, we find that it is the value of the three middle word-positions of "A Word from the Master!" We have been led in a complete circle through three procedures related to the number 52. We began at the middle word-position (fifty-two) of the poem and returned to the three middle word-positions (51 + 52 + 53) of the same writing, fulfilling once again, the motto—*Mediocria Firma*.

This process in which one of the works "refers" to another one through the use of number correspondences is a literal and metaphorical weaving. A similar weaving process is dramatically demonstrated in the Great Invocation when a word value is employed as a word-position, which in turn, refers to another word whose value is used to find the next word-position, and so on. This process, as we saw in chapter 4, leads to an endless word loop comprised of the words "the Light of God."

Although not identical, these three writings demonstrate a similar weaving pattern. Figure 9.1 illustrates this interweaving as each work points to the next one based on the middle word of the poem. It is here at the middle of "A Word from the Master" that we find a clue to a larger pattern of weaving which involves the middle word "what" (52) in word-position 52. Thus, 104 (52 + 52) is the Essence Value of the middle word-position of the poem.

A closer examination of the Great Invocation reveals that its first word "From" and last word "Earth" have identical values of 52 (52 + 52 = 104). Symbolically speaking, the combined values of the first and last words of the Great Invocation equal the Essence Value of the middle position of the poem. The symbolism infers a fundamental relationship between beginnings, endings, and midpoints. This immediately brings to mind combined functions of George Wither's epigram of Janus and *Mediocria Firma*. This phenomenon displays a weaving pattern in which the middle of one work connects to the beginning and ending of another work. This is quite interesting— and it gets better because Psalm 46 is also part of this weaving phenomenon, only in a reverse manner.

Psalm 46 is connected to the Great Invocation through the combined sum of the ESC values of its first and last words. The first word, "God" (25) plus the last word, "refuge" (60) equal 85. The number 85 is the Essence Value of the middle word of the Great Invocation ("is" 28 + 57). These interweaving patterns are illustrated in figure 9.2. Also refer to appendix A, 1-3.

Figure 9.2. Word Weaving.

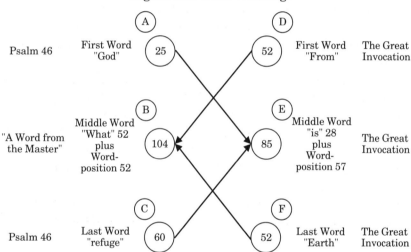

An interesting feature not shown in the diagram is the fact that the Essence Value of "is" in the Great Invocation (E), added to the first and last words of Psalm 46 (A and C respectively), equals the Essence Value of the middle word "mooved" of Psalm 46. Thus, Psalm 46 symbolically points to the middle of the Great Invocation based on the sum of its first and last words. Furthermore, the sum of all three elements points to the Essence Value of the middle word of Psalm 46. This is exactly opposite of the connecting method between the Great Invocation and "A Word from the Master."

- First and last words of Great Invocation =
  middle Essence Value of "A Word from the Master."

- First and last words of Psalm 46 =
  middle Essence Value of the Great invocation.
- First and last word of Psalm 46 + Essence Value of middle
  word of Great Invocation = Essence Value of middle word of
  Psalm 46.

Another way of describing this interrelationship is that the
Essence Value sum of the two middle word-positions equals the
sum of the two sets of first and last words as shown in the following equation: B + E = A + C + D + F (104 + 85 = 25 + 60 + 52 + 52
or 189 = 189). In other words, the three works are numerically balanced based on the number 189.

Another interesting mathematical feature of these interwoven
works is that the elements in the left column of figure 9.2 (A + B +
C) equal 189. That is, the first word of the psalm, middle Essence
Value of the poem, and the last word of the psalm equal 189.
Likewise, in the right column the elements (D + E + F) also equal
189. Here the elements are all from the Great Invocation.
Obviously, the number 189 is important in some way.

The number 189 may simply be an arbitrary number which
symbolizes an "equivalency" pointing to a *common* author of all
three writings. I believe the number 189 *is* such a symbol, however
the number itself is *not* arbitrary.

Dawkins points out that Bacon used two other mottos besides
Mediocria Firma, namely, *Plus Ultra* and *Moniti Meliora*.

> ...he personally selected and used two other mottos as having an espe-
> cial bearing on his aims and objects in life. One was *Plus Ultra* ("More
> Beyond"), and the other was *Moniti meliora* ("Being instructed, to bet-
> ter [things]").[1]

Our primary interest in these two additional mottos involves their
gematria values using the ESC system. We use the Elizabethan system based on the premise that the gematria values of these three
mottos are meant to communicate the link between the modern
English gematria values of the Great Invocation and "A Word from
the Master," and the writings of Francis Bacon. All three mottos
appear in the following table.

The key to the gematria interpretation of these three mottos lies
in the average of their combined numeric value. We find that 396

plus 171 equals 567 and 567 divided by 3 equals 189! The number 189 which pervades the interwoven relationship between Psalm 46, the Great Invocation, and "A Word from the Master" is the number representing the *synthesized gematria value of the three mottos employed by Francis Bacon.*

Table 9.1. Three Mottos.

Motto	ESC AN Value	ESC RAN Value
Mediocria Firma	119	74
Plus Ultra	132	33
Moniti Meliora	145	64
Totals	396	171

Furthermore, the RAN value 171 represents the total word-position value of the three middle words of the Great Invocation. The RAN value 171 divided by 3 equals 57. This is the value of the middle word-position of the Great Invocation. The AN value 396 divided by 3 is 132. Recall in chapter 4 we combined the values of Rakoczi based on the AN, RAN, and root values, 83, 38, and 11 respectively and found their total to be 132. Assuming that Rakoczi is the author of these three writings, we can symbolically "remove" him by subtracting 132 from 189. The result is 57. This is a very familiar number which corresponds to the words ROSE and VEILED. Consequently, Rakoczi is veiled in these three writings, as the poem says, like "the voiceless fragrance of a Rose" which equals 132 RAN!

THE HEART OF THE LION

Another mystery confronts us by the fact that the number 189 equals the value of the phrase "the heart of the Lion" which refers to Regulus, the brightest star in the constellation Leo. At first glance this correspondence does not seem relevant to our subject, however it bears investigating because Leo and the lion theme play a considerable role in the earlier research associated with my first book.

According to DK, the astrological energy of Leo was active when the human race was created:

> Cycles passed and when at a later date the sun was in Leo (approximately eighteen million years ago) the first instances of coordination between brain and mind took place and the human being was definitely self-conscious. He registered his individuality.[2]
>
> Several triangles of force were active when individualisation took place and the "Lions, the divine and tawny orange Flames" came into being and thus humanity arrived upon the planet.[3]

Notice the reference to the tawny lions. This implies the influence of the star Regulus in some mysterious way. Although the Tibetan has much to say about Leo, he only mentions Regulus in relation to Sirius:

> The influences of Sirius, three in number, are focussed in Regulus, which is, as you know, a star of the first magnitude and which is frequently called "the heart of the Lion." There is more real occultism hidden in the names given to the various stars by astronomers down the ages than has yet been realised, and here you have a case in point.[4]

As the above extract clearly states, Sirius is closely connected with Leo and Regulus. In fact the Tibetan informs us that, "Leo, in the cosmic sense (and apart from our solar system altogether) is ruled by Sirius."[5]

The name Regulus has a value of 103 (AN) which is the number of words in "A Word from the Master." Furthermore, the number 103 is also the value of Shakespeare (ESC) and Mercury (AN), two important aspects of this study. More importantly perhaps, is the symbolism attached to the name Regulus which means kingly. As the heart of the Lion implies, Regulus occupies a central location within the constellation Leo. Hence, by applying the Law of Correspondences to this king or ruler *at the center*, we are confronted once more by the all-important place which the center holds in relation to metaphysics, philosophy, and esoteric studies in general and the writings of the Master R in particular.

In an essay on Leo, Alice Bailey emphasizes the importance of the number 5 in association with this fifth sign of the zodiac. She states that "it is in Leo that man becomes what is occultly called the five-pointed star, for that star stands as the symbol of individualisation."[6] We see from this remark by Alice Bailey the great importance the number 5 has in relation to Leo and to humanity. The five-pointed star is the symbol of Man and the five initiations which liberate a human being from the wheel of death and rebirth.

Referring back to figure 9.2 (page 155), note that it is made up of six elements; however, in order for elements B and E to depict their combined value of 189, they must be joined to form one element. This means that figure 9.2 is reduced from six elements to five elements as shown in the following diagram.

Figure 9.3. The Heart of the Lion.

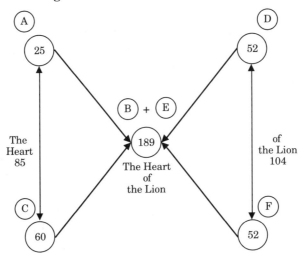

Figure 9.3 symbolically depicts the star Regulus, the heart of the Lion, created by the convergence of the first and last word values of Psalm 46 (A + C) and the Great Invocation (D + F). The truly remarkable aspect of this configuration concerns the AN value of the phrase "the Heart" (33 + 52) which equals 85 because this number is the Essence Value of *the heart* of the Great Invocation ("is" 28 plus word-position 57 equals 85.). As illustrated in figures 9.2 and 9.3, the number 85 is derived from the first and last word values of Psalm 46. The same figures demonstrate that the number 104 is derived from the first and last words of the Great Invocation. Paralleling the pattern of Psalm 46, this sum of the first and last words of the Great

Invocation equals the Essence Value of the middle or *heart* of "A Word from the Master." The heart of the poem is represented by the word "where" 52, in the middle word-position 52. In this case the word "heart" literally applies because its AN value is 52, thus equaling the value of "where!" In summary, the middle word-position of "A Word from the Master" is literally the *heart* (52) and the middle Essence Value of the Great Invocation is *the heart* (85).

It is quite remarkable that this phrase "the heart of the Lion" can be broken down into two phrases ("the heart"—85 and "of the Lion"—104) which numerologically correspond to the first and last word values of Psalm 46 and the Great Invocation respectively. The curious feature of the phrase "of the Lion" (figure 9.3) is that it appears to be an identification. Astrologically we know that the Lion is Leo, but from a numerological viewpoint "the Lion" has a more intriguing meaning because this phrase equals 83—the AN value of RAKOCZI. As a result, we can substitute "Rakoczi" in place of "the Lion" since they both equal 83. Thus, the middle Essence Value of "A Word from the Master" can mean "Of Rakoczi" and the first and last words of the Great Invocation can mean "Of Rakoczi" (21 + 85 = 104). Moreover, in regard to the Great Invocation, the first word (52), the last word (52), and the Essence Value of the middle position (85) can be deciphered to read "the Heart of Rakoczi" (33 + 52 + 21 + 83 = 189)! Furthermore, as figure 9.2 demonstrates, the combined Essence Value of the middle positions of "A Word from the Master" and the Great Invocation (B + E) equals the same number (189) as does the combined value of the first and last words of Psalm 46 and the Essence Value of the middle position of "A Word from the Master" (A + C + B). In effect, this word weaving is telling us that we are viewing the writings which are "the heart of Rakoczi" (189) and the synthesized gematria value of Francis Bacon's three mottos (189).

Whether there is more to all this beyond the numeric correspondences themselves remains to be seen. Obviously, the Master DK has left much unsaid in his reference to Regulus, but the fact that He mentioned it at all is a hint that there is much more to the cosmic relationship between Sirius, Leo, Regulus, and our Earth than can be revealed to the uninitiated. On the other hand, the fact that the Tibetan *did* provide some information on these topics implies an invitation to explore them more deeply, which we will do in chapter 12.

The fact that these three works appear woven together is reinforced further by the following example. Table 9.2 contains the Essence Values for the first, middle, and last words of the three writings. These Essence Values are combined for each work and the grand total for all three is displayed at the bottom of the table. As you can see, the sum of 1,073 reduces to a root of 11—the value of "Rakoczi."

Taking each writing individually, the total Essence Value of the three words from Psalm 46 is 457. This number is a combination of three elements. The Essence Value of the middle word equals 170. This is a combination of "Francis" (67 ESC) and "Shakespeare" (103 ESC). The Essence Values of the first and last word-positions combine to equal 287. Recall that this number is intimately connected to the First Folio of Shakespeare and is the ESC value of the strange word "honorificabilitudinitatibus" in *Love's Labor's Lost*. It is significant that the first and last words of a Psalm associated with Shakespeare combine numerically to equal the value of a "nonsense" word in *Love's Labor's Lost* which, in turn, is associated with Francis Bacon and the Rosicrucians. Additionally, according to Masonic lore, the number 287 is the year in which St. Alban is said to have founded Freemasonry. (These points are discussed in chapter 6.)

Table 9.2. First, Middle, and Last Essence Values.

Writing	First Word	Middle Word	Last Word	Totals	Meaning
Psalm 46	God 26	mooved 170	refuge 261	457	Francis Shakspeare Honorific.
The Great Invocation	From 53	is 85	Earth 165	303	St. Alban's Martyrdom Masonic Number
A Word from the Master	My 39	what 104	Silence 170	313	Master R Lord of Civilization
Totals	118	359	596	1073	Root Value = 11 Rakoczi

This sudden re-emergence of the Masonic theme brings us to the next set of numbers in table 9.2. Combining the first, middle, and last Essence Values of the Great Invocation yields another major Masonic number—303. This is the year in which St. Alban is said to have been martyred! Whether these years are valid or not is beside the point at this stage. The fact that these numbers have appeared in the first place is reason enough to give one pause to consider the implications of it all.

Referring to "A Word from the Master," we find the first word to be "My" (38 AN). Its Essence Value is 39. The last word of the poem is "Silence" (67 AN). Silence occupies position 103 and its Essence Value is 170. Curiously, the final Essence Value of "A Word from the Master" equals the middle Essence Value of Psalm 46—and what's more, it also can be read as "Francis Shakespeare!"

Finally, the first, last, and middle Essence Values of "A Word from the Master" combine to equal 313 (39 + 104 + 170). This is the numeric equivalent of "Master R, Lord of Civilization." I believe we have moved a notch beyond the realm of coincidence.

If you are not so sure, I will leave you with one more set of numbers. These numbers represent the values of the first, middle, and last words of all three writings. This set of numbers does not include the word-position values, only the word values themselves. They appear in the following table.

Table 9.3. First, Middle, and Last Word Values.

Writing	First Word	Middle Word	Last Word	Totals
Psalm 46	God 25	mooved 69	refuge 60	154
The Great Invocation	From 52	is 28	Earth 52	132
A Word from the Master	My 38	what 52	Silence 67	157
Totals	115	149	179	443

The number in the bottom right cell of table 9.3 (443) should be jumping up and down and screaming for your attention. It just happens to be the identical number of the total letters comprising the

Great Invocation. The message is beginning to come through loud and clear: These three writings are connected by a common source. The first, middle, and last words, and word-positions are significant. They relate to the number 189 whose factors are 3 x 3 x 3 x 7and to their author, Rakoczi, the Lord of Civilization on ray Three and the Master on ray Seven. Yet beyond the enormous imprint of his genius in these three works, there is another level of meaning beyond the authorship question. We will examine that deeper level in the coming chapters.

Notes

1. Dawkins, *The Master*, part 2, 4.
2. Bailey, *A Treatise on White Magic*, 440.
3. Bailey, *Esoteric Astrology*, 301.
4. Ibid., 300.
5. Ibid., 299.
6. Alice A. Bailey, *The Labours of Hercules*, 49.

THE SYNTHETIC TRIPLET

The Voice that speaks within the silence can be heard: "The power that reaches from the highest point has reached the lowest. The Plan can now be known. The Whole can stand revealed."

Esoteric Psychology, vol. II, 47.

SYNTHESIS

At this particular time in our planetary Scheme, the seventh Ray of Ceremonial Law or Order is regarded as a major ray of synthesis, and one on which the Mahachohan is blending His work.[1]

This statement by Djwhal Khul describes the work of the Master R. He is a Chohan (one level beyond a Master) on the seventh ray and is the Mahachohan, or Lord of Civilization, working with the third ray. Those who work with the seventh ray bring spirit and matter together; they blend and synthesize. The advanced seventh ray workers of the Hierarchy ultimately strive to materialize spirit and spiritualize matter. The synthesized result transforms life in the physical world. The Life hidden within the material form is unshackled and brought into the full light of day for all to see. Thus, the materialization of spirit spiritualizes matter and transforms all that it contacts in the world of physical reality.

In effect, most of what we have demonstrated in regard to Psalm 46, the Great Invocation, and "A Word from the Master" involves working with the form. We have examined the letters, words, phrases, word-positions, arrangements, and numbers associated with these three literary works.

We have detected a complex array of word clues, numbers, and symbolic themes linking Master R, Francis Bacon, Psalm 46, the Great Invocation, and "A Word from the Master." In effect, the three works are woven into an interconnected pattern of various numeric ciphers and symbolic meanings. The concepts related to those ciphers and word clues form a tightly grouped pattern dominated by three major themes, the middle or center (*Mediocria Firma*), Sirius, and Hermes.

These powerful indicators strongly suggest that the Master R composed and arranged all three writings. With this in mind it is quite possible that by treating the three writings as *one unit*—the Synthetic Triplet—a definitive answer will be discovered as to who is at the CENTER of this 500 year old puzzle. We will do this by placing the three writings in chronological sequence as shown in the following table.

Table 10.1. 417 Words.

Writings	Year	Individual Totals	Synthesized Total
Psalm 46	1611	201 Words	1 - 201
The Great Invocation	1945	113 Words	202 - 314
A Word from the Master	1993	103 Words	315 - 417
Total	383	417 Words	417 Words

Let's begin by examining the number of words in the Synthetic Triplet. The total number of words equals 417. In order to synthesize these three works, we divide their total number of words by 3. This procedure will provide the average number of words. Dividing 417 by 3 results in 139. This number can be thought of as their common source of numeric energy. This fact is striking because Thoth-Hermes has an AN value of 139. Considering the fact that Hermes is often referred to as "Thrice Greatest," it is obvious why so many hermetic concepts and references occur in these three writings.

166

Another numeric correspondence relates to three specific tarot cards—"The High Priestess," "The Star," and "The Sun." The combined RAN values of the titles of these three cards are 139. These cards are directly related to Sirius, closely related to each other, and extensively discussed in *Sacred Vessel of the Mysteries*. The High Priestess (Arcanum 2) represents Isis Veiled, The Star (Arcanum 17) is Isis Unveiled, and The Sun (Arcanum 19) is the veiling factor hiding the sun Sirius:

> When we discover The Star veiled by The Sun (card) at the center of the Great Invocation, we see "Isis Unveiled." We then realize that The Star is the sun Sirius. The numerological value of "the sun Sirius" (182) equals The Star (91) doubled (2 x 91 = 182). In addition, we can also state that 182 equals 91 + 91 or 9191, which translates into ISIS (using RAN values 9 for I and 1 for S). The numerological values of the three crucial elements ["Isis Veiled," "Isis Unveiled," and "the sun Sirius," JB] equal 443, which is the number of letters contained in the Great Invocation. This means that the true nature of the Great Invocation (Isis Veiled as The High Priestess) is revealed as a Word of Power related to the sun Sirius when the veil of Isis is removed (Isis Unveiled, The Star).[2]

This summation demonstrates the importance of the number 139. It must also be noted that the sum of these three major arcana cards equals 38, the value of "Rakoczi" (The High Priestess—2, The Star—17, and The Sun—19).

The next term equated to 139 is "Cosmic Christ" (AN). The Ageless Wisdom teaches that Sirius corresponds to the energy of the Cosmic Christ. The three tarot cards depict a story of unveiling the sun Sirius which represents the universal Cosmic Christ aspect, while Thoth-Hermes is the facilitator of that unveiling process. Thoth-Hermes is the Magician, the One Who uses number and alphabets to reveal the beauty and intelligence of God's creation. It is Thoth-Hermes who instructs in the art of using words of power, mantrams, and prayers in the magical work of transformation. This is all seventh ray activity.

The esoteric numeric meaning of 417 (3 x 139), as represented by the total words of the Synthetic Triplet, sums up quite well the overriding theme of revelation, light, and initiation emanating from Sirius, the prototypal Cosmic Christ overlighting our solar system. This theme of Light and Redemption through Initiation has been taught in mystery schools throughout the centuries, from ancient Egyptian times up to the present era. In respect to ancient Egypt, Schwaller de Lubicz calls it "Sacred Science." He refers to the puzzlement of Egyptologists to understand what factor contributed to the worldview of the Egyptians, who saw complete unity between worldly and spiritual powers. That factor, says Schwaller de Lubicz, is a sacred science which—

> ...comprehends cause and effect as a single entity: *sacred science*, the preeminently *sacerdotal science*, which since the beginnings of the empire was the "science of Thoth," *Master of divine words and sacred writings*. This science, written on papyrus scrolls, included the myth as well as the religious rituals, medicine, geometry, astronomy, and the laws of everyday life and justice. These sacred books were kept in the sanctuaries of the Egyptian temples and were accessible only to the highest religious and royal authorities.[3]

This passage by Schwaller de Lubicz again establishes the tremendous role played by Thoth-Hermes in regard to the sciences and the arts.

Drawing this subject back to the more immediate theme, these qualities which characterized the life of Thoth-Hermes apply to much of Francis Bacon's outer work, not to mention the esoteric work he produced during his life. The lineage of life expression and quality personified in Thoth-Hermes is evident in the life of Francis Bacon (and others like him). The Renaissance in Italy during the fifteenth century was triggered by the discovery of the ancient writings of Thoth-Hermes (*Corpus Hermeticum, The Stobaeus,* and *The Asclepius*), Pythagoras, Plato, Aristotle, and many other Greco-Roman, Jewish, and Islamic philosophers. This great era of awakening from the Dark Ages soon spread throughout Europe. This phenomenal growth of knowledge and learning also stimulated interest in the ancient Mysteries after many centuries of relative obscurity and eventually led to the founding of the Rosicrucians and Freemasons in the sixteenth century.

A passage from *Sacred Vessel of the Mysteries* adds further weight to the theory that some common thread, some continuous trace of authorship runs through the three writings in question:

The Egyptians first gave Thoth the attribute of "Thrice Great," and it was as Hermes that he later became known as Hermes Trismegistus, the Thrice Greatest. Antoine Faivre traces the historical evolution of Hermes from Thoth, to Thoth-Hermes, to Hermes-Mercury and finally to Hermes Trismegistus in his informative book, *The Eternal Hermes*....

"The Suda...[=Suidas] recognized it [the title, Trismegistus, JB] as the sign of the Trinity, an idea supposedly brought to mankind by Hermes...In a treatise dated 1736 and published under the pseudonym of Pyrophilus, one reads that this number is an allusion to the three alchemical principles of salt, sulphur, and mercury. It is most often interpreted as meaning 'great philosopher, priest, and king'."

These examples of the threefoldness of Hermes reinforce the idea that the Great Invocation is truly Hermetic since so much numeric symbolism is unveiled by dividing it into three parts and examining the esoteric information revealed by the middle letter, word, and phrase.

Later, while discussing Hermes as Mercury, Faivre comments on St. Augustine's opinions on Hermes-Mercury:

"In the same City of God, Augustine suggests an etymology for the name 'Mercurius' which he says means *medius currens* (running in the middle), 'because language "runs" like a sort of mediator between men'."

St. Augustine's idea of Mercury "running in the middle" is quite remarkable in relation to the Great Invocation for the following reason. The name "Hermes-Mercury" equals 171 (AN) and this number, as you may recall, is the value of the three word-positions at the exact middle of the Great Invocation, namely "God is known" (56 + 57 + 58 = 171). This cannot work with Thoth-Hermes because it equals 139 (AN); nor does it work with Hermes Trismegistus, for it equals 247 (AN). Only Hermes-Mercury (171) can be found "running in the middle" of the Great Invocation.[4]

This extract is quite remarkable in light of what has been discovered about the middle of Psalm 46, the middle of "A Word from the Master," and the middle of the Great Invocation. Not only is Hermes linked with the concept of the number 3, but also he is related to the concept of middle. When St. Augustine says that Mercurius relates to *medius currens* or that which runs in the middle, a door is suddenly opened which leads into a whole new world of possibilities. Let's explore these possibilities further by applying the three aspects of beginning, middle, and end to this synthesized trinity of writings.

Identifying the the first and last words of the Synthetic Triplet is easy (see appendix A). The first word of Psalm 46 is "God" and the final word of "A Word from the Master" is "Silence." These two words contain much food for thought as representative of the alpha and omega of existence. God is the beginning of all things. The universe comes into being and when the cycle of God's manifestation is complete there is Silence. There is creation and dissolution. Djwhal Khul describes this process in the following passage:

> Again in the solar system itself similar action will eventuate at the close of a Mahamanvantara [solar cycle JB]. The Logos will withdraw within Himself, abstracting His three major principles....From the usual physical standpoint, the light of the system will go out....All will be reabsorbed within the Absolute....The reverberations of the WORD will die away, and the "Silence of the High Places" will reign supreme.[5]

There is God (the Logos), God's creation, (the solar systems and planets), and the withdrawing of God's Life-giving energy (the reigning of the Silence). The trinity concept is fundamental to most religions and many philosophies. It is a major foundation stone of the Ageless Wisdom. The Tibetan places enormous emphasis on it, especially when he discusses the triplicity tenet in terms of "triangles" of energy relationship.

We have already demonstrated how three apparently independent writings are composed in such a way that they reflect this philosophical model of beginning, middle, and end. The previous passage by DK describes the first and last words of the Synthetic Triplet — *God* and *Silence* respectively. Now let's identify the middle of the Synthetic Triplet. (You may want to use appendix A to follow the procedure.) As usual, we divide the number of words in the triplet by 2 in order to find the median or middle point of the whole. Dividing 417 by 2 yields 208.5. This means that the middle word-position of the triplet is 209 and that there are 208 words before and after the word located in word-position 209. Since Psalm 46 contains 201 words, we must continue our count into the Great Invocation (the next writing in chronological sequence) in order to identify word-position 209. Consequently, the eighth word of the Great Invocation is the median of the entire triplet. This word-position contains the word "Mind."

This word is perfect for completing the triplicity of first, middle, and final words. We now have in order of their word-positions, "God, Mind, Silence." These three words represent the synthetic triplicity of Psalm 46, the Great Invocation, and "A Word from the Master."

Here is what DK has to say about the Mind:

> I would ask you to remember that, in our planetary development, the emphasis of the entire evolutionary process is on the MIND and on the various aspects of the mind—intelligence, mental perception, the Son of Mind, the lower mind, the abstract mind, the mind as will, the Universal Mind. The three which are of major importance and which form an esoteric triangle requiring to be brought into a vital inter-relation are the Son of Mind, the abstract mind, and the Universal Mind. They are, when fully related and active, the factors which engineer divine purpose and step it down into such form that we call it the hierarchical Plan and can act upon it. Only when the initiate has attained, through monadic contact, a touch of the Universal Mind can the Purpose be sensed by him; this involves also the development of the abstract mind, plus the residue of mental perception which the Son of Mind (the soul) has bequeathed to him; through all this unfoldment he can join the group who are the Formulators of the Plan.6

This passage could not be clearer in its presentation of Mind as the primary factor in our planetary development. This is the reason "Mind" holds the central place in the Synthetic Triplet.

In the composition of the Great Invocation, the middle letter, word, and phrase emphasize Sirius as a central factor of importance. This is because Sirius is the source of manas or mind in our solar system and consequently, our Earth. Additionally, the human race was created with help from Sirius and it was the MIND principle which was instilled into animal man resulting in the creation of the individualized human soul and the new kingdom of humanity. This soul is also called the Son of Mind.

As the previous extract shows, mind exists in various degrees from individual intelligence and commonsense reasoning all the way up to Universal Mind or the Mind of God. I believe all these aspects of Mind can be applied when interpreting the meaning of "Mind" as the middle word of the triplet. Thus, as the Tibetan has pointed out and as the Synthetic Triplet demonstrates—Mind is CENTRAL to the evolutionary Plan for Earth.

Generally speaking, we might interpret these three words as follows: in the beginning was the Word (Logos), *God* in manifestation. During at least one part of that manifestation, the *Mind* principle and its development took the central role on Earth as the most important factor in evolutionary development. At the end of this mysterious process of evolution, God withdraws all life from outer manifestation and only *Silence* remains.

Numerically speaking, the word Mind has an AN value of 40. This number does not play a vital role in anything discussed up to this point; however, its Essence Value (209 + 40) equals 249. This value appears to have little meaning until we realize that 249 is the product of 3 times 83. The number 83 equals RAKOCZI. In other words, 249 is "Rakoczi" three times. Rakoczi is *central to all three writings*—Psalm 46, the Great Invocation, and "A Word from the Master." You may not have noticed, but these factors, 3 and 83, appear in table 10.1. They are veiled within the number 383. This is the total number of years spanning the publication of Psalm 46, the Great Invocation, and "A Word from the Master"—1611 up to and including 1993 encompasses exactly *383 years*. Not only does this number refer to Rakoczi 3 times, but these are also the same digits located in figure 5.7 on page 94. This number 383 appears in *Sacred Vessel* in relation to Regulus and Sirius.[7] One of its correspondences is "the star Regulus, the heart of the Lion."As usual, there is more.

My earlier work uncovered valuable information connected to the three middle words of the Great Invocation. If that information was placed there deliberately, it is very possible that similar information is located immediately before and behind the word "Mind" in position 209.

Positions 208, 209, and 210 hold the three middle words of the Synthetic Triplet. These positions contain the words, "the," "Mind," and "of." The AN total of these three words is 94 (33 + 40 + 21). The number 94 corresponds to the name "Master R." As a result, these three words, when placed alongside the gematria correspondence of their combined value (94), symbolically read *"the Mind of Master R."*

Figure 10.1. The Mind of Master R.

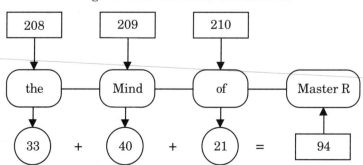

Just as the middle word and three middle words are important cipher keys in the Great Invocation, we are finding that the same is true with the Synthetic Triplet. As we know, the middle letter of the Great Invocation is significant. Let's investigate, therefore, whether this is also true with regard to the middle letter of the Synthetic Triplet. We have a minor problem. There are 1622 characters in the Synthetic Triplet. As a result, there is not a singular median because 1622 divided by 2 equals 811. Statistically, this means the median is shared by the two closest values to the middle of the distribution. Consequently, the median is found at positions 811 *and* 812. In effect, there are 810 characters before and after the two characters which share the midpoint. Therefore, the result of this procedure yields the letters "E" and "F" as the two characters at the midpoint of the Synthetic Triplet. The letters E and F are letters 5 and 6 of the English alphabet. Their combined sum is 11. The number 11 is the root value of "Rakoczi."

The important symbolism of the numbers 5 and 6 is discussed in chapter 7 in relation to the twenty-one key words. The fact that the fifth and sixth letters of the alphabet are the middle letters of all three writings is highly significant. Chapter 11 will demonstrate the high degree of symbolic relevance attached to the presence of these two particular letters—*the fifth and sixth*—at the midpoint of the synthesized triplet. Once again we are forced to admit that *Mediocria Firma* applies to this fascinating tapestry of words.

We might stop to ask ourselves if this is a mere coincidence. If it is, it's huge. Adding the mountain of related numbers we have already climbed to get to this summit of synthesis, I believe we have crossed the boundary line of coincidence and entered the territory of amazement.

Let's try to put this into perspective. We began with a curious phenomenon in the 1611 King James Bible wherein Psalm 46 contains the words "shake" and "speare" forty-six positions from beginning and end. Various researchers believe this to be one small piece of evidence, among many others, that Francis Bacon wrote or influenced the Shakepearean literature.

The Great Invocation is a prayer used all over the world for invoking right human relations and peace. It was given to the world in 1945 by the Tibetan teacher, Djwhal Khul. My earlier research demonstrates that this prayer contains symbolic numbers encoded into its words and phrases.

In 1993 Peter Dawkins was impressed to write a poem which he believes was inspired by the Master R. This poem, "A Word from the Master," contains coded information related to Francis Bacon.

Although none of these three writings show any indication of being connected, they appear to have a common source—Master Rakoczi. Numbers related to his name and title have surfaced repeatedly. Symbols related to the interests of Francis Bacon (such as the rose, Athena, the cross, the ship metaphor, and Signature of Sirius) appear in the Great Invocation. These correspondences lend weight to the Tibetan's statement that Master R once lived as Francis Bacon.

These three writings display a high degree of interconnectedness through their beginning, ending, and middle words. Their combined fusion into one unit, the Synthetic Triplet, demonstrates to a remarkable degree the presence of the Master R's identity. And now the final blow to doubt.

In the last chapter we saw how the number 189 related the first, middle, and last words of the three works. Let's apply the same principle to the Synthetic Triplet. The first word is "God" from the psalm. The middle word is "Mind" from the Great Invocation. The last word is "Silence" from the poem. The combined gematria sum of "God," "Mind," and "Silence" (25 + 40 + 67) equals 132 which is the exact sum of the combined AN, RAN, and root value of "Rakoczi" (83 + 38 + 11)! Hence, "Rakoczi" is the alpha, midpoint, and omega of Psalm 46, the Great Invocation, and "A Word from the Master." He is at the heart of them all.

Notes

1. Bailey, *Initiation, Human and Solar*, 181.
2. Berges, *Sacred Vessel of the Mysteries*, 144.
3. R. A. Schwaller de Lubicz, *Sacred Science*, 7.
4. Berges, *Sacred Vessel of the Mysteries*, 268-9.
5. Bailey, *A Treatise on Cosmic Fire*, 86-7.
6. Alice A. Bailey, *Telepathy and the Etheric Vehicle*, 71.
7. For a discussion of the number 383 see *Sacred Vessel of the Mysteries*, The Lions Emerge pp. 208-14.

GOD OF LIGHT WITHIN

Forth through the chalice gross and dark that forms the foundation
shines the light supernal, till all who see the radiation cry out within
themselves: "Behold, a God is here."

The Rays and the Initiations, 768.

In the Great Invocation, the numbers 5, 6, 56, and 65 play a role in its esoteric meaning. An analysis of the numbers 5 and 6 in my earlier research was initiated because of the twenty-one key words in the Great Invocation. As described in chapter 7, six words are labeled "Celibate" since they do not reproduce themselves and five words are labeled "Non-celibate" because they produce ten off-spring. Thus, the numbers 5 and 6 were examined in some detail. One of the analyses identified the words of the Great Invocation located in positions 5, 6, 56, and 65 (these last two being the two possible combinations of 5 and 6). The four words in those positions are "Light," "within," "God," and "of." The root values of these four words combine to equal 33. This is the cipher number of Bacon and it is also the number of times the word "Francis" appears on page 56 of *The First Part of King Henry the Fourth*. With these points in mind, we begin to see the relevance of the fifth and sixth letters of the alphabet located at the middle of the Synthetic Triplet. The information to follow will expand and solidify the highly symbolic importance of this statistical fact.

The words in these four positions can be read a number of ways including the "God of Light within." We just closed the last chapter by revealing that the first, middle, and last words of the Synthetic Triplet combine to equal 132. Additionally, we found that the AN, RAN, and root value of "Rakoczi" also equal 132. Now we must add another item to this group because the word-positions for "God of Light within" also total 132! Table 11.1 below is the original table from *Sacred Vessel of the Mysteries*.

Table 11.1. God of Light Within.

Word Position	Word	Root Value
5	light	11
6	within	11
56	God (8)	11
65	of (3)	(8 + 3)
132	Totals	33

In effect, the "God of Light within" the Great Invocation corresponds to Rakoczi. We can interpret this to mean that Rakoczi is the "god" or creator of the English translation of the Great Invocation. Adding this new information to what we already know concerning the presence of the Master R in the Synthetic Triplet and in all the other examples to this point is truly doubt shattering.

It is vitally important to keep all this in perspective because certainly Master R is not a god and is not the Creator. We are dealing with esoteric material and therefore it has various levels of meaning. Because of this, the "God of Light" can and must be interpreted at various levels in order to comprehend the deeper meanings and implications of this material. Holding this in mind, "God of Light" is a phrase which can be understood in several ways.

One of the interpretations of the God of Light concerns Hermes. Although we have discussed Hermes Trismegistus previously, the following extract will reinforce that information:

There is a meaningful message contained in the positions occupied by these four words within the Great Invocation. The words combine to form the phrase "God of Light within."... the combined total of their four positions in the Great Invocation equals 132....This God of Light was known as Thoth to the ancient Egyptians, Hermes to the Greeks, and Mercury to the Romans....

Djwhal Khul says that it was "...Hermes, Who initiated the process of enlightenment for our race, the Aryan [fifth root-race, JB]." In the book *The Reappearance of the Christ*, in a discussion of various Teachers of the ancient world, the Tibetan states that at "some unknown date Hermes came and, so the records say, was the first to proclaim Himself as 'the Light of the World'."[1]

The above passage indicates that Hermes plays a crucial role in bringing Light to the human race. Let's apply esoteric numerology to this theme. The total root value of the phrase "God of Light within" equals 33 (table 11.1).

From a metaphysical standpoint the number 33 is symbolically related to the age at which Jesus Christ was crucified and resurrected. The Tibetan states that the Christ also proclaimed, like Hermes, that He was the Light of the world. Hence, the number 33 symbolizes liberation into the full Light of God, thus becoming a God of Light. This spiritual liberation was also applied to the Masonic idea of freedom to pursue the Light of Knowledge and Truth; thus the term Freemasonry. Using the ESC system, the word "free" equals 33. This relates to that ultimate liberation of the thirty-third degree of Masonry in which the candidate is freed from the bodily structure of the thirty-two prior degrees and rises into the Light of God's freedom. As just stated, this is the symbol of the Christ's liberation from the "body" of Jesus at the age of thirty-three. This same idea is symbolized by the pillaging of Solomon's Temple by the pharaoh Shishak thirty-three years after its construction. In each instance, a temple or bodily form is destroyed in order to release the spirit into the Light of freedom. Curiously, the Ageless Wisdom identifies the fourth initiation as the Crucifixion or Renunciation and 4 x 33 equals 132, the number at the center of our discussion.

Since the number 33 symbolizes liberation into spiritual Light and Hermes symbolizes the Light of the World, we will take the value 33 and the value of Hermes, 68 (AN) and multiply them. Esoterically, this means that the energy of freedom or liberation is absorbed by Hermes 33 times, thus indicating His initiation into the spiritual world. This results in the number 2244. As noted above, the name "Bacon" also equals 33 (ESC) and therefore corresponds to "God of Light within." Thus, the number 2244 applies equally to Hermes and Bacon. This equivalency suggests that Francis Bacon corresponds numerically, at least, with Hermes and they both are associated with Masonry through the Light of freedom.

Let's test this numerological correspondence further. Using the modern English alphabet, the RAN value of Bacon equals 17. We also know that the total value of the word-positions comprising "God of Light within" equals 132 (5 + 6 + 56 + 65). Curiously, the result of multiplying 132 by 17 *also equals* 2244.[2] This might be a coincidence, but remember this only works because these four particular words (God, of, Light, within) are located in the exact positions within the Great Invocation which result in their word-positions totaling 132. Thus Bacon (33) x Hermes (68) = 2244 and Bacon (17) x God of Light within (132) = 2244. Bacon corresponds to Hermes, the "God of Light within."

For those readers who still feel skeptical about this peculiar numeric equivalency of Bacon and Hermes, we will attempt to lay your doubts to rest by employing a deciphering technique from my earlier research with the Great Invocation. This method separates a four digit number into two sets of two digit numbers. The resulting two digit numbers are then used to reference word-positions in the Great Invocation. Because we have established an interwoven connection between Psalm 46, the Great Invocation, and "A Word from the Master," we are going to use all three writings in this procedure.

We will now apply that method using the number 2244. The first step is to split 2244 into two numbers, 22 and 44. The next step is to identify the words located in positions 22 and 44 in each writing. The third step is to calculate their AN and RAN values. The last step is to find the sum of all six words. The results of this procedure are displayed in table 11.2 on the following page.

Table 11.2. Numbers 22 and 44.

Writing	Word	AN value	RAN value
Psalm 46	WP 22 removed	77	32
	WP 44 the	32	14
The Great Invocation	WP 22 descend	54	27
	WP 44 May	39	12
A Word from the Master	WP 22 9.3=R.U	39	12
	WP 44 A	1	1
	Totals	242	98

The two sums at the bottom of table 11.2 tell the story. The numbers 242 and 98 are the AN and RAN values of the three names—Thoth-Hermes-Mercury! Significantly, number 242 is derived from the factors 11 and 22. This is important because the numbers 11 and 22 are specifically used by the Tibetan in relation to the adept (22) and the adept using energy (11). (See page 146.) If any god of the ancient world signifies the adept using energy, it is certainly—Thoth-Hermes-Mercury. Furthermore, when 11 and 22 are added together they equal 33—the root value of the "God of Light within," the ESC value of "Bacon," the symbolic age of Jesus at the crucifixion and resurrection, and the degrees of Masonry.

What can all this mean? Why does Hermes keep entering the picture? And why is Bacon associated with Light? For a clue to the answer, let's turn once again to Penn Leary's book *The Second Cryptographic Shakespeare*:

Mrs. Henry Pott, writing in *Francis Bacon and his Secret Society* (1891), says: "It is worthy of notice that the Bacon family in early times spelt their name *Becon* or *Beacon*"...

As reported by Nathanial Holmes (*The Authorship of Shakespeare, 1887*) Sir John Davies published a book of poems in 1621. In it is the

following anagram to Bacon:
"To the Right Honorable Sir Francis Bacon, Knight, Lord High
Chancellor of England.

{Bacone.

Anagr^{m.}   {

{Beacon.

Thy vertuous Name and Office joyne with Fate,
To make thee the bright Beacon of the State."3

Leary goes on to explain that in Elizabethan times, the name
Bacon and the word "beacon" were pronounced the same way and
therefore Bacon could be a pun for beacon or a guiding light.
Consequently, "God of Light within" is a beacon and also Bacon. The
number 2244 corresponds to both Hermes and Bacon because they
both signify LIGHT.

We now know that the Master R is related to this phrase in two
ways. First, by a numeric correlation between the phrase and the
total value of "Rakoczi"—132. Second, by the esoteric information
that Master R was Francis Bacon in a previous life—a life in which
Bacon was characterized as a "beacon" of light.

Following up on this double meaning, let's perform one more
arithmetic operation on the phrase "God of Light within." Up to this
point we have only dealt with its total root value (33) and total word-
position value (132). Calculating its AN value results in the number
186 (26 + 21 + 56 + 83). Thus, the Essence Value of "God of Light
within" equals 318 (132 + 186).

We derive the "double" meaning of this value by dividing it in
two. In this way we are employing arithmetic to symbolically demonstrate the dual relationship which Master R has in relation to the
phrase "God of Light within." Remarkably, this simple division
results in the number 159 which is the AN value of "Master
Rakoczi." Consequently, "Master Rakoczi" is related to the Essence
Value of "God of Light within" in two ways (2 x 159).

Before continuing further it must be noted that the AN value of
"God of Light within" (186) is equal to the name "Master Djwhal
Khul"! This marks the second location within the Great Invocation
in which DK is symbolically present. (The other location involves
the middle word "is." See chapter 5.) Once again, this points to the
Tibetan's cooperative work with Master R in producing this invocation for humanity's use.

Continuing our analysis, it is obvious that the numbers 5 and 6 (along with 56 and 65) have a dual meaning here. First, they are symbolic of the path of perfection or the Way of Initiation which always and inevitably leads to the Light. In addition, they are pointers to the Master R as the God of Light within the Great Invocation. In effect, this means that Master R is the creator "God" of the English translation of the Great Invocation. He is the Light, the Beacon, or BACON, now known as Master Rakoczi, illuminating the words of this hermetic sound formula.

SUMMATION

Our examination of the evidence to this point makes a strong case for concluding that the Master R had a definite influence on the composition and coding of the Great Invocation. The question is, why? Why would a Master of the Hierarchy, indeed one of the department Heads—the Mahachohan—expend the time and energy to do such a thing? What value is there in knowing the Master Rakoczi designed the Great Invocation?

On the surface, accepting this idea as a fact seems rather trivial and even distracting in light of the many problems facing humanity and the Hierarchy at this time. Nonetheless, the numbers are real, their correspondences are clear, and the themes are consistent and persistent. Consequently, we are forced to look beyond the obvious meaning to deeper levels. This is the nature of the esoteric—its study and practice results in penetration to deeper layers of understanding; to increased intensity of Light.

We started with words. We have been led to numbers, patterns, and correspondences which we have interpreted. Those interpretations strongly suggest the authorship of the Great Invocation to be that of the Master R. Yet, the material uncovered in *Sacred Vessel of the Mysteries* unmistakably reveals the Great Invocation as a repository of esoteric information which transcends any one individual. Thus, this new discovery of authorship is an addendum, a completion of the record so to speak. It does not necessarily complete all there is to know about the Great Invocation, but it closes one aspect of the story.

We can now think of the Great Invocation as more than a prayer given to humanity for its use in times of crisis. The Great Invocation can now be seen in greater perspective as the fully integrated centerpiece of the Plan. Knowing that the great Chohan of the seventh ray and Lord of Civilization may have designed and composed it adds to our understanding of how the Hierarchy operates in concert to achieve its ends. It suggests continuity of work over the centuries. We think of work and accomplishment in terms of one lifetime, but this project of the Master R and other members of the Hierarchy displays a work in progress over many lifetimes—indeed a work which transcends the human world completely.

In fact, there is the possibility that the Great Invocation was designed and composed in group formation with the Master R presiding over the final English version which was finally dictated to Alice Bailey by Djwhal Khul. Actually, the question of which member of the Hierarchy translated the Great Invocation into English is beside the point. For whatever reason we may surmise, specific symbols and numbers are present which consistently refer to the Master R. If these numbers and symbols referred to another Master in the Hierarchy, we would have no choice but to accept that information and attempt to interpret its meaning just as we have done in regard to Master Rakoczi.

Speaking esoterically, strictly in terms of ray energy, it is logical that the Master of the seventh Ray of Ceremonial Order should be the one to design a sound formula; for ray seven deals with hermetic procedures. It is also logical that a Master who once lived as Francis Bacon should be given the task of translating the Great Invocation into English. After all, Bacon had a great command of the English language, may have written the works attributed to Shakespeare, and had an interest in and knowledge of cryptography.

But why the codes and word patterns, not only in the Great Invocation, but also in the Psalm and the poem? I believe there are several reasons for this:

1. To show the source of the writing.
2. To train the mind in synthetic thinking. The manner in which this material is intertwined demands more than one dimension of thinking. Left brain logic is necessary but will not lead to solutions here. Only whole brain thinking can penetrate the deeper meanings and hidden relationships in the material presented so far. Left and right brain function-

ing result in synthetic thinking patterns which see in wholes and know through the transcendence of linearity.

The ray energy of the Master R—ray seven—is the energy which joins and relates spirit to matter. In the realm of thought we have had to use the left, logic side and the right, intuitive side of the brain in order to produce results. We have had to think logically and abstractly. Ray seven produces right relationship by bridging these opposites, thus producing an integral and holistic approach and attitude leading to synthesis.

3. To teach and inform about the Plan and our role in that Plan. This is the big picture. Getting this is critical for moving into the new millennium with hope, courage and meaning. Humanity is ready for a new, more complete context for its life on Earth. The coming revelation of the twenty-first century will demand an entirely new paradigm in human thought. How do we fit into the cosmic scheme of things?

Now a note of caution. We must keep in mind that even though names related to Master R are embedded in these works, it does not mean he represents the goal of our search. No Master of the Hierarchy draws attention to his own identity for ego's sake. These Great Ones are far beyond such vain human traits. I believe the Master R is simply guiding our feet in the right direction. In effect, the message is quite similar to the words of the poem "A Word from the Master": "The intention of my work is that you should seek and by seeking discover me and by discovering me know me. My essence is Silence." Putting this into my own words, we are being told, "Seek me. Give me your attention so that I may point the way, the Lighted Way to Liberation." The Master R, like all the great teachers of wisdom, is a living example of this Way.

The hints provided to this point tell us that the Way is toward the Light in the East. This is the Way of Initiation, a graded series of revelations leading ultimately to the Great White Lodge on Sirius. The divine Guide along that Way is symbolized by Hermes who, according to the Tibetan, first proclaimed, "I am the Light of the World." Later, the Christ repeated these same words. Every Avatar and Divine Messenger Who comes into the world is a Light on the Path to Freedom. Essentially every human being who achieves freedom from the wheel of rebirth and the chains of matter becomes a Light. We come from Light and we return to Light; our very souls are made of Light substance. In our world the Highest Light, the One Who stands above all others is Sanat Kumara: the Ancient of Days, the Lord of the World, the prototypal Avatar of the World.

In a curiously worded sentence reminiscent of his reference to Hermes as the Light of the World and the bringer of enlightenment to our current fifth race, Djwhal Khul states:

> The Buddha...acts today as the agent of that great Life in Whom we live and move and have our being, *Who is Himself the true Light of the World and the planetary Enlightener.*[My emphasis, JB] I refer to the Ancient of Days (as He is called in the Old Testament), to the God of Love, to Sanat Kumara, the Eternal Youth, the One Who holds all men in life and Who is carrying His whole creation along the path of evolution to its consummation—a consummation of which we have not as yet the faintest idea.[4]

By using suggestively similar phraseology, DK is drawing a parallel between Sanat Kumara and Hermes. From a gematria standpoint, this association is powerful because the numbers constituting the name "Sanat Kumara" are all 5s and 6s. Sanat equals 55 (AN) and Kumara equals 65 (AN). Consequently, it is very significant that the words comprising the phrase, "God of Light within" are located in word-positions 65, 55, 5, and 6. This fact clearly demonstrates that Sanat Kumara is ultimately the God of Light within the Great Invocation. It is now time to follow the Light to another level—Sanat Kumara, the originating God of Light within our planet.

Notes

1. Berges, *Sacred Vessel of the Mysteries*, 97. Note that at the time of that writing, I had no knowledge of the numbers and ciphers in Psalm 46 and no knowledge of Peter Dawkin's poem, "A Word from the Master."

2. Note that the three values of Rakoczi (83, 38, 11) also equal 132. Thus Bacon (17) times Rakoczi (132) equals 2244.

3. Leary, *The Second Cryptographic Shakespeare*, 130-1.

4. Bailey, *The Externalisation of the Hierarchy*, 464.

THE PRIMORDIAL LIGHT
OF THE WORLD

Sanat Kumara has created this planet and all that moves and lives therein in order to bring about a planetary synthesis and an integrated system whereby a tremendous solar revelation can be seen.

The Rays and the Initiations, 717.

The last chapter ended by pointing out that the ultimate God of Light is our planetary Logos, presently incarnated in the form of Sanat Kumara. We have explored the God of Light from several perspectives. This Being is symbolically represented by the name "Bacon" or "Beacon," as Master R lighting the way to deeper discoveries within the framework of the Synthetic Triplet. The God of Light is also represented by Hermes and the Christ, for They were Avatars Who brought enlightenment to humanity. Along with these two great Messengers of Light, we cannot forget the Buddha, the Enlightened One of the East and other Light Bearers such as Moses, Muhammad, Krishna, and Lao Tse. Each and all of these Great Ones have brought humanity Light.

The key to understanding the power of the Great Invocation is that all human beings already have that Light within them. It is that soul which was imbued in animal-man by the original God of Light, Sanat Kumara. When we sound the Great Invocation, we are setting in motion a powerful and ancient prayer which energizes the light within us. The God of Light within the Great Invocation is the synthetic symbol of every Being Who has achieved Enlightenment on our planet.

Every Messenger and Avatar of the spiritual Hierarchy enters the world of human living in order to awaken the primordial light within each person. That tiny, individualized light of the soul is a replica of the Primordial Light of the World, the One we call Sanat Kumara. Age after age, cycle after cycle, He sends His Messengers into the world to fan the millions of tiny human flames into blazing Beacons of Light. Each and every one of us has a God of Light within ourselves. We are that God of Light because we were all created by the Primordial Light of the World Who came to Earth on a mission of unknown purpose. Portions of this purpose are gradually revealed to the Hierarchy and formulated into what the Tibetan calls the Plan. We are an integral part of that Plan and in order to gain a fuller appreciation of its magnitude and importance in our present lives, we must try to fathom in some small measure the nature and purpose of Sanat Kumara.

The primary means available for this exploration is the teaching given by Djwhal Khul. Using this as a foundation, we may glean some understanding of our place on this planet at this time. As you will see, the Great Invocation contains a hidden clue to the present hour of opportunity for the human race, but in order to appreciate who we are, we must see from where we have come.

The Ageless Wisdom presents us with an intriguing view of the world and the creation of humanity. It teaches that man was created in a special way. In short, humanity was born out of crisis.

In general, the story begins about twenty million years ago. Minerals, plants, and animals had evolved to a degree of refinement allowing for the creation of a fourth kind of life. The mineral, plant, and animal kingdoms all displayed degrees of intelligence, but they were not designed to think and to have a sense of self, distinct from other lifeforms. This new kingdom of nature would be composed of creatures with "self" awareness and would display intelligence at a higher level through the possession of mind. These creatures would be given the ability to think, reason, and create through the use of the mind and a sense of individuality. It was time to create Man.

The planetary Beings overseeing the development of the Earth's lifeforms had a problem—the mental principle, although present in the animal forms chosen to contain the mind, remained inactive. For whatever reasons (which are not totally clear), the substance, the genetic material available, just wasn't able to initiate mental activity and self-consciousness in the animals selected as the vehicles for the human kingdom.

Finally, we are told that the lead member of this project made a bold decision. He would enter into this genetic material directly and stabilize the organism "in the field." This decision entailed a stupendous sacrifice on the part of this Being. It meant that He would have to leave His high level of existence and enter the confined conditions of life in matter. Thus, according to the Ageless Wisdom, there is much truth to the phrase *Deus ex machina*—God has entered His creation in an act of redemption.

So this great Being, Sanat Kumara, somehow immersed Himself in the actual substance, the genetic building blocks, which constituted the physical form of the third root-race, the Lemurian. This Being did not come alone, but brought 104 Assistants with Him, and together they created the human race.

As mentioned in previous chapters, Sanat Kumara is the original Savior or Avatar of the Earth. His decision to leave the lofty world of spirit and descend into matter has set the tone for the redemptive process on our planet and consequently, world saviors are redeemers. Every Savior, Avatar, and Messenger who brings Light to our physical world from higher dimensions is mirroring the "descent" from higher dimensions of the One known as the Great Sacrifice, Sanat Kumara. The recurring numeric values related to Hermes (and the variations of his name) are symbols pointing to the prototypal Avatar, Sanat Kumara, Who is the true God of Light in the Great Invocation.

From our human standpoint, Sanat Kumara's incarnation on Earth is the most important spiritual occurrence of the Earth's history to date—it marks the creation of humanity. Granting that much of this remains a mystery, the entry of Sanat Kumara onto the physical plane of existence was His conscious choice. Many students of the Ageless Wisdom are familiar with this story of humanity's creation and the continued presence of Sanat Kumara, the Lord of the World, on Earth.

We may rightfully ask how this knowledge helps us understand our place in the world. The answers to several questions are somewhat clarified by this information. For instance, the great sacrifice Sanat Kumara and His Assistants made by entering these lower planes of consciousness established the keynote of sacrifice in our own lives. This is expressed in its simplest form by the aphorism, "It is better to give than to receive." Sooner or later most human beings realize the enormous satisfaction in giving and sacrificing in order to help others. Service lies at the heart of the human soul. This is only one attribute out of many which were instilled in humanity when we were created; so the great sacrifice made by Sanat Kumara is replicated billions of times in each human soul. As above, so below. The macrocosm is reflected in the microcosm and the sacrificial descent of God is reflected in each one of His creations.

Apparently, something had gone terribly wrong if such a seemingly drastic measure was taken by this great Being. The esoteric teachings state that if this intervention had not occurred, the animal forms destined to become human beings would have never developed properly. The great Purpose for which the Earth was created would not be realized if the human kingdom could not reach its planned potential. Thus, the ideal of sacrifice and compassion for all living things was laid down for us all at the very beginning of our creation as a race. Every Savior, Avatar, and Boddhisatva exemplifies this compassionate attitude of the Lord of the World, the Great Sacrifice.

The other aspect of Sanat Kumara's work involves redemption. The substance of which all life on Earth is composed is said to be tainted in some way. This may be part of the cause for the non-response of the animal kingdom to the efforts to stimulate the mental principle instilled in them. Beyond this, however, the Tibetan states that the degeneration of forms, resulting in disease and death is the result of the inadequacy of the material used to create the biological forms on our planet.

Humanity is to be the instrument through which Sanat Kumara redeems, refines, or upgrades the building blocks of life. Human beings are destined to be the potential collective saviors of the three lower kingdoms of nature—the mineral, plant, and animal kingdoms. It is abundantly evident that we are rapidly responding to this enormous task by the many groups throughout the world dedicated to understanding and caring for the environment and its lifeforms.

All these factors contribute to our sense of meaning and purpose within God's Plan for Earth. These serve us well and provide the religious and ethical foundation upon which most of civilization is built. In non-esoteric terms, we, as the human race, are cooperating with God in making the world a better place. We are slowly learning how to feed and shelter those in need, provide education and work for people, build economic and political systems based on freedom, and to eliminate racial, religious, and gender prejudices. As a human family we are emerging out of our separative tribal consciousness into a global group consciousness.

Even while this mass movement toward a more unified world-view proceeds, many are already contemplating our place in the cosmos. We increasingly look toward the heavens and wonder why we are here and whether we are alone in the universe. Clearly, humanity is ready to receive answers to these questions, just like a child wants to know who lives outside his home. It is time to expand the envelope of our worldview to include other worlds, both physically and other-dimensionally. The next phase of the Plan may very well involve the introduction of humanity to new and unimagined forms of life which will break through the boundaries of our isolation in an apparently empty universe. I believe the Great Invocation is a principal key for unlocking the door separating humanity from the rest of creation. It is not the only key, but it is a most powerful one.

We must ever keep in mind that the Great Invocation was prepared by Beings of much greater Intelligence than ourselves. It has been in the possession of Sanat Kumara and His Aides since their arrival on Earth. Until 1945 they were the only Beings on our planet to sound it, but by June of 1945 the Christ and members of the Hierarchy were also granted permission to use the Great Invocation.

Djwhal Khul has stated that the Great Invocation is the most important tool humanity has for invoking the reappearance of the Christ, the next World Teacher. This event is an integral part of the Plan; however, the Great Invocation was not created explicitly for invoking the World Teacher of the twenty-first century. The translation of the Great Invocation into English, from its original seven sounds in the higher worlds, is an extremely recent event. Humanity's current use of the Great Invocation is the final culminating phase of a planned distribution of this sound formula to all the conscious lives on this planet. We must remember that Sanat Kumara and the other Great Lives in Shamballa have been sounding the Great Invocation (in some unknown form) for millions of years. All we have been told is that the Great Invocation is ancient, "one of the oldest prayers ever known" and "so ancient that they [the seven original symbols, JB] are without date or background of any kind." The implications are that this ancient mantric sound originates outside our planet and even beyond our solar system.

At the heart of this mystery stands our planetary Logos Who has taken the form known as Sanat Kumara, the Lord of the World. We are told that He has a special relationship to the Lord of Sirius. The Ageless Wisdom also teaches that Sanat Kumara is in incarnation in order to take the fourth cosmic initiation, the crucifixion. In astrological terms this situation is described as His being crucified on the Fixed Cross. The Fixed Cross signs are Taurus, Leo, Scorpio, and Aquarius. As discussed in chapter 9, Leo was at the height of its influence when humanity became self-conscious.

The many numeric clues and esoteric hints suggest that the Great Invocation is of Sirian origin and a word formula related to Hermes, the God of numbers, alphabets, and Words of Power. Somehow, this Great Cosmic Invocation was given to Sanat Kumara and His Assistants in Shamballa millions of years ago and has been sounded by these Exalted Beings even to this day.

Consequently, several major themes have emerged through the number clues associated with the Great Invocation. These themes are Sanat Kumara, Sirius, Hermes, and Leo. Each of these topics contains their own set of sub-themes, but the most important point to grasp is that they are all held together by the Great Invocation. The symbolic structure and gematria of the Great Invocation is the touchstone allowing us to gather some very large concepts. All of these themes have been discussed in *Sacred Vessel of the Mysteries* to some extent. Here is a list of the themes and the concepts attached to them:

1. Sirius governs Leo.
2. Sirius governs Scorpio.
3. Sirius governs our solar system.
4. Sanat Kumara has a special relationship with the Lord of Sirius.
5. Sanat Kumara is the Avatar of Earth.
6. Without the help of Sirius, Sanat Kumara could not have incarnated on Earth. This event occurred during a time when the energy of Leo was very active.

7. DK compares Sanat Kumara to the Light of the World, a title associated with the god Hermes, who proclaimed, "I am the Light of the World."
8. Hermes is the god of numbers, alphabets, and words of power, among other things.
9. The Great Invocation is a Word of Power composed of words which reflect deep, numerically symbolic associations with each of these themes.

I hope to amplify these themes in this chapter in order to integrate them into a meaningful description of our place in this vast unfolding Plan. Although I will deal with each theme independently, it is almost impossible to avoid discussing one without discussing another due to the interwoven nature of their relationships. Nevertheless, we will begin with Sirius.

SANAT KUMARA AND SIRIUS

Considering all the information which has emerged in this study in relation to Sirius, it is noteworthy that the Tibetan states, "There is a relationship of very ancient date between our Lord of the World, Sanat Kumara, and the Lord of Sirius."[1] Also, "He is the Custodian of the will of the Great White Lodge on Sirius."[2] These two statements definitely link Sanat Kumara to Sirius in a special way.

This is the point where we must stay focused on the concept of systems which are sub-systems of larger ones. In regard to Sirius, our solar system, although independent and distinct, is a corporate part of the Sirian system. In turn, our planetary Logos is a corporate part of our solar Logos. Hence, our planetary Logos presently incarnated as Sanat Kumara is unavoidably linked to Sirius (as are we all). What is unusual is the fact that our planetary Logos appears to be in a special situation in relation to Sirius. In mundane terms this might be compared to an average worker in a large corporation who is performing a special project for the CEO. The Tibetan acknowledges this rarity by stating:

It might be considered by those with a sound sense of occult proportion that our tiny planet with its planetary Logos (one of the "imperfect Gods" of The Secret Doctrine) would be too small to enter in the slightest way into the consciousness of that Supreme Illumined Entity

[Sirius, JB] Who is greater even than our Solar Logos. Such, however, is the case.3

From these few scraps of information we are presented with a picture of Sanat Kumara as a Being of some special genius or quality Who is given a task involving the will of the Great White Lodge on Sirius. We must assume that Sanat Kumara is special in some way. Otherwise, why would a Being of lesser development, relative to the solar Logos and other more advanced planetary Beings within our solar system, be given a special task to perform involving the will of the Great White Lodge on Sirius?

A further clue to this state of affairs may be found in another statement by Djwhal Khul. In this extract the Tibetan is referring to a time in the future when peace and tranquility will be brought to Earth:

> When this happens, our planet will no longer be known as the planet of sorrow and of pain, but will be distinguished by a quality of tranquillity and by an aura of calm potency wherein the will of God (to be demonstrated in the next solar system) will be focussed; this—in some mysterious way—will enable the solar Logos (not the planetary Logos) to bring the first great divine aspect, that of Will or Power, into expression throughout the solar system. Instead, therefore, of the statement which explains our present solar system, "God is Love," we shall have a dynamic expression of the will-to-good—an energy which will have been generated to some extent upon our Earth. This is the reward which the present Earth humanity will reap, and this is the consummation of the preordained task of our planetary Logos. He undertook, when He came into incarnation (through the medium of our little planet), to aid the work of the Solar Logos in expressing the will aspect of divinity.4

The point of importance to our discussion is "the preordained task of our planetary Logos." Our planetary Logos, (presumably through His present incarnation as Sanat Kumara) is to serve the solar Logos in His task of "expressing the will aspect of divinity." Furthermore, our Earth humanity will reap the reward of this endeavor. The following extract by the Tibetan provides more light on this subject:

> For the sake of clarity, yet at the same time speaking symbolically, Sanat Kumara might be regarded as a personal disciple of the Solar Logos, with all that that indicates of cosmic responsibility....
> It is...far more difficult and practically impossible to say anything anent this Path which is trodden by Those Great Beings Who are in training for Solar Logoi. Of These, Sanat Kumara is One.5

This information aids our understanding a great deal. Apparently, our planetary Logos holds the responsibility of anchoring a small measure of the future Will aspect of the solar Logos on Earth as part of His training to become a solar Logos in the future. At the same time, the Tibetan tells us that our planetary Logos is a "personal disciple" (in human terms) of the solar Logos.

Holding this thought in mind, we note the following statement by DK in which he is describing the goal of a solar Logos:

> His problem concerns itself with the development of the principle of cosmic Will which will make Him what has been called a "Lion of Cosmic Will."[6]

Is this the special task given to Sanat Kumara by the Lord of Sirius—to help our solar Logos become a "Lion of Cosmic Will?" As already stated by DK, the Earth is to become the focal point for the expression of Will "throughout our present solar system....This is the reward which the present humanity will reap."

SANAT KUMARA AND LEO

Djwhal Khul's use of the word "lion" in relation to the development of Cosmic Will by our solar Logos brings the zodiacal sign, Leo into the discussion. Recall that in chapter 9, which deals with the interlinking of Psalm 46, the Great Invocation, and "A Word from the Master," the subject of Leo and the star Regulus arose. We discovered a remarkable numeric equivalence in which the beginning, middle, and end of the three writings all totaled 189. We saw that one meaning of this number pertained to the three mottos employed by Francis Bacon. On a larger scale we found that this number is the AN value of the phrase "the Heart of the Lion." The emergence of a number related to Leo is significant because of DK's remark that Leo was in its ascendancy when Sanat Kumara incarnated as the planetary Avatar and created the human kingdom. Hence, the statement:

> Several major triangles of force were active when individualisation took place and the "Lions, the divine and tawny orange Flames" came into being and thus humanity arrived upon the planet.[7]

Combining the information in this extract with the previous one concerning the "Lion of Cosmic Will" indicates that lion symbolism plays some part in the goal of the solar Logos, the incarnation of the planetary Logos on Earth, and the consequent creation of humanity. Apparently, our planetary Logos carries the special energy of self-will via Leo:

> Leo, which is the will of the self-conscious Entity to manifest, holds the clue or key to the entire problem of self-conscious being, whether it is the will-to-be of a planetary Logos, of a group or of a man. The self-consciousness of man is inherent in the planet itself, which is the life expression of a fully self-conscious Being. The use of the will through the Shamballa centre involves the conscious use of that energy by the planetary Logos; this is evoking response today from the world of men in terms of will, both higher and lower.8

Additionally, the Tibetan comments that the highest ray energy, the monadic ray of our planetary Logos, is that of ray one. This energy is expressed through three constellations—Aries, Leo, and Capricorn. Our concern is with Leo, but it should be pointed out that Aries controls this first ray energy at this time and this triangle of signs wields a great influence on our Earth today. The point, however, is that Leo expresses ray one energy. Taken together a picture emerges in which our planetary Logos, Whose ultimate ray energy is ray one, has an important role to play in helping our solar Logos become a "Lion of Cosmic Will." This process may have begun when Sanat Kumara created the "Lions, the divine and tawny orange Flames" and Leo was in its ascendancy eighteen million years ago.

Today humanity has matured to the point where Sanat Kumara and His Aides in Shamballa can transmit this ray one energy directly into the human kingdom without it first being "diluted" by the Hierarchy. This first occurred in 1925. Unfortunately, that energy transmission contributed to the outbreak of World War II. Ray one (Will and Power) energy is very potent in destroying any form which is inadequate for the expression of a heightened spiritual energy. Hence, those forms, whether physical forms or mental forms (institutionalized principles and ideals of society) which were not adequate for the new incoming ideas, met with destruction.

A second release of the Shamballa energy occurred in 1975. That transmission did not result in a world war, but we have seen the destruction of tyranny on a large scale these past twenty-five years, including the disintegration of the Communist dictatorships in Europe. It appears that humanity is adapting to the direct release of Shamballa energy into its midst.

Another Shamballa impact occurred in May, 2000. It will be very interesting to see the effects of this third release of the first ray on humanity in the coming years.

These direct contacts with ray one are proof that the evolutionary process set in motion eighteen million years ago is bearing fruit. As the Tibetan has said, our Earth humanity will reap the benefits of the divine Will as it manifests on our tiny planet. We are witnessing the beginning of this process today.

Returning to the lion theme associated with the Will and Leo, DK supplies another hint, although it is rather obscure. He states that:

> The influences of Sirius, three in number, are focussed in Regulus, which is, as you know, a star of the first magnitude and which is frequently called "the heart of the Lion." There is more real occultism hidden in the names given to the various stars by astronomers down the ages than has yet been realised, and here you have a case in point.[9]

This extract is discussed in my earlier work, but the main point for our purposes here is the phrase which DK has placed between the quotation marks—"the heart of the Lion." In this passage, the Tibetan is making the point that three influences of Sirius are focussed through the brightest star within the constellation Leo, which is Regulus, "the heart of the Lion." Elsewhere he states that Sirius governs Leo: "Leo, in the cosmic sense (and apart from our solar system altogether) is ruled by Sirius."[10]

Now let's examine the numbers associated with these phrases:

- The heart of the Lion equals 189 AN.
- Lion of Cosmic Will equals 189 AN.
- 105 Kumaras (84 AN) equals 189 AN (105 + 84).

As indicated above, the key topics of this discussion all equal 189. The first item relates to Leo and Regulus, the second item relates to the goal of our solar Logos, and the third item relates to Sanat Kumara and the 104 Kumaras Who came to Earth. The number 189 supports the idea that Sanat Kumara and His 104 Assistants incarnated during the "time" of Leo the Lion in order to initiate a Plan to establish divine Will in the solar system through planet Earth. This Plan is part of an effort to advance the evolution of our solar Logos, (and by default, our solar system) to the level at which He will be called a "Lion of Cosmic Will." Our planetary Logos is well-suited for this task because His highest spiritual energy (monadic) is that of the First Ray of Will, Power, and Purpose. This may be why Sanat Kumara is the Custodian of the Will of the Great White Lodge on Sirius. This, perhaps, is the special relationship that our planetary Logos has with the Lord of Sirius.

Strangely enough, this relationship is highlighted in DK's remarks about a triangle of force which was active when individualization took place under the influence of Leo. (This extract directly follows the quotation regarding the tawny lions in note 7.) The Tibetan states:

> I would touch here briefly upon one triangle: The Sun (second ray), Jupiter (second ray) and Venus (fifth ray). It will be apparent to you that we here have another sphere of influence of major importance, governed by Leo.[11]

On the face of it, this extract simply indicates that Leo was active at the time of individualization and consequently, three planets associated with it based on astrological rulership and ray energies were also activated. Leo is ruled by the Sun (exoterically). The Sun is a ray two planet (astrologically, the Sun is referred to as a planet) and is therefore related to Jupiter which is also a ray two planet. Venus is included because it is a ray five planet and Leo transmits ray five energy to Earth. All these planetary relationships concern corresponding astrological and ray energies.

Beneath the astrological aspect of DK's remarks is a numeric component which demonstrates that Sirius and Sanat Kumara are symbolically veiled behind this triangle of the Sun, Jupiter, and Venus. He is discussing the various triangles of energy which were active when the tawny lions (humanity) came into being. We know that this event occurred because our planetary Logos took physical/etheric form as Sanat Kumara and that this was only made possible through the direct help of the Lord of Sirius. These esoteric facts are borne out by the combined numerical value of these three celestial bodies which equals 267 (AN) and 78 (RAN). The number

267 corresponds to "Sirius the Cosmic Christ" and 78 corresponds to "the planetary Logos"! Hence, the gematria values of three planets active at the time of individualization and directly related to Leo express the numeric values corresponding to Sirius and our planetary Logos. Just to complete the picture, the RAN value of "Sirius the Cosmic Christ" equals 105—the number of Kumaras Who came to Earth (104) accompanying Sanat Kumara Himself.

Let's bring this discussion to full circle by recalling the discovery, in chapter 9, of the number 189 in the combined beginning, middle, and last words of Psalm 46, the Great Invocation, and "A Word from the Master" (figure 9.2). Whether by accident or design, this number 189 summarizes the coming of Sanat Kumara to Earth as part of a cosmic Plan. This idea emerged when, in chapter 9, we discovered that the number 189 also referred to "the Heart of the Lion" (figure 9.3) and was therefore associated with Leo. The cosmic proportions of this Plan suggested by Leo and Regulus are actually present, but veiled at a deeper level than that shown in figure 9.3. That same diagram is shown in figure 12.1 with the addition of terms corresponding to the RAN values of 85 and 104. These results do not negate those obtained earlier in any way—they simply expand and add to what has already been discovered. Furthermore, these new conclusions reinforce everything we have discussed to this point pertaining to the incarnation of Sanat Kumara.

Figure 12.1. Mission of Sanat Kumara.

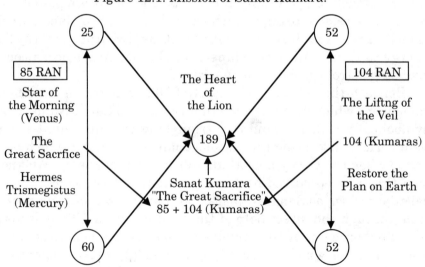

The numbers in this diagram include all the major elements in the story of Sanat Kumara's mission on Earth. The left side of figure 12.1 contains the title "Star of the Morning." This is another name for Venus. Next, we find "the Great Sacrifice." We now know that this refers to Sanat Kumara, the incarnation of the planetary Logos of Earth. Finally, we see the name "Hermes Trismegistus" and we know that one of his names is Mercury. Continuing with a quote from Djwhal Khul, we find the following:

> It was the activity of Venus—under the influence of Gemini—which produced the great crisis of the individualisation when the two kingdoms "approached" each other. Venus, Mercury and the Earth then set up a magnetic field which made the intervention of the Great Lodge on Sirius and the dual stimulation of Gemini effective in producing significant results of which the fourth kingdom in nature is the expression.[12]

This extract is monumental in terms of the information it contains which parallels the items listed in figure 12.1. Venus, *the Star of the Morning*, Mercury, as *Hermes Trismegistus*, and Earth, represented by *The Great Sacrifice*, Sanat Kumara, formed a "magnetic field" which made the intervention of the Great White Lodge on Sirius and the dual stimulation of Gemini effective in creating the human kingdom on Earth.

SANAT KUMARA AND GEMINI

The new addition to these now familiar themes is Gemini. Along with Leo, it appears that Gemini has also been a key factor in the mission of Sanat Kumara. As the next extract makes clear, Sirius once more emerges as a primary influence on our Earth:

> Gemini—forms a point of entrance for cosmic energy from Sirius....
> It might be profitable to you to bear in mind at this point what I have often told you, that the great White Lodge on Sirius is the spiritual prototype of the great White Lodge on Earth, of which modern Masonry is the distorted reflection, just as the personality is a distorted reflection of the soul. I would also remind you again of the relation between Gemini and Masonry to which reference has frequently been made.[13]

From this quotation we see that our White Lodge (spiritual

Hierarchy) is modelled after the great White Lodge on Sirius; and continuing the chain, Masonry is a lesser reflection of the spiritual Hierarchy of Earth. The link between Masonry and Sirius is strengthened in the following statement by the Tibetan:

> Masonry, as originally instituted far back in the very night of time and long ante-dating the Jewish dispensation, was organised under direct Sirian influence and modelled as far as possible on certain Sirian institutions and bearing a slight resemblance also to our hierarchical life.[14]

Let's gather some of these loose threads. Chapter 4 discusses the distinct Masonic symbols connected to Dr. John Dee's titlepage for his book about the art of navigation. The influence of Dee's philosophy on Bacon is obvious in Bacon's titlepage to *The Advancement of Learning*, depicting the two pillars of Masonry with a ship sailing between them. Adding in DK's linkage of Masonry, Sirius, and Gemini, we see that all the elements are included and that the new factor of Gemini is connected to Masonry. The completion of this chain comes through the planetary ruler of Gemini which is *Mercury*. In fact, the linked elements are even more compelling because the esoteric and hierarchical rulers of Gemini are *Venus* and the *Earth*, respectively. (In the esoteric astrology taught by the Tibetan, each zodiacal sign has three planetary rulers.) This explains DK's statement that Venus, Mercury, and the Earth formed "a magnetic field which made the intervention of the Great Lodge on Sirius" and Gemini effective in the creation of the human race. As we now know, the incarnation of the planetary Logos as Sanat Kumara was also necessary for the completion of this cosmic Work.

The symbolism of Gemini's glyph (II) refers to duality. This duality is symbolized by two stars in the constellation named after the twins, Castor and Pollux. These two represent the duality of the immortal soul and mortal personality. They also represent, among other things, the inherent dualism of life on Earth, such as day and night, good and evil, life and death, male and female, etc. The following commentary by the Tibetan brings together several factors of importance in our study:

> The formless nature of the influences of Gemini is strikingly borne out if the significance of Masonry is studied. This world-wide institution

was—as I have earlier told you—organised under the influence and impulse of this sign and is governed by it in a most unusual manner. The format or exoteric symbolism of Masonry has frequently been changed during the millennia of years through which it has been active. Its present Jewish colouring is relatively modern and not necessarily enduring, but its significance and its history of unfoldment are the history of the indwelling Christ consciousness and of that inner light, and this must unalterably be continued. That which has entered through the two pillars of Hercules, the disciples (Jachin and Boaz), and through the sign Gemini, has entered to stay.[15]

The axis upon which this entire passage turns is the question of what exactly has "entered [our planet] to stay?" It appears to be the indwelling Christ consciousness.

Let's retrieve an earlier statement by the Tibetan located at the beginning of this section: "Gemini—forms a point of entrance for cosmic energy from Sirius." Sirius is the middle principle of a cosmic energy triangle governing our solar system (and six others). This triangle consists of seven stars of the Great Bear (the Big Dipper), seven stars of the Pleiades, and Sirius. The Ageless Wisdom teaches that the Great Bear, the Pleiades, and Sirius are often represented as the cosmic Father, the cosmic Mother, and the cosmic Son (cosmic Christ), respectively. (More about this important cosmic triangle can be found in my first book, as well as in the books of Alice Bailey.) This cosmic triplicity is supremely important in the cosmology presented by the Tibetan. Although Sirius is the only celestial object out of the three which plays a major role in this study and my earlier research, the power of this cosmic triangle cannot be overstated. That is why the following short story is so amazing in its implications.

A startling discovery occurred several years ago while I was looking at a star map. As I looked at the relative positions of these three important celestial star groups, I realized that they appeared to form a pattern similar to the Signature of Sirius (fig. 4.3). The Pleiades, seven stars of the Great Bear (the Big Dipper), and Sirius formed a triangle when joined by three lines. Even more amazing, however, was that in order to encompass the seven stars of the dipper, a smaller triangle had to be drawn. It was then that I realized that this playful exercise essentially produced the same pattern as the Signature of Sirius. Obviously, this is only a symbolic representation of the all-important esoteric link between these three massive astronomical star groups, but nevertheless it is there. (This symbol

overlaid on a star map appears in appendix D.) Apparently, we are
being reminded that even though Sirius is vital to the present
unfolding Plan, we cannot forget that the Great Bear and the
Pleiades form an integral triangle with Sirius in the overall structure of cosmic relationships affecting our planet.

Before proceeding, I want to point out that the topics discussed
in this chapter are deep and complex. They cannot be fully understood at our present degree of knowledge. Consequently, I am limiting the discussion as much as possible to those essentials which pertain to the Great Work of our planetary Logos (incarnated as Sanat
Kumara) and His Mission on Earth. Even this cursory investigation
of the matter reveals enormous complexities and vast interrelationships at planetary and cosmic levels of existence. More advanced students of esoteric cosmology may see opportunities for exploring these
deeper levels, but for the sake of the "group reader" I am limiting
the temptation to delve into the more complex possibilities.

Continuing with Gemini, the Tibetan states that Gemini forms
a triangle of energy with the Great Bear and the Pleiades:

> Because the Ray of Love-Wisdom, the second ray, pours through
> Gemini it becomes apparent how true is the occult teaching that love
> underlies the entire universe. God is love, we are assured, and this
> statement is both an exoteric and an esoteric truth. This underlying
> love of Deity reaches our solar system primarily through Gemini,
> which forms, with the constellation of the Great Bear and the
> Pleiades, a cosmic triangle. This is the triangle of the cosmic Christ
> and is the esoteric symbol lying behind the cosmic Cross. There is
> ever the eternal triangle to be found behind the fourfold phenomenal
> appearance.[16]

The reason that Sirius is not mentioned as part of this cosmic Christ
Triangle is because Gemini has already received cosmic Christ energy from Sirius (as quoted at the beginning of this section). Gemini
now becomes the agent of Sirian energy and takes the place of Sirius
in this "stepped down" energy triangle consisting of the other two
constellations of the Great Bear and the Pleiades. This is illustrated in figure 12.2 by the upper and lower triangles. Armed with this
information, we now understand why Gemini played such a crucial
role in the coming of Sanat Kumara as the Avatar, the planetary
Christ. It is because Gemini distributes (with the help of the Great
Bear and the Pleiades) the Cosmic Christ energy of Love-Wisdom

Figure 12.2. Triangle of the Cosmic Christ.

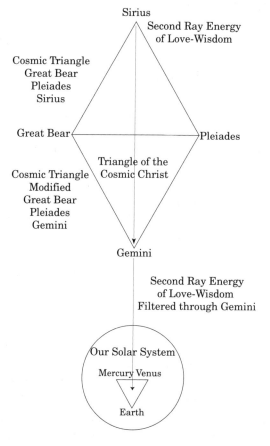

from Sirius; hence, also the roles of Mercury and Venus (the exoteric and esoteric rulers of Gemini) which aid the planetary Logos in making "the Great Sacrifice" as the prototypal Avatar, Sanat Kumara. Remember, as explained earlier, these elements are present in the left column of figure 12.1.

THE THREE COSMIC CROSSES

In the previous quotation, Djwhal Khul ends by referring to the "cosmic Cross" and the "fourfold phenomenal appearance." This refers to the Mutable Cross, of which the four signs are Gemini, Virgo, Sagittarius, and Pisces.

The Tibetan describes the three crosses of astrology in terms of the second aspect of the cosmic triangle, the cosmic Christ aspect. This means that the grouping of the zodiacal signs into the three crosses is based on the characteristics of the second aspect of the esoteric trinity. This represents the soul, the qualities of love and consciousness, and the supervision of the building of forms in the lower material worlds. The three crosses contain the following signs:

> Mutable Cross—*Gemini*, Virgo, Sagittarius, Pisces
> Fixed Cross—*Taurus*, Leo, Scorpio, Aquarius
> Cardinal Cross—*Aries*, Cancer, Libra, Capricorn

Gemini, Taurus, and Aries are the governing signs of the three crosses. I have placed the crosses according to the order of their evolutionary development as given by the Tibetan. The following names of these crosses are given by DK:

> Mutable Cross—"The Cross of the Hidden Christ."
> Fixed Cross—"The Cross of the Crucified Christ."
> Cardinal Cross—"The Cross of the Risen Christ."

As you can see for yourself, these titles describe the evolution of the Christ Consciousness. Describing this process in the broadest way, at the beginning of the evolutionary process in the physical world, the Christ or soul is hidden in each individual. Through much pain and suffering each person learns by experience that sacrifice for others is the key to the meaning of life. This opens the way for the stage of the Crucified Christ. Selfish desire gives way to selfless service to others. Eventually, the individual is liberated from the wheel of rebirth, of birth and death in the world of matter. She or he begins transiting out of the world of human living into the world of souls, known as the spiritual Hierarchy. This is the stage of the Risen Christ. As in all esoteric processes these stages apply to the human and cosmic levels of existence.

While discussing the Mutable Cross in relation to human evolution, the Tibetan calls it "the cross of the Son of God, the incarnating Christ...the Cross of the planetary Christ."[17] Of particular interest to us is the fact that the term "planetary Christ" equals 189! As figure 12.1 indicates, this corresponds to the value at the center of the diagram, for it sheds light on the nature and quality of the role played by Sanat Kumara as the incarnated *planetary Christ* Who, as the outer manifestation of the planetary Logos, is the prototypal "Word made flesh."

In accordance with the Mutable Cross, we see that by coming into incarnation under the influence of Sirius and Gemini, the planetary Logos set Himself up as a conduit (Sanat Kumara) for the entry of cosmic energy from Sirius—the energy of the Cosmic Christ—Love-Wisdom. In this way the seeds of the Christ Consciousness were initially hidden in the newborn human race where they remain to this day. It is the work of this cross to "transform animal man into an aspirant" and to nurture and develop the "life of the indwelling Christ, the hidden Soul or Lord of Being."[18] Thus, the energy of Sirius was channeled through Gemini, Venus, and Mercury to Earth. Djwhal Khul tells us that our planetary Logos was prepared to perform this service because He had already mastered the Mutable Cross (in the cosmic sense) in a previous solar system before our Earth ever existed. Our planetary Logos is now moving forward in His own evolution in this current solar system by "mounting" the Fixed Cross. He is doing this through the embodied Presence known as Sanat Kumara:

> From the angle of the supreme Masters on Sirius, our planetary Logos, Sanat Kumara, is still on the Fixed Cross; He mounted the Mutable Cross in the first solar system; the Fixed Cross still holds Him in this solar system "fixed in His place"; in the next solar system, He will transfer Himself to the Cardinal Cross, and from "thence return to that High Place from whence He came."[19]

We will discuss the Fixed Cross shortly, but first let's examine the numbers associated with the Mutable Cross. The gematria touched upon through the values of the four signs of the Mutable Cross is quite fascinating. The AN value of the names of the four signs Gemini, Virgo, Sagittarius, and Pisces equals 343. This number is significant because it is the result of 7 to the third power or 7 x 7 x 7. While discussing the number 777 the Tibetan states:

> Primarily this number applies to the planetary Logos of our scheme and not so much to other schemes. Each Heavenly Man has His number and the number of our Heavenly Man lies hid in the above three figures.[20]

This number 777 is discussed extensively in my previous work as it plays a vital role in the composition of the Great Invocation. Here, I believe the number 343, representing the Mutable Cross, indicates the completion of the cycle which prepares the form—the physical, emotional, and mental bodies of the individual—for the emergence of the hidden Christ into the light of day. The number 343 symbolizes the number of cycles and root-races which the planetary Logos utilizes for His evolutionary unfoldment in our Earth Scheme. This will be fully discussed in the next chapter, but for now it is enough to know that this number is a powerful indicator of the cyclic activity of the Great Work of the planetary Logos. It might be said that this number related to the Mutable Cross signs represents the vast planetary field of service encompassed by our Logos. This field is comprised of the kingdoms of nature, including the human, and the 343 world cycles through which these life streams pass in their evolutionary development.

This brings us to the Fixed Cross, the cross of the Crucified Christ. If the Mutable Cross numbers symbolize the field of service of the Logos, then the Fixed Cross is the means of carrying out that service. As stated many times already by the Master DK, this is described as a redemptive or saving process. A fair analogy might be that the substance of the physical plane, the atoms themselves, are inhibited or corrupted in some way and need to be subjected to an energizing process which will free that substance and allow its full functioning. Consequently, the planetary Logos has incarnated as Sanat Kumara in order to upgrade this relatively imperfect matter. Hence, such work is described as a redemptive process and is related to the Fixed Cross—the cross of the Crucified Christ. Thus, DK's statement:

> This theme of redemption (which underlies all the initiatory processes) is hidden in the karmic responsibilities of Sanat Kumara. ....This little planet is essentially unique in its purpose and its techniques, and that on it and within it (if you could but penetrate below the surface) a great redemptive experiment is going forward; its prime implementing factors and its scientific agents are the "sons of mind who choose to be the sons of men and yet for all eternity remain the Sons of God." These "sons of mind" were chosen, in that far distant time when the fourth kingdom in nature came into being, to carry forward the science of redemption.[21]

This statement simply means that we human beings are the evolutionary creation of ancient and advanced cosmic Beings who "descended" to our tiny planet from higher dimensions and other worlds in order to carry out an experiment in evolution at the physical dimension of creation. This is part of the cosmic Plan involving our solar system, the Earth, and Sirius.

The Fixed Cross provides an abundance of esoteric numeric symbolism. This is altogether appropriate in light of the importance of this cross in the present cyclic work of Sanat Kumara. Speaking strictly in terms of numeric symbolism, of the four signs comprising the Fixed Cross, Scorpio and Leo are discussed at some length in *Sacred Vessel of the Mysteries* (Aquarius emerged to some degree and Taurus not at all). Seen from this angle, Taurus appears to be veiled or silent in regard to the esoteric features of the Great Invocation. This is because, according to DK, Taurus is connected more to the Great Bear (cosmic Will) and the Pleiades (cosmic Intelligence) than to Sirius (cosmic Love-Wisdom).

It is this perception of connectivity which makes the study of esotericism so difficult, for at much higher levels of consciousness the cosmic connections are clear and all the zodiacal signs, the Great Bear, the Pleiades, and Sirius, along with our solar system and other systems are seen as a vast Unity. Our vision is severely restricted and we suffer consequently from the illusion of separation and fragmentation. In fact, the Ageless Wisdom teaches that Taurus and all the other zodiacal signs form a part of that vast cosmic Entity called the One About Whom Naught May Be Said, but from our limited angle, Taurus simply does not appear to play a large part in the esoteric numbers associated with the Great Invocation. That in itself tells us something, because a large body of evidence clearly shows that the Great Invocation has a distinct focus on Sirius rather than on the Great Bear or the Pleiades. Consequently, Taurus would not appear to have a direct relation to the Great Invocation. (It should be noted that preliminary research indicates that Taurus may have some deeper, less obvious relation to the Great Invocation.)

Moving on, we find that the Fixed Cross signs, as a whole, exhibit numerical associations with the the Great Invocation. This relationship is evidenced in the numeric sum of these four signs which equals 334. We already know that the Great Invocation contains 443 letters. Note that both these sums contain the identical digits (3 and

4). The digits of these two numbers are mutually connected to the number 7. Recall that this is the number of Athena. Obviously, 3 + 4 = 7, but more to our point, 7 - 3 = 4 and 7 - 4 = 3. Consequently, the subtraction of either number from 7 results in the manifestation of its counterpart. Metaphysically speaking, an energy relationship exists between these two numbers based on 7.

A simple extension of this basic arithmetic demonstrates that 777 - 334 = 443 and 777 - 443 = 334. Hence, by adding these two numbers together they equal 777—the number(s) of the planetary Logos. We can interpret this to mean that the number of our Logos (working through Sanat Kumara) is found through the combined energies of the Fixed Cross and the Great Invocation. This means that the Great Invocation, Sanat Kumara, and the Fixed Cross form a triangular relationship signaled by the numbers related to them.

Figure 12.3. Numbers Related to Sanat Kumara.

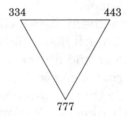

We are already somewhat familiar with the energies of the Great Invocation represented by its 443 letters. We are also familiar with the number(s) 777. Now let's examine the energies revealed through the combined numeric values of the horizontal and vertical arms of the Fixed Cross.

Figure 12.4. The Fixed Cross.

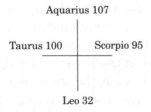

THE PRIMORDIAL LIGHT OF THE WORLD

Although we could go into deeper levels of numerological analysis of these signs, I am confining my comments to the AN values of each arm of the Fixed Cross. Obviously, we could go into a much deeper analysis of the individual signs, but these will suffice to make the point. The Taurus/Scorpio horizontal arm has an AN value of 195. This is the value of "The High Priestess," the second major trump card of the Tarot (chapter 8). From an esoteric angle this meaning is very appropriate. The Tibetan states that Scorpio governs the path of discipleship and Taurus is the sign of Illumination which is the result of initiation into the Mysteries. "The High Priestess," as discussed in chapter 8, is the veiled Isis who guards the door of initiation.

The vertical arm of the Fixed Cross consists of Leo/Aquarius. The AN value of these two signs equals 139. This number has also been discussed in chapter 10. This number corresponds to "Hermes-Thoth" and "Cosmic Christ." The former is not only the archetypal God of Light, but esoterically is Sanat Kumara, the planetary Hermes. In a similar vein, Sanat Kumara is also the planetary Christ, the prototypal Avatar of our planet. On the cosmic scale Sanat Kumara is a lower reflection of that higher cosmic Christ triangle composed of Gemini (transferring agent for Sirius), the Great Bear, and the Pleiades (fig. 12.2).

This point is driven home even more forcefully by the fact that 139 is also the combined RAN value of the three tarot cards "The High Priestess" (87), "The Sun" (24), and "The Star" (28). These are also discussed in chapter 10. In effect, all these elements are wrapped within the Great Invocation and have been discussed here and in my previous book. The point is that Sanat Kumara, as the embodied representative of our planetary Logos, has incarnated on the Fixed Cross of the crucified Christ. He is the primordial Light of the World, Hermes; He is the planetary Christ/Avatar and constant reminder of the greater Cosmic Christ represented in one sense as Gemini (along with the Great Bear and the Pleiades), but in the highest sense as Sirius, the star of Initiation.

The Cardinal Cross is the final stage of evolutionary unfoldment on the human and cosmic scale. In an earlier extract (p. 203n19) the Tibetan states that our planetary Logos will transfer to the Cardinal Cross in the future solar system. The AN value of the Cardinal Cross signs equals 235. Appropriately, this number has never appeared in this book or my previous one because it concerns the distant future when an entirely new solar system will be manifesting. Symbolically, the number 235 does not concern us.

HERMES TRISMEGISTUS: HUMAN, PLANETARY, AND COSMIC

We have said much about Hermes already and an entire chapter is devoted to this mysterious Being in *Sacred Vessel of the Mysteries*. I mention this merely to point out the continuity and apparent importance of the theme. The attention paid to Hermes is prompted by the numbers which persistently appear in the Great Invocation and "A Word from the Master" which equate to the the various names of this Being. Chapter 11 closed with a quote by Djwhal Khul in which he alludes to an association between Sanat Kumara and Hermes; the implication being that the Lord of the World is a planetary Representative or Agent of Hermes, the God of Light. This idea lends credence to the theory that the Great Invocation is a Cosmic Sound created by a cosmic Entity called Hermes, Who is associated with Sirius. Within the context of the esoteric and hermetic tenet, "As above, so below," this is not so far-fetched. After all, the gods of antiquity are human personifications of divine and semi-divine Entities Who originate in higher dimensions associated with Earth as well as other worlds beyond our planet. This very concept is demonstrated by the embodiment of the planetary Logos, a *cosmic* Entity, in the physical/etheric *terrestrial* form of Sanat Kumara.

Let's examine the three expressions of Hermes as they are symbolically represented in this material. Chapter 11 demonstrated the influence of the Masters R and DK within the Great Invocation through the gematria related to the phrase "God of Light within." In effect, these two Masters of the Wisdom are the messengers of the Hierarchy who have buried their message within the words of the Great Invocation. They represent the human aspect of Hermes because of their close affiliation with the human kingdom relative to great cosmic Lives Who passed the human stage millions of years ago. We are told that such Lives exist in Shamballa and other similar centers on other worlds and in other solar systems. The Master Djwhal Khul, in particular, is the messenger of the Hierarchy at this time in relation to the giving out of the modern presentation of the Ageless Wisdom. The Master R also plays a similar role, although his work is very much hidden behind the scenes.

Whether by accident or design, a fascinating numerological fact directly relates the work of Djwhal Khul as the messenger of the Hierarchy to Hermes or Mercury. Here is a statement by DK which demonstrates this connection. "On November 19th, 1919, I made my first contact with A.A.B. (much to her distress and dismay), and I have worked steadily with her ever since."22 Examining this date closely, we find that it gives us the number 19 three times. There is the November day "19" and the year "1919." When we convert November to its number as the eleventh month, the result is 11. When combined (11 + 19 + 19 + 19), these numbers total 68 which is the AN value for Hermes. Furthermore, 3 x 19 equals 57 which is the value of Gemini. The Tibetan states:

> Gemini is pre-eminently the sign of the messenger, and this sign produces many of the messengers of God as they appear down the ages, the revealers of new divine truths and the intermediaries between the fourth and fifth kingdoms.23

Generally speaking, we can easily place the Tibetan in the category of a "messenger of God" and a revealer of "new divine truths." And he is certainly an intermediary between the "fourth and fifth kingdoms," humanity and the Hierarchy respectively. The giving of this date by Djwhal Khul is a perfect example of hiding esoteric information in plain sight. This is a technique used throughout the Tibetan's writings as well as in other esoteric and occult works throughout the centuries and it certainly applies to the Synthetic Triplet.

Having explored the human expression of Hermes through the Masters R and DK, let's proceed to the level of the planetary Hermes. This is represented by the embodiment of the planetary Logos in the form of Sanat Kumara. It is at this crucial stage that the impact of numbers and their esoteric correspondences emerge. The Tibetan states that "Christ said (as have all the Sons of God Who know the true significance of the Fixed Cross), 'I am the Light of the world.'"24 Although the Christ, Buddha, and Hermes have all made this proclamation, they were responding to the Light emanating from Sanat Kumara, the Lord of the World. We know that

Sanat Kumara is now on the Fixed Cross and therefore, we can apply this same principle to Him. As part of our solar system, Sanat Kumara responds to the Light of the solar Logos. Furthermore, due to our planetary Logos having a special relationship to the Lord of Sirius, He must be responding to the Greatest Light influencing our solar system—Sirius, the Cosmic Hermes.

The esoteric numerology of this relationship is found in the following diagram (fig.12.5). You will notice that the diagram contains two sets of identical numbers corresponding to Sirius and Scorpio/Leo. When either set is combined with the value of Sanat

Figure 12.5. Planetary and Cosmic Hermes.

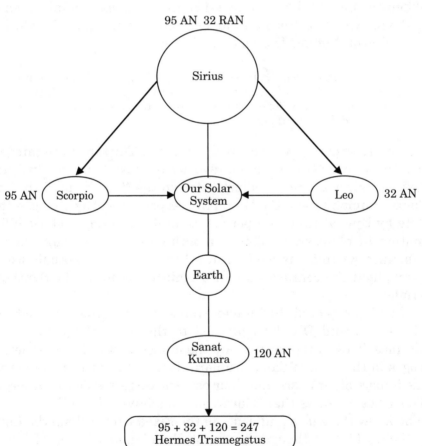

Kumara, the result is 247, "Hermes Trismegistus." Several factors have come together here. The Tibetan states that Sirius governs not only our own solar system, but it also governs Scorpio and Leo, two signs of the Fixed Cross. Peculiarly, the AN and RAN values of Sirius equal 95 and 32. These two values equal the AN values of Scorpio and Leo respectively. Sanat Kumara is on the Fixed Cross and consequently, when the value of His name is combined with two of the Fixed Cross signs governed by Sirius, the result—247 equals the name "Hermes Trismegistus." In addition, our planetary Logos has a special relationship to Sirius and therefore, if the values for Sirius and Sanat Kumara are combined (excluding Scorpio and Leo), the result is still the same—247.

There is more to this particular number example. In my first book, I discussed the code numbers 14 and 17 which DK gave as clues to the creative Hierarchies associated with the Path to Sirius. I concluded that these two numbers were related to the signs Leo (14) and Scorpio (17). (These are not the gematria values of these signs, but are numbers based on calculations found in my first book. Space does not allow going into this here.) Creative Hierarchies are the various types of group Lives which enter into the planetary worlds to aid in the evolutionary process. For instance, Leo rules the first Creative Hierarchy associated with the highest group of Lives in our solar system, the planetary Logoi. Humanity is the fourth creative Hierarchy and is associated with Scorpio.

The point of this very brief mention of these two creative Hierarchies is that they also relate to Hermes. The declaration, "I am the Light of the World" has an AN value of 238. The two numbers 14 and 17, when multiplied, equal 238. Consequently, the two signs Leo (32) and Scorpio (95) are again related to Sirius (32 RAN, 95 AN). Naturally, when the value of the name Sanat Kumara (120) is added to Leo (32) and Scorpio (95), they also total 247—Hermes Trismegistus.

Figure 12.6. Sanat Kumara and Hermes.

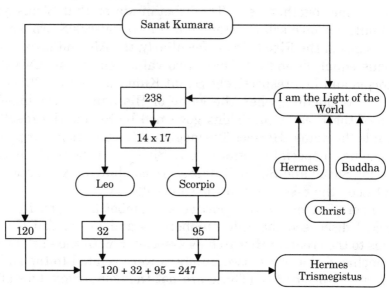

SUMMATION

The numbers and corresponding themes explored in this chapter make clear that Sanat Kumara is the Hermetic God of Light of our planet. He is a cosmic Entity temporarily (relative to our human reckoning of time) functioning in a planetary role as the Avatar for Earth and Hermetic Messenger of Light. He is a Mediator between the cosmic Light of Sirius and the lesser lights of Earth. He incorporates within His Being the Fixed Cross signs of Leo and Scorpio. These are symbolically rendered into the name Hermes Trismegistus (fig. 12.5).

The energies of both these signs are already active in the human kingdom. Symbolically speaking, Hermes Trismegistus is interacting with the world of human living in a potent way. Leo was active during individualization and continues to create that sensitivity in the human species which will make it responsive and responsible to the lower kingdoms of nature. This increasing sensitivity of the God-man (as DK describes it) will allow humanity to fulfill its role of group Avatar to the natural world. In effect, Sanat Kumara will achieve part of His success as the planetary Avatar through humanity.

This success in Leo will be paralleled by its opposite sign on the

Fixed Cross, Aquarius. The increasing sensitivity of the individual spreads out to include others, thus leading to the group consciousness of Aquarius along with the sensitivity acquired through Leo. As a result, Aquarius is esoterically described as the sign of the world server. It is also the governing sign of the new age for the next 2,150 years. The effect of the Leo-Aquarius arm can already be seen working within the human kingdom through the environmental movement and the work of many scientists and researchers with the animal kingdom.

Scorpio has been especially active in the twentieth century as the tests and trials of the world wars and globalization have challenged humanity's survival. These tests and trials will continue into the twenty-first century, challenging the leaders in every field of human endeavor to work together in a cooperative spirit and resist the temptations of materialism and selfishness. This continued push toward globalization, while maintaining respect for the individual, will someday lead to the activation of the opposite sign Taurus. This will release the Illuminating Light of Hermes in ever increasing brightness. Taurus is the controlling sign of the Fixed Cross and thus is the most veiled. Its powerful Light can only gradually emerge as the other three signs of the Fixed Cross perform their work when activated through humanity's response to their energies.

This, I believe, is why Aquarius and Taurus are less visible in terms of the numeric symbolism of the Great Invocation and its connection to Sanat Kumara. The energies of Leo and Scorpio must be integrated by the human kingdom before Aquarius and Taurus can emerge and be available for human use. This is why the mantric energies of the Great Invocation are so vitally important—they contain the correct formula for the ordered unfolding of the Plan.

As figure 12.5 shows, above Leo and Scorpio stands Sirius. Again the symbolism is there to see. The numbers 95 and 32 match those of Scorpio and Leo. As Sirius symbolically stands above Gemini in the Cosmic Cross, pouring Love-Wisdom into that constellation (fig. 12.2), this great Light also stands above Scorpio and Leo. Not only is Sirius "above" these constellations in terms of the hierarchy of cosmic energy relationships, but from the human standpoint, Sirius is veiled behind the astrological energies of Leo, Scorpio, and Gemini. Hence, we see that the archetypal energy of Hermes can be recognized from at least three levels.

Figure 12.7. Three Levels of Hermes.

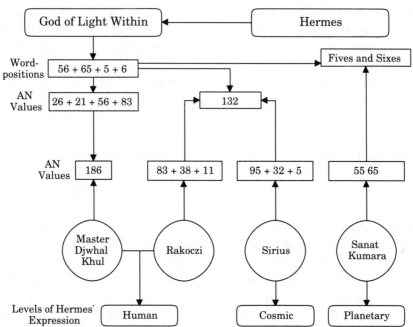

Chapter 11 described the Hermetic presence within the Great Invocation of "Master Djwhal Khul" and "Master Rakoczi" through the numbers associated with their names. These "names" correlate to the "God of Light within." These two great Teachers of the Hierarchy can each be thought of as a transhuman Hermes. Sanat Kumara is present through the fives and sixes associated with His name and the word-positions of "God of Light Within."

Sanat Kumara can be thought of as the planetary Hermes, the Messenger of Light Who has come to our physical world from higher cosmic worlds. The Tibetan offers a clue to the ultimate controlling factor in the incarnation of our planetary Logos as Sanat Kumara. That controlling factor is Sirius because Sirius governs Leo and Scorpio. And as the numbers indicate, Sanat Kumara (being on the Fixed Cross) is initially utilizing the energies of Leo and Scorpio prior to Aquarius and Taurus. Consequently, we might say that Sirius is the cosmic Hermes distributing its cosmic Light through a zodiacal filtering circuit outside our solar system and a planetary circuit within our solar system prior to its reception on Earth.

Figures 12.2 and 12.5 illustrate this process. (Note that there are other energy circuits associated with Sirius, but I have only discussed those related to the number clues evident in our study.) Thus, Sanat Kumara emerges as the Avatar, the Hermetic Messenger of Sirius, mediating between the Redeeming Light of Sirius and the lesser lights which must be saved on Earth—the imprisoned lives of the human, animal, vegetable, and mineral kingdoms.

Our planetary Logos is on at least two tracks. In the current incarnation as Sanat Kumara, He is working on the Sirian Plan for redeeming the imprisoned lives on Earth. An intrinsic part of that Plan involves an accelerated means of liberation known as initiation. Through the revelatory experience of initiation instituted by Sirius, Sanat Kumara is the agent of the Sirian initiatory process. Again, following the Way of Hermes, initiation is a process of emergence into ever increasing Light. Each initiation increases the Light and consequently the Life of the Initiate. Thus, the prisoners of the planet are released into greater Light and Life because, as the Tibetan states, Light and Life are interchangeable within the confines of our planet.[25]

The role of Gemini emerges more clearly in relation to Sanat Kumara in two ways. First, Gemini steps down the cosmic ray energy of Love-Wisdom which emanates from Sirius. This is the energy of the Cosmic Christ. Because Sanat Kumara is the incarnating Avatar, the planetary Christ, it is not only natural, but perhaps necessary for Him to align with the energy of Sirius via Gemini.

Second, the Great Work of redemption on Earth can be rapidly accelerated through the process of initiation. According to the Tibetan, Masonry was originally used as a means of introducing young humanity to the Mysteries of life. These Mysteries hold the clues to man's origin and destiny through the symbols of color, sound, and number which can be expressed through ritual. As discussed earlier, Masonry originates in the Sirian system and Gemini is the cosmic filter through which Sirian energy flows into our solar system and our planet. Hence, Masonry is saturated in the highly charged energy of the sun Sirius via Gemini.

The second track which our planetary Logos is traveling relates to our solar Logos. This involves the cosmic evolutionary path of our planetary Logos. This is known as the "Way of the Higher Evolution." There are seven possible paths which the Masters of the

Hierarchy can take. The sixth one is called the path of the Solar Logos. The Tibetan says that our planetary Logos is on this path:

> It is... difficult and practically impossible to say anything anent this Path which is trodden by Those Great Beings Who are in training for Solar Logoi. Of These, Sanat Kumara is One. Not all the planetary Logoi tread the Path of Solar Logoi, for just as exalted positions await Them elsewhere in the universe.[26]

Through this information, it is obvious that Sanat Kumara works closely with the solar Logos and as pointed out early in this chapter, He is helping the solar Logos develop an embryonic aspect of spiritual Will on Earth. This activity of our Logos is apparently meant to plant a seed of the Will energy in the present solar system which can be cultivated in the third solar system some time in the distant future.

Now more to the point. As mentioned earlier in this chapter, our solar Logos is working to become what DK terms a "Lion of Cosmic Will." This phrase has a value of 189 which matches the phrase "the heart of the Lion." This latter phrase refers to the star Regulus in the middle of the constellation Leo. Hold this thought for a moment and recall that in chapter 9, mention was made about the incarnation of Sanat Kumara. DK stated that: "'Lions, the divine and tawny orange Flames' came into being and thus humanity arrived upon the planet." It is now clear that since our planetary Logos is on the same path as the solar Logos, He is also associated in some way with lions or the leonine energy of Leo.[27] This, I believe, is a subtle clue which tells us that a cosmic school for the training of those on the sixth path may exist in the Regulus star system and therefore is saturated with the energy of Leo, the Lion.

This may explain why the tawny lions are mentioned in relation to Sanat Kumara's incarnation on Earth. He is a Pupil in the school which is training cosmic Beings Who will someday have the "coded" title of "Lion of Cosmic Will." At the same time He is an "understudy" of our solar Logos and a planetary Builder in our solar system. It appears obvious that "the heart of the Lion" is also coded with quotation marks by the Tibetan to draw the very subtle connection between the work of our solar Logos and the cosmic training of our planetary Logos in the sixth Path school for solar Logoi on Regulus. The convergence of these two phrases along with the interwoven pattern of Psalm 46, the Great Invocation and "A Word from the Master" all relate to the number 189. This could be purely coincidental, but the material itself provides a logical basis for the correspondences existing in all these elements. As figure 12.8 illustrates, the Law of Correspondences is solidly integrated into this entire occult presentation.

Figure 12.8. Energy Alignments of Sanat Kumara.

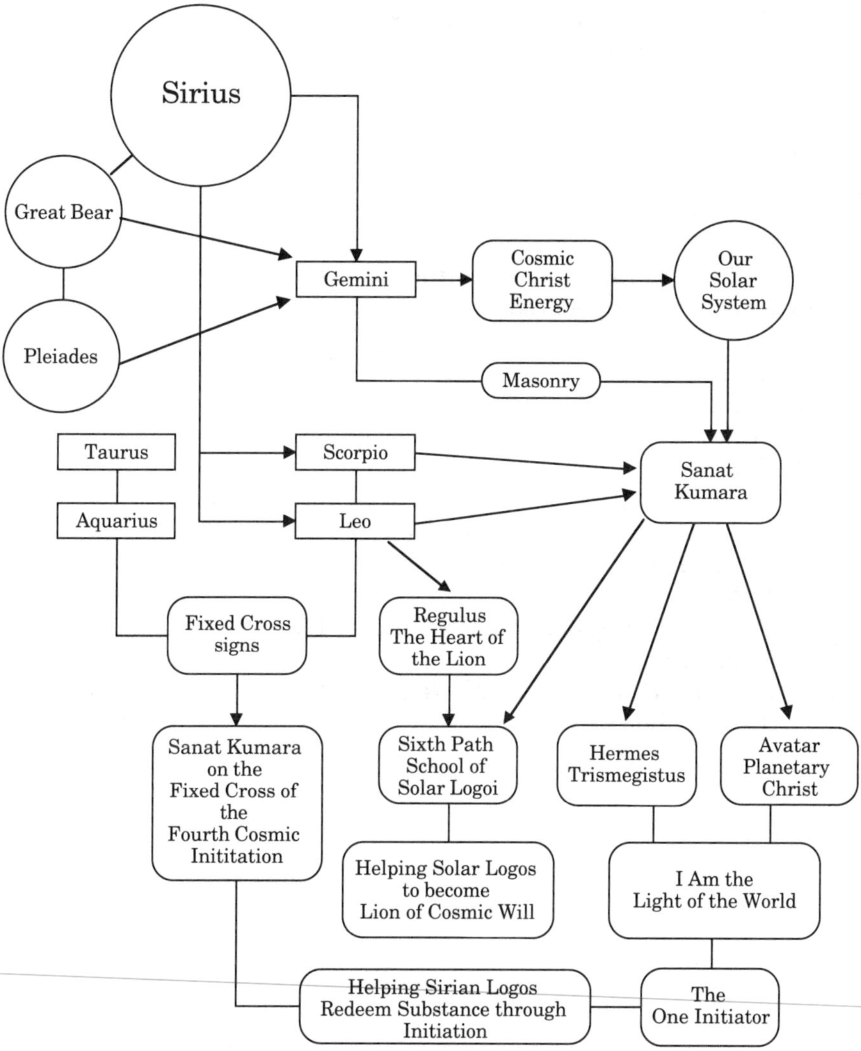

Please note that the sizes and shapes of the objects in this diagram are purely for emphasis. They should be interpreted only within the context of their relationship to Sanat Kumara as described in this chapter.

Notes

1. Alice A. Bailey, *The Rays and the Initiations*, 414.
2. Ibid., 130.
3. Ibid., 413-14.
4. Ibid., 654.
5. Ibid., 421-2.
6. Bailey, *A Treatise on Cosmic Fire*, 305-6.
7. Bailey, *Esoteric Astrology*, 301.
8. Ibid., 439-40.
9. Ibid., 300.
10. Ibid., 299.
11. Ibid., 301.
12. Ibid., 355.
13. Ibid., 349-50.
14. Bailey, *The Rays and the Initiations*, 418.
15. Bailey, *Esoteric Astrology*, 346.
16. Ibid., 348.
17. Ibid., 121.
18. Ibid., 553, 554.
19. Bailey, *The Rays and the Initiations*, 693.
20. Bailey, *A Treatise on Cosmic Fire*, 306.
21. Bailey, *Discipleship in the New Age*, vol. II, 385-6.
22. Bailey, *The Externalisation of the Hierarchy*, 631.
23. Bailey, *Esoteric Astrology*, 354.
24. Ibid., 565.
25. Bailey, *The Rays and the Initiations*, 143.
26. Ibid., 421-2.
27. See *Sacred Vessel of the Mysteries*, 208-18 for further discussion of Leo and lion symbolism.

113:

THE HIDDEN KEY

The process of stimulation of the human Egos by means of graded instructions...is instituted during every fourth round, and its peculiar interest lies in the fact that the emphasis for the fourth Creative Hierarchy in every fourth chain and globe during the fourth round is laid upon the fourth initiation, that of the Crucifixion.

Initiation, Human and Solar, 94.

THE 113 UNIT CYCLE

One of the most subtle and occult aspects of the Ageless Wisdom concerns the correspondences which exist between numbers. Using Venus and Earth as examples, the Tibetan indicates in the following extract that number correspondences are the outer symbol of a deeper relationship between cosmic Entities. Numbers somehow provide a means of communication and energy exchange between planetary and solar Lives:

The key is hidden in the fact that between the number of a globe in a chain and its corresponding chain lies a method of communication. The same is true likewise of the correspondence between a chain of globes and a scheme of analogous number. The connection between Venus and the Earth lies hid in number, and it took a moment of mysterious alignment between a globe, its corresponding chain and the scheme of allied number to effect the momentous occurrence known as the coming of the Lords of Flame. It occurred in the third rootrace in the fourth round....The chain was the fourth

219

chain and the globe, the fourth. The fourth chain in the Venus scheme and the fourth globe in that chain were closely involved in the transaction.[1]

This discussion of schemes, chains, and globes will be explained shortly, but the main point to grasp here is the importance of number symbolism in esotericism. The Law of Correspondences is universal to the esoteric aspect of most religions and philosophies and the Ageless Wisdom is no exception. In fact, it is probably more visible in Djwhal Khul's modern presentation of the Ageless Wisdom than in the sacred texts of most religions. With this concept in mind, we may find it easier to examine the idea that the number 113 is a significant numeric symbol mysteriously connected to the coming of Sanat Kumara to Earth and His creation of humanity.

Sacred Vessel of the Mysteries contains a section which explains how the 113 words of the Great Invocation correlate to the number of root-races which transpired between the time of Sanat Kumara's arrival in the fourth Earth chain and His final "descent" into incarnation on the planet. This correlation is a major finding suggesting that the number 113 is a key to establishing a cosmic timetable for restoring the Plan on Earth. In fact, the Tibetan states that such a timetable exists, as plainly seen in the following remarks:

> The final stanza of the "Invocation for Power and Light," as it is called in the Archives of the Masters, is apparently simple. It has, in these Archives, an indicatory symbol beside it which indicates the era or period in human history during which it can and should be used. It is interesting to us to note that the evolution of humanity is in line with the indicated timing.[2]

In order to grasp the significance of this "indicatory symbol" and humanity's readiness to use the Great Invocation, let's review the septenary (sevenfold division) cosmology of the Ageless Wisdom. This concept is based on the triple nature of the One Life. The One Life divides Itself into the basic trinity, and out of this trinity—A, B, C—comes a lesser trinity—a, b, c. In turn, this lesser trinity generates four additional combinations—ab, ac, bc, and abc. From this series of steps we see that there are seven outer or exoteric combinations, an intermediate or esoteric three (A, B, C) and an ultimate ONE. This metaphysical unfoldment relates to the Pythagorean "ten of perfection," which is finally resolved back into the unmanifest One. Even here, a triple demonstration of the One Life is set forth. The symbolism of Number is born out of this primordial combination of 1, 3, 7, and 10 (11 elements if we include the ultimate One from which all the rest emerge).

Employing this fundamental numbering system, the Ageless Wisdom philosophy divides the planes of consciousness, stars, solar systems, planets, and planetary cycles into sevens. Elements A, B, and C are not included because they are synthesizing components of the lower seven. Following the triple law, it divides these various elements three times. For instance, the ONE Cosmic Being called the "One About Whom Naught May Be Said" is first divided into seven fundamental planes of consciousness—the seven cosmic planes. These seven are divided into seven subplanes, and each of these subplanes is divided, a third time, into seven sub-subplanes. This is illustrated in the following diagram.

Figure 13.1. Divisions of the Cosmic Planes.

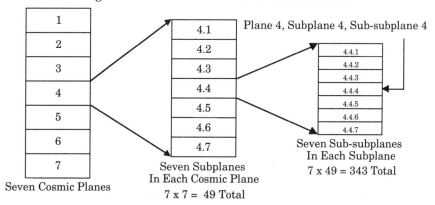

Since the seven cosmic planes (the left column) are each divided into seven subplanes (the middle column), and each of these is divided into seven sub-subplanes (the right column), it can be stated that the One About Whom Naught May Be Said contains 343 distinct levels of consciousness (7 x 7 x 7 or 7^3). The planes of consciousness of this Cosmic Life contain myriads of worlds and life forms from solar systems to atoms.

This exact formulation can be applied to a planetary scheme within a solar system. For instance, our physical world is considered

one of seven globes within the fourth cyclic expression (chain) of the
Earth Scheme. Our physical Earth belongs to the fourth chain of the
Earth Scheme which contains six other chains. The other planets in
our solar system also follow this arrangement.

Our globe is the only one of the seven globes in our fourth chain
which exists physically. The other six globes exist in dimensions or
planes of consciousness currently beyond our detection. Figure 13.2
illustrates this septenary division. Note that the column on the far
right represents 343 world periods whereas in figure 13.1, the same
column represents 343 sub-subplanes. This scale remains constant
no matter what element in the cosmology is being viewed.

Figure 13.2. Divisions of a Planetary Scheme.

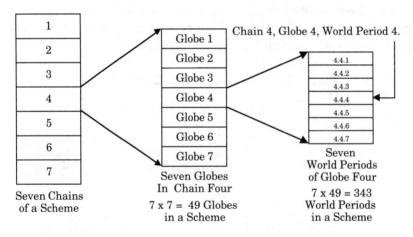

Each of these globes contains life in various forms of expression
and in different planes of consciousness, depending on the globe.
Although various kingdoms of nature exist on these globes, we are
concerned with the human kingdom, which is differentiated into
root-races. Each world period on a globe contains seven root-races
which evolve, one after the other, in a series of seven. Little is known
about the nature and forms of these root-races except for the
Lemurian, Atlantean, and Aryan races of our fourth Earth globe. An
example of this root-race cycle is depicted in figure 13.3.

Figure 13.3. Divisions of a Chain.

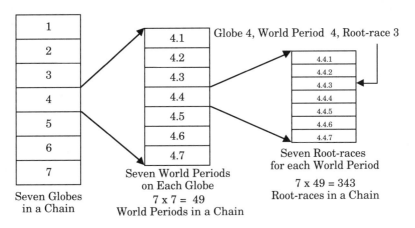

Seven Globes
in a Chain

Seven World Periods
on Each Globe
7 x 7 = 49
World Periods in a Chain

Globe 4, World Period 4, Root-race 3

Seven Root-races
for each World Period
7 x 49 = 343
Root-races in a Chain

Note once more, that the right column contains the number 343. In this last case, 343 refers to the total number of root-races which can evolve within any given chain. The point is that 343 represents the Whole no matter what scale is represented—planes, planetary schemes, world periods, etc. (It should be mentioned that not every septenary scale is illustrated in these examples.)

At the beginning of this section, I remarked that the 113 words of the Great Invocation symbolize the number of root-races that evolved between the time of Sanat Kumara's entry into the fourth Earth chain of globes to when he took etheric form on our planet. Here is the extract in which Djwhal Khul gives the all-important information revealing the 113 unit cycle:

> The statement that the great Kumara or the One Initiator came to this planet from Venus is true in so far as it embodies the fact that He came to this dense planet (the fourth) in the fourth chain from that chain in our scheme which is called the "Venus" chain, and which is the second chain. He came via the second globe in our chain; His scarcely felt vibration was sensed (occultly) in the second round [specifically, the second world period of the second globe, JB], but only in the third root-race of the fourth round [fourth world period of globe four, JB] did conditions permit of His physical incarnation and of His coming as the Avatar.[3]

The detailed steps of this event are shown in the following diagram (figure 13.4). Note that the portion of the diagram above the dotted line illustrates the seven chains of our Earth Scheme with seven globes attached to each chain. This is the same scale as that of figure 13.2. The portion below the dotted line matches the scale depicted in figure 13.3.

This lower section of figure 13.4 is a blow-up of chain 4, the Earth, from globe 2 through globe 4 as shown in the middle of the upper section of the diagram. As you can see, this detailed rendering of chain 4 begins in world period 2 and extends into our present world period 4.[4]

The arrow on the left which extends down to the box labeled R2 is the point at which Sanat Kumara came to our fourth chain. The box labeled R2 means root-race 2. The circle to the immediate right of this box contains the letters "SK" indicating that Sanat Kumara entered our fourth chain at this juncture.

There are another series of boxes running horizontally below the columns of circles. These boxes represent the globes and are labeled G1, G2, etc. The world periods are labeled above the columns of circles. World Period 2 is shown from the coming of Sanat Kumara (SK) through circle 40; World Period 3 extends from circle 41 through circle 89; World Period 4 begins at circle 90 and extends up to our present time period, depicted as circle 115.

In order to identify when Sanat Kumara came to the fourth chain, locate the circle labeled SK. Note that it is in the area of World Period 2. It is in the horizontal row labeled R2 and in the column labeled G2. Thus, Sanat Kumara came to our fourth chain during World Period 2, root-race 2, on globe 2.

The root-races evolve according to their numbers R1 through R7. They follow one globe at a time. Therefore, root-race 3 (R3) is marked circle 1 (immediately below SK). Root-race 4 (circle 2) continues down the column labeled G2 or globe 2. When the seventh root-race is completed on globe 2 (G2), the cycle repeats itself on globe 3 with root-race 1. Hence, circle 6 marks the first root-race of globe 3. Note that we are still in World Period 2. When the seventh root-race on the seventh globe completes its evolution, the World Period ends. This is shown two times in figure 13.4, by circles 40 and 41 and circles 89 and 90. Each instance depicts the end of one World Period and the beginning of another.

Putting these technical details aside, the important aspect to grasp is Djwhal Khul's deliberate pinpointing (see previous extract)

Figure 13.4. Descent of Sanat Kumara.

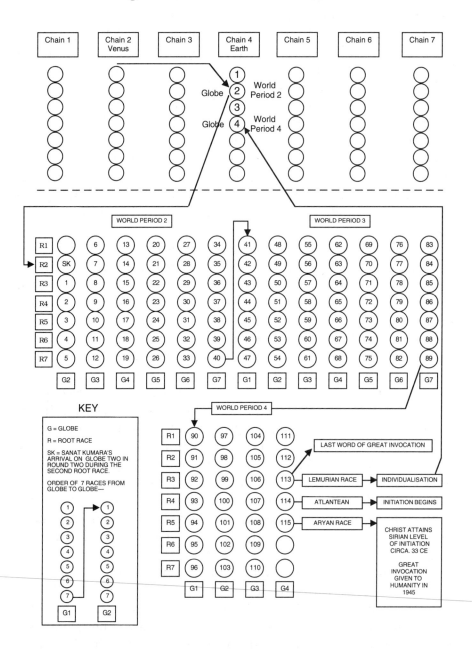

of Sanat Kumara's arrival in chain 4 and His incarnation and consequent creation of humanity (individualization) in world period 4, and root-race 3. Note these three numbers 4,4,3. These digits combine to form 443—the total quantity of letters in the Great Invocation. These "markers" have allowed us to unveil the number 113 by counting back to the time of Sanat Kumara's arrival in our fourth chain. And as we now know, this vital cyclic number is built into the Great Invocation by its exact number of words—113.

Although we can only speculate about the meaning of this peculiar circumstance, it hints at some deeper significance, some valuable information concerning the nature of this, our current period of planetary activity. Perhaps by taking a wider view of these vast septenary cycles, we can gain a greater perspective on our place in the scheme of creation.

However occult it may be, there is a pattern here. Tracing the root-races backward from the third Lemurian root-race (the time of humanity's inception) reveals that Sanat Kumara arrived in our fourth Earth chain in the second world period, the second globe, and the second root-race—*all twos*. This specific placement of the inception of the cosmic "gestation" period of Sanat Kumara means that the midpoint was reached during the third world period, the third globe, and the third root-race—*all threes* (labeled circle 57 in figure 13.4). Carrying this exercise a bit further reveals that the root-race immediately following the creation of the human family occurred in the fourth world period, the fourth globe, and the fourth root-race—*all fours*. This is labeled circle 114, the Atlantean root-race in figure 13.4.

It is certainly possible that all this means nothing, but quite often number patterns such as these indicate some deeper significance which is not immediately obvious. In this instance it appears as though the numbers 2 and 4 are important. It is significant, therefore, that the Tibetan tells us that the planet Venus is Scheme 2 and the Earth is Scheme 4. This is important because we are also told that the Logos of Venus played an important role in helping Sanat Kumara proceed with His incarnation as our planetary Avatar. Consequently, another 113 unit cycle most likely extends from our own planetary scheme to the Venus Scheme. We will not follow that esoteric trail here, but it is a deep subject worthy of further investigation at a later time.

A REDEMPTIVE EVENT IN PROGRESS

The transfer of Sanat Kumara from the second chain of the Earth Scheme to the fourth chain signifies the beginning of a momentous event in planetary evolution. As already mentioned, this great cosmic Being has chosen to submit to a cosmic initiation entailing a great sacrifice. There are at least two reasons for Venus' involvement with our planetary Logos and consequently Sanat Kumara, Who is the personified focal point of the Logos at this time. First, the planetary Logos of Venus is the polar opposite of the planetary Logos of Earth based on positive and negative electrical charges. Our planetary Logos is the positive pole and the Venusian Logos is the negative pole. Venus is said to be the Earth's "alter ego." These two Beings share a cosmic affinity. Second, the Venusian Logos has already experienced the initiation process and therefore, is at a more advanced stage of evolution than our Logos. Thus, when the time came for the individualization of humanity on Earth, the Venusian Logos aided the Earth in this planetary event. Recall that this accelerated mode of evolution—initiation—originates in the Sirian solar system and is being applied to our solar system. Venus was the first planet to utilize the method and Earth is the second.

According to the Tibetan, Sanat Kumara is preparing for the fourth cosmic initiation which involves immersion in substance in order to redeem it by purification. This means that the number 4 holds tremendous meaning for all life on our planet. Consider this: we are the fourth Scheme in a solar system consisting of etheric substance of the fourth order. The planetary Logos of this fourth Scheme has taken form as Sanat Kumara in the fourth chain, during the fourth round, in order to redeem the material substance comprising the fourth globe (of physical matter); which means that He entered that fourth globe in the fourth world period of the fourth round. Humanity was created during the third root-race. As we already know, this was a momentous event, but it involves a 3 and not a 4. One would logically assume that humanity should have been created during the fourth root-race in order to work out the numeric correspondence to its conclusion. The clue to understanding this lies in the fact that the creation of humanity was *an effect* of Sanat Kumara's achieving a major cosmic initiation. (The Tibetan does not identify it, but we assume the third, since DK has already revealed that Sanat Kumara is preparing for the fourth.) Humanity was not the cause of Sanat Kumara's initiation achievement and, therefore, the fourth root-race was not involved. It is interesting to note, however, that the *third* root-race was the effect of His taking the *third* cosmic initiation. From the larger perspective, the number 4 is still vital to our investigation because the fourth initiation confronts Sanat Kumara and we, the fourth kingdom of nature, are living on the fourth globe, in the fourth world period, of the fourth round, of the fourth chain, of the fourth Earth Scheme in a solar system of the fourth order. So let's find out why the number 4 is vitally important to our understanding of our role on Earth.

In order make this easier to understand please refer to figure 13.5. This diagram depicts a sequence of events leading up to the creation of humanity. It is very similar to figure 13.4 except that the root-races are overlaid onto the words of the Great Invocation to illustrate their correlation. Begin reading figure 13.5 from the lowest of the three large boxes on the left side of the diagram. These three boxes describe Sanat Kumara's arrival in our fourth chain. The main section of the diagram depicts all the root-races which transpired in each of the three world periods. These world periods are bounded by bold lines. Note the "sandwiching" effect in which the words of the Great Invocation lie *between* the time of Sanat Kumara's arrival and the opening of the door of initiation to humanity in the fourth world period of the fourth globe during the fourth root-race. This is shown in figure 13.5 by the left hand box containing 2-2-2 and the bottom box containing 4-4-4.

Figures 13.4 and 13.5 clearly show that exactly 113 root-race cycles transpired until the human kingdom was created, during the Lemurian root-race. The Tibetan also tells us that Sanat Kumara achieved a major initiation at the same time:

> ...when individualisation took place during the Lemurian, or the third root race, and the human family in this cycle definitely came into manifestation, it signified a major initiation for our Heavenly Man [in the form of Sanat Kumara, JB].[5]

Hence, the 113 unit cycle represents a time of preparation for *initiation*. This idea is reinforced by the fact that after Sanat Kumara's achieved initiation experience, the symbolic door of initiation was opened for humanity during the next root-race. Obviously, it is all

Figure 13.5 The Great Invocation and Root-race Overlay.

Incarnation process begins Chain 4 World Period 2 Globe 2 Root-race 3

Sanat Kumara arrives in World Period 2 Globe 2 Root-race 2 **2-2-2**

Sanat Kumara transfers His Life Expression from Chain 2 to Chain 4.

From W2 G2 R3	the W2 G2 R4	point W2 G2 R5	of W2 G2 R6	Light W2 G2 R7	within W2 G3 R1	the W2 G3 R2
Mind W2 G3 R3	of W2 G3 R4	God W2 G3 R5	Let W2 G3 R6	light W2 G3 R7	stream W2 G4 R1	forth W2 G4 R2
into W2 G4 R3	the W2 G4 R4	minds W2 G4 R5	of W2 G4 R6	men W2 G4 R7	Let W2 G5 R1	Light W2 G5 R2
descend W2 G5 R3	on W2 G5 R4	Earth W2 G5 R5	From W2 G5 R6	the W2 G5 R7	point W2 G6 R1	of W2 G6 R2
Love W2 G6 R3	within W2 G6 R4	the W2 G6 R5	Heart W2 G6 R6	of W2 G6 R7	God W2 G7 R1	Let W2 G7 R2
love W2 G7 R3	stream W2 G7 R4	forth W2 G7 R5	into W2 G7 R6	the W2 G7 R7	hearts W3 G1 R1	of W3 G1 R2
men W3 G1 R3	May W3 G1 R4	Christ W3 G1 R5	return W3 G1 R6	to W3 G1 R7	Earth W3 G2 R1	From W3 G2 R2
the W3 G2 R3	centre W3 G2 R4	where W3 G2 R5	the W3 G2 R6	Will W3 G2 R7	of W3 G3 R1	God W3 G3 R2
			is W3 G3 R3			

Midpoint of the cycle **3-3-3**

known W3 G3 R4	Let W3 G3 R5	purpose W3 G3 R6	guide W3 G3 R7	the W3 G4 R1	little W3 G4 R2	wills W3 G4 R3
of W3 G4 R4	men W3 G4 R5	The W3 G4 R6	purpose W3 G4 R7	which W3 G5 R1	the W3 G5 R2	Masters W3 G5 R3
know W3 G5 R4	and W3 G5 R5	serve W3 G5 R6	From W3 G5 R7	the W3 G6 R1	centre W3 G6 R2	which W3 G6 R3
we W3 G6 R4	call W3 G6 R5	the W3 G6 R6	race W3 G6 R7	of W3 G7 R1	men W3 G7 R2	Let W3 G7 R3
the W3 G7 R4	Plan W3 G7 R5	of W3 G7 R6	Love W3 G7 R7	and W4 G1 R1	Light W4 G1 R2	work W4 G1 R3
out W4 G1 R4	And W4 G1 R5	may W4 G1 R6	it W4 G1 R7	seal W4 G2 R1	the W4 G2 R2	door W4 G2 R3
where W4 G2 R4	evil W4 G2 R5	dwells W4 G2 R6	Let W4 G2 R7	Light W4 G3 R1	and W4 G3 R2	Love W4 G3 R3
and W4 G3 R4	Power W4 G3 R5	restore W4 G3 R6	the W4 G3 R7	Plan W4 G4 R1	on W4 G4 R2	Earth W4 G4 R3

Door of Initiation opens

Incarnation process completed after 113 root-races in World Period 4, Globe 4, Root-race 3-----**4-4-3**

The next root-race 4 marks the midpoint of Earth Scheme 4. Chain 4, World Period 4, Globe 4, Root-race 4 ------ **4-4-4** about INITIATION. The 113 root-races mark Sanat Kumara's preparation for initiation, culminating in His achieved initiation during the 113th root-race (Lemuria) following His arrival in our chain.

With His initiation completed, human beings were offered the opportunity of initiation for the first time in the fourth root-race. Sanat Kumara is known as the First Initiator. He is present in our world as part of His own initiation and since we are all part of this One Life, we too can experience the same essential process, but on a smaller scale. The following extract reiterates the great significance of the number 4 for our world:

> As you know, the first human being out of that "centre which we call the race of men" to achieve this point was the Christ; in that first great demonstration of His point of attainment (through the medium of what was then a new type of initiation) the Christ was joined by the Buddha....This third initiation was taken in a fourth ray Ashram, the Ray of Harmony through Conflict. This Ashram had taken form and attained functioning activity some time earlier. You can see, under the Law of Correspondences, why this was so. The first human being in the fourth kingdom in nature to take this initiation did so in a fourth ray Ashram and then, esoterically speaking, "the Way lay open toward the Cross"...The fourth initiation then became a possibility.[6]

Please note the numbers embedded in DK's words. The Christ and the Buddha were the first members of the *fourth* kingdom of nature to achieve the third initiation. A *fourth* ray ashram had already been created for new initiates and the Christ and the Buddha were the first members of that ashram to achieve the *third* initiation. The numbers are 4-4-3, the total letters contained in the Great Invocation. Notice also, that because of this success in the evolutionary growth of humanity (through the Buddha and the Christ), the way lay open for the fourth initiation, the Way of the Cross. Furthermore, a great alignment of the number 4 enabled Sanat Kumara to take the *third* cosmic initiation, on the *fourth* globe in the *fourth* world period, and create humanity—the *fourth* kingdom of nature. Thus, what DK is describing in the previous quotation is a reflection, in the human world, of the higher initiatory experience of Sanat Kumara.

Both of these enormous events are identified by the numbers 4-4-3: the first one at the planetary scale, the second at the human scale, and both symbolized in the Great Invocation by its 443 letters! This prepared the way for Him to work toward the fourth cosmic initiation. This is made clear in the following statement by the Tibetan regarding our planetary Logos:

> He is in physical incarnation [as Sanat Kumara, JB]. He is midway through His career upon the cosmic Path of Initiation, and consequently is to take the fourth Initiation in this chain.7

This cosmic esoteric fact concerning Sanat Kumara is dramatically illustrated in figure 13.6 which depicts all seven chains of the Earth Scheme of our planetary Logos. The large square at the intersection of the cross represents our present physical Earth globe, the fourth globe of the fourth Earth chain. The black square at the exact center of the entire diagram depicts the fourth Atlantean root-race, when the door of initiation was opened to humanity. This was the point when the Buddha and the Christ took the third initiation. The Great Work of Sanat Kumara and His Aides finally began to bear fruit. Not only was Sanat Kumara in the process of initiation, but the human kingdom itself was producing souls capable of bypassing the slower evolutionary process of growth and taking the more rapid path of initiation.

This event at the very heart of our planetary scheme signals a major spiritual success for Sanat Kumara as well as humanity. Because human beings could liberate themselves from the human kingdom and advance into the Kingdom of Souls, the Hierarchy, it meant that work toward the fourth cosmic initiation could proceed for Him. Continuing from the previous extract we find:

> Well may this globe, therefore, be considered the globe of sorrow and of pain, for through it our planetary Logos is undergoing that which the mystic calls "the Crucifixion."
>
> The cells in His body—those cells through which He feels, and senses, and experiences,—are, in this world period, rent by pain and suffering, for His is the consciousness at the centre of the Body, and theirs is the capacity to suffer, so that by means of them He may learn the meaning of systemic dispassion, be dissociated from all forms and material substance, and upon the cross of matter eventually find liberation and the freedom of the Spirit.8

Figure 13.6. The Cross of Sanat Kumara.

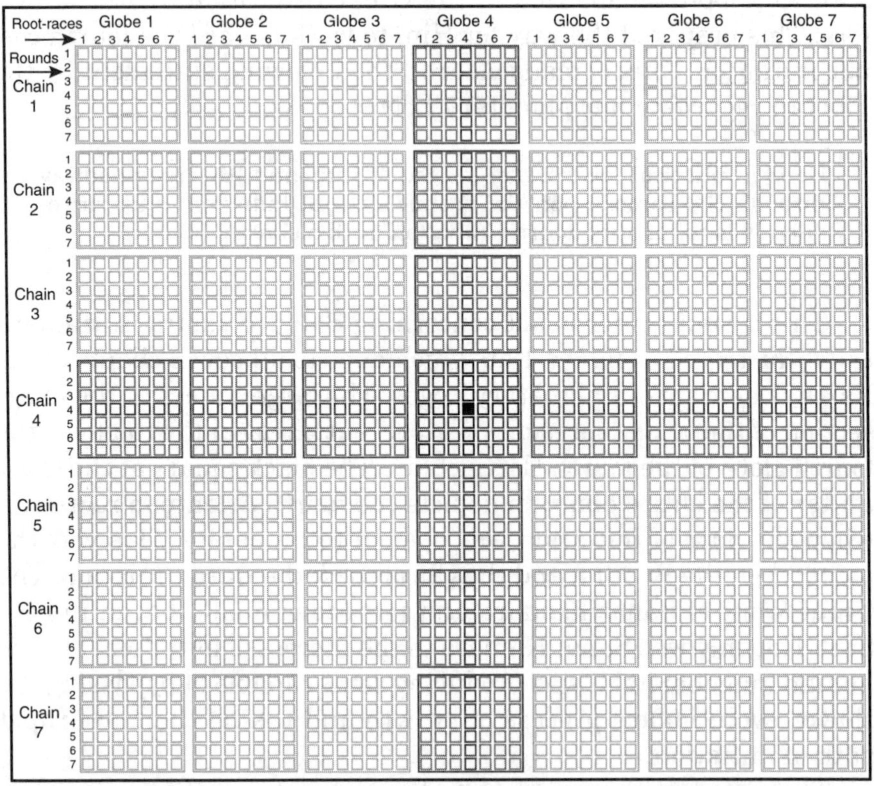

The horizontal rows indicate the 7 chains of the Earth Scheme. Each vertical column represents 1 of the 7 globes in each chain. Each of these globes is broken down into the 7 root-races which manifest during a world period on a globe. These are identified by the numbers immediately below the labels for the globes. The small numbers running vertically down the left side of the chart indicate the rounds. These run horizontally across the chart from globe to globe. For instance, at the end of the 7th root-race on globe 7 of chain 1, the cycle begins once more, returning to globe 1 in the next sequential round of that same chain. This continues until all 7 rounds in a chain are completed. At that stage evolution proceeds to the next chain in the series and repeats the entire 7 round cycle. Note: This graphic depiction of the planetary process is a detailed view of the more general illustrations in figures 13.2 and 13.3.

In terms of the root-races, the small box immediately to the left of the black box (the Atlantean root-race) represents the third Lemurian root-race, when humanity was created. The box to the immediate right of the Atlantean root-race is our current fifth root-race. We, today, are the first human race following the Atlantean mid-point of the entire 343 root-races of the Earth chain.

Counting all the root-races in the fourth chain, the Atlantean root-race is number 172. This number corresponds to the value of the name "the Cosmic Christ." The Lemurian root-race is number 171. This number has already been discussed in earlier chapters. Briefly, the sum of the three middle word-positions of the Great Invocation equals 171. Those three words are "God is known." Indeed, the incarnation of Sanat Kumara during the Lemurian root-race drives home the meaning of those three words at a deeper level—for God had materialized in the physical/etheric world. Our current fifth root-race is number 173 in the chain. The title "Great Invocation" has a gematria value of 173. This fact is amazingly appropriate since *our root-race is the first human race to sound the Great Invocation.*

The esoteric symbolism of three numbers, 171, 172, and 173 is profound. "The Celestial Ship" (171) of Sanat Kumara arrives on Earth. He establishes Himself as "the Cosmic Christ" (172) incarnate in substance, thus reflecting the Cosmic Christ in the higher worlds. He then institutes the process of initiation during the 172nd root-race, again reflecting the Cosmic Christ. One of the first of those Initiates was the Christ, the current Head of the Hierarchy. Later, the Christ becomes the first Being outside Shamballa to sound the "Great Invocation" (173) during the 173rd root-race. Our current era marks the completion of a vast cyclic Plan for anchoring the divine energy of the Cosmic Christ on Earth through the agency of humanity. In the words of the Tibetan: "The first aim and the primary aim is to establish, through the medium of humanity, an outpost of the Consciousness of God in the solar system."[9]

Notes

1. Bailey, *A Treatise on Cosmic Fire*, 299-300.
2. Bailey, *Discipleship in the New Age*, vol. II, 157.
3. Bailey, *A Treatise on Cosmic Fire*, 371.
4. Technically speaking, a world period applies to the seven root-races which evolve on a globe within a chain. A round applies to forty-nine root-races which evolve in a series of seven globes. Therefore, a world period is one-seventh of a round. I am using the term world period because it serves as a better identifier of specific root-races on specific globes.
5. Bailey, *Initiation, Human and Solar*, 181.
6. Bailey, *The Rays and the Initiations*, 385-6.

7. Bailey, *A Treatise on Cosmic Fire*, 384.
8. Ibid., 384.
9. Bailey, *Esoteric Psychology*, vol. II, 217.

555

RESTORE

THE PLAN ON EARTH

This has been an epoch of crisis, and the great moment for which the Hierarchy has been preparing ever since it was founded upon the Earth.

The Rays and the Initiations, 236. Written September, 1944

This final chapter is devoted to the last five words of the Great Invocation. These five words, "restore the Plan on Earth," occupy word-positions 109 through 113. When added together, these five positions equal 555.

Before discussing the coded meaning of 555, it may prove useful to examine the word "restore." Although it is subtle, I believe it has a connection to the early work of the Master R during his incarnation as Francis Bacon. Recall that in chapter 2 reference was made to the unfinished work of Francis Bacon known as the *Great Instauration*. When Bacon conceived the idea of the *Great Instauration*, he believed this would contribute to the English phase of the Renaissance which had begun two hundred years earlier in Italy. The darkness of ignorance which had descended over Europe following the fall of the Roman Empire was being dispelled. There was a revival of the great learning achieved during the classical period of the Greek and Roman Empires. Although unbeknownst to him at the time, Bacon's visioned contribution to the Renaissance was part of the final phase of a vaster Hierarchically inspired Plan stretching back into the night of time. When the words of the Great Invocation state "restore the Plan on Earth," the implications uncovered by information discussed in the last two chapters is that the Plan actually began when Sanat Kumara arrived on globe 2 of our fourth chain. We are fortunate to be living in the world at this time because we may be witnesses to a major climaxing phase of this cosmic Plan.

Bacon may only have sensed a small portion of this Plan in 1610, but after more than 300 years of mental and spiritual development, the Master R now understands the magnitude of the Plan to a much larger degree. The point is that the Bacon life experience is now a corporate part of the consciousness of Master Rakoczi. As a Master of the Wisdom, he is able to access, if necessary, the detailed knowledge of his lifetime as Francis Bacon or any other of his previous lives. Along with this capacity to draw on past experiences, the Master R has undergone various initiations which have revealed more of Sanat Kumara's purpose for humanity and Earth. He is certainly not unique in this, because we are told in the Tibetan's teaching that such knowledge becomes part of the consciousness of all human beings who achieve the fifth initiation and enter the spiritual Hierarchy. The revelation is even greater for those like Master R who have also taken the sixth initiation.

At various points in this study, evidence has surfaced which indicates that the Masters Rakoczi and Djwhal Khul have worked in cooperation to present the English version of the Great Invocation to humanity. I believe there are subtle hints of this cooperative work scattered through the eighteen books written by the Tibetan through Alice Bailey.

We will focus on one particular instance of this here because it involves the word "restore." This quotation appears earlier in chapter 4 and originates from *A Treatise on White Magic*. The extract reads as follows:

> This period has been occultly called the "age of restoration of what has been broken by the fall."[1]

This brief remark by the Tibetan offers numeric evidence that Master R may have worked (at least some of the time) with Djwhal Khul, but *hidden in the background*. Part of that silent work may have involved the composition of the Great Invocation.

There are several subtle, but important hints here as to the origin of this short passage. First, DK states "this period has been occultly called." We might ponder on *who* has called this period the "age of restoration." Second, DK states that it has been *occultly* described. This means that the statement appearing in quotation marks may have some *hidden* meaning. Finally, the actual words which describe our period are given as the "age of restoration of what has been broken by the fall." This occult phrase contains the word "restoration" and resembles the final stanza of the Great Invocation which calls for the restoration of the Plan. At the same time, the concept of "restoration" has a familiar ring to it when juxtaposed with Bacon's concept of the *Great Instauration*, or as rendered in modern English, the Great *Restoration*. *A Treatise on White Magic*, however, was first published in 1934, eleven years before the Great Invocation was transcribed by Alice Bailey. Let's examine the gematria of these two lines of text.

Table 14.1. Restoration of the Plan.

Quotation	AN	RAN	Qty. of Words	Qty. of Letters
Let Light and Love and Power restore the Plan on Earth	519	213	11	44
age of restoration of what has been broken by the fall	471	201	11	44

As table 14.1 shows, these two sets of statements do not match numerologically, but both of these phrases contain eleven words and forty-four letters. This is an important clue signaling an occult or hidden connection between them. The gematria values of the extract from *A Treatise on White Magic*, however, provide a direct occult connection to the Master R. The number 471 is equal to 3 x 157. The number 157 equals the RAN value of the Latin inscription on the titlepage to Bacon's *Advancement and Proficience of Learning*, published in 1640 (see chapter 4); one of the books which formed part of the unfinished multi-volume series *Great Instauration*. This phrase is *"Multi pertransibunt & augebitur Scientia."* As earlier pointed out, this translates as "many shall pass through and learning shall be increased." Number 157 also equals "Fra. Rosi Crosse" (Fraternity of the Rosy Cross). This is also the value of the four words (of, God, known, the) immediately surrounding the middle word of the cross of the Great Invocation (see fig. 6.2). Furthermore, 157 equals the RAN value of the formal name of the Great Invocation as given by Djwhal Khul: "The Invocation for Power and Light" (see chapter 4). We see that this occult statement ascribed by DK to someone beside himself links directly to the work of Francis Bacon in the seventeenth century and the Great Invocation in the twentieth century. But that's not all.

The RAN value of "age of restoration of what has been broken by the fall" equals 201. Interestingly, this value equals the number of words in Psalm 46. The number 201 is 3 x 67. Thus, the ESC value of "Francis" emerges one more time.

As in most everything else we have examined in this material, the numbers 157 and 67 have other correspondences which pertain to planetary and cosmic themes related to Sanat Kumara. The number 157 also correlates to "the human soul" and "the Great Sacrifice." We now know that this latter title refers to Sanat Kumara Who created the human kingdom—the human soul. The number 67 correlates to "the Place of peace" and "the Initiator." These refer to the sacred center, Shamballa, from where Sanat Kumara acts, among other things, as "the Initiator" into the Mysteries originating on Sirius. This brings us to the last of the numeric correspondences, "the Great Goddess" and the "Throne of Isis" which both equal 157 AN and 67 RAN. These terms refer to Sirius, which the Egyptians identified with the great goddess, Isis.

In summary, this analysis reveals that a phrase quoted by the Tibetan in the early 1930's is similar in meaning to the final eleven words of the Great Invocation. Additionally, both phrases have the same number of words and letters yet were published eleven years apart. The 1930's phrase, according to Djwhal Khul, comes from some other source besides himself and the gematria values of that phrase have direct correspondences to literary works written by Francis Bacon. As a final observation, it is interesting to note that the word "restore" has an AN value of 100 which matches "Francis Bacon" (ESC) and it is located in word-position 109. This means the

Essence Value of "restore" equals 209. This is the middle word-position of the Synthetic Triplet which contains the word "mind." Consequently, the AN value of the word "restore" not only equals the name "Francis Bacon," but the Essence Value matches the middle word-position of three works theoretically linked to the Master R. This subtle use of the word "restore," along with the phrase offered by the Tibetan, raises the distinct possibility that some of the occult information found in the books given by the the Tibetan came from the Master R.

THE HUMAN CYCLE OF 113

Humanity is playing a central role in the restoration process now under way. Today we are at a climaxing point in restoring the Plan on Earth. The 113 words of the Great Invocation clearly demonstrate this fact and identify the present century as the day of opportunity for the successful completion of this restoration. To clarify this theory, we must look at one more example of the septenary scale. This involves the division of a world period into root-races.

Figure 14.1. Divisions of a World Period.

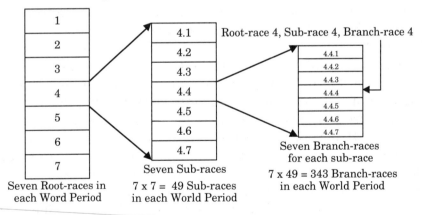

As figure 14.1 shows, each world period consists of seven root-races and just as all the previous examples in chapter 13 illustrate (figs 13.1, 13.2, 13.3), every root-race can also be subdivided twice. These two subdivisions are called "sub-races" and "branch-races," and as the diagram shows, they each consist of seven parts.

The Tibetan offers little information about the nature of branch-races except that they do exist as part of the cyclic expression of Sanat Kumara. Although DK has never explicitly stated the precise "time" of individualization in the Lemurian root-race, in terms of sub-races or branch-races, I believe at least one logical number clue is present within the Great Invocation which reveals this information.

The words associated with this number are the final five words of the Great Invocation—"restore the Plan on Earth." These five words are located in positions 109, 110, 111, 112, and 113. The sum of these five word-positions equals 555. In light of the symbolic importance of the three digits—444, which represent the middle of the fourth Earth chain and the time of the opening of the door of initiation in Atlantis, the number 555 appears most interesting. (See figure 13.5 in last chapter.)

Of all the various number themes associated with the Great Invocation, the number 5 is the most prominent and it is significant that these final five words—"restore the Plan on Earth"—have a root value of 5. These five words serve two purposes. First, by the simple meaning of the words themselves, we hear a command, "Restore the Plan on Earth." This alerts us that something momentous is in process on our planet. Second, by calculating the sum of the positions occupied by these five words within the Great Invocation, a number cipher (555) is obtained. Although Sirius is not the main focus of this aspect of our study, it is important to mention that the numeric value (257 RAN) of these five words, corresponds to— "Sirius, the Star of Sensitivity, governing the Hierarchy." This is a reminder of the essential spiritual influence of Sirius on our planetary purpose and the resulting Plan implemented by the Hierarchy.

Rather than viewing 555 as five hundred and fifty-five, this number can be read as three distinct 5s. As mentioned several times already, the Hierarchical archives contain an "indicatory symbol" marking the earliest point in time when the Great Invocation could be used by humanity. I believe the digits 5-5-5 are the clue to the meaning of that indicatory symbol. Let me explain.

The Tibetan identifies the majority of the present human population as the fifth root-race. He has also identified portions of our present humanity as the fifth sub-race of the fifth root-race. We know that humanity first sounded the Great Invocation in 1945. I am suggesting that the group of individuals who first used the Great

Invocation represented a segment of the fifth branch-race, fifth sub-race, and the fifth root-race. In effect, 5-5-5 can be deciphered as the fifth root-race, the fifth sub-race, and the fifth branch-race. This specific "time marker," 5-5-5, represents the culmination of a 113 unit cycle measured in branch-race units.

This theory can be tested through the use of the principle of *Mediocria Firma*. We have seen many instances of symbolic coding based on the middle point. Proceeding on the premise that the middle point of the 113 unit cycle is important, I have overlaid the 113 words of the Great Invocation onto branch-races of the third, fourth, and fifth root-races.

Most importantly, I have aligned the middle word of the Great Invocation with the fourth branch-race of the fourth sub-race of the fourth root-race. This alignment of 4-4-4 represents the closest approximation to the midpoint of evolution for our entire Earth chain. And because ours is the middle chain within the entire scheme, this 4-4-4 configuration represents the midpoint of the entire Earth Scheme. As figure 14.2 clearly shows, this alignment places the incarnation of Sanat Kumara at 3-3-3 (third root-race, third sub-race, third branch-race). Equating one word of the Great Invocation with the one branch-race, exactly 113 branch-race cycles later the final symbolic word of the Great Invocation is grounded, and thus completed in its final form for human use (5-5-4 in fig. 14.2). Symbolically speaking, the completed version of the Great Invocation was finally given to Alice Bailey by Djwhal Khul in the fifth branch-race of the fifth sub-race of the fifth root-race. Whether symbolically or literally, humanity initially sounded the Great Invocation in the 5-5-5 cycle, completing a vast preparatory phase by the human kingdom for its destined part in the Plan.

Thus, the words of the Great Invocation serve as a time-line which clearly establishes the occurrence of three major planetary events. The first event marks individualization during the Lemurian epoch, the second marks the establishment of initiation in the Atlantean epoch, and the third marks the emergence into physical form of the fifth kingdom (Hierarchy) on Earth in the present epoch. This third event lies in the immediate future and it consists of three phases—the reappearance of the Christ, the externalization of the spiritual Hierarchy, and the subsequent re-establishment of the Mysteries of Initiation.

Figure 14.2. 113 Branch-races.

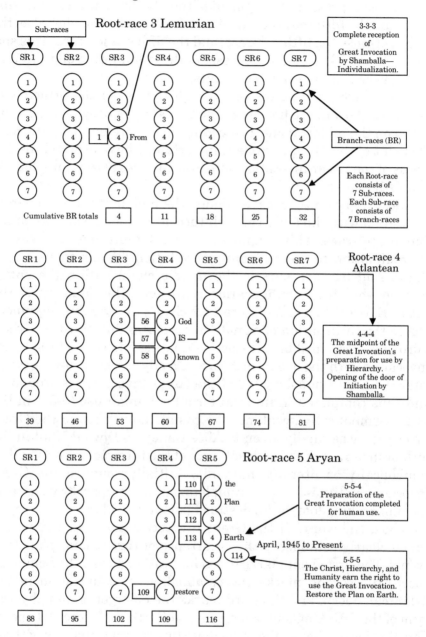

Figure 14.3. The Great Invocation and Branch-race Overlay.

Root-race 3, Lemurian

[box] 3RR / 3SR / 3BR

Individualization occurs during third branch-race. Coded 333.

"From" marks beginning of 113 branch-race cycle. Coded 334 "Heart" marks end of Root-race 3.

"of" marks beginning of Root-race 4, Atlantean.

Middle of Great Invocation and Atlantean Race Coded 4-4-4

Buddha and Christ take third initiation after fourth branch-race.

"the" marks end of Root-race 4

"race" marks beginning of Root-race 5, Aryan

The 113 branch-race cycle concludes with the fifth root-race, fifth sub-race, fourth branch-race marked by the word "Earth."

The Great Invocation is given to AAB in April, 1945 for human use. Coded 555.

[bottom box] 5RR / 5SR / 5BR

From 3SR 4BR	the 3SR 5BR	point 3SR 6BR	of 3SR 7BR	Light 4SR 1BR	within 4SR 2BR	the 4SR 3BR
Mind 4SR 4BR	of 4SR 5BR	God 4SR 6BR	Let 4SR 7BR	light 5SR 1BR	stream 5SR 2BR	forth 5SR 3BR
into 5SR 4BR	the 5SR 5BR	minds 5SR 6BR	of 5SR 7BR	men 6SR 1BR	Let 6SR 2BR	Light 6SR 3BR
descend 6SR 4BR	on 6SR 5BR	Earth 6SR 6BR	From 6SR 7BR	the 7SR 1BR	point 7SR 2BR	of 7SR 3BR
Love 7SR 4BR	within 7SR 5BR	the 7SR 6BR	Heart 7SR 7BR	of 1SR 1BR	God 1SR 2BR	Let 1SR 3BR
love 1SR 4BR	stream 1SR 5BR	forth 1SR 6BR	into 1SR 7BR	the 2SR 1BR	hearts 2SR 2BR	of 2SR 3BR
men 2SR 4BR	May 2SR 5BR	Christ 2SR 6BR	return 2SR 7BR	to 3SR 1BR	Earth 3SR 2BR	From 3SR 3BR
the 3SR 4BR	centre 3SR 5BR	where 3SR 6BR	the 3SR 7BR	Will 4SR 1BR	of 4SR 2BR	God 4SR 3BR
			is 4SR 4BR	4-4-4	Mediocria Firma	
known 4SR 5BR	Let 4SR 6BR	purpose 4SR 7BR	guide 5SR 1BR	the 5SR 2BR	little 5SR 3BR	wills 5SR 4BR
of 5SR 5BR	men 5SR 6BR	The 5SR 7BR	purpose 6SR 1BR	which 6SR 2BR	the 6SR 3BR	Masters 6SR 4BR
know 6SR 5BR	and 6SR 6BR	serve 6SR 7BR	From 7SR 1BR	the 7SR 2BR	centre 7SR 3BR	which 7SR 4BR
we 7SR 5BR	call 7SR 6BR	the 7SR 7BR	race 1SR 1BR	of 1SR 2BR	men 1SR 3BR	Let 1SR 4BR
the 1SR 5BR	Plan 1SR 6BR	of 1SR 7BR	Love 2SR 1BR	and 2SR 2BR	Light 2SR 3BR	work 2SR 4BR
out 2SR 5BR	And 2SR 6BR	may 2SR 7BR	it 3SR 1BR	seal 3SR 2BR	the 3SR 3BR	door 3SR 4BR
where 3SR 5BR	evil 3SR 6BR	dwells 3SR 7BR	Let 4SR 1BR	Light 4SR 2BR	and 4SR 3BR	Love 4SR 4BR
and 4SR 5BR	Power 4SR 6BR	restore 4SR 7BR	the 5SR 1BR	Plan 5SR 2BR	on 5SR 3BR	Earth 5SR 4BR

These Mysteries were first taught to humanity when the process of initiation was instituted by the Hierarchy in the middle of the Atlantean root-race. Note in figures 14.2 and 14.3 that the middle word of the Great Invocation has been correlated with the middle of the Atlantean fourth sub-race—the fourth branch-race. Here the symbolic construction of the Great Invocation shines brightly. At the exact midpoint of the fourth world period, young humanity would shortly be able to advance into greater Light. The human kingdom had finally produced individual souls capable of spiritual growth beyond the boundaries of the human world. As described earlier, the Buddha and the Christ were soon to take the third initiation which would confirm Their entry and transition into the Hierarchy. The experiment of initiation, already a success in the Venus Scheme, was now ready to move forward in the Earth Scheme. This is confirmed by Djwhal Khul in the following passage:

> It has been emphasised many times in the occult teachings that the process of initiation, as it is usually understood, is an abnormal and not a normal one....This particular mode of developing the consciousness of the human family was initiated by the Hierarchy during the Atlantean root-race at the latter end of the fourth sub-race.[2]

Figure 14.2 illustrates this by showing the phrase "God is known" at the middle of the fourth Atlantean sub-race. These words imply that, with the door of initiation into the Mysteries now open to humanity, God can be known.

Figure 14.3 displays how the words of the Great Invocation span eighteen million years—between the coming of Sanat Kumara (with the consequent creation of humanity) and 1945 when the Great Invocation was given to Alice Bailey during the fifth root-race, fifth sub-race, fifth branch-race. (Note that figures 13.5 and 14.3 are identical except for scale; the former is based on root-races and the latter is based on branch-races.)

The immense importance of the midpoint is once again demonstrated graphically in the following diagram (fig. 14.4). This illustration is identical to figure 13.6 except for scale; now we are looking at round 4, with all the root-races, sub-races and branch-races which have manifested in the past, are manifesting now, and will manifest in the future. A cautionary note is necessary here because we can only conceive of these races in terms of our space/time three dimensional world, the fourth globe. The other globes depicted in

Figure 14.4. 2401 Branch-races of the Fourth Round.

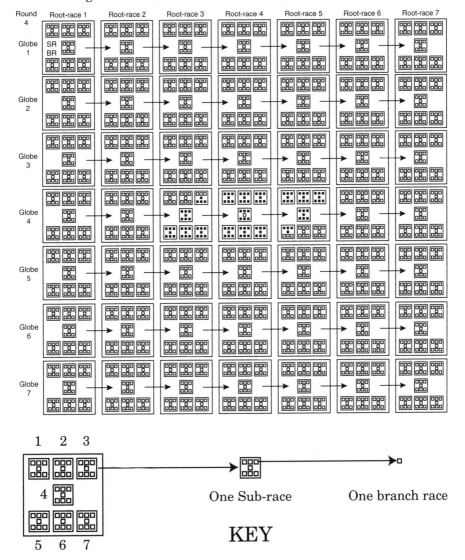

KEY

One Sub-race   One branch race

The numbers 1 - 7 in the key above show the order of manifestation of each sub-race within a root-race in the main diagram. The branch-races within a sub-race follow the same number pattern. The arrows in the main diagram indicate the movement of each root-race through each globe. When seven root-races have manifested on one globe, the process begins again on the next globe beginning with the first root-race.

figure 14.4 (and other similar diagrams) are not on the physical plane. Therefore, it is almost impossible for us to comprehend the nature of the "races" or lifeforms on those globes. Additionally, the terms "past" and "future" do not apply to them in the same way as the time sense applies to our fourth (space/time) globe.

The primary concern for us in this chapter is the *symbolism attached to the numeric place which our fourth globe root-races, sub-races, and branch-races hold in relation to the entire scheme of seven globes.* In order to accentuate this point, I have identified the 113 branch-races which have manifested since humanity's creation. These are marked in black in figures 14.4 (except for the exact middle branch-race of the fourth sub-race of the fourth root-race). For the sake of clarity, I have reproduced globe 4 from figure 14.4 and placed it below in figure 14.5. In the previous extract the Tibetan states: "the human family was initiated by the Hierarchy during the Atlantean root-race at the latter end of the fourth sub-race." Recalling the importance of *Mediocria Firma*, we should now have a greater appreciation of the significance and magnitude of the midpoint in planetary and cosmic terms. That fourth sub-race is at the exact center of figure 14.4.

Figure 14.5. Races 333 to 555.

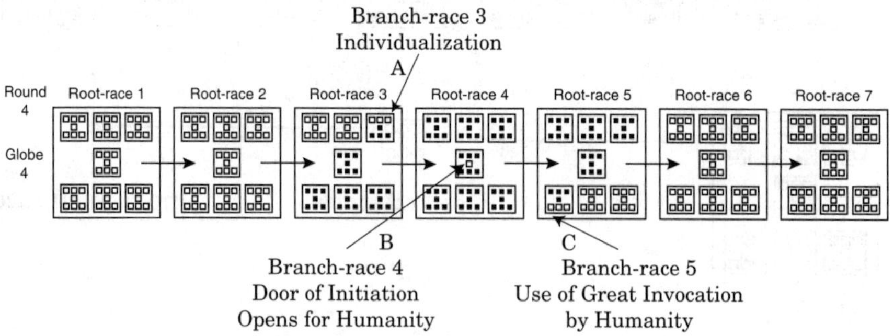

Branch-race 3
Individualization
A

| Round 4 | Root-race 1 | Root-race 2 | Root-race 3 | Root-race 4 | Root-race 5 | Root-race 6 | Root-race 7 |

Globe 4

B
Branch-race 4
Door of Initiation
Opens for Humanity

C
Branch-race 5
Use of Great Invocation
by Humanity

The number of branch-races between Individualization and Humanity's use of the Great Invocation is 113.

Figures 14.4 and 14.5 graphically illustrate the *centrality* of the period bridging the time between individualization and the current fifth sub-race. This eighteen million year period spans root-race 3, sub-race 3, branch-race 3 and root-race 5, sub-race 5, and branch-race 5. As figure 14.5 demonstrates, exactly 113 branch-races have passed since the time of Sanat Kumara's incarnation and creation of humanity and the giving of the Great Invocation to the Christ, the Hierarchy, and finally to Humanity.

I believe the 113 words of the Great Invocation are meant to show us that our use of the Great Invocation is inextricably related to the coming of Sanat Kumara to the fourth physical globe, our Earth. In receiving and using the Great Invocation, we are participating in an event of cosmic proportions. Here, I am paraphrasing the Tibetan's own words when he was explaining the significance of the Great Invocation and its use by humanity in 1945. This momentous event is indicated by arrow C in figure 14.5. Arrow A points to the Lemurian third branch-race of the third sub-race—3-3-3. and arrow B points to the Atlantean fourth branch-race of the fourth sub-race—4-4-4.

Because the animal kingdom, the third kingdom in nature, was being employed to provide the bodies for the newly created human souls, the third branch-race may be a more precise estimation of when Sanat Kumara took form on our planet and created the human race. Following the Law of Correspondences, it makes perfect sense that the first human souls embodied in animal forms of the third kingdom should do so during the third branch of the third sub-race of the third root-race.[3]

THE FIFTH ROOT-RACE

The current time period in human history is meant to emphasize the development of the human mind. This is because each root-race develops the particular principle matching its order of evolution. We are currently the fifth root-race, so this means we are evolving the fifth or mental principle. As explained earlier, each root-race has seven sub-races. According to the Ageless Wisdom, the fifth sub-race of the fifth root-race is represented by Western civilization. Consequently, modern civilization holds the reasoning principle with its logical left brain orientation in high esteem, resulting in an emphasis on education, science, and technology. Our current civilization, the good and the bad, is largely the result of the philosophers, theologians, artists, scientists, and inventors of the past 1,000 years. These pioneering thinkers inherited much of their knowledge from the Greek, Roman, and Byzantine civilizations going back to 500 BCE, and the early Greek philosophers learned much from the ancient Egyptians.

This period of world growth reflects only one particular cycle of history, for it is well recognized that Eastern civilizations of an earlier era have also influenced the evolution of humanity. The past millennium, however, represents that part of the cyclic period of human history in which the European civilization expanded to the Americas and Australia. This expansion represents the fifth sub-race of the fifth root-race. This double influence of the mental principle was the fuel for the rapid growth of the Industrial Revolution and the breathtaking scientific and technological advances of the twentieth and twenty-first centuries. Unfortunately, this double dose of the mental principle has also contributed to environmental destruction and the disruption of other cultures and societies.

In order to avoid any misunderstanding in regard to the use of the word "race," we must emphasize once again that our doubled fifth race civilization is really a matter of consciousness and not physical body type. The fact that the fifth sub-race emerged from Europe simply means that the initiating impetus for this quality of consciousness, with its emphasis on the mind, logic, reason, and scientific observation, had its beginnings in that geographic location. Europe was the incubator for the new-born fifth sub-race consciousness which spread around the world, creating our modern global civilization in little more than 200 years. In a passage written by the Tibetan during or just after World War II, he is very clear in his definition of "race:"

> Today in our Aryan age and race, we see the vital expression of this fifth ray energy [mental ability, JB]. When I use the word "race" I deal not with man-made or pseudo-scientific differentiations of nations and races or types. I deal with a state of consciousness which is the Aryan or mental consciousness or state of thinking; this finds its exponents and its "race members" in every nation, without any distinction or omissions. This I would have you carefully remember, for there is no new race in process of appearing, from the territorial angle; there is only a general distribution of those persons who have what have been called the sixth root race characteristics [more refined sense of understanding, JB]. This state of consciousness will find its expression in people as far apart racially as the Japanese and the American or the Negro and the Russian. It posits an ability to function with clarity upon the mental plane, to collate information, rightly to interpret and relate

that information, and to create the needed thoughtforms or concepts for those interpretations.[4]

Having clarified this position, we can proceed to the more esoteric aspect of present day humanity. This involves the number 113 once again. We have established that after transferring from the second chain to the fourth chain, globe two, 113 root-race cycles transpired before Sanat Kumara took form and created the human kingdom on globe four, our physical Earth. We have also seen that from the time of humanity's creation to the time we received the Great Invocation, 113 branch-races transpired.

As just discussed, even though root-races and their divisions manifest through human bodies, these are merely the vehicles for expressing a particular quality of consciousness. In other words, the races are the means whereby the planetary Logos (now manifesting as Sanat Kumara) develops His consciousness on a cosmic scale. Consequently, we should be able to correlate the 113 races to the planes of consciousness in order to establish the quality of consciousness that Sanat Kumara is currently bringing to perfection.

Referring back to figure 13.1, note that there are 343 possible sub-subplanes within the seven cosmic planes. Beginning with the densest physical plane (the atoms composing your body and this book) designated as number 1 and counting "up," we discover a fascinating bit of information. The 115th sub-subplane is the fifth sub-subplane of the fifth subplane of the fifth cosmic mental plane—5-5-5. As figure 14.6 shows, our current fifth root-race correlates with that exact sub-subplane. Refer to figure 13.4 for a detailed view of this concept. Imagine that each numbered circle is a sub-subplane and a root-race simultaneously. Counting up toward 115 is the same as moving to higher planes of consciousness. When circle 115 is reached, it thus corresponds to the mental sub-subplane illustrated in figure 14.6 on the following page.

This is the reason for Djwhal Khul's remark that "This Invocation will have a potent appeal to mankind." Modern day humanity resonates to the fifth principle of mind more than any other root-race in history, and as we know, the Great Invocation is based on the number 5. Repeating the earlier extract:

It [the Great Invocation, JB] has, in these Archives, an indicatory symbol beside it which indicates the era or period in human history during which it can and should be used. It is interesting to us to note that the evolution of humanity is in line with the indicated timing.[5]

Figure 14.6. The Fifth Race of Mind Development.

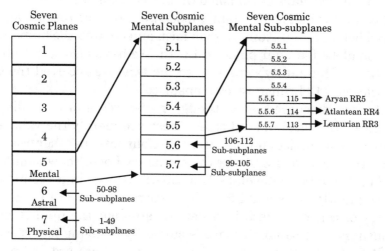

Once humanity was established as a distinct kingdom of nature, the 113 unit cycle proceeded once more with the branch-races as the unit of measure (figure 14.2). Thus, counting smaller units (branch-races instead of root-races), the very next branch-race following the final 113th corresponds to the fifth branch-race of the fifth sub-race of the fifth root-race. Consequently, the 5-5-5 of the planes (right column of figure 14.6) corresponds not only to the fifth root-race, but more precisely to the *fifth branch-race within the fifth sub-race within the fifth root-race—555!*

Hence, the indicatory symbol may very well indicate the fifth branch-race of our present era. We don't know how to define a branch-race within a sub-race, but the important point lies in the number symbolism which identifies it. The 5-5-5 equates with the total word-position value of "restore the Plan on Earth"—555. A major new phase of the Plan began when the Great Invocation was anchored on the human level, in human words, in a form which modern humans could understand.

What began millions of years ago with the 113 steps into incarnation by Sanat Kumara is coming to fulfillment today at the human level. After Sanat Kumara arrived in our world and created the human race, the first phase of the 113 unit cycle was completed. This was measured in root-races. Then began the second phase of the 113 unit cycle, measured in branch-races. The giving of the Great Invocation to humanity signaled the completion of 113 branch-races by the human kingdom. The first 113 unit cycle resulted in the incarnation of the *planetary* Avatar known as Sanat Kumara. The second 113 unit human cycle measured in branch-races is now complete. This successful completion will result in the incarnation of the *human* Avatar known as the Christ, for it is stated by Djwhal Khul that in 1945, the Christ announced that He intended to incarnate in the world in physical form once again. As a result of this decision, He was given permission to use the Great Invocation, the ancient Sound translated exactly into 113 English words.

SUMMATION

We have covered a tremendous amount of technical information in these final two chapters and a summation will be helpful. Here are the main points:

1. The planetary Logos of the Earth is currently incarnated in etheric form. He is called Sanat Kumara and is located at the planetary center known as Shamballa.
2. Sanat Kumara incarnated about eighteen million years ago during the third Lemurian root-race. He came with 104 other Kumaras, but because He is the Leader, He is designated the "First" Kumara, or "Sanat."
3. He was enabled to incarnate through help from the planetary Logos of Venus. As a result, Sanat Kumara transferred from the second Earth chain (which resonates to the second Venusian Scheme) to the fourth chain, the present chain of globes of which our physical Earth is the fourth globe in the series.
4. His coming was by His own choice and entailed a huge sacrifice; thus, He is also given the name "The Great Sacrifice." Consequently, Sanat Kumara is also an Avatar, One Who leaves an exalted realm for a lower realm in order to save the suffering lives imprisoned there.

5. The incarnation of the planetary Logos in the form of Sanat Kumara is His training process for a cosmic initiation. Sanat Kumara is working toward the fourth cosmic initiation known as the Great Renunciation or the Crucifixion. The cross symbolizes this spiritual event, which is the reason He is described as being on the Fixed Cross.

6. All Saviors and Avatars associated with our Earth Scheme Who appear in human form are reflections of the original prototypal Avatar, Sanat Kumara.

7. The Beings of Shamballa along with Sanat Kumara have been sounding the Great Invocation for millions of years.

8. The 113 words of the Great Invocation symbolize the 113 root-race cycles which transpired between the time of Sanat Kumara's arrival in our fourth chain, globe two and His incarnation on the physical globe four with the consequent creation of the Human kingdom.

9. Exactly 113 branch-races transpired between the creation of humanity and the giving of the Great Invocation to the Christ and soon afterward, to humanity in 1945.

10. There appears to be a gestation period, or developmental cycle related to the number 113 which involves the penetration of spirit into the depths of material substance.

11. This developmental stage represents the planetary aspect of the cosmic Plan of Sirius. The human kingdom has been brought up to a definite point of readiness for consciously working with the Plan. That Plan relates to the redemption of the kingdoms of nature by humanity. We are to become the planetary *group* savior of this planet.

12. One of the latter preparatory phases of this Plan began in the fifteenth century when the Renaissance swept across Europe. Francis Bacon played a large role in that rebirth in England and later as Saint Germain in France and as the "old professor" in revolutionary America. He continues to influence Europe and world civilization as the Master R, the Lord of Civilization.

13. The spiritual Hierarchy and Shamballa are preparing for the reappearance of the Christ, Who will be the World Teacher for the Aquarian Age. In order to help Him in that task, Sanat Kumara permitted the Christ and the Hierarchy

to use the Great Invocation. This occurred in 1945. Up to that moment, no Being outside Shamballa had ever been permitted to use it, except for Sanat Kumara and the senior Members of His Council.

14. As two of the five Masters working directly on the final readiness phase of the planetary Plan, the Masters R and DK translated the Great Invocation into English and coded it with the story of humanity's origin, destiny, and divine cosmic relationships.

15. The Great Invocation represents a highly charged concentration of cosmic energy designed for the alchemical transformation of material substance. Apparently, Sanat Kumara volunteered to deliver it to the physical world personally.

16. The form of the Great Invocation sounded by humanity is a microcosmic version of this ancient mantram of cosmic origin and scale. The original intent was that this mantric vibration would eventually be sounded by human beings living at the densest level of matter in our solar system. That intent has been fulfilled and now the Plan can be restored on Earth. The incarnation of Sanat Kumara was the beginning phase of that restoration.

17. After millions of years of evolution, all three major planetary centers—Shamballa, Hierarchy, and Humanity—are finally sounding the Great Invocation. As a result, the major implementing factors of the Plan are in place and rapidly preparing for a new phase of planetary expression.

The true Purpose of Sanat Kumara is gradually revealed to the members of the Hierarchy through a graded series of initiations. We are also told that Sanat Kumara is the Custodian of the Will of the Lord of Sirius. The implications are that there is an overall Purpose for the entire Earth Scheme which includes many different evolutionary lives, including humanity, and a second Purpose pertaining mainly to the Human Kingdom. This latter Purpose involves a Sirian Plan for human evolution of which Sanat Kumara is the Custodian. Naturally, this concept of dual planetary Purposes is purely theoretical, but this theory is conceptually based on conclusions drawn from an analysis of the occult clues found in the writings of the Tibetan and Master R. The fact that so many clues exist, which hold together in a consistent pattern, tells us that certain conclusions can be drawn if we simply have the desire to search for the answers.

The twenty million year Plan of Sirius began with the creation of the human kingdom and reached a crucial midpoint when the One we now call the Christ achieved the third initiation in the Atlantean root-race. This Plan reached its crowning phase when the Christ achieved the Sirian level of initiation (the seventh) these past 2,000 years. Today this Plan is in its final phase which can be divided into four parts:

1. The giving out of the Great Invocation to Hierarchy and Humanity in 1945.
2. The impending reappearance of the Christ as the World Teacher.
3. The emergence of some members of the Hierarchy into physical plane living.
4. The restoration of the Sirian Mysteries.

Today is the day of opportunity, the time when a "new Heaven and a new Earth" can be created. The Sirian Plan initiated more than eighteen millions years ago is coming to full flower in our time. The fifth branch-race of the fifth sub-race of the fifth root-race has been brought into direct contact with the ancient sound of the Great Invocation. Each time someone sounds the words of the Great Invocation and reaches the final phrase "restore the Plan on Earth," the number represented by this racial cycle—555—is brought into alignment with the final five words—555—resulting in a synchronized meshing of human and divine will. Through this invocative chorus, the Plan which was begun millions of years ago under the direction of the Lords of Sirius and implemented by the incarnation of our planetary Logos in the form of Sanat Kumara and his 104 divine Assistants, can be fulfilled.

Finally, recall that five members of the Hierarchy (Master Morya, Master Koot Hoomi, Master R, Master DK, and an unnamed Master) are especially involved in this final phase of the Plan. I do not want the reader to finish this book with the thought that Master R is the only member of the Hierarchy with such advanced knowledge. I want to leave you with the broad and realistic vision of a cooperative network of enlightened, compassionate transhuman

Beings who are working toward the success of the final phase of a Plan of cosmic proportions—a Plan which may very well have originated in that *primary* Hierarchical Center known as Sirius.

Utilizing the same techniques as in *Sacred Vessel of the Mysteries*, the evidence strongly suggests that the Master R was very much involved in creating the English translation of the Great Invocation given to Alice Bailey by the Master Djwhal Khul in April, 1945.

On the surface, this evidence suggests that the Master R is drawing attention to himself as the God of Light within the Great Invocation. He is, I believe, the creative genius of the word structure of the Great Invocation and all its symbolic coding. This conclusion has already been made clear. But to suggest from the evidence that Master R is an egotist because his name and Francis Bacon's name appear within it, is totally misguided. This, I believe, is a superficial interpretation of that evidence, for surely such an advanced and enlightened transhuman is far beyond any egotistical attitude of self-glorification or ego-inflation. Logically, the interpretive powers of the mind must not end there, but are called to a deeper level. The wisdom-centered nature of the higher mind and intuition must be invoked to penetrate to the true significance of these coded words, for the lower self-centered mind will only see a self-centered ego coded in these words or else, deception and nonsense.

We are being challenged to open our eyes to the much larger picture and the glorious destiny awaiting us as a human family. Through these many-layered numbers spread before us, we are being given a glimpse of the destined Plan which awaits our recognition. This brilliant tapestry of interwoven numbers and symbols is wondrous to behold. The profound complexity of the interlocking elements overwhelms the mind and leaves us with a humbling sense of having touched something beautiful beyond measure or description. Having contacted and experienced such creative genius, it is difficult to believe that the Masters Rakoczi and Djwhal Khul did not deliberately create a true work of esoteric art. With these hidden foundations brought into the light of day, let us build toward the heavens and Restore the Plan on Earth.

Notes

1. Bailey, *A Treatise on White Magic*, 409.
2. Bailey, *Initiation, Human and Solar*, 94.
3. The pinpointing of Sanat Kumara's entry onto the physical/ether-ic plane, in terms of human races correlating to number 3, raises some interesting thoughts in regard to the Moon chain, the chain of globes which existed just prior to our Earth chain. The Moon chain was the third chain. We are told by the Ageless Wisdom that some type of failure in evolution occurred at that time and the entire chain was brought to an abrupt and apparently catastrophic end before it completed its full evolutionary cycle. This event is a deep mystery involving our planetary Logos.

   This subject is too complex to delve into with any degree of confidence that such an effort will reward us with dependable facts. Despite this, I believe that the presence of the number 3 in relation to the creation of humanity may shed a small light on the mystery of the Moon chain failure.

   The correlation of the third root, sub, and branch-races with the third Moon chain may have something to do with the fulfillment of planetary karma. The Tibetan says that "On the moon chain individualisation took place during the fifth race of the third round." (Bailey, *A Treatise on Cosmic Fire*, 459.) More specifically, individualization took place on the third Moon chain, during the third round, in the fifth root-race. This occurred on the fourth globe. Consequently, we are dealing with numbers 3, 4, and 5 which correlate to the 3-3-3, 4-4-4, and 5-5-5 pattern we see in the Earth chain in relation to the branch-races.

   On our chain, the fourth, individualization took place in the fourth round, and the third race (third sub-race, third branch-race). As we have seen, 113 branch-races have transpired between the creation of humanity and the giving of the Great Invocation to our current fifth root-race, fifth sub-race, and fifth branch-race.

   The Tibetan notes that individualization occurred during the third chain (the Moon) in the the fifth race, but some catastrophic event occurred which interrupted evolution in that chain. In the very next fourth chain, the human kingdom is created in the third root-race, is able to take initiation in the fourth root-race, and finally sounds the Great Invocation in the fifth root-race. This comparison evokes a sense of retracing or recapitulating the events of the failed Moon chain by the planetary Logos. In both instances, although the reference scales are different, there is a correspondence between 3 and 5. After all, there are exactly 113 branch-races between 3-3-3 (third root-race, sub-race, and branch-race,— the theoretical arrival of Sanat Kumara) and 5-5-5 (fifth root-race, sub-race, and branch-race—the time humanity began to use the Great Invocation, 1945). Perhaps this is part of what "restore the Plan on Earth" means. The Plan, on a larger scale, was disrupted during the third Moon chain and the restoration commenced "on Earth" when Sanat Kumara came to our world as the prototypal Avatar. He entered the material world to make up the time lost due to the Moon chain failure.

4. Bailey, *The Rays and the Initiations*, 593-4.
5. Bailey, *Discipleship in the New Age*, vol. II, 157.

APPENDICES

APPENDIX A1

PSALM 46

#	Word	Value	#	Word	Value	#	Word	Value
1	God	25	68	of	20	135	in	22
2	is	27	69	the	32	136	the	32
3	our	51	70	Tabernacles	95	137	earth	50
4	refuge	60	71	of	20	138	He	13
5	and	18	72	the	32	139	maketh	55
6	strength	106	73	most	62	140	warres	79
7	a	1	74	High	32	141	to	33
8	very	65	75	God	25	142	cease	32
9	present	92	76	is	27	143	vnto	66
10	helpe	44	77	in	22	144	the	32
11	in	22	78	the	32	145	end	22
12	trouble	88	79	midst	62	146	of	20
13	Therfore	96	80	of	20	147	the	32
14	will	52	81	her	30	148	earth	50
15	not	46	82	she	31	149	hee	18
16	we	26	83	shal	49	150	breaketh	67
17	feare	34	84	not	46	151	the	32
18	though	76	85	be	7	152	bow	37
19	the	32	86	moued	55	153	and	18
20	earth	50	87	God	25	154	cutteth	93
21	be	7	88	shall	49	155	the	32
22	remoued	77	89	helpe	39	156	speare	61
23	and	18	90	her	30	157	in	22
24	though	76	91	and	18	158	sunder	77
25	the	32	92	that	47	159	he	13
26	mountaines	124	93	right	60	160	burneth	84
27	be	7	94	early	57	161	the	32
28	caried	39	95	The	32	162	chariot	71
29	into	55	96	heathen	59	163	in	22
30	the	32	97	raged	34	164	the	32
31	midst	62	98	the	32	165	fire	37
32	of	20	99	kingdomes	92	166	Be	7
33	the	32	100	were	48	167	stil	57
34	sea	24	101	mooued	69	168	and	18
35	Though	76	102	he	13	169	know	58
36	the	32	103	vttered	89	170	that	47
37	waters	81	104	his	35	171	I	9
38	thereof	74	105	voyce	65	172	am	13
39	roare	54	106	the	32	173	God	25
40	and	18	107	earth	50	174	I	9
41	be	7	108	melted	56	175	will	52
42	troubled	92	109	The	32	176	bee	12
43	though	76	110	Lord	46	177	exalted	67
44	the	32	111	of	20	178	among	47
45	mountaines	124	112	hosts	59	179	the	32
46	shake	42	113	is	27	180	heathen	59
47	with	57	114	with	57	181	I	9
48	the	32	115	vs	38	182	will	52
49	swelling	95	116	the	32	183	be	7
50	thereof	74	117	God	25	184	exalted	67
51	There	54	118	of	20	185	in	22
52	is	27	119	Iacob	29	186	the	32
53	a	1	120	is	27	187	earth	50
54	riuer	6	121	our	51	188	The	32
55	the	32	122	refuge	60	189	Lord	46
56	streames	90	123	Come	34	190	of	20
57	wherof	76	124	behold	44	191	hosts	59
58	shall	49	125	the	32	192	is	27
59	make	28	126	workes	85	193	with	57
60	glad	23	127	of	20	194	vs	38
61	the	32	128	the	32	195	the	32
62	citie	45	129	Lord	46	196	God	25
63	of	20	130	what	49	197	of	20
64	God	25	131	desolations	126	198	Iacob	29
65	the	32	132	hee	18	199	is	27
66	holy	56	133	hath	36	200	our	51
67	place	35	134	made	22	201	refuge	60

THE GREAT INVOCATION

1	From	52		58	known	77
2	the	33		59	Let	37
3	point	74		60	purpose	110
4	of	21		61	guide	46
5	Light	56		62	the	33
6	within	83		63	little	78
7	the	33		64	wills	75
8	Mind	40		65	of	21
9	of	21		66	men	32
10	God	26		67	The	33
11	Let	37		68	purpose	110
12	light	56		69	which	51
13	stream	76		70	the	33
14	forth	67		71	Masters	95
15	into	58		72	know	63
16	the	33		73	and	19
17	minds	59		74	serve	69
18	of	21		75	From	52
19	men	32		76	the	33
20	Let	37		77	centre	65
21	Light	56		78	which	51
22	descend	54		79	we	28
23	on	29		80	call	28
24	Earth	52		81	the	33
25	From	52		82	race	27
26	the	33		83	of	21
27	point	74	57 IS 28	84	men	32
28	of	21		85	Let	37
29	Love	54		86	the	33
30	within	83		87	Plan	43
31	the	33		88	of	21
32	Heart	52		89	Love	54
33	of	21		90	and	19
34	God	26		91	Light	56
35	Let	37		92	work	67
36	love	54		93	out	56
37	stream	76		94	And	19
38	forth	67		95	may	39
39	into	58		96	it	29
40	the	33		97	seal	37
41	hearts	71		98	the	33
42	of	21		99	door	52
43	men	32		100	where	59
44	May	39		101	evil	48
45	Christ	77		102	dwells	75
46	return	96		103	Let	37
47	to	35		104	Light	56
48	Earth	52		105	and	19
49	From	52		106	Love	54
50	the	33		107	and	19
51	centre	65		108	Power	77
52	where	59		109	restore	100
53	the	33		110	the	33
54	Will	56		111	Plan	43
55	of	21		112	on	29
56	God	26		113	Earth	52

A WORD FROM THE MASTER

#	Word	Value			#	Word	Value
1	My	38			53	may	39
2	name	33			54	be	7
3	is	28			55	My	38
4	a	1			56	life	32
5	mask	44			57	is	28
6	I	9			58	my	38
7	am	14			59	work	67
8	one	34			60	and	19
9	yet	50			61	my	38
10	more	51			62	love	54
11	than	43			63	I	9
12	one	34			64	cannot	67
13	My	38			65	name	33
14	name	33			66	myself	80
15	is	28			67	as	20
16	a	1			68	the	33
17	cipher	59			69	intention	120
18	it	29			70	of	21
19	is	28			71	my	38
20	1.9 = S.I.	28			72	work	67
21	and	19			73	is	28
22	9.3 = R.U.	39			74	that	49
23	C.R.C.	24			75	you	61
24	is	28			76	should	79
25	an	15		52 what 52	77	seek	40
26	epigram	69			78	and	19
27	Saint-Germain	130			79	by	27
28	is	28			80	seeking	70
29	a	1			81	discover	95
30	pseudonym	132			82	me	18
31	My	38			83	and	19
32	life	32			84	by	27
33	is	28			85	discovering	125
34	my	38			86	me	18
35	own	52			87	know	63
36	yet	50			88	me	18
37	my	38			89	My	38
38	life	32			90	essence	70
39	is	28			91	is	28
40	that	49			92	Silence	67
41	of	21			93	like	37
42	all	25			94	the	33
43	souls	86			95	voiceless	109
44	a	1			96	fragrance	73
45	parable	55			97	of	21
46	of	21			98	a	1
47	what	52			99	Rose	57
48	is	28			100	Who	46
49	what	52			101	can	18
50	was	43			102	name	33
51	and	19			103	Silence	67

SYMBOLIC NUMBER GLOSSARY

11 Root value of Rakoczi.

19 Gematria value of the letter "S," the middle letter of the Great Invocation.

A number sacred to the Egyptians, esoteric Islamic philosophy, and the Ageless Wisdom. It signifies the cosmological totality of the seven rays and the twelve constellations of the zodiac.

A variation of this number appears in "A Word from the Master" in the form of 1.9. In this form it is a cipher number representing the letters AI and/or SI. AI relates to Francis Bacon and SI relates to Sirius. See 9.3 and 1993.

21 Quantity of key words in the Great Invocation.

Quantity of different letters comprising the words of the Great Invocation. Letters B, J, Q, X, and Z are not present.

Quantity of letters in the cipher alphabet used by Francis Bacon.

27 The line number in *Love's Labor's Lost* in which the word "honorificabilitudinitatibus" appears. See 136, 151, and 287.

RAN value of Horus.

28 AN value of "IS," the middle word of the Great Invocation.

RAN value of "Master DK."

RAN value of "The Star," the seventeenth major card of the Tarot. See 91.

33 ESC value of Bacon. Related to the age of Jesus during His crucifixion and resurrection, and the age of King Solomon's Temple when it was first pillaged.

38 RAN value of Rakoczi.

49 AN value of Athena, the Muse of Francis Bacon.

52 Key numeric connector between Psalm 46, the Great Invocation, and "A Word from the Master."

AN value of the middle word "what" in "A Word from the Master."

AN value of the word "heart."

Number of letters comprising the eleven Celibate and Non-celibate key words of the Great Invocation.

57 Middle word-position of the Great Invocation.

ESC value of Fra. Bacon. (Brother Bacon).

67 ESC value of Francis.

RAN value of the four words surrounding "IS" in the Great Invocation pattern of the Maltese/Templar cross (fig. 6.2).

77 Greek gematria value of Athena, the Muse of Francis Bacon.

83 AN value of Rakoczi.

85 Essence Value of the middle word-position (57) of the Great Invocation—57 + 28 (IS).

Essence Value of the middle word-position (26) of the essential fifty-one words (containing no duplicates) of the Great Invocation—26 + 59 (WHERE).

AN value of "the heart." The gematria value of this phrase is significant in relation to the Essence Values of IS and WHERE because they are both at "the heart" of the Great Invocation.

91 AN value of "Master DK."

AN value of "The Star," the seventeenth major card of the Tarot. The digits 9 and 1 can be read as I and S, thus spelling "IS" the middle word of the Great Invocation.

93 This number appears in "A Word from the Master" in the form of 9.3. In this form it is a cipher number representing the letters IC and/or RU. IC relates to a cipher created by Francis Bacon and RU relates to Sirius.

94 AN value of "Master R."

AN value of the three middle words of the Synthetic Triplet, "the mind of."

95 AN value of Sirius. 5 x 19.

100 ESC value of Francis Bacon.

Word-position in the Great Invocation whose Essence Value equals 159—Master Rakoczi.

104 AN value of "of the Lion."

Essence Value of middle word-position of "A Word from the Master."

AN value of the first and last words of the Great Invocation.

113 Total words of the Great Invocation.

124 ESC value of "W. Shakespeare" and "Rosicrucian."

126 ESC value of Boteswaine.

Cipher number signifying the location of the word "Boteswaine" in the First Folio—page 1 on line 26.

132 Sum of the word-positions in the Great Invocation based upon the numbers 5 and 6 and their combinations, 56 and 65. (5 + 6 + 56 + 65). Hence the four words—Light, within, God, of.

Gematria sum of the first, middle, and last words of the Synthetic Triplet—God, Mind, Silence.

Gematria sum of the AN, RAN, and root values of Rakoczi.

136 AN value of "the God of Light." These four words form the Signature of Sirius in the Great Invocation. See figure 4.3.

Relates to Shakespeare's sonnet 136, Napier's logarithm, and zero.

Page number in *Love's Labor's Lost* where the word "honorificabilitudinitatibus" appears.

151 Word-position in *Love's Labor's Lost* where "honorificabilitudinitatibus" appears.

157 ESC value of "Fra Rosi Crosse" (Brotherhood of the Rosy Cross). See 287.

AN value of the four words surrounding "IS" in the Great Invocation pattern of the Maltese/Templar cross (figure 6.2).

RAN value of the Latin phrase appearing on the titlepage of Bacon's *Advancement and Proficience of Learning,* published in 1640. This phrase is *"Multi pertransibunt & augebitur Scientia."*

159 AN value of Master Rakoczi.

Essence Value of word-position 100 in the Great Invocation.

171 AN value of the three middle word-positions in the Great Invocation.

Relates to the ship and Isis themes.

186 AN value of "God of Light within."

AN value of Master Djwhal Khul.

189 A number interlinking Psalm 46, the Great Invocation, and "A Word from the Master."

The average ESC value of Francis Bacon's three mottos, *Mediocria Firma, Moniti Meliora,* and *Plus Ultra.*

AN value of "the heart of the Lion." This relates to the star Regulus in Leo.

201 Total words in Psalm 46.

3 x 67 (Francis).

RAN value of the phrase "age of restoration of what has been broken by the fall." This phrase is subtly connected with Bacon's unfinished work *The Great Instauration* (meaning the great restoration).

209 Middle word-position of the Synthetic Triplet containing the word "Mind."

231 Total AN value of the Non-celibate key words in the Great Invocation.

238 AN value of the phrase attributed to Hermes and Christ, "I am the Light of the world."

Result of 14 x 17. These two numbers are ciphers given by Djwhal Khul which are related to the Path to Sirius.

242 AN value of Thoth-Hermes-Mercury.

The result of 11 x 22.

249 Essence Value of the middle word-position of the Synthetic Triplet.

287 Essence Value of the first and last words of Psalm 46, "God" and "refuge." (Based on ESC.)

Number of letters in the sections "To the Reader" and "Principal Actors" in the First Folio of Shakespeare.

ESC value of "honorificabilitudinitatibus."

RKC value of "Fra. Rosi Cross." Related to 157.

The year (A.D.) in which St. Alban is said to have founded Freemasonry in Britain.

There are three K's in the Great Invocation. The second or middle K is located in letter-position 287. The letter K equals 11 and consequently 3 x 11 equals 33, the cipher number of Bacon.

303 The year (A.D.) in which St. Alban is said to have been martyred. A cipher number for "Bacon" when the null character, zero, is removed.

Combined total of the three middle word-positions of Psalm 46, 100 + 101 + 102.

313 AN value of "The Invocation for Power and Light." This is the actual name of the Great Invocation.

AN value of "Master R, Lord of Civilization."

318 Essence Value of "God of Light within."

2 x 159.

334 AN value of the Fixed Cross signs: "Taurus, Leo, Scorpio, Aquarius."

342 Sum of the elements identifying the location of "honorificabilitudinitatibus" in *Love's Labor's Lost*. These are 136 (page), 27 and 28 (lines), and 151 (word-position).

18 x 19. These two factors are the ratio connected with the human canon discovered in ancient Egyptian temple art by E. A. Schwaller de Lubicz.

343 7 x 7 x 7. Related to Athena through the number 7.

Signifies a complete cycle of manifestation according to the Ageless Wisdom philosophy.

Relates to Sanat Kumara. Djwhal Khul states that the digits 777 are associated with Sanat Kumara.

AN value of the Mutable Cross signs: "Gemini, Virgo, Sagittarius, Pisces."

417 Total quantity of words in the Synthetic Triplet.

443 Total quantity of letters in the Great Invocation.

AN value of the first, middle, and last words of Psalm 46, the Great Invocation, and "A Word from the Master."

471 AN value of the phrase "age of restoration of what has been broken by the fall."

3 x 157.

505 Sum of the last five word-positions in "A Word from the Master."

515 Greek gematria value of Athena. By placing a decimal point after the 1, this whole number becomes 51.5. A circle divided into 7 parts contains approximately 51.5 degrees in each section. Thus the connection to Athena. Related to 49, 77, 343.

555 Sum of the last five word-positions in the Great Invocation.

777 The number (read as three 7s) related to Sanat Kumara.

Related to Athena. See chapter 4.

993 Final page number of the First Folio which should be printed as 399, since the previous page is 398. Many Baconian researchers believe this is a deliberate misprint, and hence, a cipher number created by Francis Bacon.

1122 Sum of the last five word-positions, quantity of words, root values, and letters in the Great Invocation and "A Word from the Master." See table 8.8.

1622 Quantity of letters in the Synthetic Triplet.

1993 A year derived from the cipher numbers, 1.9. and 9.3. which are found in "A Word from the Master."
Related to Sirius by substituting the letters S (1), I (9), R (9), and U (3) for the numbers 1, 9, 9, 3. SIRU are the letters required to spell Sirius. The additional I and S are duplicates of the original letters I and S.

2244 33 x 68, Bacon (ESC) times Hermes.
17 x 132, Bacon (RAN) x 132 (value of word-positions 56, 65, 5, and 6 in Great Invocation—"God of Light within").
The AN values of the words located in positions 22 and 44 in Psalm 46, the Great Invocation, and "A Word from the Master" yield a sum of 242—the AN value of "Thoth-Hermes-Mercury."

2310 Total ESC value of Francis Bacon based on the number of times the name appears in *The First Part of King Henry the Fourth.*

MULTIPLE NUMBERS

5, 6, 56, 65

The word-positions in the Great Invocation of the four words—Light, within, God, of. Related to 132.

The phrase, "God of Light within" is formed from these four numbers. This phrase has several levels of meaning, including Hermes and Sanat Kumara.

This set of four numbers is based on the numbers 5 and 6. These two numbers symbolize the liberation of the human being at the fifth initiation when form (6), is brought to perfection. According to esoteric symbolism, the six-pointed star (the human being) must become the five-pointed star (the initiated Master). Prior to achieving mastery at the fifth initiation, the constitution of a human being consists of the monad, soul, and personality. The personality, in turn, is composed of the mind, emotions, etheric body and physical body. After the fourth initiation the soul is absorbed into the monad. Thus, at the time of the fifth initiation the perfected human being is an expression of the monad and personality, with its four vehicles of mind, emotion, etheric and physical bodies. This is the five-pointed star. This is only one of various possible interpretations of the relationship between numbers 5 and 6.

222, 333, 444, 555

This series of three digit numbers generally correspond to root-race and branch-race cycles. These special numbers act as cyclic time markers which establish important points in the history of our planet.

The number 222 signifies the arrival of Sanat Kumara to our fourth Earth chain on globe 2, round 2, root-race 2.

The following three numbers relate to root-races. Each digit of each number correlates to a root-race, a sub-race, and a branch-race respectively. The number 333 correlates to the time when Sanat Kumara created the human kingdom. The number 444 represents the period marking the midpoint between the creation of humanity (333) and our present, modern humanity (555).

Exactly 113 branch-races have elapsed between the creation of humanity and the current human race. This 113 unit cycle is represented by the 113 words in the Great Invocation.

1
Laying the Foundation

"It is the most stupendous utterance of all time. I do not hesitate to use the most extreme superlatives I can find."[1] These words of Foster Bailey, the husband of Alice A. Bailey (AAB), describe the Great Invocation in an article appearing in *The Beacon* magazine in 1951. Foster Bailey continues:

> I well remember the strain of the days before the morning when, as the sun rose, Mrs. Bailey brought me the words of this Invocation as she had written them to the exact dictation of the Tibetan.[2] It was an occasion of the most complete at-one-ment with him that she had probably ever achieved.[3]

Most people seeing the Great Invocation for the first time experience it as a beautiful prayer dedicated to all humanity. It calls for the restoration of God's Plan on Earth through the invoking of spiritual Light, Love, and Power. However, behind this selfless world prayer is a fascinating story and history. The Great Invocation did not simply appear out of a vacuum, but like most things was born through crisis—a crisis of worldwide proportions involving the basic freedom of humanity. The Great Invocation carries a simple message with which all people can identify—no matter what their background may be. The power of these words lies in their simplicity. Yet, these seemingly simple words carry a potency and a message that reaches to the very depths of our planetary existence. There are hidden layers to these words that await discovery. In order to appreciate this world prayer at its deeper levels we must first explore some of the background of Alice A. Bailey and her relationship to Djwhal Khul (DK), also known as the Tibetan. We will also need to learn some of the fundamental aspects of the ageless wisdom philosophy recorded by AAB. First we begin with the two persons who collaborated in bringing the Great Invocation to humanity.

Alice A. Bailey

Alice Bailey was born in Manchester, England in 1880, as Alice La Trobe-Bateman. Both her parents died by the time she was eight years old, and as a result Alice and her sister lived with their grandparents in Moor Park, Surrey, England. In her autobiography, AAB describes the first twenty years of her life as "completely disciplined by people or by the social conventions of the time."[4] Indeed, Alice and her sister were educated by various governesses and were later sent to a finishing school in London.

After her schooling, Alice worked as an evangelist for the British army in Ireland and India. During this period of her life she describes herself as "forcefully preaching the old-time religion."[5] It was in India that she met her first husband, Walter Evans. Eventually they married and settled in America where Walter studied theology and was ordained in the Episcopal Church. When Walter was assigned his first church, Alice soon found herself teaching Bible classes and performing all the necessary duties of a minister's wife.

By 1915, however, Alice and Walter Evans separated due to Walter's uncontrollable temper and abusive behavior. By then they were living in California, and Alice was supporting her three daughters by working in a sardine factory. It was at this point in her life that Alice, now thirty-five, came into contact with Theosophy through two English women who befriended her. Alice spent the next several years working hard at the factory while studying the many new ideas of Theosophy, which she struggled to integrate with the strict Christian ideas of her upbringing.

As she tells the story, it was not long before she was studying *The Secret Doctrine* of Helena P. Blavatsky (HPB) with the help of two other women who had been Blavatsky's personal students. Before long Alice joined the Theosophical Lodge in Pacific Grove, California where she began teaching classes in Theosophy.

At this point in the story we must mention that from the time Alice Bailey was a teenager she had been under the guidance of a mysterious man who visited her on at least two occasions—once in England in 1895 and again in India in 1906. Although he offered guidance and advice, he never demanded Alice's obedience. It was in 1918 that Alice learned the identity of this mysterious man, for she saw his portrait hanging in the shrine room of the Theosophical Lodge to which she had just been admitted after several years of study. He was known as the Master Koot Humi (KH) and the fact that Alice Bailey claimed to have been under His guidance since adolescence created an uproar in the lodge. After all, Alice was only a neophyte and why would such a great Teacher as KH contact such a new student of the Ageless Wisdom? As AAB explains:

> Believing that they would be pleased and not intending in the very least to be boastful I said, in all innocence, "Oh, then, He must be my Master, for I've talked with Him and been under His guidance ever since." This person looked at me and said, with rather a withering inflection, "Am I to understand that you believe yourself to be a disciple?"[6]

This incident initiated Alice into the glamours and controversies which so often surround the subject of guides and gurus. Mrs. Bailey never used her association with any Master of the Wisdom to inflate her own ego; on the contrary, she did her utmost to downplay such relationships, because they only hindered her service activities. (I recommend reading *The Unfinished Autobiography* in order to get a complete picture of AAB's attitudes concerning such matters.) As we shall see, this entire issue soon became critical in Alice's life.

The year 1919 proved to be quite momentous for AAB for several reasons. First she met Foster Bailey who she eventually married after being granted a divorce from Walter Evans. Alice and Foster became quite active in the Theosophical Society and their work together was the beginning of a partnership which would eventually lead them to New York City and the founding of Lucis Trust and the Arcane School. The other important event that year was Alice's contact with the Tibetan Teacher Djwhal Khul. As AAB explains:

I now come to a happening in my life about which I hesitate to speak. It concerns the work which I have done for the past twenty-seven years. This work has received world-wide recognition and has evoked world-wide curiosity. It has also brought me some ridicule and suspicion, but surprisingly little, and I have been quite able to understand it because I started by being very suspicious myself.[7]

It was in November 1919 that I made my first contact with The Tibetan. I had sent the children off to school and thought I would snatch a few minutes to myself and went out on to the hill close to the house. I sat down and began thinking and then suddenly I sat startled and attentive. I heard what I thought was a clear note of music which sounded from the sky, through the hill and in me. Then I heard a voice which said, "There are some books which it is desired should be written for the public. You can write them. Will you do so?" Without a moment's notice I said, "Certainly not. I'm not a darned psychic and I don't want to be drawn into anything like that."[8]

Despite her wariness, and after much soul searching AAB agreed to work with the Tibetan, serving as His amanuensis and secretary. Although AAB was a student of the ageless wisdom, she never claimed authorship for eighteen of the twenty-four books that bear her name. As she explains:

Today, as the result of twenty-seven years work with the Tibetan I can snap into telepathic relation with Him without the slightest trouble. I can and do preserve my own mental integrity all the time and I can always argue with Him if it seems to me, at times, that—as an Occidental—I may know better than He does as regards points of presentation. When we have an argument along any line I invariably write as He wants the text written, though He is apt to modify His presentation after discussion with me. If He does not change His wording and point of view, I do not change what He had said in any way.[9]

Their work together lasted for thirty years until Alice A. Bailey died in 1949. By the time of her transition AAB had accomplished a great deal in the field of spiritual and esoteric study beyond the work she did with DK. Along with Foster and other dedicated co-workers Alice Bailey created the Lucis Trust, the Arcane School, World Goodwill, the Triangles network, and other service activities.[10]

Djwhal Khul and the Hierarchy

Undoubtedly, the most controversial aspect of Alice Bailey's work was her claim that the majority of the books she wrote were actually dictated to her by a Tibetan Master of Wisdom named Djwhal Khul. It is not the intention of this book to debate the existence or non-existence of Djwhal Khul. Such matters are best left to the personal feelings of each individual. However, in order to put the Great Invocation into the proper perspective it is important to relate some of the background of the Tibetan Teacher.

In brief, H. P. Blavatsky, founder of the Theosophical Society, introduced the idea of a spiritual brotherhood which guides the evolution of humanity from behind the scenes of world events. These guides are known as the spiritual Hierarchy, or simply the Hierarchy. Much has been written about this brotherhood, both positive and negative. Members of this band of spiritual guides are known as the Masters of Wisdom or Lords of Compassion.[11] Two of the most well known Masters of the Theosophical movement are the Masters Morya and Koot Humi. All of these advanced souls have lived as human beings but have evolved beyond the physical plane of existence. According to the ageless wisdom, They exist at a level of expanded awareness beyond the normal range of human activity. The spiritual Hierarchy can be thought of as the Kingdom of God. The function of the Hierarchy in general is to oversee the evolution of life on the planet; in particular it guides the evolution of human consciousness according to the Plan of God.

Almost invariably when students of the ageless wisdom discuss evolution they are talking about the growth of consciousness, not about evolution in the Darwinian sense. They are talking about the evolution of consciousness, not bodies. The form is ready and only awaits spirit to bring it to completeness. This is the message of Christ, Buddha, Mohammed, Moses, Krishna, Lao Tse, and many other teachers sent forth from the Hierarchy. Hierarchy is non-sectarian; Hierarchy transcends religious forms. The kingdoms which the Hierarchy guides are the mineral, vegetable, animal, and human. Humanity represents the fourth kingdom in nature and Hierarchy is the fifth.

The most advanced member of this Hierarchy is the Christ. According to the ageless wisdom, the term "Christ" or anointed one is a position indicating the leader of Hierarchy. This idea is the same as the office of president in a government or corporation, in that different individuals hold the office at various times. The Master Jesus sacrificed His life so that the One now called the Christ could work through Him in Palestine 2,000 years ago. The Master Jesus is the leader of all Christianity, while the Christ as head of the spiritual Hierarchy presides over all worldwide activities (including religions) that work toward human betterment.

According to the books written by Alice Bailey, the Tibetan Master Djwhal Khul is also a member of this spiritual Hierarchy. One aspect of His role in the immediate Plan is to bridge the religious and philosophical beliefs of the East and West in order to prepare the world for a global civilization which respects the rights of the individual while at the same time provides for the overall needs of society. At this point it is best to let DK speak for himself from an extract first published in August of 1914, which appears in each of his books written through AAB:

> Suffice it to say, that I am a Tibetan disciple of a certain degree, and this tells you but little, for all are disciples from the humblest aspirant up to, and beyond, the Christ Himself. I live in a physical body like other men, on the borders of Tibet, and at times (from the exoteric standpoint) preside over a large group of Tibetan lamas, when my other duties permit. It is this fact that has caused it to be reported that I am an abbot of this particular lamasery. Those associated with me in the work of the Hierarchy (and all true disciples are associated in this work) know me by still another name and office. A.A.B. knows who I am and recognises me by two of my names.
>
> I am a brother of yours, who has travelled a little longer upon the Path than has the average student, and has therefore incurred greater responsibil-

ities. I am one who has wrestled and fought his way into a greater measure of light than has the aspirant who will read this article, and I must therefore act

as a transmitter of the light, no matter what the cost. I am not an old man, as age counts among the teachers, yet I am not young or inexperienced. My work is to teach and spread the knowledge of the Ageless Wisdom wherever I can find response, and I have been doing this for many years. I seek also to help the Master M. and the Master K.H. whenever opportunity offers, for I have been long connected with Them and with Their work. In all the above, I have told you much; yet at the same time I have told you nothing which would lead you to offer me that blind obedience and the foolish devotion which the emotional aspirant offers to the Guru and Master Whom he is as yet unable to contact. Nor will he make that desired contact until he has transmuted emotional devotion into unselfish service to humanity,—not to the Master.

The books that I have written are sent out with no claim for their acceptance. They may, or may not, be correct, true and useful. It is for you to ascertain their truth by right practice and by the exercise of the intuition. Neither I nor A.A.B. is the least interested in having them acclaimed as inspired writings, or in having anyone speak of them (with bated breath) as being the work of one of the Masters. If they present truth in such a way that it follows sequentially upon that already offered in the world teachings, if the information given raises the aspiration and the will-to-serve from the plane of the emotions to that of the mind (the plane whereon the Masters can be found) then they will have served their purpose. If the teaching conveyed calls forth a response from the illumined mind of the worker in the world, and brings a flashing forth of his intuition, then let that teaching be accepted. But not otherwise. If the statements meet with eventual corroboration, or are deemed true under the test of the Law of Correspondences, then that is well and good. But should this not be so, let not the student accept what is said.[12]

The subject matter covered in the eighteen books on which AAB and DK collaborated is vast, but one of the most important themes covered in their work together concerned the reappearance of a World Teacher, called the Christ. It should be noted that the Christ does not represent any one religion, but serves all humanity. According to DK, the reappearance of the Christ will inaugurate the new age of Aquarius and represent a major evolutionary advance in consciousness for humanity. The Great Invocation plays a central role in this coming event.

The Great Invocation was given to humanity in order to aid in the return of the World Teacher. The Tibetan asked those who felt dedicated to His work to:

> Prepare men for the reappearance of the Christ. This is your first and greatest duty. The most important part of that work is teaching men—on a large scale—to use the Invocation so that it becomes a world prayer and focuses the invocative demand of humanity.[13]

Alice Bailey was completely dedicated to the work of preparing humanity for the coming of a World Teacher through promoting right human relations and goodwill throughout the world via the service activities of the Lucis Trust. Although she died before commenting on the Great Invocation in her autobiography, she was well aware of the importance of the Great Invocation relative to the spiritual preparation of humanity prior to the coming of the Christ. This was implicit through her thirty years of close work with the Tibetan. During this time He dictated much material to her concerning the critical world events of the twentieth century. (Details of the events leading up to the public release of the Great Invocation will be covered fully as we proceed.)

The primary aim of this book is to show that the Great Invocation is much more than a prayer of great vision and hope for a better world (as if this were not enough); for underlying the outer structure of the words are clues and codes revealing an even larger vision, a vision of a vast intelligent Life of superhuman dimensions in which we human beings find ourselves living—St. Paul's "One in Whom we live and move and have our being." Through the use of esoteric numerology we will demonstrate how the ideas and mysteries of the ageless wisdom are woven into the very word fabric of the Great Invocation.

The Ageless Wisdom View of God

Each form, from that of the tiniest atom to that of a vast constellation, is an embodiment of a life, which expresses itself as consciousness, awareness, and responsive sentiency through the medium of some type of response mechanism. Thus we have the establishing of a universe of lives, interacting and interrelated, all of them conscious, some of them self-conscious, and others group-conscious, but all grounded in the universal mind, all possessing souls, and all presenting aspects of the divine Life.[14]

The teachings presented by the Tibetan in the Alice Bailey books describe all life in the universe as being conscious at some level, whether it is the consciousness of an atom or a galaxy, a plant or a human, an animal or a planet. The term "God" is relative in this model of reality. At the universal level, the ageless wisdom recognizes the existence of an intelligent, loving, and purposeful Being Who created and sustains the universe. If the universe is thought of as the singular expression of God universal, then the next step in understanding this concept is to think of the galaxies as sub-systems operating within the corporate body of the universal God.

Modern astronomy now knows there are many billions of galaxies contained within the universe. The ageless wisdom concept views galaxies as integrated life systems having the same fundamental characteristics as the original universal Creator, namely will, love, and intelligence. This threefold aspect is an integral part of all the components of the universe, and corresponds to the trinity concept of Christianity—Father, Son, and Holy Spirit.

Table 1. Basic Triplicities.

First Aspect	Second Aspect	Third Aspect
Father	Son	Mother
Will	Love	Holy Spirit
Spirit	Soul	Body
Life	Consciousness	Form

In effect, the ageless wisdom recognizes galaxies as whole living conscious life forms operating on a scale beyond any human being's power to comprehend. An entity expressing itself through a galactic body structure composed of stars, planets, and other celestial objects is literally alive and functioning at its own level of consciousness and intelligent purposes. What these may be we have no way of knowing. An important point to understand at this stage is that relative to us humans, a galaxy is a God. It is not the supreme universal God, but it is Godlike relative to our level of evolution.

The next level of organization in this model of reality pertains to related groups of stars within the galaxies themselves.[15] The Tibetan mentions in his writings that our solar system, along with six other solar systems, comprise part of the "body" of a cosmic entity He calls the "One About Whom Naught May Be Said." In addition to these seven solar systems, Djwhal Khul frequently discusses three other star groups of primary importance to our tiny Earth and solar system. These are the seven stars of the Big Dipper within Ursa Major (which DK simply refers to as the Great Bear), the Pleiades, and the star Sirius. These three star systems are said to govern and control the seven solar systems. To this vast array of cosmic solar Lives we must add one more celestial group, the twelve constellations of the zodiac. Our solar system, along with the six others in our local system, are governed by the Great Bear, the Pleiades, and Sirius via the twelve star groupings known as the zodiacal constellations. These act as cosmic filters between the seven solar systems and the three governing constellations. All of these make up the celestial system known as the "One About Whom Naught May Be Said."

Relatively speaking, this collection of star systems (three transmitting, twelve intermediate, and seven receiving solar systems) is the ruling Intelligence or God in which we, on our tiny planet Earth, live and have our being. It is very important to remember, however, that each one of these celestial units is an independent, Self-conscious, Intelligent Life living within the corporate sphere of influence of a greater Life. These, including ourselves, are all systems and sub-systems existing as part of an infinite Hierarchy of Universal Life.

Djwhal Khul has revealed a wondrous and mind-reeling description of our place in the universal scheme of things. Although He has revealed much about the One About Whom Naught May Be Said (a cosmic Logos), there are many unknowns, plenty of unanswered questions, and a mind-boggling array of complex relationships existing between the various parts of this celestial Mystery. Despite these daunting complexities, the presented vision is undeniably awe-inspiring and beautiful when approached with an open mind and a willingness to examine it in depth.

Descending this dizzying cosmic scale of life we finally arrive at our own solar system. Our solar system is also a living conscious Entity of cosmic proportions relative to human existence. This Being is called the solar Logos. Sometimes the Tibetan refers to the solar Logos as "The Grand Man of the Heavens." We live within the body of this Being and come under Its laws. Within the living structure of the solar Logos are other cosmic Beings called "planetary Logoi" (sometimes referred to as "Heavenly Men"). Our Earth is one of these Logoi. Our planetary Logos is a conscious, living, loving intelligence who is OUR GOD. Some names given to our planetary Logos are the Ancient of Days, Melchizedek, and Sanat Kumara, a Sanskrit name that will be discussed in greater detail later on.

Our Earth, like all the other cosmic entities discussed to this point, is a consciously evolving Being living in cooperative group relationship with the other planetary Beings in our solar system. We are given to believe that definite communication goes on between the planetary Logoi and the solar Logos. Communication goes on at higher levels as well—at stellar levels and beyond. The entire universe is alive and conscious at innumerable levels of awareness and evolution. Philosophically considered, this model is called Hylozoism and is explained by DK as follows:

> This posits a living substance, composed of a multiplicity of sentient lives which are continuously swept into expression by the "breath of the divine Life." This theory recognises not so-called inorganic matter anywhere in the universe, and emphasizes the fact that all forms are built up of infinitesimal lives, which in their totality—great or small—constitute a Life, and that these composite lives, in their turn, are a corporate part of a still greater Life. Thus eventually we have that great scale of lives, manifesting in greater expression and reaching all the way from the tiny life called the atom (with which science deals) up to that vast atomic life which we call a solar system.[16]

A brief definition of Hylozoism states:

> From the Greek *Hyle* ("matter") and *zoe* ("life"). A doctrine predicating life of all matter. Held by many early philosophers, among them Thales, (Q.V.), suggestions of the view are to be found in most philosophies which find the world to be teleologically ordered. If all living forms are sentient to some degree, Hylozoism becomes a sub-class of Panpsychism.[17]

Pursuing Panpsychism we find:

> From the Greek *pan* and *psyche* meaning that everything is possessed of soul. The doctrine that everything is possessed of life is termed Hylozoism....Although Panpsychism makes a stronger claim, the distinction between possessing soul (or sentience) and possessing life is difficult to maintain in practice.[18]

I am going into some detail here because the ageless wisdom stresses the fundamental importance of life, consciousness, and form as the basis of all existence. When it is said that a galaxy or solar system is an integrated life form this does not simply mean that these are random collections of dead matter that just happened to become organized into orbiting whirlpools of new stars and planets. No, the theory suggests that the form of a solar system, for instance, is only the outer visible manifestation—the physical body so to speak. This solar system is also conscious. It experiences the cosmos as a distinct living Entity and furthermore, this Entity is evolving in ways beyond our ability to comprehend.

The same holds true for our Earth. All these celestial systems are living, evolving souls with physically manifested "bodies," whether they are planetary, solar, or cosmic. This idea relates to the world soul of Plato (428-348 BCE) and the Neoplatonic school of Plotinus (205-270 CE):

> In Plotinus, who in his own way systematized the Platonic themes, the world soul is an emanation from God, the One, by way of the Nous or intelligible world, and contains the physical world as its body.[19]

Earth—Who's In Charge?

Up to this point we have seen that the ageless wisdom describes a hierarchical organization to the universe. Apparently, the cosmos contains vast centers of unique and distinct intelligent life forms most of which exist in dimensions beyond the physical universe. This hierarchical organization is reflected on our own planet Earth in the form of centers of consciousness. These centers comprise intelligent, purposeful Entities living at various levels or planes of consciousness. There are three primary centers which directly relate to the Great Invocation. These three centers are Shamballa, Hierarchy, and Humanity. The ageless wisdom teaches that each of these centers represents a definite aspect of the planetary Logos of the Earth, Who is referred to as Sanat Kumara, the Lord of the World. It is important to remember that every whole system (center) is composed of sub-systems which are also conscious and evolving within the greater system. Therefore, Shamballa, Hierarchy, and Humanity are specific centers of existence containing living beings at various levels of evolutionary development. Relative to each other Shamballa is the most advanced, the Hierarchy is intermediate and Humanity is least evolved. As already mentioned, the Hierarchy is made up of Masters and Teachers Who were once humans that evolved beyond the human center, so we will briefly describe Shamballa and Humanity.

Shamballa

The center called Shamballa is the directing agency of the Earth's purpose within the solar system. The Beings who live within the consciousness sphere of Shamballa are very highly evolved, and most of them have gone through the human experience in bodily form millions of years ago, before the Earth existed in its present form. The Beings who exist in Shamballa work closely with Sanat Kumara—they work intimately with the purposes and will of God. The will and purpose of Sanat Kumara include all the kingdoms of nature on Earth including humanity. Certain of the Masters in the Hierarchy work specifically with that part of Sanat Kumara's purpose which concerns human evolution. This purpose is transmitted to the Hierarchy from Shamballa where it is developed into an immediate Plan for humanity. The Plan is then worked out through various Masters and their groups within the Hierarchy, and also groups of human beings living in the outer world.

Humanity

The third major center of importance in the life expression of Sanat Kumara is humanity itself. Humanity is the key to the success of the present evolutionary plan of Earth. According to the ageless wisdom the human center is just now coming into its real operational phase relative to the other two centers of Shamballa and Hierarchy. The human center is the first kingdom of nature in which consciousness of individual self is said to manifest. Apparently humanity is needed to help fulfill the plans and purposes of Sanat Kumara, and Hierarchy is assigned to guide us through this critical stage of human evolution.

The human center undergoes psychological development that is assessed by Hierarchy and Shamballa in terms of groups. Generally speaking, humanity is phasing between adolescence and young adulthood. We are in a transition phase, and at a crisis point in our group development, which is obvious to many people everywhere at this time. Chapter 2 will focus on this crisis in relation to the Great Invocation.

Initiation

The subject of initiation is another key factor of the ageless wisdom. It is vital to have a basic understanding of initiation in order to appreciate the enormous implications of the Great Invocation in relation to the current world crisis facing humanity.

Simply put, initiation means entering into something new. Often initiation is the beginning of a new life experience. It can be likened to a rite of passage, such as when an adolescent becomes an adult by reaching a symbolic age in a given culture, or when particular religious sacraments are performed signifying an entering into some sacred spiritual commitment, such as baptism or communion. Another example might be joining a secret society in which the individual is initiated by having to undergo some form of discipline in order to be accepted and given knowledge only known by the members. All these examples and many others can be applied to the term initiation; however, the Master DK places initiation on an entirely different level of understanding.

Initiation might be defined in two ways. It is first of all the entering into a
new and wider dimensional world by the expansion of a man's consciousness
so that he can include and encompass that which he now excludes, and from
which he normally separates himself in his thinking and acts. It is, secondly,
the entering into man of those energies which are distinctive of the soul and of
the soul alone,—the forces of intelligent love, and of spiritual will. These are
dynamic energies, and they actuate all who are liberated souls.[20]

When we think of initiation our minds tend to create elaborate scenes of dramatic ceremony and ritual, perhaps drawing images from Hollywood. And although
ceremony and ritual play a large role in religion and Masonic work, the Tibetan
downplays the importance of the dramatic enactment involved with initiation.

Initiation has been so frequently presented as being a ceremony that I have felt
it necessary to offset strenuously that erroneous significance.
    Initiation is only a ceremony in so far that there comes a climax-
ing point in the initiatory process in which the disciple's consciousness becomes dramatically aware of the personnel of the Hierarchy
and of his own position in relation to it. This realisation he symbolis-
es to himself—successively and on an increasingly large scale—as a
great rhythmic ceremonial of progressive revelation in which he, as a
candidate, is the centre of the hierarchical stage....I am not here saying that the teachings given in the past by various occult groups, or
in my book Initiation, Human and Solar, are not correct or do not
recount accurately what the candidate believes has taken place. The
point I seek to make is that the ceremonial aspect is due to the
thoughtform-making capacity of the disciple.21

The names given to the five initiations closely follow the five main events in the
life of Jesus as presented in the Gospels. The Tibetan alluded to the relationship
between the initiations and the events in the life of Jesus in the book *Initiation,
Human and Solar.* In 1937 Alice Bailey wrote her own book entitled *From
Bethlehem to Calvary* which clearly defines each one of the five initiations in relation to the Gospel story. In the introduction to her book, Alice Bailey describes each
initiation succinctly:

    1.   The Birth at Bethlehem, to which Christ called Nicodemus, saying,
"Except a man be born again, he cannot see the kingdom of God."
    2.   The Baptism in Jordan. This is the baptism to which John the Baptist
referred us, telling us that the baptism of the Holy Spirit and of fire must be
administered to us by Christ.
    3.   The Transfiguration. There perfection is for the first time demon-
strated, and there the divine possibility of such perfection is proven to the disciples. The command goes forth to us, "Be ye therefore perfect even as your
Father which is in heaven is perfect."
    4.   The Crucifixion. This is called the Great Renunciation, in the Orient,
with its lesson of sacrifice and its call to the death of the lower nature. This was
the lesson which St. Paul knew and the goal towards which he strove. "I die
daily," he said, for only in the practice of death daily undergone can the final

Death be met and endured.

   5.   The Resurrection and Ascension,[22] the final triumph which enables the initiate to sing and to know the meaning of the words: "Oh death, where is thy sting? Oh grave, where is thy victory?"[23]

Following is a table showing the five initiations with their names as given by Djwhal Khul.

Table 2. The Five Initiations.

Initiation	Name	Stage
First	Birth	Aspirant
Second	Baptism	Probationer
Third	Transfiguration	Disciple
Fourth	Renunciation	Adept
Fifth	Revelation	Master

One of the objectives of Djwhal Khul's writing project with Alice Bailey was to clarify the subject of initiation and remove many distorted ideas surrounding this important and sacred spiritual topic. Unfortunately, much of the glamour, claim making, and misinformation arose through basic misunderstanding of spiritual, theosophical, and occult literature that was easily becoming available to thousands of people at the turn of the twentieth century. Most of this increased interest was due to rapid advances in education and technology which allowed anyone with the time, money, and education to access esoteric literature at an unprecedented speed and volume. In fact, this is even more so today.

   We can hardly scratch the surface of initiation here except to give a general idea of this topic according to Djwhal Khul's books and in relation to the Great Invocation. From the Tibetan's viewpoint, initiation concerns a fundamental and realized expansion of consciousness resulting in an unmistakable altering of the initiate's comprehension and attitude to life. The emphasis is on service to humanity and the greater Whole and any changes in the material aspect of the initiate's life are secondary. In other words, what we commonly hold to be initiations are dim reflections in the outer world of a deep and profound transformation of the soul within the form. The initiate now sees the world with new eyes and can no longer return to the person he or she was before initiation occurred.

   This concept is amply illustrated in Christianity, the Mystery Religions of the Greco-Roman world, and by a good number of ancient philosophers who understood the process of spiritual rebirth. Rebirth into the new life was part of the ancient Mysteries even before Christianity officially proclaimed this sacred process of being born again (into the kingdom of God), as described in the Gospel story. In his book *The Ancient Mysteries, A Sourcebook*, editor Marvin W. Meyer offers several fine examples of the power of initiation.

Just how the initiates into the mysteries appropriated this power we do not know, but they may have understood themselves to have experienced an immediate or mystical encounter with the divine. At times this experience seems to have entailed an approach to death and a return to life. Sometimes, as in the Eleusinian and Egyptian mysteries, the *mystai* underwent dramatic rituals of darkness and death and emerged afterward into new light and life. In several texts the initiates are specifically declared to be reborn....

In a literary fragment attributed to Plutarch (in Stobaeus, *Anthology* [*Anthologion*] 4.52.49), the experience of death is compared with initiation into great mysteries. Plutarch initially notes the similarity of the Greek verbs *teleutan* (to die) and *teleisthai* (to be initiated) and then observes that people who die and people who are initiated go through comparable transformations.[24]

Djwhal Khul uses similar language when He describes the experience and results of the first initiation called the "Birth at Bethlehem."

The "new man" who has come to birth at the first initiation must and will tread the occult or scientific way, which inevitably leads him out of the world of mysticism into the scientific and assured perception of God as life or energy.

The first initiation marks the beginning of a totally new life and mode of living; it marks the commencement of a new manner of thinking and of conscious perception.[25]

Beyond the individual level of experience, initiation plays an important role in the spiritual evolution of our planet in terms of the group experience. The human race is very significant in relation to the plans and purposes of Sanat Kumara, the planetary Logos, and His position relative to the greater purpose of the solar Logos. As difficult and far-fetched as this may sound to many people, the ageless wisdom stresses the importance of the human role in the Plan of God. Initiation is important in this regard because it is the process by which the conscious awareness of the individual initiate is expanded. As more human beings take initiation there is a cumulative effect in the mass of humanity. This process of initiation builds slowly in the early phase of human spiritual evolution and gradually accelerates as the cumulative effect of more advanced humans begins to radiate into the mass population of the Earth.

Each one of these expansions *reveals* more knowledge of the true nature, meaning, and purpose of life on our planet. These revelations are gradual and cumulative, as each initiation is undergone by the initiate.

You have to bear in mind that each initiation enables the initiate to "see ahead" a little further, for revelation is always a constant factor in human experience.[26]

The first three initiations are meant to purify and integrate the individual so that their lives become transformed and filled with light and understanding or wisdom. Increasingly, more is revealed about the nature and purpose of the planetary Life we call God and which DK calls Sanat Kumara, and Jesus called the "Father." The third initiation is really considered the first initiation by the Hierarchy because the first two are considered as preparations for the third. The third initiation marks the initiate's entrance into the spiritual kingdom of God or the Hierarchy—the fifth kingdom of nature. It is the beginning of a transition between the human kingdom and the spiritual kingdom which is consummated at the fourth initiation.

The fourth initiation is in the words of the Master DK, "a culminating experience and a point of entrance into a new life for which all the past has been a preparation."[27] This initiation of Renunciation marks the point of renouncing all contact with the world of human living because the initiate has mastered all that the human world has to offer. The initiate has nothing more to learn in this world and thus, is liberated into a new realm of experience. In the life of Jesus the fourth initiation was the crucifixion.

At the fifth great expansion of consciousness the initiate experiences what is called the "Revelation" initiation. Djwhal Khul says little about this initiation except:

> It is not possible for me here to indicate the nature of the revelation which is accorded to the initiate of the fifth initiation. It is too closely related to Shamballa, and I have not myself done more this life than take the fifth initiation and climb the Mount of Ascension. The revelation for me is not completed
>
> and—in any case—my lips are sealed.[28]

According to DK our modern civilization is on the brink of a major spiritual rejuvenation which will once again restore initiation to a prominent role in the spiritual life of humanity.

> In the era which lies ahead, after the reappearance of the Christ, hundreds of thousands of men and women everywhere will pass through some one or other of the great expansions of consciousness.[29]

In other words, after the Christ returns as the World Teacher, a heightened spiritual atmosphere will exist in the world that will allow many more people to advance in their spiritual lives than is now possible. Alice Bailey describes this process of mass initiation in this way:

> Humanity stands today upon the path of probation. The way of purification is being trodden by the masses, and we are in process of purging ourselves from evil and materialism. When this process is completed, many will find themselves ready to make preparation for the first of the initiations, and to undergo the new Birth.[30]

Alice Bailey wrote those words in 1937. Today as we approach the year 2000 humanity is closer to a time of great spiritual transformation. Crisis is always a part of the process of initiation. Initiation is a time of intense catharsis, turmoil, and upheaval. The Great Invocation is an important link in the spiritual development of humanity because it invokes the spiritual forces of Light, Love, and Will, which lead to liberation from the thralldom of materialism and separatism. The human family is deeply and profoundly involved in an evolutionary process of cosmic proportions. As we will discover later on, the process of initiation is a forcing process and an experiment that extends far beyond our planet. Sanat Kumara and Shamballa, the Christ and the Hierarchy, Humanity and the Great Invocation are all connected by the common golden thread of initiation. We are all being subjected to a loving but forced process of accelerated growth and expansion of consciousness that will transform our lives dramatically if successful. The Great Invocation is an extraordinary gift of power given to us now in our hour of trial, to aid our passage through the dangerous waters of rapid global change.

The Seven Rays

The subject of the seven rays forms a major part of the teaching offered by the Tibetan in his work with AAB. These rays are simply distinct qualities of energy that permeate our entire solar system and which are said to emanate from the constellation of Ursa Major (the Great Bear). The seven rays originate from the seven stars making up the Big Dipper. The Big Dipper is actually a group of stars contained within Ursa Major. An interesting fact related to this idea comes from Robert Burnham Jr. in his *Burnham's Celestial Handbook*.[31] Mr. Burnham describes the Big Dipper as a moving cluster of stars (more than seven) which are all related as a group, and not simply a pattern of totally unrelated stars as seen from Earth. Further, as of 1978—the publication date—Burnham points out that the Ursa Major cluster is the closest known star cluster to the Earth.

Having said all that, DK ascribes tremendous importance to these seven rays of energy. He says:

> I wonder sometimes if any of you realise the epoch-making importance of the teaching which I have given out anent the seven rays as manifesting energies...With all that I have given you concerning the seven rays and the seven Ray Lords, much more can be discovered; these seven great Lives can be seen and known as the informing essences and the active energies in all that is manifested and tangible upon the physical plane, as well as on all the planes of divine expression.[32]

The seven rays are:

Ray 1–Will or Power
Ray 2–Love-Wisdom
Ray 3–Active Intelligence
Ray 4–Harmony Through Conflict and Beauty
Ray 5–Concrete Knowledge and Science
Ray 6–Devotion and Idealism
Ray 7–Ceremonial Order

The subject of the seven rays is large and complex and we will limit our discussion of the seven rays to their connection with the Great Invocation. Humanity comes under the influence of various ray energies according to cycles existing beyond our current level of understanding, but governed by universal laws and principles. Djwhal Khul indicates some of these cyclic periods in relation to the twentieth century crisis in which the Great Invocation appeared. The relationship between the seven rays and the Great Invocation is important because it gives us a broader understanding of recent historical events. This more inclusive perspective adds meaning to the dizzying swirl of crises which has characterized the twentieth century.

With these basic principles and terms set in place, we are now ready to put the Great Invocation into historical perspective.

Notes

1. Foster Bailey, "The Great Invocation," *The Beacon* Vol. XXX No. 3-4 (June-July 1951): 86. Note: The Beacon is a bi-monthly magazine containing articles of esoteric and spiritual topics published by Lucis Publishing.
2. Another name used by AAB for the Master Djwhal Khul.
3. Ibid., 87.
4. Alice A. Bailey, *The Unfinished Autobiography*, 26.
5. Ibid., 80.
6. Ibid., 155.
7. Ibid., 161.
8. Ibid., 162-63.
9. Ibid., 167-68.
10. Further information concerning these services can be obtained by writing to Lucis Trust, 120 Wall St., 24th floor, New York, NY 10005.
11. The term "Masters of Wisdom" also denotes those spiritual teachers of the Hierarchy who are more developed on the mental side, while the "Lords of Compassion" are those Masters who have developed more on the feeling side. Naturally, this is all relative to human understanding, and words are poor substitutes for explaining levels of growth beyond the current range of human evolution. It might be said that some souls evolve more toward the heart and others develop more toward the head, but all exist as wise and loving teachers and guides.
12. Alice A. Bailey, *The Externalisation of the Hierarchy*, vii-viii.
13. Ibid., 641.
14. Alice A. Bailey, *Esoteric Psychology*, vol. I, 136.
15. It should be noted that astronomers recognize the fact that galaxies tend to exist in group formation. I mention this because the wisdom teachings given by DK emphasize the concept of group living and interrelationships at all levels of existence.
16. Ibid., 149.
17. W.L. Reese, *Dictionary of Philosophy and Religion*, s.v. "Hylozoism."
18. Ibid., s.v. "Panpsychism."
19. Ibid., s.v. "World Soul."
20. Alice A. Bailey, *Esoteric Psychology*, vol. II, 12.
21. Alice A. Bailey, *The Rays and the Initiations*, 530-31.
22. DK calls this fifth stage of initiation the Revelation.
23. Bailey, *From Bethlehem to Calvary*, 22-23.
24. Marvin W. Meyer, ed. *The Ancient Mysteries, A Sourcebook*, 8.

25.   Bailey, *The Rays and the Initiations,* 666-67.
26.   Ibid., 703.
27.   Ibid., 697.
28.   Ibid., 707.
29.   Alice A. Bailey, *The Reappearance of the Christ*, 127.
30.   Alice A. Bailey, *From Bethlehem to Calvary,* 23.
31.   Robert Burnham Jr., *Burnham's Celestial Handbook,* vol. 3, 1947.
32.   Alice A. Bailey, *Esoteric Healing*, 583.

2 - Historical Overview
The Invocation for Power and Light
Stanzas One and Two

The Great Invocation consists of three different and distinct prayers or invocations given by the Master Djwhal Khul over a ten year period, from 1935 to 1945. What is known today as the Great Invocation is referred to by DK as "the final stanza of the 'Invocation for Power and Light...' "[1] The Tibetan's use of the word "stanza" may cause some confusion because we often use the word stanza to refer to a specific part of one poem, prayer or song. But DK's use of "stanza" refers to the three parts He gave to Alice Bailey in 1935, 1940, and 1945. From His standpoint, the three parts or stanzas are one invocation. Most people today are only familiar with the (third) part currently used, which is widely known as the Great Invocation, and this third part is the subject of this book. The third stanza of the Invocation for Power and Light follows:

From the point of Light within the Mind of God
Let light stream forth into the minds of men.
Let Light descend on Earth.
From the point of Love within the Heart of God
Let love stream forth into the hearts of men.
May Christ return to Earth.
From the centre where the Will of God is known
Let purpose guide the little wills of men—
The purpose which the Masters know and serve.
From the centre which we call the race of men
Let the Plan of Love and Light work out
And may it seal the door where evil dwells.
Let Light and Love and Power restore the Plan on Earth.

This world prayer, now spoken by millions of people all over the world, was given to Alice A. Bailey by Djwhal Khul on April 17, 1945 (the date appearing in *Externalisation of the Hierarchy*, p. 488). From that time until November 1949 when AAB made her transition, DK provided some analysis and interpretation of the Great Invocation, along with suggestions for its use and distribution.

Before discussing the third stanza, however, a historical overview of the extreme and profound circumstances surrounding its release is necessary because, according to the Tibetan, humanity had reached the most critical point in its evolution. An ancient conflict, which originated in Atlantis between material and spiritual forces, was re-emerging in the twentieth century. As explained by DK, in the ancient conflict the spiritual forces "won," but only by destroying Atlantis, and not because of humanity's spiritual strength.[2] After this intervention by the higher spiritual Guides of the planet, the Hierarchy withdrew from open contact with humanity leaving it free to work out its own destiny with only occasional appearances by spiritual teachers who came into the world to guide and teach through religion, philosophy or other means.

The First World War was part of this karmic reaction, and by 1935 the Hierarchy was hopeful that humanity had matured enough to choose the spiritual way over materialism. It was under these circumstances that the first stanza of the Great Invocation was made available for humanity's use. But according to DK, by 1939 the situation was as follows:

> The test to which humanity was to be subjected and which is today the controlling factor was whether—it would consecrate that knowledge and its scientific and mental attainment to group good or to selfish ends, to material issues or to spiritual incentives and impulses. This ancient conflict has now been carried through into another field of human expression, that of the mind and—as the race has progressed and the personalities of human beings have reached a high stage of integration and achievement—the conflict has become acute, the issues clearer and the ranging of the opponents into two clearly defined groups is now so complete that the final struggle has become possible.[3]

With brief background setting the stage, following are the first two stanzas:

Let the Forces of Light bring illumination to mankind.
Let the Spirit of Peace be spread abroad.
May men of goodwill everywhere meet in a spirit of cooperation.
May forgiveness on the part of all men be the keynote at this time.
Let power attend the efforts of the Great Ones.
So let it be, and help us to do our part.   Stanza One 1935

Let the Lords of Liberation issue forth.
Let Them bring succour to the sons of men.
Let the Rider from the Secret Place come forth,
And coming, save.
Come forth, O Mighty One.

Let the souls of men awaken to the Light,
And may they stand with massed intent.
Let the fiat of the Lord go forth:
The end of woe has come!
Come forth, O Mighty One.
The hour of service of the Saving Force has now arrived.
Let it be spread abroad, O Mighty One.

Let Light and Love and Power and Death
Fulfil the purpose of the Coming One.

The WILL to save is here.
The LOVE to carry forth the work is widely spread abroad.
The ACTIVE AID of all who know the truth is also here.
Come forth, O Mighty One and blend these three.
Construct a great defending wall.
The rule of evil *now* must end.   Stanza Two 1940[4]

When DK communicated the first stanza in 1935, there was great opportunity and hope on the part of the Hierarchy that humanity was ready for a spiritual renaissance that would result in international cooperation and world peace. In a message to AAB on October 10, 1934 DK wrote:

> Esoterically speaking, a point of contact, a moment of "spiritual intercourse," is imminent, and *out of that moment a new world can be born....*
> If this spiritual contact can be brought about, it means that the Hierarchy will no longer be hidden and unknown, but will be recognised as present upon the physical plane. This would at first be necessarily on a small scale.[5]

This communication was followed by the April, 1935 message entitled "A Challenging Opportunity" in which the first stanza was given. This invocation "...will set up a rhythm and a momentum of great potency."[6]

Apparently, humanity was not responding to calls for goodwill, international cooperation, and world peace. In September of 1939 Djwhal Khul wrote that powerful spiritual energy involving the will of God had been directly released upon the world by certain advanced Beings in Shamballa. Although this energy was having some positive effects on humanity, it was also stimulating the aggressive forces within some very powerful personalities. DK names such men as Mussolini, Hitler, Lenin, Stalin, and Franco as "...expressions of the Shamballa force."[7] The main point to bear in mind is that humanity was being greatly stimulated by powerful energies. Unfortunately, humanity was not responding as well as had been expected or hoped by the spiritual guides of the planet in Hierarchy and Shamballa, for much ancient karma of humanity was being worked out. In other words, humanity was being subjected to increased pressure to face the mistakes and injustices of the past and move forward spiritually as one human family. The stress of this "accelerated growth process" was apparently too much to handle for many people. To make matters worse, certain aggressive personalities who DK claimed were being influenced by evil forces soon took advantage of the situation.

By November of 1939 the world crisis was at a boiling point.

> The situation is serious. Sea and air and land are arrayed against the Forces of Light; they are the agents of material substance and can be used potently against the spiritual Forces....The Members of the Hierarchy are hard put to it to turn the tide in favour of that true and more spiritual civilisation which is on the way.[8]
> The World Crisis was, as you know, inevitable, but physical warfare could have been avoided if right psychological methods had been employed,...and if the spirit of sacrifice had also been demonstrated by the world aspirants. The

need for group sacrifice has not met with adequate response, except in those cases where it has been imposed by governments upon their nationals. Such is the sorry history of what is taking place today.[9]

On June 30, 1940 DK gave the second stanza of the Great Invocation. In this message DK did not bandy words but called for all spiritually minded people, aspirants, and disciples to stand up for freedom and fight the forces of evil. This was a wake-up call alerting humanity that the use of prayers alone for peace was futile, and could no longer be effective without definite action.

> Will you use prayers for peace, and then patiently wait for the forces of good to fight your battle and for God to do the work? I tell you that your prayers and your wishes are unavailing when divorced from right and potent action.[10]

At the end of this message Djwhal Khul commented that the first stanza was not used as potently as it should have been.

> The Great Invocation was rendered relatively powerless, from the angle of dynamic usefulness, because the majority of those who used it turned it into a peace prayer. It was instead a great spiritually militant invocative demand. This must not happen with this Stanza of Invocation. It is a demand; it is also an authoritative affirmation of existent fact; it sets in motion agencies and forces hitherto quiescent, and these can change the face of the world battlefield; it invokes the Prince of Peace, but He carries a sword, and the effects of His activity may prove surprising to those who see only the needs of the form aspect of humanity.[11]

The Prince of Peace mentioned in the quotation above is the "the Rider from the Secret Place." Attention is drawn to this remark in order to show how DK is reiterating that certain illusions and glamours in the beliefs of spiritually minded people may be surrounding the ideal of the Christ and the Hierarchy in regard to war and the need to combat evil forces which threaten human liberty. It is also an indication of the possibility that humanity can call forth this Rider if the invocative demand is coupled with positive action. This somewhat mystical reference to the Rider is a prelude to the more direct appeal for the reappearance of the Christ which became possible once the tide of WWII was turned in favor of the Allies.

According to DK, this turning point came between December of 1941 and April 1942. It was during this period that America entered the war after the Japanese attack on Pearl Harbor. Having been forced to drop its neutral position, the USA was able to mobilize its national will and resources to fight the Axis forces. In a message dated December, 1941 DK states:

> The determination and the inner purpose of humanity will be so definite during the period when the Sun will begin to move northward—from December 25th until June 22nd, 1942—that the future of humanity for many hundreds of years will be decided.[12]

DK next urges all his students to use and distribute both stanzas of the Great Invocation for,

...one will invoke the Rider from the secret place...the other will invoke the Lords of Liberation.

The blended invocation and the united call from the different levels of the human consciousness will bring a mighty appeal to bear upon the hidden Centres of the "Saving Force." It is this united appeal which must now be organised.[13]

The combined efforts of all those who stood against the Axis powers were apparently succeeding from the viewpoint of DK because in a message dated August, 1942 He stated:

The critical point is now passed, and the humanitarian grasp of the issues involved, and the unity existing among the Allied Nations, guarantee the inevitable defeat of the Axis Powers.[14]

DK gives some indication of how important the use of the Great Invocation was in the following passages from August 9, 1945 entitled "The Release of Atomic Energy." He discusses the profound effects of splitting the atom and the fact that the race between the Allies and the Axis to develop a bomb caused "enormous tension in hierarchical circles."[15] If they [Axis] had succeeded "it would have led to a major planetary disaster."[17] Djwhal Khul states further that:

You will now understand the meaning of the words used by so many of you in the second of the Great Invocations: *The hour of service of the saving force has now arrived.* This "saving force" is the energy which science has released into the world for the destruction, first of all, of those who continue (if they do) to defy the Forces of Light working through the United Nations.[17]

Finally, comes a relatively shocking passage:

The evil forces were closer to success than any of you have ever dreamed. They were so close to success in 1942 that there were four months when the members of the spiritual Hierarchy had made every possible arrangement to withdraw from human contact for an indefinite and unforeseen period of time...

The necessity to withdraw was averted. I may not say in what manner, beyond telling you that the Lords of Liberation took certain unexpected steps. This They were led to do owing to the invocative powers of humanity, used consciously by all those upon the side of the will-to-good and unconsciously by all men of goodwill.[18]

According to this information, the use of the first two stanzas of the Great Invocation along with the enormous efforts of the Allies combined to defeat the Axis powers and the Forces of Darkness. The final passage through this planetary crisis led to the decision of the Rider to now come forth, and this in turn led to the giving out of the third and final stanza of the Great Invocation. This third stanza is the most potent of the three, and according to Djwhal Khul sums up the complete new teachings of the Christ (formerly called the Rider) for the Aquarian Age.

The Great Invocation: Stanza Three

Each epoch has its own word. This word is as a key to the lock. Ancient Teachings continually spoke about a potent word which was contained in a precise and brief formula. Immutable, like a crystal of known composition, it is impossible to alter in any way the words of these formulas: impossible either to lengthen or to shorten. The guaranty of Cosmos is in the casting of these words.[19]

The third stanza appears next and it is printed in every book written by Alice Bailey. The format as laid out in those books is the one that will be used to explore the deeper aspects of the Great Invocation later in this book. It appears as follows:

> From the point of Light within the Mind of God
> Let light stream forth into the minds of men.
> Let Light descend on Earth.
> From the point of Love within the Heart of God
> Let love stream forth into the hearts of men.
> May Christ return to Earth.
> From the centre where the Will of God is known
> Let purpose guide the little wills of men—
> The purpose which the Masters know and serve.
> From the centre which we call the race of men
> Let the Plan of Love and Light work out
> And may it seal the door where evil dwells.
> Let Light and Love and Power restore the Plan on Earth.

From what is written by Djwhal Khul about the Great Invocation, this third stanza is the most powerful and significant prayer ever used on our planet. In *The Reappearance of the Christ* DK says:

The agony of the war, and the distress of the entire human family led Christ, in the year 1945, to come to a great decision—a decision which found expression in two most important statements. He announced to the assembled spiritual Hierarchy and to all His servants and disciples on Earth that He had decided to emerge again into physical contact with humanity, *if* they would bring about the initial stages of establishing right human relations; secondly, He gave to the world (for the use of the "man in the street") one of the oldest prayers ever known, but one which hitherto had not been permitted to be used except by the most exalted, spiritual Beings. He used it Himself for the first time, we are told, at the time of the Full Moon of June, 1945, which is recognised as the Full Moon of the Christ, just as the Full Moon of May is that of the Buddha. It was not easy to translate these ancient phrases (so ancient that they are without date or background of any kind) into modern words, but it has been done, and the Great Invocation, which may eventually become the world prayer, was pronounced by Him and taken down by His disciples.[20] Two things are especially interesting about this passage: first, the fact that the "phrases" are of very ancient origin, and second, the fact that the Christ was only permitted to use the Great Invocation in June of 1945, for prior to this date only "the most exalted spiritual Beings" had used it.

These two points indicate the great potency and importance of this invocation. These statements make clear we are not dealing with an ordinary prayer created just recently at a time of humanity's need.

> If one may venture to speak in such terms (reverent and symbolical), the reward accorded to the Christ, as He announced His decision [to reappear in the world, JB] as final and irrevocable, was the permission or rather the right to use a certain great Invocation—never before granted....The right to use certain great Words of Power or "Stanzas of Direction" is never lightly accorded. The decision of Christ to appear again among men, bringing His disciples with Him, drew forth this permission from the Lord of the World, the Ancient of Days.[21]

This quotation lays further emphasis on the tremendous magnitude of this invocation by showing that the Lord of the World, Sanat Kumara Himself, granted permission for the Christ to use it. This special permission, along with the facts of the invocation's ancient origin and use only by "exalted spiritual Beings" until 1945, adds a whole new perspective and significance to this sacred "Stanza of Direction." But, before we investigate these deeper and larger issues it is best to examine the words themselves, for much food for thought exists on the outer surface of this invocation that provides nourishment to the soul.

Commentaries On the Great Invocation

Since 1949 some articles about the Great Invocation have been written by various students of the esoteric philosophy taught by Djwhal Khul through AAB; however, the literature available on the Great Invocation is not extensive. No books are written specifically about the Great Invocation alone, although individual chapters and discussions appear in some esoteric and spiritual books as part of a wider topic. World Goodwill[22] produces a 16-page pamphlet entitled *The Great Invocation: The Use and Significance of the Great Invocation.*One of the earliest commentaries on the Great Invocation is an article written by Foster Bailey which appeared in the June-July 1951 issue of *The Beacon.* In this article Mr. Bailey interprets the invocation by the various stanzas. An extensive extract from this article gives not only a fine analysis of portions of the Great Invocation, but also serves as a typical example of how the Great Invocation is usually interpreted:

> In the first stanza the words "From the point of Light within the Mind of God" are a direct reference to the divine source of light which is the Universal Soul. This Soul includes all souls in all kingdoms, and is the source of light for the animal soul and for the individual human soul and for the soul of humanity as a whole....
> In the second stanza the words "From the point of Love within the Heart of God" refer specifically to the occult Hierarchy of the planet, of which the

Christ is the Head....

The combined effect of the merging of this light and love in the form of spiritual energy, as invoked by these two stanzas, produces that loving understanding which fecundates the hearts of all men....

The third stanza deals with "The centre where the Will of God is known." This is Shamballa, the centre from Which the Hierarchy draws its life; the centre from which the Christ and those standing closest around him draw the knowledge of the Plan....It is the focal point on this planet for the reception of the direct potency of the will of God....

The fourth stanza specifically directs the invoked energies into that centre

of the divine manifestation which is humanity as a whole. The Invocation conforms to the fundamental Plan itself in its recognition that it is only humanity in its own right and by its own evolution and spiritual effort, which can bring the Divine plan into manifestation on this planet....

The Invocation closes with a powerful mantric series of words that gathers up its meaning and focuses it on the exact point of the ultimate purpose. This restoring of the Plan on earth by humanity itself with the aid of the Christ and the Hierarchy, is the grand climax of the whole evolutionary process to date.[23]

Foster Bailey's commentary provides a wonderful beginning for an exploration of some basic principles of the ageless wisdom. The Great Invocation is appealing to so many people because it contains the fundamental qualities found in most of the world's religions. In stanza one the Mind of God is stated to be the source of spiritual Light, and the call goes forth for this Light to enter into the human world providing spiritual guidance and wisdom to all humanity. Foster Bailey relates this universal Light to the "Universal Soul" which refers back to the world soul of Plato and Plotinus.

Table 3. Triplicities of the Great Invocation.

Great Invocation	Stanza One	Stanza Two	Stanza Three
Ageless Wisdom	Light	Love	Will
	Mind of God	Heart of God	Will of God
Greek	Nous	Logos	Pneuma
Christian	Holy Spirit	Son	Father
Hindu	Brahma	Vishnu	Shiva
Mahayana Buddhist	Nirmanakaya	Sambhogakaya	Dharmakaya
Egyptian	Isis	Horus	Osiris

Reference is made in the second stanza to the Heart of God, and the broad and sweeping theme of Love. The invocation calls for Christ to return to Earth. Many religions recognize the principle of divine intervention through a savior. Christianity teaches the second coming of Christ; the Jews await the Messiah; the Buddhists expect the future Buddha to appear as Maitreya, and the Islamic faith speaks of the coming Imam Mahdi. This stanza also relates directly to Hierarchy which represents the Heart of God with the Christ as its Leader. Stanza three deals with the Will of God and relates to Shamballa. These aspects of the Great Invocation appear in table 3 along with corresponding representations of deity from various religions and philosophies.

Foster Bailey offers further commentary on the Great Invocation in two of his books. In *Things To Come*, he points out the power and importance of the three aspects in relation to humanity:

> The Great Invocation is unique in that it invokes all three divine aspects in one spoken world-wide prayer. Light invokes the third aspect, love invokes the second aspect and will invokes the first aspect. All three will eventually be lived by in the human family. The potency of all three combined is unimaginably tremendous....
>
> The Great Invocation as a whole acts as a word of power. The words themselves are a divine energy vehicle. When pronounced clearly and intelligently this energy is released. Therefore, The Invocation prevails in its own right if only it is used.[24]

In another book by Foster Bailey entitled *Reflections*, he comments briefly on the need for cooperation between human beings:

> A key word for the Great Invocation is *cooperate*, not merely follow. The Christ uses the Great Invocation to hasten God's Plan and to evoke spiritual potency for his work and when we rightly use the Great Invocation we are cooperating with him.[25]

The themes of the three aspects, the Christ, humanity, and cooperation are all central and vital to the meaning of the Great Invocation. Mary Bailey (who later married Foster after Alice's death), retired president of Lucis Trust, discusses the Great Invocation in her book, *A Learning Experience*. Discussing the importance of the three aspects of light, love, and power, she says:

> We need a much deeper and more inclusive understanding of the three basic energies the Invocation presents, because they, in turn, embody the significance of the Christ's work throughout the Aquarian era.[26]

Without the cooperation of humanity—freely given—the Plan of God cannot succeed. This idea is brought out in stanzas four and five which link the restoration of the Plan to humanity. The human race has come of age and must now accept its responsibility as a co-partner in the evolutionary process of our world. This increasing sense of responsibility is evident in the environmental and world population crises, to name only two areas of global concern. The Christ, representing all humanity, is said to use the Great Invocation daily. If it is accepted that this world prayer is a vital factor in the spiritual evolution of the world, then the effect of people saying the Great Invocation at least once a day becomes a powerful service in cooperation with the Christ and the Hierarchy, as well as with Sanat Kumara and Shamballa.

Invocation as a Tool for Spiritual Emergence

Prayer has always played a part in the life of humanity. The appeal to a Higher Force, to God, is an intrinsic part of all religions. The concept of invocation as explained by Djwhal Khul involves a greater use of the mind and the will than in the past, especially as it has been applied to religious practice. In discussing the possibility of a world religion in the next century, DK states that such a religion will be based on the "science of invocation and evocation."

> The science of invocation and evocation will take the place of what we now call "prayer" and "worship." Be not disturbed by the use of the word "science." It is not the cold and heartless intellectual thing so oft depicted. It is in reality the intelligent organisation of spiritual energy and of the forces of love, and these, when effective, will evoke the response of spiritual Beings Who can again walk openly among men, and thus establish a close relation and a constant communication between humanity and the spiritual Hierarchy.[27]

Djwhal Khul goes on to explain that in the future the practice of invocation will fall into two parts. The first part will involve large numbers of people trained to invoke those spiritual forces of the planet Who, when called, will approach humanity; this involves the Hierarchy of Masters and the Christ. Along with this invocative appeal to Hierarchy is the demand for "light, liberation, and understanding." The idea is to raise the level of approach to God and the spiritual Hierarchy from a purely personal, emotional, devotional level to a point that is mental and less emotional yet filled with compassion and heart energy. This is meant to be an act of invocative service.

Djwhal Khul describes the second part of prayer as an invocative psycho-spiritual tool of greater potency and conscious direction than available today. DK says:

> There will also be the skilled work of invocation as practised by those who have trained their minds through right meditation, who know the potency of formulas, mantrams and invocations and who work consciously. They will increasingly use certain great formulas of words which will later be given to the race, just as the Lord's Prayer was given by the Christ, and as the New Invocation has been given out for use at this time by the Hierarchy.[28]

When the Lord of the World gave the Christ permission to use this ancient invocation, DK referred to this decision by saying, "The right to use great Words of Power or 'Stanzas of Direction' is never lightly accorded." This indicates the magnitude, power, and sacredness of the Great Invocation, and at the same time it demonstrates the tremendous importance of Christ's decision to reappear in the world. It is a mantram of ancient origin and able, if used properly, to effect great spiritual change. The Tibetan defines mantrams in this way:

> A mantram is a combination of sounds, of words and of phrases that, through virtue of certain rhythmic effects, achieve results that would not be possible apart from them....
>
> The potency of a mantram depends upon the point in evolution of the man who employs it. Uttered by an ordinary man it serves to stimulate the good within his bodies, to protect him, and it will also prove of beneficent influence upon his environment. Uttered by an adept or initiate its possibilities for good are infinite and far-reaching.[29]

Referring specifically to the Great Invocation DK goes even further.

> No one can use this Invocation or prayer for illumination and for love without causing powerful changes in his own attitudes; his life intention, character and goals will be changed and his life will be altered and made spiritually useful.[30]

In a video-taped interview,[31] Mary Bailey tells the story of the night Alice Bailey received the Great Invocation from Djwhal Khul. According to the story, Djwhal Khul was so intent on the words of the invocation being exact that He almost materialized in the dictation room in order to accomplish the transmission. This was something that had never been considered in all the years of their work together as far as anyone knows. Apparently, this particular mantram was so important, it had to be recorded as close to the ancient phrases as possible using specific English wording.

Beyond the obvious fact that this invocation is a mantram, a "Word of Power," and a "Stanza of Direction," is the suggestion that its use will not only affect the one who uses it but, perhaps more importantly, it will stimulate and accelerate the spiritual evolution of the entire planet.

> For the reception of this last part or final stanza of the great hierarchical "Invocation for Power and Light," all previous teaching you have received and all your earlier meditation work was simply an elementary prelude. In receiving this Invocation, in its use and distribution, you have been participating in a cosmic event of tremendous importance.[32]

The fact that this Great Invocation was not a mantram suddenly formulated in order to meet the spiritual needs of humanity during recent world crises is another indicator that it has some deeper, more fundamental relationship to the Plan and purpose of our planet. Evidence of this can be found in the following quotation:

> The final stanza of the "Invocation for Power and Light," as it is called in the Archives of the Masters, is apparently simple. It has, in these Archives, an indicatory symbol beside it which indicates the era or period in human histo-

ry during which it can and should be used. It is interesting to us to note that the evolution of humanity is in line with the indicated timing.[33]

The possible implications and significance of this statement by DK will be explored in chapter 4. For now, it is enough to know that sufficient reason exists to explore the Great Invocation for any clues that may reveal an esoteric meaning lying behind the words of its outer form.

Notes

1.   Alice A. Bailey, *Discipleship In the New Age,* vol. II, 157.
2.   See Bailey, *The Externalisation of the Hierarchy,* 123.
3.   Ibid., 125.
4.   Ibid., v.
5.   Ibid., 21.
6.   Ibid., 26.
7.   Ibid., 133.
8.   Ibid., 171.
9.   Ibid., 171.
10.   Ibid., 233.
11.   Ibid., 250-51.
12.   Ibid., 337.
13.   Ibid., 338.
14.   Ibid., 367.
15.   Ibid., 493.
16.   Ibid., 493.
17.   Ibid., 497.
18.   Ibid., 493-94.
19.   *New Era Community*, 42-43.
20.   Bailey, *The Reappearance of the Christ*, 30-31.
21.   Ibid., 72-73.
22.   World Goodwill is a branch of Lucis Trust, the umbrella organization which oversees the publication of the Alice A. Bailey books, the operation of the Arcane School, and various other service activities.
23.   Foster Bailey, "The Great Invocation," *The Beacon* Vol. XXX No. 3-4 (June-July 1951): 81, 82, 83.
24.   Foster Bailey, *Things To Come*, 127.
25.   Foster Bailey, *Reflections*, 115.
26.   Mary Bailey, *A Learning Experience*, 114.
27.   Bailey, *The Reappearance of the Christ*, 151.
28.   Ibid., 152.
29.   Alice A. Bailey, *A Treatise on Cosmic Fire*, n. 926.
30.   Bailey, *Discipleship in the New Age*, vol. II, 168.
31.   Mary Bailey, *Bridge to the Future*, video, 1984.

SIGNATURE OF SIRIUS TRANSFERRED TO THE COSMIC TRIANGLE OF THE GREAT BEAR, THE PLEIADES, AND SIRIUS

GLOSSARY

Acrostic. Word play in which the first letters of a series of lines in a poem or narrative spell a name, epigram or motto.

Ageless Wisdom. The name given to a transcendent teaching which forms the basis of all religion, science, art, and philosophy. It is a secret science of life purportedly given to humanity by divine Instructors and taught in the ancient mystery schools of initiation.

AN. Acronym for Alpha Number.

AN Method. A numerological method of converting letters to numbers using the natural order of the alphabet wherein A = 1 and Z = 26. For instance, the letter J equals 10 or has an AN value of 10 using this numerological method because it is the tenth letter of the alphabet.

AN Value. Alpha Number Value. The sum of a word or phrase derived using the AN method. For instance, the AN value of the word "Isis" equals 56 (9 + 19 + 9 + 19).

Aquarian Age. Sometimes referred to as the New Age. This is a cycle of approximately 2,150 years in which the Sun appears in the constellation of Aquarius due to the precession of the equinox. The Aquarian Age is characterized by group activities, brotherhood, humanitarianism, and the use of the mind.

Ashram. A Sanskrit term for a group of spiritual students gathered around a teacher or guru.

In the Ageless Wisdom, a specific type of group consciousness comprised of spiritual aspirants and disciples dedicated to a common goal. There are various levels and kinds of ashrams but they all have an advanced

spiritual teacher as a leader. Ashrams are places of activity and work
for the betterment of the world, not places of guru worship. Ashrams are
not necessarily located on the physical plane.

Astral. Emotional or desire nature. A quality of consciousness or plane of
existence in which most souls find themselves after death. Usually considered a plane of glamour and illusion.

Atlantis. An ancient civilization of advanced technology that was
destroyed through greed, ignorance, and the misuse of science. In the
Ageless Wisdom this is the generic term applied to the fourth root-race.

Baconian. An individual who believes that Francis Bacon wrote the works
of Shakespeare. Baconians believe that the works of Shakespeare contain coded information in the form of acrostics and numbers related to
the name "Francis Bacon" or to interests and causes which Bacon sup-
ported, i.e. Masonry and the Rosicrucians.

Branch-race. A smaller unit within a sub-race. There are seven branch-
races in each sub-race. Although branch-races are definitely part of the
the Ageless Wisdom teaching, there is no definitive example of how to
identify a branch-race in the current world or in history.

Causal Body. Also called the egoic lotus. Symbolically the "command center" of the incarnating soul from lifetime to lifetime. When a human
being incarnates on the physical plane, it is from the causal body on
the higher mental plane from which it emerges. Following death, the
human soul ultimately returns to the causal body after various experiences on the astral and lower mental planes. The causal body houses or
stores the thousands of experiences of a human being over many lifetimes. Thus, it is a vessel of the accumulated wisdom of the ages.

Central Spiritual Sun. That aspect of any solar Logos which relates to
the Monad or life of that cosmic Entity. The first aspect of a solar Logos
is associated with the highest Will and Purpose.

Chain. That part of a planetary scheme which comprises a series of seven
globes. Each globe is a specific dimensional "locale" in which a planetary
Logos experiences evolutionary life and works out some particular purpose generally called God's Plan. Since the seven globes are connected
in a series they are referred to as a chain. Seven chains equal one planetary scheme.

Christ. The supreme Teacher of Humanity and Leader of the spiritual
Hierarchy. The Christ is a title for the One Who holds that high position of leadership in the Hierarchy. Through the ages there existed various advanced souls Who headed the Hierarchy. In the Ageless Wisdom,
the Christ is not limited to the role of a religious figure, but is the
supreme spiritual Leader and Teacher Who transcends all religions and
philosophies.

Christ Principle. 1. Associated with the soul and the second aspect of the
basic triplicity of the Ageless Wisdom. 2. Consciousness, the product of

spirit and substance. 3. The evolutionary force which propels consciousness growth.

Cipher. Any code based on a particular key which is substituted for the actual text of a message or other writing.

Creative Hierarchy. A life stream interacting with the various planes of consciousness for purposes of furthering the evolutionary development of entire planets and solar systems. There are twelve Creative Hierarchies, each associated with a particular constellation of the zodiac. Only seven Creative Hierarchies are actively manifesting in our solar system. One of these is the human Hierarchy of which the human kingdom is a lower reflection.

Cryptology. The science and study of codes; encoding and decoding information in various forms

Cryptography. The science and art of encoding and decoding messages in written form. Creating secret messages.

Disciple. Any person who is committed to spiritual growth regardless of religious affiliation. The Ageless Wisdom extends the definition of disciple to include any person who is working for the betterment of the human condition and not just for personal gain.

ESC. Elizabethan Simple Cipher. A cipher system employed during the Elizabethan age. Each letter of the twenty-four letter English alphabet was assigned the numbers 1-24 according to the natural order of the letters. Because there were no spelling rules in that time, words could be spelled in ways which allowed their total ESC value to equal number values meaningful only to those who knew the key. The ESC system can be used according to the modern AN and RAN methods; the only difference being that there are twenty-four letters and not twenty-six.

Esoteric Astrology. Astrology of the soul rather than the personality. This form of astrology is developed by Djwhal Khul in the book by the same title, in which emphasis is placed on spiritual development rather than the mundane events of the outer life such as career, money, relationships, etc.

Essence Value. A number value produced by adding together the AN or RAN value of a word and the word-position number of that word within any given writing. For instance, the first word of the Great Invocation is "From." Its word-position value is 1 and its AN value is 52. Therefore, its Essence Value is 53 (1 + 52 = 53). An Essence Value can be used in any cipher system, such as ESC.

Etheric. A specific type of substance lying just beyond the range of the five physical senses. Etheric matter is still considered part of the world of form despite its invisibility to ordinary sense perception. The ethers are divided into four distinct types. All physical objects have an etheric counterpart which is the underlying structural network carrying life and consciousness to the outer world.

Factor. Two or more numbers associated through the product of their multiplication. For instance, 2 and 3 are factors of 6. In esoteric numerology a word or phrase is subjectively linked to the factors which interact to give it birth.

First Aspect. That part of the basic triplicity of the Ageless Wisdom relating to pure Spirit, Non-duality, Will, the Christian Father of the Trinity, and the Monad.

Gematria. The specific conversion of letters to numbers in order to penetrate into the inner meaning and correspondences between terms, names, and phrases. As in esoteric astrology, this form of numerology focuses on spiritual qualities and subjective relationships rather than on outer mundane affairs.

Globe. A specific world located in a particular dimension or plane of consciousness. For instance, the Earth globe is located on the dense physical plane. A globe exists as one unit in a series of seven globes called a chain.

Hierarchy. 1. In general, the great chain of being found throughout the universe in which life systems contain lesser systems and are themselves contained within greater systems. All systems are alive, conscious, and intelligent, pursuing their own growth as part of some greater whole system. 2. The spiritual Hierarchy of the Earth is a second aspect center of activity led by the Christ and comprised of Beings Who have evolved through the human stage of consciousness. All the Members of the Hierarchy were once human beings. The purpose of the Hierarchy is to oversee planetary evolution in all the kingdoms of nature including the human. The Hierarchy never interferes with humanity's free will. It guides and teaches, leaving humanity the freedom to make its choices based on the spiritual principles expressed through the various religions and philosophies made available throughout the ages.

Individualization. The evolutionary method of creating individual and distinct souls with the free will to pursue life in relative freedom. This planetary event occurred about eighteen million years ago and resulted in the creation of the human kingdom. This initiative by Sanat Kumara and 104 other Kumaras began about twenty million years ago but took two million years to achieve success. Sirius was involved in the crisis of individualization because it involved the initiation of our planetary Logos.

Initiation. A special form of consciousness expansion employed to accelerate evolution. There are nine possible initiations available on our planet. Completion of the first five initiations liberates a person from the human kingdom and allows full entry into the Hierarchy. Initiation originates on Sirius, and the Christ is the most advanced Sirian Initiate Whose soul originated on Earth.

Invocation. 1. A prayer or mantram. 2. The act of calling forth some higher power to intervene in a time of crisis.

Karma. The result of cause and effect. Karma can be positive or negative.
Karma exists at many levels: cosmic, systemic, planetary, racial, national, familial, and individual. All karma in our solar system is governed
by Sirius.

Key Word. A term created for the specific analysis of the Great Invocation.
It is a word in the Great Invocation which is capitalized, excluding the
words which begin each line. There are twenty-one key words in the
Great Invocation.

Kumaras. Beings of a higher order of life than humans or members of the
Hierarchy. Kumaras are associated with interplanetary levels of activ-
ity. Sanat Kumara, and the Kumaras Who incarnated on Earth with
Him, passed through the human stage of evolution before the Earth
ever existed. They are now world Builders, Creators, and sometimes
Saviors on a universal scale.

Law of Correspondences. Also called the Law of Analogy. A method for
investigating the possible relationships existing between apparently
unconnected objects, people, energies, ideas, or events. The Ageless
Wisdom teaches that objective forms including thoughtforms are actually connected at a deeper subjective, archetypal level. This law helps
penetrate and interpret the concepts and energy patterns found at these
abstract and intuitive planes of consciousness.

Lemuria. The third root-race. The first race of human beings created after
the process of individualization was completed.

Lords of the Flame. Another name for that class of Beings Who brought
manas or mind to animal man. Generally speaking, these are also called
the Kumaras.

Maltese cross. An equal-armed cross in which the arms are arrow-shaped
and pointing inward, converging at a central point. See Templar cross.

Manas. Sanskrit for the "mind principle." This is divided into two aspects:
higher mind, producing abstract thought and wisdom, and lower mind,
producing concrete thought and knowledge. It was the principle of
manas which the Lords of the Flame or the Kumaras instilled in the
Lemurian race. The manasic principle was successfully "individualized"
resulting in the self-conscious human soul or individual. These individualized units of consciousness resulted in the human kingdom.

Mantram. Sanskrit for prayer; also called mantra. More specifically, the
Ageless Wisdom teaches that mantrams produce powerful effects when
sounded according to a particular rhythm. The Great Invocation is a
mantram of high potency when sounded with complete mental concentration and focused intent.

Master. A member of the spiritual Hierarchy Who was formerly a human
being. These advanced souls are called Masters because they have

learned all the lessons which the human experience can teach. They have transcended the human level of living by mastering every aspect of the human condition. They now work toward mastering higher levels of existence.

Master Jesus. A Member of the Hierarchy Who leads the Christian religion in all its aspects. This Master was overshadowed by the Christ in Palestine 2,000 years ago. Jesus and the One Who is known as the Christ are two separate and distinct Beings.

Master Number. 1. In traditional numerology, 11 and 22 are considered master numbers, although some numerologists use 11, 22, 33, 44, 55, 66, 77, 88, and 99 as master numbers. This book uses only the numbers 11 and 22. 2. Master numbers are not reduced to single digits (1 + 1 = 2 or 2 + 2 = 4) in esoteric numerology (or traditional numerology, in most cases); as root values they symbolize the use and control of energy. For instance, the word "light" equals 56 or 29 depending on whether the AN or RAN method is used to determine its numeric value. However, its root value is 11 by either method (5 + 6 or 2 + 9). Thus, the word "light" is not reduced to 2 (1 + 1) because it is a master number. Note that not every word reduces to a master number when it is subjected to both the AN and RAN methods. For instance, the word "Isis" equals 56 (AN) and 20 (RAN). Therefore, its root value for the AN method is the master number 11; but its root value for the RAN method is 2 because 2 + 0 = 2.

Monad. The divine spark of a human being. It corresponds to the first aspect of the basic triplicity of the Ageless Wisdom. The monad also corresponds to the Father aspect of the trinity.

Non-sacred Planet. A term used to differentiate the spiritual evolution of the planetary Logoi in our solar system; a planetary Logos Who has not yet taken one of the higher cosmic initiations. The Earth is a non-sacred planet, but our planetary Logos, through the incarnation of Sanat Kumara, is currently undergoing that particular initiatory process which will make our planet sacred. Technically, the Earth is already a sacred planet, but until this can be practically expressed at the physical level through the manifesting kingdoms (especially the human), the Earth is still considered a non-sacred planet. The other non-sacred planets in our solar system are the Sun, the Moon, Mars, and Pluto.

Perfect Number. Any number which equals the sum of its factors, not counting itself. For instance, 6 is a perfect number. Its factors are 1, 2, and 3 (1 x 6 and 2 x 3). Thus 1 + 2 + 3 = 6. The first three perfect numbers are 6, 28 and 496.

Personality. 1. The form manifestation of the soul. The personality is the instrument used by the soul to contact the lower mental, astral, and physical planes of consciousness. 2. The personality is a type of consciousness which is self-centered. It represents a stage of consciousness growth wherein individuality is developed.

Piscean Age. The 2,150 year zodiacal cycle which is now ending as the Sun precesses into the constellation of Aquarius. The Piscean era was characterized by faith, devotion, idealism, sacrifice, individual effort, and emotions.

Plane. 1. A level or dimension of consciousness. Each plane has its own characteristics. For instance, the astral plane is based on emotions and feelings; the mental plane is a world of thoughts and thoughtforms. 2. The Ageless Wisdom describes 343 possible planes of consciousness. There are seven cosmic planes. Each cosmic plane is divided into seven subplanes, called systemic planes. Each one of the seven systemic planes is divided once more into seven subplanes. Thus, there are 7 x 7 x 7 planes of consciousness (343) recognized at this time by the Ageless Wisdom. Consequently, the densest level of substance in which consciousness can express itself can be notated as the 343rd sub-subplane of the entire known spectrum of consciousness.

Precession. The apparent backward motion of the sun through the twelve signs of the zodiac due to the wobble of the Earth's axis. This wobble shifts the apparent position of the sun backward, relative to the zodiacal signs about one degree every seventy years. It takes approximately 25,880 years for the sun to complete one revolution through all the constellations of the zodiac. The beginning of an age, such as the age of Aquarius, is measured by the year when the sun enters the first degree of a sign on the vernal equinox or first day of spring.

Planetary Logos. A cosmic Entity Who ensouls or manifests through a planet. Such a planetary Logos manifests through a planetary scheme of worlds. The planetary Logos of the Earth Scheme is currently incarnated as Sanat Kumara.

Planetary Scheme. The entire series of worlds through which a planetary Logos creates and manifests during the cyclic activity of a solar system.

Pyramidal Number. A number which is the sum of a series of square numbers. For instance, 14 is a pyramidal number because it is the sum of 1 x 1, 2 x 2 and 3 x 3 or 1 + 4 + 9. Fourteen wooden cubes can be arranged in the form of a pyramid by placing 9 cubes in a square (3 x 3) at the base, 4 cubes on top of these (2 x 2), and 1 cube at the apex (1 x 1).

RAN. Acronym for Reduced Alpha Number.

RAN Method. A numerological method of converting letters to numbers using the reduced values of the alphabet. For instance, the letter J is the 10th letter of the alphabet, but instead of counting J as 10 it is reduced to 1 by adding 1 + 0. Thus the letter J = 1 or has a RAN value of 1 as opposed to its AN value which equals 10.

RAN Value. Reduced Alpha Number Value. The sum of a word or phrase

derived using the RAN method. For instance, the RAN value of the
word "Isis" equals 20 (9 + 1 + 9 + 1).

Root Value. A numerological term applied to the lowest number to which
any word or phrase can be reduced. For instance, the word "god" has an
AN value of 26 (7 (g) + 15 (o) + 4 (d)), a RAN value of 17 (7 (g) + 6 (o) +
4 (d)) and a root value of 8 (2 + 6 or 1 + 7). No matter what the AN or
RAN value of any word or phrase is, it can always be reduced to a root
number.

Root-race. 1. A distinct type of consciousness development seeded into a
particular group of souls living in human form. The physical race in
which a particular quality of consciousness develops is irrelevant
because a root-race has no relation to racial body type. For instance,
the current fifth root-race is developing lower manas or the ability to
use the concrete, logical, reasoning faculty. The ability to integrate
doing, feeling, and thinking (manas) into a smoothly operating personality is the present goal for the humanity of the modern world. This is
fifth root-race consciousness. Each root-race is the means by which a
planetary Logos experiences, develops, and synthesizes a particular
principle or quality of consciousness. The collective psychological fruit
of a root-race is absorbed by the planetary Logos as part of His own
growth experience in the cosmos. 2. Each globe produces seven root-
races. On the Earth globe the first two root-races were etheric. The first
physical plane root-race was the Lemurian, but technically it is referred
to as the third root-race. This group of humans developed the ability to
integrate basic survival instincts and physical plane activity. The
Atlantean root-race, the fourth, developed and integrated the emotional and feeling principle with that already developed by the Lemurian
race. Our current humanity is the Aryan fifth root-race. It is combining
the physical, emotional, and mental principles into one integrated unit
of consciousness, called the personality. This is being accomplished
through the rapid spread of education and technology throughout the
world. NOTE: Hitler used the Aryan idea to spread his insanely distorted and evil philosophy of the superman. *This was, still is, and
always will be a complete misuse and distortion of the root-race concept.*
To repeat, root-race has nothing to do with the color of a person's skin
or their ethnic background; it is simply a term used to describe the overall development of human consciousness.

Round. A cycle of experience which encompasses the passage of seven root-
races through seven globes of a chain. Ideally, since there are seven
rounds in every chain this means each globe will eventually host forty-
nine root-races. Taken as a whole, one chain of seven rounds will host
343 root-races, or 7 root-races x 7 globes x 7 rounds = one chain.

Sacred Planet. The definition of a planetary Logos Who has taken a particular cosmic initiation resulting in His liberation from lower cosmic

planes of consciousness, and His consequential expansion into higher cosmic levels of experience and life.

Sanat Kumara. 1. The incarnated planetary Logos of the Earth. In terms analogous to the human experience, Sanat Kumara is the personality incarnation of the soul of the planetary Logos. 2. Loosely translated from Sanskrit, Sanat means "first" and Kumara means "eternal youth" or "born with difficulty." Sanat Kumara is also called Melchizedek, The Lord of the World, The Great Sacrifice, and The Ancient of Days.

Scheme. The Ageless Wisdom philosophy applies the term scheme to the entire evolution of any given planet in our solar system. The evolutionary phases of a planetary scheme encompass seven chains. Each chain is composed of seven globes. Therefore, the evolutionary cycle of an entire planetary scheme consists of forty-nine globes.

Second Aspect. A term referring to the soul or middle aspect of the basic triplicity of the Ageless Wisdom. It is the Christ principle and the Cosmic Christ. In terms of the Christian trinity, it is the Son. It also corresponds to Love-Wisdom and Universal Consciousness.

Seven Rays. The seven distinct cosmic energies which constitute all life and planes of consciousness as we know it in our solar system and in the One About Whom Naught May Be Said. The seven rays are: the first Ray of Will and Purpose, the second Ray of Love-Wisdom, the third Ray of Intelligent Activity, the fourth Ray of Harmony Through Conflict or Beauty, the fifth Ray of Science and Concrete Knowledge, the sixth Ray of Devotion and Idealism, and the seventh Ray of Ritual and Order.

Shamballa. The highest spiritual center of our planet, the focal point of Sanat Kumara, and the supreme ruling spiritual Council for all the kingdoms of our planet. This is the center where the Will of God is known. According to the Ageless Wisdom, Shamballa is located on the highest physical etheric plane somewhere in central Asia. Shamballa is related to the First Aspect of the basic triplicity.

Shekinah. A Hebrew term generally translated as divine Intelligence, Sophia, Wisdom, and spiritual Light. This is the divine feminine principle and is related to the third aspect of the basic triplicity.

Sirian Cross. 1. An equal-armed cross related to the star system of Sirius. 2. A graphic symbol used to decode specific sections of the Great Invocation using esoteric numerology or gematria.

Sirius. 1. The most influential cosmic source of spiritual energy in our solar system. 2. The fifth closest known star to our solar system, 8.7 light years from Earth. There are at least two, maybe three stars in the Sirian system; Sirius A, the main star and Sirius B, a white dwarf which orbits the much larger Sirius A approximately once every fifty years. There is some evidence that a third star is part of the Sirian system but this has not yet been proven.

Solar Logos. A cosmic Entity that ensouls an entire solar system when in physical manifestation. The Ageless Wisdom teaches that our solar Logos will manifest three times. During each manifestation one aspect of the basic triplicity will be perfected. Our solar logos has already manifested in an earlier cycle. That first solar system perfected the third aspect of Intelligence. Our present solar system is the second manifestation of the solar Logos in which the second aspect of Love-Wisdom is being brought to perfection. The third solar system will perfect the first aspect of the basic triplicity, that of Will.

Soul. The second aspect of the basic triplicity of the Ageless Wisdom. The soul is consciousness itself. The chief characteristic of the soul is group relationship. Soul consciousness corresponds to the Christ principle, the Son—the product of divine (Father) spirit and divine (Mother) substance.

Spiritual Triad. 1. The manifestation of the monad on the three planes of atma—spiritual will, buddhi—spiritual love-wisdom and manas—spiritual mind. The spiritual triad is the human correspondence to the three aspects of the basic triplicity of the Ageless Wisdom. As far as is known this triplicity is universal. 2. The human personality, constituted of mind, emotion, and physical body is the lower reflection of the spiritual triad. The lower concrete mind corresponds to higher spiritual, abstract mind, emotions correspond to spiritual love-wisdom, and physical/etheric activities correspond to spiritual will. 3. The soul is the middle principle partaking of both spirit and personality qualities.

Square Number. When any whole number is multiplied by itself, the result is called a square number. For instance, 9 is a square number, being the product of the factors 3 x 3.

Sub-race. A smaller unit within a root-race. There are seven sub-races in each root-race. Sub-races incorporate large regions or continents which transcend national boundaries. For instance, Europe can be considered a sub-race. As in the case with branch-races, there are no strict guidelines available which clearly demarcate sub-races. These races and their subdivisions primarily indicate the general trend of social consciousness of large regions transcending national borders.

Templar Cross. An equal-armed cross in which the arms are triangular and pointing inward (figure 1.1). This cross is similar to a Maltese cross except that the outer edges of the arms are flat and not indented or notched. See Maltese cross. *Coil's Masonic Encylopedia* defines the pattern of the two crosses depicted in figure 1.1 as variant of the Maltese cross. According to *Coil's*, this pattern was adopted by the modern Order of the Knights Templar.

Tetrahedral Number. The sum of a series of triangular numbers. For instance, 20 is a tetrahedral number because it is the sum of the first four triangular numbers 1, 3, 6, and 10 (1 + 3 + 6 + 10 = 20). For instance twenty oranges can be arranged in the form of a tetrahedron by placing 10 in a triangular pattern at the base, a triangular pattern of 6 on top of these, 3 on top of these, and 1 at the apex. The resultant pile of fruit is a tetrahedron or a four-sided object consisting of 20 oranges.

The Great Work. 1. Traditionally, the alchemical process of transmuting lead into gold. 2. Symbolically, it is a transformative process applied to any situation requiring release from unnecessary limitations into an expanded state where new growth can proceed. 3. The spiritual path of redemption. The release of the soul that is identified with material form and thus trapped on the wheel of rebirth or what Christianity considers sin. The Great Work of redemption is transmuting, transforming, and ultimately transfiguring. It involves the process of initiation and consequent release and spiritual evolution of the individual into a greater life, which cannot be accurately described, but only experienced. The Great Work is individual, group, planetary, and cosmic in scope.

Third Aspect. That part of the basic triplicity relating to divine Substance, Intelligence, the divine Feminine, and the Christian Holy Spirit of the Trinity. In the human being it corresponds to the spiritualized personality.

Triangular Number. Any number which is the result of the addition of the numbers one through x. For instance, 10 is a triangular number because it is the result of the addition of the numbers 1 through 4 (1 + 2 + 3 + 4 = 10). Thus, the numbers 10 and 4 have a numeric relationship. The number 14 is not a triangular number because 1 through 4 equals 10 and 1 through 5 equals 15 (1 + 2 + 3 + 4 + 5 = 15). Thus 10 and 15 are triangular numbers, but 14 is not. Triangular numbers are inherently related to the number which produces them.

Word of Power. A mantram or sound formula capable of effecting spiritual, psychological, and physical change when used with the correct note and rhythm. The Great Invocation is a word of power specifically designed to be effective when used with mental concentration and spiritual intent.

Word-position. A term identifying the numeric order a word occupies relative to any given writing. For instance, the Great Invocation is composed of 113 words. The word "From" is the first word and thus occupies word-position 1. The word "Earth" is the last word and thus occupies word-position 113.

World Period. A smaller unit within a round. A world period is that portion of a round on one particular globe. A round describes the passage of forty-nine root-races through seven globes. A world period describes the passage of seven root-races on only one particular globe within a round. For instance, in round five, the third globe (in the chain of seven) is experiencing its fifth world period. In turn, globe four will experience its fifth world period in the same fifth round.

WORKS CITED

Bailey, Alice A. *A Treatise on Cosmic Fire*. 1925. Reprint, New York: Lucis Publishing Co., 1964.

———. *A Treatise on the Seven Rays*. Vol. II. *Esoteric Psychology*. 1942. Reprint, New York: Lucis Publishing Co., 1966.

———. *A Treatise on the Seven Rays*. Vol. III. *Esoteric Astrology*. 1951. Reprint, New York: Lucis Publishing Co., 1970.

———. *A Treatise on the Seven Rays*. Vol. V. *The Rays and the Initiations*. 1960. Reprint, New York: Lucis Publishing Co., 1970.

———. *A Treatise on White Magic*. 1934. Reprint, New York: Lucis Publishing Co., 1979.

———. *Discipleship in the New Age*. Vol. I. 1944. Reprint, New York: Lucis Publishing Co., 1966.

———. *Discipleship in the New Age*. Vol. II. 1955. Reprint, New York: Lucis Publishing Co., 1968.

———. *Initiation, Human and Solar*. 1922. Reprint, New York: Lucis Publishing Co., 1970.

———. *The Externalisation of the Hierarchy*. 1957. Reprint, New York: Lucis Publishing Co., 1968.

———. *The Labours of Hercules*. 1957-58. Reprint. New York: Lucis Publishing Co., 1977.

———. *The Reappearance of the Christ*. 1948. Reprint, New York: Lucis Publishing Co., 1969.

———. *The Unfinished Autobiography*. 1951. Reprint, New York: Lucis Publishing Co., 1951.

———. *Telepathy and the Etheric Vehicle*. 1950. Reprint, New York: Lucis Publishing Co., 1971.

Berges, John. *Sacred Vessel of the Mysteries*. Egg Harbor Township, NJ: Planetwork Press, 1997.

Blavatsky, Helena P. *The Secret Doctrine*. Adyar ed. 6 vols. Adyar, India: Theosophical Publishing House, 1962.

Cedarcrans, Lucille. *The Synthetic Ashram*. Whittier, CA: Wisdom Impressions, 1997.

Coil, Henry Wilson, 33°. *Coil's Masonic Encyclopedia*, revised ed., Allen E. Roberts, 33°. Richmond, VA: Macoy Publishing & Masonic Supply

Co., Inc., 1995.

Dawkins, Peter. *Arcadia*. Warwick, England, UK: Francis Bacon Research Trust, 1988.

———.*The Master*, parts 1 and 2. Warwick, England, UK: Francis Bacon Research Trust, 1993.

———.*The Virgin Ideal*. Warwick, England, UK: Francis Bacon Research Trust, 1982.

Guinagh, Kevin. *Dictionary of Foreign Phrases and Abbreviations*. New York: Pocket Books, 1966.

Hall, Manly P. *The Initiates of Greece and Rome*. Los Angeles: The Philosophical Research Society, Inc., 1981.

———. *The Secret Teachings of All Ages*. Reprint black and white facsimile of Golden Ann. ed. Los Angeles: The Philosophical Research Society, Inc., 1977.

Harold, Edmund. *Master Your Vibration*. Devon, UK: The Spiritual Venturer's Education Trust, 1981.

Higgins, Godfrey. *Anacalypsis* in 2 vols. 1833. Reprint Kila, MT: Kessenger Publishing Co. n.d.

Hollenbach, Karl F. *Francis Rosicross*. Ekron, KY: Dunsinane Hill Publications, 1996.

Johnson, Edward D. *Bacon-Shakespeare Coincidences*, 2d ed. London: The Francis Bacon Society, 1950.

———. *Francis Bacon's Maze*. London: The Francis Bacon Society, 1961.

Kilvet, Ian Scott, ed., *British Writers,* Vol. 1, *Francis Bacon*, by Brian Vickers. New York: Charles Scribner's Sons, 1979.

Leadbeater, C. W. *The Masters and the Path*. 1925. Reprint, Adyar, Madras, India: The Theosophical Publishing House, 1965.

Leary, Penn. *The Second Cryptographic Shakespeare*, 2d ed. Omaha, NE: Westchester House Publishers, 1990.

Pennick, Nigel. *Magical Alphabets*. York Beach, ME: Samuel Weiser, Inc., 1992.

Schwaller de Lubicz, R. A. *Sacred Science*. Rochester, VT: Inner Traditions International, 1988. First published in French under the title *Le Roi de la théocratie Pharaonique* by Flammarion, 1961.

———.*The Temple of Man*. Rochester, VT: Inner Traditions International, 1998. First published in French under the title *Le Temple de l'homme* by Éditions Dervy, 1957,1993, 1998.

Shakespeare, William. *Mr. William Shakespeares Comedies, Histories, & Tragedies: A Facsimile of the First Folio, 1623*. New York and London: Routledge, 1998.

Taylor, Michael. *Master R: Lord of Our Civilization*, 3d ed. Christchurch, NZ: The Rawley Trust, 1997.

The Holy Bible. *King James Version*, 1611 ed. A word-for-word reprint of the "First Edition of the Authorized Version." Nashville: Thomas Nelson Publishers, n.d.

Numbers
2-2-2 and 4-4-4
  Sanat Kumara, 228
2 and 4
  Venus and Earth, 226
3
  humanity, 227-228
  humanity's creation, 256
3-3-3
  incarnation of Sanat Kumara, 241
3-3-3 to 5-5-5
  113 branch-races, 246-247
3-4-5
  Moon and Earth chains, 256
4
  importance of, 228
  importance to Earth, 227
4-4-3
  coded time markers, 226
  letters of Great Invocation, 231
  meaning of, 230
  reveal key number 113, 226
4-4-4
  Mediocria Firma, 241
  meaning of, 240
5
  Great Invocation, 240
5-5-5
  branch-race five, 250
  Great Invocation, 241
  meaning of, 241
  time marker of Great Invocation, 240
5 and 6
  dual meaning, 180
  Great Invocation, 119-120
  key words, 174
  number 132, 119-120
  Sanat Kumara, 183
  Synthetic Triplet, 172
  word-positions in Great Invocation, 174
6, 5 Theme
  Great Invocation and "A Word from the
    Master", 148
7
  334 and 443, 206
  symbolism of Athena, 60
11 and 22
  Thoth-Hermes-Mercury, 146, 178
14 and 17
  creative Hierarchies, 211
  duplex rotary motion, 98-99
  number 287, 99
  Path to Sirius, 98-99
18 and 19
  Egyptians, 105
  Great Invocation, 104

The Knowledge Book, 134
  meaning of relationship, 106
  spiritual boundary, 106
19
  "The Boat of Mystery which Plows the
    Ocean", 92
  causal body, 106
  Egyptian art, 104-105
  Egyptians, 104
  Great Invocation and Sirius, 104
  Horus and honorificabilitudinitatibus,
    104
  letter S, 91
  Sirius, 105
  zodiac and the seven rays, 146
1.9 and 9.3, 14
  Dawkins interpretation, 127
  letter equivalents, 127
  Sirius, 127
  year 1993, 131
22,
  trinity, zodiac, and the seven rays, 146
27,
  Horus, 103
28
  Great Invocation, 58
  middle word "is", 58
33
  God of Light within, root value of, 174
  Jesus, 176
  Masonic degree and Bacon, 87
  Masonry, 176
  Solomon's Temple, 176
33 and 34
  Bacon and Cross of the Great Invocation,
    147
  number 1122, 147
33 and 68
  symbolic arithmetic, 176-177
33
  fourth initiation, and number 132, 176
49
  Athena, 61
50 year orbit
  Sirius B, 132-133
51
  Great Invocation and Athena, 61
52
  key middle word-position, 152
  link between Great Invocation and King
    Henry IV, 118
  Three Works, linked by, 152-154
  "A Word from the Master", 152-154
55
  Bacon, 86
  Psalm 46, 86

57
  "Fra. Bacon", 93
  middle position of Great Invocation, 60
  symbolism of Athena, 60
  three letter T's, 92
  "veiled", 92
67
  "Francis", 84
  Psalm 46, 84
69
  ESC value of "mooved" in Psalm 46, 84
77
  Athena, 60
83 38 pattern
  Djwhal Khul and Rakoczi, 95
  Rakoczi, 94
  triple meaning, 94-95
85
  the heart, 159
  middle word of Great Invocation, 155
91
  "Is", 87
  "The Star", 87
  "The Star" Tarot card, 87-88
94
  "Master R", 171
95
  "Sirius", 91
100
  "Francis Bacon", 87
  letter C and Bacon, 121
103
  gematria of, 158
105
  Kumaras Who came to Earth, 196
  Sirius the Cosmic Christ, 196
113
  Great Invocation and root-races, 223
  key to the Plan, 220
  numeric symbol, 220
  occult pattern, 226
  related to initiation, 228-230
113 root-races
  meaning of, 230
113 unit cycle
  results of, 251
  two phases of, 250-251
124
  Great Invocation and related Bacon
     themes, 122
132
  "God of Light within", 175
  number 33 and fourth initiation, 176
  numbers 5 and 6, 119-120
  Rakoczi, 119, 173
  Synthetic Triplet, 173

Three Works
  Rakoczi, 173
136, 102
  "C.R.C. is an epigram", 130
  gematria values related to, 130
  Signature of Sirius, 68
  Sonnet 136, 68
138
  Janus epigram and Psalm 46, 83
139
  "Cosmic Christ", 166, 207
  "Hermes-Thoth", 207
  " The High Priestess, The Star, The Sun",
     166 ,207
  Leo-Aquarius, 207
  meaning of, 165
  Synthetic Triplet, 165
  "Thoth-Hermes", 165, 166
151 and 136
  honorificabilitudinitatibus, 100
157
  471 and Bacon, 238
  Cross of the Great Invocation, 101-102
  "Fra. Rosi Crosse", 101
  Great Invocation and ship metaphor, 72
  Multi pertransibunt & augebitur Scienta,
     238
  many gematria links, 238
  page correspondence, 77n.20
157 and 67
  gematria links, 238
159
  "Master Rakoczi", 128, 179
171
  "the celestial ship", 92
  equivalent gematria phrases, 87
  God is known, 233
  honorificabilitudinitatibus, 104
  Lemurian root-race, 233
  meaning of, 69, 233
171, 172, and 173
  esoteric symbolism of, 233
171 and 303
  Great Invocation and Psalm 46, 88
172
  Atlantean root-race, 233
  the Cosmic Christ, 233
173
  fifth root-race, 233
  Great Invocation, 233
176
  "the Boat of Mystery which Ploughs the
     Ocean", 103-104
  "the light which ever shineth in the
     East", 103-104
  meaning of, 76

186
"Master Djwhal Khul", 179
189
arithmetic factors and Master R, 163
gematria phrases, 194
"the heart of Rakoczi", 160
"the heart of the Lion", 157
interweaves Three Works, 156
Mottos of Francis Bacon, 157
"planetary Christ", 202
rays Three and Seven, 163
Sanat Kumara and Leo, 192
Sanat Kumara, Leo, and Will, 194
    cosmic meaning, 196
    incarnation of Sanat Kumara, 196
195
"The High Priestess", 137, 207
"Taurus-Scorpio", 207
203
"Light from Sirius", 139
Master R, 141
"My Essence is Silence", 139
222
Great Invocation and "A Word from the Master", 129
"A Word from the Master", 129
226
Great invocation and Athena, 61
231
related to 21, 116
235
Cardinal Cross, 207-208
242
"Thoth-Hermes-Mercury", 146, 178
247
"Hermes Trismegistus", 211
249
3 x 83, 171
middle Essence Value of Synthetic Triplet, 171
Rakoczi, 171
266
ray Five, 148
267 and 78
gematria values, 196
285
"the central spiritual sun" and 19, 91
multiples of 19, 91
287
Bacon/Shakespeare, 99
First Folio, 99, 100
"Fra. Rosi Crosse", 101
"honorificabilitudinitatibus", 100
Letter K and Great Invocation, 107
Masonry, 101
numbers 14 and 17, 99

numbers 151 and 136, 100
Psalm 46, 161
"Sirius the Great White Lodge", 99
303
Janus epigram, 86
Masonic number, 86
Psalm 46, 86, 161-162
St. Alban, 86
313
"Invocation for Power and Light", 124
"Master R, Lord of Civilization", 124
"A Word from the Master", 162
334
Fixed Cross signs, 205
334 and 443
Fixed Cross and Great Invocation, 205-206
number 7, 206
342
honorificabilitudinitatibus and the Great Invocation, 104
343
meaning of, 204, 223
Mutable Cross signs, 203
Pallas, 60
383
Rakoczi, 171
"The star Regulus, the heart of the Lion", 171
years encompassing Synthetic Triplet, 171
436
relation to Multi pertransibunt & augebitur Scienta and "the door of Initiation", 73
437
"The Boat of Mystery which Ploughs the Ocean", 92
443
veiling factor, 166
457
Psalm 46, 161
471
"age of restoration of what has been broken by the fall", 237
linked to Bacon's titlepage, 237-238
number 157 and Bacon, 237-238
515
Parthenos, 61
550 year cycle
ray two, 134
Sirius B, 133
summation, 134
555
Great Invocation, 240, 254
last five words of Great Invocation, 235

(555 continued)
  Restore the Plan on Earth, 143
777
  Great invocation and Athena, 61
  Great Invocation and Fixed Cross, 206
993
  arithmetic operations on, 111
  coded page numbers, 110-111
  conclusion of arithmetic operations, 112
  First Folio, 110
  key words link to Bacon, 119
  Mediocria Firma, 111
  number 433 and Psalm 46, 111-112
993 and 433
  Psalm 46, 111-112
1122
  numbers 33 and 34, 147
  relation to Great Invocation and "A Word
    from the Master", 145-148
  number 242 , 145
  number 33, 145
2244
  Bacon and Rakoczi, 183n.2
  Bacon, Francis, 177
  viewed as 22 and 44, 177-178
2310
  conclusion to key words link to Bacon,
    116-117
  "Francis Bacon" in *King Henry IV*, 115
  a number bridge, 113

AA signature
  Signature of Sirius, 62
AA symbol, 77
  Apollo and Athena, 59
  Athena, 59
  authors using it, 59
  Dawkins comments on, 59-60
Academy of Dr. John Dee, 28
acronyms, 52
acrostics
  common Elizabethan practice, 32
  example of, 31
Advancement and Proficience of Learning
  cipher types named by Bacon, 33
  titlepage symbolism, 70-73
    full-sailed ship, 70-72
Ageless Wisdom
  definition, 2
  God explained, 3, *274-77*
  number correspondences, 219
  release of secret teachings, 146-147
  septenary unfoldment of creation, 220-
    221
  sevenfold divisions of, 221
  story of creation, 185-186

  human kingdom, 185
  kingdoms of nature, 185
  mental principle, 185-186
    Sanat Kumara's great sacrifice, 186
  trinity concept, 169
Age of restoration of what has been broken
    by the fall
  AN value, 237
  Bacon, 238
  Djwhal Khul statement analyzed, 237
  Master R connection, 237
  Psalm 46 and Francis, 238
  RAN value, 238
  restoration and instauration, 237
  summation, 238-239

Alpha Number
  See also AN
American flag
  the old professor, 36
Ampersand in gematria, 78n.24
AN
  method explained, 46
  origin of term, 45
Anagrammatic meaning
  honorificabilitudinitatibus, 100
Apollo
  AA symbol, 59
  God of Light, 64
Apophthegms, 25
Aquarius
  group consciousness and service, 213
  humanity, 212-213
Areopagus, meaning of, 39n.19
  See also English Areopagus
Argo
  Athena, 69, 70
  Bacon, 70
  vessel of wisdom, 75
  the celestial ship, 69
  the Queen of Heaven, 74
Ark
  "the Boat of Mystery which Ploughs the
    Ocean", 74
  esoteric meaning of, 74
  parallels in writings of Berges/Dawkins,
    74-75
  ship metaphor, 74
Athena, 56
  77 and 49, 60-61
  AA symbol, 59
  Argo, 69, 70
  Bacon, 33-34
  Bacon's Muse, 59
  Elizabeth I, 77n.17
  Goddess of Wisdom, 62

Great Invocation and AA symbol, 61
Great Invocation and septenary cross,
    61-62
helmet of, 60
Muse of Bacon's inner circle, 60
the Queen of Heaven, 70
spear-shaker, 60
spelling of, 59
structure of Great Invocation, 60
veil of, 60
Athena and Elizabeth I
Shekinah feminine archetype, 76
Athena and Isis
feminine principle, 69-70
ship metaphor, 69-70
Atlantean fourth root-race
door of initiation first opened, 231
importance of, 244
number 172, 233
Authorship question regarding Great
    Invocation, 53-54
Avatars' statement
"I am the Light of the World", 209-210
"A Word from the Master", 126
AN value of title, 129
capitalized words, 135
    gematria results, 136-140
    gematria values, 135
    key elements, 136-137
capitalized words, reason for, 139-140
CRC, 130
decipherment of line 3, 127-128
decipherment of line 4, 130
final five words
    Bacon and Shakespeare, 141
    deciphered, 140-141
Great Invocation
    agreement between, 145
    final five words, 140-148
    final five words compared, 143-144
    numbers 5 and 21, 143
    synthesis of final five words, 145-148
heart of, 159-160
key to *Mediocria Firma*, 152
last two words examined, 140
Master R, Lord of Civilization, 162
middle word-position, 152, 154
number 313, 162
number 52, 152-54
number of words, 144-145
"of Rakoczi", 160
poem by Dawkins, 34
Regulus and Leo, 136
Saint-Germain within, 144-145
Sirius, 136
summary of findings, 151

Thoth-Hermes-Mercury, 136-137

Bacon
ESC root value, 109
ESC value, 84
RAN value, 109
veiled in Great Invocation, 93
Bacon, Francis
Apophthegms, 25
admiration by peers, 23
"age of restoration of what has been bro-
    ken by the fall", 238
Argo, 70
Aristotle and Plato, 22
Athena, 33-34, 59
attracted to St. Alban, 35
Bacon's name in Cross pattern, 108-109
Bacon's name in *King Henry IV*, 109
birth date, 22
ciphers systems used, 47-52
codes and ciphers, 12
cryptographic birth story, 29-30
cryptography and, 29
cryptography, use of, 40
    extends to Master R, 40
death of, 25
education, 22
Elizabeth I and, 23
Elizabeth I his mother, 29
ESC value and "restore", 238-239
esoteric work of, 167
faked death, 25
father's death, 23
Great Instauration, 24, 57
    and English Renaissance, 235
George Wither, 82
God of Light within, 177
an initiate, 27
intellectual talents, 24-25
interest in mathematics, 67
James I, 23. 81
King James Bible and, 25
Literary and Professional Works, 24
law career, 23
Master R, 6
Master R connection, 43
mottos
    Mediocria Firma, 76
    Plus Ultra, 156
    Moniti Meliora, 156
Muse of, 62
New Atlantis, 25
Novum Organum, 24
number 2244, 177
opening of his tomb, 25
Promus, 25

(Bacon, Francis continued)
  parents, 22
  Paris, duties in, 22-23
  philosophical leanings, 22
  the Plan, 236
  political career, 23
  Psalm 46, 86
  ray Seven, 24
  reformer, 57
  reformer of science and law, 24
  rise to power, 23
  Rosicrucians, 57
  searching for in Great Invocation, 120-
    121, 122-123
    concluding remarks about, 123-124
  Shakespeare, 6
  Shakespearean literature, 21
  Shakespeare, Rosicrucians, Masonry, 43
  span of work, 11-12
  spelling of "Bacon", 178-179
  St. Alban, 87
  his stated purpose, 24
  The Advancement of Learning, 24
  themes associated with, 14
  three mottos of, 156
  use of twenty-one letter alphabet, 66, 110
    twenty-one key words in Great
      Invocation, 114
  Verulam, 60
  writings, 23-24
Bacon and Cross of the Great Invocation
  numbers 33, 34, and 1122, 147
Bacon and Dee
  gematria values, 99
Bacon and Great Invocation
  twenty-one letters, 142
Bacon and Master R
  hyphenation use, 145
Bacon and Saint Germain
  comments by Hall, Manly P., 36
Bacon and Shakespeare
  "A Word from the Master", 141
Baconians
  Psalm 46, 82
Bacon/Shakespeare
  287, 99
Bacon-Shakespeare Coincidences
  hyphenation example, 52
Bacon-Shakespeare question, 21
  Hall, Manly P. conclusion, 26
Bacon's Heraldic Achievement
  Centurion symbolism, 87
  Masonic symbolism on, 87
Bailey, Alice A.
  books of, 8, 18n.4
  Djwhal Khul, 8

Djwhal Khul's English, 41
  five-pointed star, 158-159
  Great Invocation, 6
  Leo essay, 158-159
  life of, *269-71*
  work with Djwhal Khul, 8
Beacon
  God of Light within, 179
Berges and Harold
  Christchurch connection to Master R, 16
Berges/Dawkins
  ark parallels in writings of, 74-75
Biliteral cipher, description, 39n.24
Blue Lodge
  AN and RAN values, 94
  Masonic term, 94
"The Boat of Mystery which Ploughs the
  Ocean"
  AN value, 72
  Ark, 74
  "The light which ever shineth in the
    East", 76
  number 176, 103-104
  multiple of 19, 92
  third initiation, 73
Books dictated by Djwhal Khul
  presence of obscure words—anent, e'en,
    oft, whilst, 42
"Boteswaine"
  ESC value, 112
  first word in First Folio, 112
Brahma third aspect
  Shekinah, 76
Branch-race five
  5-5-5, 250
Branch-races, 240
Branch-races, 113
  3-3-3 to 5-5-5, 246-247
Branch-race three of Lemuria
  third animal kingdom, 247
Briggs, Henry and logarithms, 67
"The Brother from Sirius"
  AN value, 148
  ray Five, 148

Cardano, Geronimo, 27
  cryptographic system, 27
  description, 27
  influence on Dee, 27
Cardinal Cross
  obscure gematria value, 207-208
  Risen Christ, 202
  signs, 202
    AN value, 207
Castor and Pollux
  meaning, 198

Causal body and number 19, 106
Cedarcrans, Lucille
  Master R, 37
  Nature of the Soul, 37
  received The Wisdom teachings, 37
"The celestial boat"
  AN value, 72
"The celestial ship"
  AN value, 62, 92
  Argo, 69
  meaning of, 69
Celibate key words, 115
Center, importance of, 158
"The central spiritual Sun"
  AN value and meaning, 91
Centurion symbolism
  Bacon's Heraldic Achievement, 87
  letter C, 87
  Psalm 46, 87
Chohan of ray Seven
  Freemasonry and, 35
  Master R, 35
Christ
  first use of Great Invocation, 9-10
  link to Thoth, 139
  reappearance, 9
  redemption, 57
  the rose, 57
Christ, reappearance of
  five Masters involved, 96
Christ and Buddha
  third initiation, 230
Christ and Master R
  high spiritual status, 38
Christchurch, 15
  Berges and Harold, 16
  conference site, 15
  Edmund Harold, 15-16
  meeting with artist described, 16
Christ Consciousness
  astrological crosses describe, 202
  evolution of, 202
Christian Rosicross
  Master R, 35
Cipher device
  Mediocria Firma, 84
Cipher methods
  acronyms, 52
    and Masonry, 52
  capitalization, use of, 52
  "A Word from the Master", 135
  dates, 209
  hyphenation, 144-145
  hyphenation, example of, 52
  italics, 52
  separating four digits, 177

  applied to 2244, 177-178
  word placement, 52
  word placement example, 121
Ciphers
  Bacon and Shakespeare, 26
Cipher types, 31
Cipher types named by Bacon, 33
Circle of the Greeks
  Athena, 61
Coded page numbers
  993, 110-111
  First Folio, 110
  King Henry IV, 109-110
  Love's Labor's Lost, 102
  The Tempest, 112
Coded time markers
  4-4-3, 226
Codes
  Great Invocation, 1
Colel, 72
  and *Sacred Vessel of the Mysteries*,
    77n.21
*Collection of Emblemes, Ancient and
    Moderne*, 82-83
  Janus epigram, 83
College of the Six Days' Work
  New Atlantis, 25
Communication between cosmic Lives, 219
Çorak, Vedia Bülent
  The Knowledge Book, 133
"Cosmic Christ"
  AN value, 166
  Gemini, 200-201
  number 139, 207
  Sirius, 131
Cosmic Cross
  Mutable Cross, 201
Cosmic Hermes
  Sirius, 214
CRC
  rose and cross, 35-36
CRC and Thoth, 138-139
"C.R.C. is an epigram"
  and number 136, 130
Creation of humanity
  ray Five, 149
Creative Hierarchies
  description, 211
  Leo-Scorpio, 211
  numbers 14 and 17, 211
Cross and rose
  Great Invocation and, 35-36
Crosses
  Christ Consciousness, 202
  names given by Djwhal Khul, 202
  three astrological described, 201-202

(Crosses continued)
  three astrological, signs of, 202
Cross of the Great Invocation
  four words surrounding "is", 101-102
  Master R, 16
  Masters R and DK, 102
Cross pattern
  Bacon coded in, 108-109
Crucified Christ
  Fixed Cross, 202
Cryptographic birth story of Bacon, 29-30
Cryptography
  Bacon and, 29
  Cardano, Geronimo, 27
  Dee, Dr. John, 28
  Francis Bacon and, 40
  Master R
    importance of , 40-41
  Masters R and DK, 44-45
  Walsingham, 29

Dawkins, Peter
  1.9. and 9.3. interpretation, 127
  initial contact with, 15
  Letter T and 19, comments on, 92
  Master R, comments on, 35
  work, 6
Declaration of Independence
  the old professor, 36
Dedication decipherment
  Signature of Sirius, 68
  results, 68
Dedication page
  explanation of deciphered Sonnets, 66
Dee, Dr. John
  academy of, 28
  Bacon, 198
  birth date, 27
  cryptographic methods, 28
  depiction of Masonic degrees, 73-74
  Elizabeth I, 28
  English Aeropagus, 28
  library of, 28
  life of, 27
  Monas Hieroglyphica, 27-28
  Masonic symbolism, 75-76, 198
  Perfect Arte of Navigation
    relation to Multi pertransibunt &
    augebitur Scienta and "the door of
    Initiation", 73
Djwhal Khul
  Christ, reappearance of, 96
  coded date given by, 209
  comments on his relationship with AAB,
    41
  English lifetime, 42

English usage style, 41
  use of obscure English words, 41-42
evidence of English incarnation, 41-42
extract
  anchoring will of God on Earth, 191
  Aryan defined, 248-249
  Buddha, 183
  cells of Sanat Kumara, 231
  Christ and Buddha initiated, 230
  Christ's decision, 10
  Cosmic Christ triangle, 200
  date of Christ's first use of Great
    Invocation, 10
  dissolution of solar system, 169
  Earth's purpose, 204
  era when Great Invocation can be
    used, 220
  formation of new ashram , 37-38
  fourth cosmic initiation, 231
  fourth creative hierarchy, 219
  fourth initiation, 219
  fourth round, 219
  future goal for Earth, 5
  gematria, 40
  Gemini, 197
  Gemini and Masonry, 197
  Gemini and ray Two, 200
  Gemini and Sirius, 197
  Gemini as messenger, 209
  Gemini, Great Bear, and
    Pleiades triangle, 200
  globalization, 58
  Great Invocation, 8
  Hermes, 139, 176
  individualization, 192
  individualization and initiation of
    Sanat Kumara, 228
  intervention of Sirius, 197
  Invocation for Power and Light, 220
  Jachin and Boaz, 199
  Leo, 158
  Leo and Will, 193
  Leo planetary triangle, 195
  light supernal, 174
  lions, 158
  lives of Master R, 21
  Lords of Flame, 219-220
  Love, 200
  Mahachohan, 164
  Masonry and Gemini, 198-199
  Masonry and Sirius, 198
  Master R, 19, 34
  Master R, functions of, 20
  Master R, shift within Hierarchy, 20
  the middle way, 79
  mind, 170

(Djwhal Khul extracts continued)
Moon chain, 256
Mutable Cross, 202
number 4 and initiation, 230
number 777, 203
number correspondences, 219
numbers 11 and 22, 146
Path of the Solar Logoi, 216
The Plan, 2, 1, 233
planetary Logos, task of our, 191
present epoch, 235, 236
process of initiation, 244
race defined, 248-249
ray Five, 149
ray Seven, 20, 164
redemption, 204
Regulus, 158
Regulus and Sirius, 194
rosy cross, 98
Sanat Kumara, 183, 184
Sanat Kumara and
fourth initiation, 231
Sanat Kumara and Sirius, 190
Sanat Kumara and three astrological
crosses, 203
Sanat Kumara's transfer to Earth
chain described, 223
Sanat Kumara,
disciple of solar Logos, 191
Sanat Kumara, training of, 191
Sirius, 126
Sirius and Leo, 158
Sirius and our solar system, 190-191
Sirius and Regulus, 194
solar Logos, goal of, 191
spiritual awakening in 1625, 28-29
statement by, 272-73
three aspects of mind, 170
translation and
age of Great Invocation, 10
his two European incarnations, 41
Universal Mind, 170
veils, 108
Venus-Earth connection, 219-220
Venus, Mercury, Earth, 197
the Weaver, 151
work of the Master R, 19
Great Invocation, 6
liaison work, 96
numerology, use of, 54n.3
other names, 8
present in Great Invocation, 95
Rakoczi, spelling of, 95
RAN value, 95
Djwhal Khul and the Hierarchy, 271-74
Djwhal Khul and Master R

cooperation between, 95
Djwhal Khul and Master R in England, 42
Djwhal Khul and Rakoczi
83 38 pattern, 95
DK
See Djwhal Khul
"The door of Initiation"
quantity of appearances in Djwhal
Khul's writing, 77n.23
RAN value, 73
relation to Multi pertransibunt &
augebitur Scienta, 73
Royal Arch degree, 74
Duality and Gemini, 198
Duplex rotary motion
numbers 14 and 17, 98-99
Path to Sirius, 98-99

Earth
number 4, 227
purpose of and lion symbolism, 193
purpose of humanity, 5
redemptive experiment, 204
who's in charge, 277
Earth Scheme, 222
fourth chain, 222
Mediocria Firma, 246
two purposes, 253
Egyptian art
number 19, 104-105
Egyptians
number 19, 104
numbers 18 and 19, 105
Egyptian trinity
Osiris, Isis, and Horus, 103
Elizabethan alphabet, 47-48
Letters J, U, and V, 48
Elizabethan Reverse Cipher
See ERC
Elizabethan Simple Cipher
See ESC
Elizabethan spelling, 100
Elizabeth I
Athena, 77n.17
Bacon illegitimate son, 29
Bacon, Francis and, 23
confrontation with Bacon, 30
Dee, 28
Robert Dudley, 29, 30
secret marriage, 29-30
Elizabeth I and Virgin Queen
immaculate vessel, 75
English Aeropagus
description, 28
members of, 28
English usage style of Djwhal Khul, 41

Environmental movement
  Leo-Aquarius, 213
Equal-armed cross
  Great Invocation
    gematria method explained, 93
ERC
  AN and RAN values, 49-50
ESC
  AN and RAN values, 49
  basis of, 47-48
Esoteric study
  difficulties of, 205
Esoteric topics, complexity of, 200
Essence Value
  explained, 53-54
European awakening, 11
Externalization of the Hierarchy
  three stages, 241

Feminine archetype
  Shekinah, 76
Fifth root-race
  definition, 148
  number 173, 233
Final five words
  See Great Invocation and "A Word from
    the Master"
First and last words
  of Great Invocation, 154
  of Psalm 46, 155
  of Synthetic Triplet, 168
First Folio
  Bacon's name in, 32
  Ben Jonson and number 287, 99
  Coded page numbers, 110
  contains "Francis Bacon", 113
  mispaginations, 125n.2
  number 287, 99, 100
  page anomaly, 110
First, middle, and last words
  of Synthetic Triplet, 169
    AN value, 173
First, middle, and last words of three writ-
    ings examined, 162-163
The First Part of King Henry the Fourth
  See *King Henry IV*
Five-pointed star
  esoteric meaning of, 158-159
Fixed Cross
  Crucified Christ, 202
  Great Invocation, 205
  horizontal arm signs
    AN value, 207
  meaning of, 204
  numeric symbolism, 205
  redemptive process, 204

signs, 202
  AN value, 205
  Taurus, 213
  vertical arm signs
    AN value, 207
Fixed Cross and Great Invocation
  334 and 443, 205-206
Fourth cosmic initiation
  Sanat Kumara, 189
Four words surrounding "is"
  Cross of the Great Invocation, 101-102
  number 157, 102
"Fra. Bacon" and number 57, 92, 93
"Francis"
  ESC value, 84
  meaning of, 35
  Teutonic derivative, 122
"Francis Bacon"
  AN value, 122
  ESC value, 87
  in Psalm 46, 84
  word "free", 122
"Francis Bacon" in *King Henry IV*, 115-116,
    118-119
"Fra. Rosi Crosse"
  Cross of the Great Invocation, 102
  ESC value, 101
  number 157, 101
  number 287, 101
  Rosicrucians, 101
"Free"
  gematria link to Bacon, 122
Freemasonry and Chohan of ray Seven, 35
Free will and the Plan, 3
Friedman, William and Elizabeth
  acrostics in Shakespeare, 32
  conclusions on Bacon's cryptographic
    birth story, 31
"FS Biaccen" coded as "Boteswain", 112
Fundamental questions, 2

Gallup, Elizabeth Wall
  Bacon's biliteral cipher, 31
Gematria, 6-7, 44
  codes used in *Hidden Foundations*, 51
  numerology and, 46
  results involving Master R, 120
Gematria and numerology
  difference between, 46
Gematria methods
  examples of, 47
Gemini
  Castor and Pollux, 198
  Cosmic Christ energy, 200-201
  duality, 198
  role of Sanat Kumara, 215

Sanat Kumara as Avatar, 200
Sirian agent, 200
Gemini, Masonry, Sirius summation, 198
General and Rare Memorials
    interpretation of titlepage, 73-74, 75-76
    Masonic degrees, 73-74
    ships, 73
Geneva Bible, 80
    Psalm 46, 82
Global consciousness
    Humanity, 188
God
    divine Author, 7
    incarnated, 3
God and Silence, 169
Goddess of Wisdom
    Athena, 62
"God is known"
    AN value, 69
    meaning of, 233, 244
    number 171, 233
God of Light
    in each person, 185
    Hermes, 175-176
    several perspectives, 184
"The God of Light"
    Apollo, 64
    number 136, 68
    Signature of Sirius, 64
"God of Light within"
    AN value, 179
    Bacon, 177
    Beacon, 179
    Essence Value, 179
    levels of meaning, 175
    Master R, 179
    Masters R and DK, 214
    Rakoczi, 175
    root value, 174
    symbolic arithmetic, 179
    word-position value, 175
Great Instauration, 24
    Bacon and English Renaissance, 235
Great Invocation
    5 and 6, 119-120
    5-5-5, 241
    5-5-5 a time marker, 240
    actual title of, 72
    Alice A. Bailey, 6
    ancient mantram, 188-189
    Athena, 60
    51 essential words, 61
    226 essential letters, 61
    777, 61
    AA symbol, 61
    the rose, 61

septenary cross of Great invocation,
    61-62
authorship conclusions, 255
authorship question
    methods of testing theory, 53-54
Bacon veiled in, 93
clue to creator/composer, 117
codes, 1
commentaries on, *291-93*
connection to Psalm 46, 155
correlation of words and root-races, 223
cosmic event, 247
critical juncture of history, 5
cross and rose and, 35-36
deeper meaning, 1
description, 8-9
Djwhal Khul present in, 95
effects of sounding, 9, 254
English translation
    Masters involved, 6
equal-armed cross depiction, 93
    gematria method explained, 93
Essence Value of middle word, 155
first and last words of, 154
first human users of, 240-241
Fixed Cross signs, 205
Francis Bacon, 12
higher Beings, 188
humanity's use of, 188
iambic pentameter, 68
importance of the middle, 79
influence of Fixed Cross signs, 213
key to understanding, 184-185
key words explained, 113-114
    conclusion to Bacon connection, 116-117
    link to Bacon, 116
last five words, 140, 142-143
    "restore the Plan on Earth", 235
    twenty-one letters, 142
last stanza compared to "age of restoration of what has been broken by the fall", 237
layout and structure, 13
letter K, 107
letter S at the middle, 91
letters of, 120
Mediocria Firma, 79
major themes
    Hermes, 190
    Leo, 189
    Sanat Kumara, 189
    Sirius, 189
marks three planetary events, 241
Master R, 43
    cryptography in, 41

(Great Invocation continued)
   testing methods, 43-44
   Master R, discussion of role in, 180-182
   meaning of 113 words, 220, 247

   metaphorical door to mysteries, 45
   metaphysical structure, 54
   middle phrase of, 82
   middle word of
      Mediocria Firma, 241
   middle word, importance of, 54
   moving from word to word, 62-64
   multiples of 19, 91
   names associated with Master R, 124-125
   new perspective on, 180-181
   number 28, 58
   number 5, 240
   number 555, 240, 254
   the Plan, 7
   poetic meter of, 68
   in possession of Sanat Kumara, 189
   quantity of words and letters in, 53
   Rose Cross, 58
   sacred vessel, 75
   septenary theme, 62
   Sirian in origin, 93
   Sirian mantram, 189
   Sirius, 88
   Sirius and key words, 143
   "The Star" hidden at center, 88
   summation of rose symbol, 59
   as symbolic cross, 58
   Taurus role in, 205
   three elements of, 58
   three letter K's within, 120
   three middle word-positions, 69
   vessel of esoteric knowledge, 13
   Virgo, 75
   weaving process in, 154
   without date, 189
   word "Christ" in, 9
   "A Word from the Master"
      agreement between, 145
      conclusion of comparison , 145
      final five words, 140-148
      final five words 6/5 theme, 148
      final five words analysis, 147-148
      final five words compared, 143-144
      final five words root value, 147
      numbers 5 and 21, 143
      synthesis of final five words, 145-148
   word-positions 5, 6, 56, and 65, 174
   words 57 and 58, 128
   words of, 9
   words span eighteen million years, 244

   year 1993, 133
Great Invocation and "A Word from the Master"
   222, 129
   pattern of relationships, 149
   Ray Five, 148
Great Invocation and Bacon
   twenty-one letters, 142
Great Invocation and Fixed Cross
   443 and 334, 205-206
   number 777, 206
   Sanat Kumara, 206
Great Invocation and *King Henry IV*
   number 52, 118
Great Invocation and *Love's Labor's Lost*
   letters K and L, 107
Great Invocation and Psalm 46
   171 and 303, 88
   Mediocria Firma, 88
   Regulus, 159
   similar coding technique described, 87
   summary of parallels
      Mediocria Firma, 90
      middle word of Great Invocation, 90
      middle word of Psalm 46, 90
      number 171, 90
      number 303, St. Alban, 90
      Shakespeare and Francis Bacon, 90
      Sirius, 90
Great Invocation and Psalm 46, parallels
   between, 88
"The Great Sacrifice"
   Sanat Kumara, 101
"The Great White Lodge on Sirius"
   number 136 and Signature of Sirius, 103
   RAN value, 103
   Signature of Sirius, 64
Greek gematria value
   "Pallas Athena Parthenos", 60-61
Group consciousness and service
   Aquarius, 213

Hall, Manly P.
   Bacon and Saint Germain, 36
   Bacon-Shakespeare opinion, 26
   comments on Saint Germain, 36
   opinion of Bacon, 26-27
   Shakespeare's signatures, 26
Harold, Edmund
   artist from Christchurch, 16
   Christchurch, 15-16
   Master Your Vibration, 15
   Master R, 16
   meeting with artist, 16
Head of Freemasons
   Master R, 35

"The heart"
  number 85, 159
"The heart of Rakoczi"
  Three Works, 160
"The heart of the Lion"
  AN value, 157
  meaning of, 216
  Rakoczi, 160
  Sirius, 194
  summary of phrase, 160
  Three Works, formed from, 159-160
Helmet of Athena, 60
Hermes
  God of Light, 175-176
  Initiation, 182
  Middle concept, *Mediocria Firma*, 168
  persistence of theme, 208
  proclamation, 182
  Sanat Kumara and number symbolism,
    186
  Sirius, 208
  symbolic arithmetic, 176-177
  three expressions of
    cosmic, 210-212
    human, 208-209
    planetary, 209-210
"Hermes-Thoth"
  number 139, 207
"Hermes Trismegistus"
  AN value, 211
  Sanat Kumara, 211
Hermetic Agent
  Sanat Kumara, 208
Hierarchical movement
  plans for reform, 57
Hierarchy
  concern over human selfishness, 10-11
  definition, 4
  Masters of
    work, 4-5
  Messengers, 185
  Sirius, 131
"The High Priestess"
  AN value, 137
  descriptions of, 137-138
  Isis Veiled, 166, 137
  Shekinah, 137
  Tarot Arcanum, 137
  Taurus-Scorpio, 207
"The High Priestess, The Star, The Sun"
  number 139, 166, 207
  RAN value, 166
  Sirius, 166
Hi ludi F. Baconis nati tuti orbi
  honorificabilitudinitatibus, 100
  translation of, 100

Hollenbach, Karl
  commentary on name "Francis", 122
  honorificabilitudinitatibus, 100
  Rosicrucian Kay Cipher, 50
  Rosicrucian Order, 57
Honorificabilitudinitatibus
  anagrammatic meaning, 100
  Bacon, 100
  Hi ludi F. Baconis nati tuti orbi, 100
  Love's Labor's Lost, 100
  location within *Love's Labor's Lost*,
    102-103
  number 171, 104
  number 287, 100
  number 342, 103-104
  numbers 151 and 136, 100
  Psalm 46, 161
  split between two lines, 103
  summary, 106
  word placement technique, 100
Horus
  number 27, 103
  RAN value, 103
Horus and honorificabilitudinitatibus
  number 19, 104
The Human Canon
  Schwaller de Lubicz, 105
Human initiation
  Sanat Kumara, 230
Humanity, *278*
  Aquarius, 212-213
  created by cosmic initiation, 227-228
  creation of and number 3, 256
    Sirius, 170
  destiny, 5
  destiny of, 187-188
  an experiment, 205
  global consciousness, 188
  limited vision of, 205
  maturity, 4
  mental growth, 11
  new revelation, 188
  number 3, 227-228
  The Plan, 4
  restoration process, 239
  selfishness, 10-11
  tested by Scorpio, 213
Human soul
  service, 187
Hyphenation
  Saint-Germain, 144-145
Hyphenation cipher method
  Bacon-Shakespeare Coincidences, 52

"I am the Light of the World"
  Avatars' statement, 209-210

Immaculate vessel
    Elizabeth I and Virgin Queen, 75
Individualization
    Leo planetary triangle, 195
    The Sun, Jupiter, Venus, 195
Infinity sign
    Signature of Sirius, 68
Initiation
    third
        cosmic and human, 230
        Christ and Buddha, 230
Initiation
    Atlantean root-race, 231
    The Boat of Mystery which Ploughs the
        Ocean, 73
    the door of, 73
    explanation, *278-82*
    fourth cosmic, 231
    fourth cosmic and Sanat Kumara, 227
        Sanat Kumara, 231
    Hermes, 182
    human opportunity, 230
    Light and Redemption, 167
    Logos of Venus, 227
    meaning of, 73
    process of, 91-92
    redemption, 215
    Way of, 182-183
Instauration
    meaning and significance, 57-58
Invocation as a tool for spiritual emergence,
    293-95
"Invocation for Power and Light"
    AN value, 124
    number 313, 124
    stanzas one and two, *285-89*
    stanza three, *289-91*
"The Invocation for Power and Light"
    AN value, 72
"Is"
    number 91, 87
    "The Star" Tarot card, 87-88
Isis
    The High Priestess, 138
    The Queen of Heaven, 70
    Sothis, 69
Isis and Athena
    feminine principle, 69-70
    ship metaphor, 69-70
Isis and Sirius
    Ship metaphor, 69
Isis Unveiled
    The Star, 166
Isis Veiled
    The High Priestess, 166
    secret societies, 138

James I
    Bacon, 23, 81
    commissions new Bible, 80-81
Janus epigram
    clue, 83
    number 138 and Psalm 46, 83
    technique
        Mediocria Firma, 111-112
    using clue in Psalm 46, 84-85
    Wither, 82-83
Jesus
    number 33, 176
Jonson, Ben
    First Folio and number 287, 99

Karma, Law of
    Sirius, 138
Key words
    cipher bridge, 120
    Great Invocation, explained, 113-114
    Master R connection, 119
    non-celibate
        number 21, 115
        number 231, 115
        number 2310, 115
    numbers 5 and 6, 174
    review, 174
    three groups, 114-115
Key words link to Bacon
    993 and First Folio, 119
King Henry IV
    appearances of "Francis Bacon" in, 118
    appearances of Bacon's name, 109
    coded page numbers, 109-110
    word placement, 117-118
King Henry IV and Great Invocation
    conclusion to key words link to Bacon,
        116-117
King James Bible
    Bacon, 25, 80
The Knowledge Book
    Corak, Vedia Bulent, 133
    description of, 133-134
    numbers 18 and 19, 134
    Omega Gate dimension, 134
    Sirius, 134
    year 1993, 134
Kumaras Who came to Earth
    number 105, 196

Language patterns, 44
Law of Correspondences, 220, 247
    Regulus, 158
Leadbeater, C. W.
    The Masters and the Path
        lives of Master R, 20-21

Leary, Penn
  Dedication decipherment result, 66
  explanation of deciphered *Sonnets*
    Dedication page, 66
Lemurian root-race
  number 171, 233
Leo
  Bailey essay, 158-159
  human kingdom, 212
  ray One, 193
  will, 193
Leo-Aquarius, 207
  AN value, 207
  environmental movement, 213
Leo planetary triangle
  individualization, 195
Leo-Scorpio
  Creative Hierarchies, 211
  Sanat Kumara and number 247, 211
Letter C
  example of placement, 121
  Mediocria Firma technique, 121-122
Letter K
  Great Invocation, 107, 120
  number 287, 107
Letter L
  Love's Labor's Lost, 107
Letter R
  Master Rakoczi, 141
  non-celibate key words and Master R,
    117
  "A Word from the Master"
    final five words, 141
Letter S
  number 19, 91
Letter T
  and number 19, 92
  repeated three times, 92
Letters
  of Great Invocation, 120
  numeric values, 44
Letters E and F
  numbers 5 and 6, 172
  Synthetic Triplet, 172
Letters J, U, and V
  Elizabethan usage, 48
Light, 182-183
Light and Life, 215
Light and Redemption
  Initiation, 167
  mystery teachings, 166-167
"The Light of God"
  Signature of Sirius, 64
"The light which ever shineth in the East"
  number 176, 103-104
  RAN value, 76

Shekinah, 76
Lion symbolism
  cosmic Will, 192
  Earth's purpose, 193
Literary and Professional Works, 24
Logarithms
  Napier, John, 65
  Sonnet 136, 67-68
  zero, importance of, 66-67
Lord of Sirius
  planetary Logos relationship, 210
Lords of Flame
  time of arriving on Earth, 219-220
Love's Labor's Lost
  letter L, 107

Masonic symbolism
  Dee, 198
Masonry
  287 A.D., 101
  Blue Lodge, 94
  cipher methods, 52
  four degrees of, 73-74
  Master R, 19
  Mysteries, 215
  number 33, 176
  Royal Arch degree, 74
  Sirius, 99, 198
  Sirius and Gemini, 215
  White Lodge, 197-198
Master Djwhal Khul
  AN value, 179
  messenger of the Hierarchy, 208-209
Master KH
  Christ, reappearance of, 96
  Discourses
    description of, 133
    Rose Cross and Order of the Star, 133
    Year 1993, 133
Master Morya
  Christ, reappearance of, 96
Master numbers
  numerology, 47
Master R
  "age of restoration of what has been
    broken by the fall", 237
  AN value, 171
  authorship question, 54
  Bacon, 6, 180
  Bacon and Beacon, 179
  Bacon and Great Invocation connection
    methods of testing theory, 53-54
    use of "A Word from the Master", 53
  Bacon connection, 43
  Chohan of ray Seven, 35
  Christ's reappearance, 12

(Master R continued)
Christian Rosicross, 35
Christ, reappearance of, 96
cross of the Great Invocation, 16
current responsibilities, 20
description of, 92-93
drawing, 15
  artist from Christchurch, 15
  Maltese cross, 15
gematria results, 120
general manager, 19
God of Light within, 179
Great Invocation, 6, 43, 129
  level of involvement, 18
  testing methods, 43-44
Great Invocation, creator of, 180
Great Invocation, discussion of role in,
  180-182
Head of Freemasons, 35
intention of, 54
key words connection, 119
letter R, 141, 117
link to non-celibate key words, 117
lives of, 12, 21, 33
Lord of Civilization, 19
Lucille Cedarcrans, 37
masonry, 19
memory of past lives, 236
method of work, 12
names associated with in Great
  Invocation, 124-125
number 189, 163
number 203, 141
number clues, 125
past 500 years, 6
projects span many centuries, 181
Rakoczi, 6
ray Seven, 19
  and Great Invocation, 181
ray Three, 19
rays Three and Seven, 163
Saint Germain
  in courts of Europe, 36
  expert in many fields, 36
  a Mason, 36
  travels, 36
Selah, use of, 82
shift within Hierarchy, 20
Sirius, 15
St. Alban, 20
symbols related to, 56
Synthetic Triplet
  three middle words of, 171
teaching method, 182
Templar cross, 17
Three Works, veiled in, 157

veiled in Mottos of Francis Bacon, 157
work of, 164
"Master R, Lord of Civilization"
  AN value, 124
  number 313, 124
  "A Word from the Master", 162
"Master Rakoczi"
  AN value, 123, 128
  number 159, 179
"Master Rakoczi is known", 128-129
Master R and Bacon
  hyphenation use, 145
Master R and the Christ
  high spiritual status, 38
Master R: Lord of Our Civilization
  clues to lives of Master R, 33-34
  description of, 33
  St. Alban, 20
Masters M, DK, and R
Masters R and DK
  head the Synthetic Ashram, 37
  cooperation, 179
  in England, 42
  evidence of cooperation, 236-239
  God of Light within, 214
  Hermetic expression, 208
  transhuman Hermes, 214
  within Great Invocation, 214
Master Your Vibration
  Harold, Edmund, 15
Mathematics
  Bacon's interest in, 67
Mediocria Firma
  4-4-4, 241
  993, 111
  AN value, 122
  "A Word from the Master", 152
    final five words, 141
  Bacon family motto, 76
  basis of Great Invocation coding, 79
  cipher device, 84
  Earth Scheme, 246
  Great Invocation and Psalm 46, 88
  importance in Great Invocation, 76
  Janus epigram technique, 111-112
  letter R and Master R, 117
  Master R, 141
  middle word of Great Invocation, 241
  non-celibate key words and Master R,
    117
  Psalm 46, 80, 86
  translation, 76, 79
Mediocria Firma and Janus
  cipher technique reviewed, 151-152
Mediocria Firma and Janus techniques
  Three Works, 154-155

Mediocria Firma technique
  Letter C placement, 121-122
Mental development
  Root-race five, sub-race five, 248
Mercury and Venus
  meaning of names, 197
Messenger of the Hierarchy
  Djwhal Khul, 208-209
Metaphorical door to mysteries
  Great Invocation, 45
Metaphysical structure of Great Invocation, 54
Middle concept, *Mediocria Firma*
  Hermes, 168
  Three Works, 168
Middle letter
  locating in Synthetic Triplet, 172
Middle word
  of Great Invocation, 54
  of Psalm 46, 54
Middle word "is"
  AN value, 58
Middle word of Great Invocation
  number 85, 155
Middle word-position
  number 52, 152
Midpoint
  immense importance of, 244
Mind
  AN value, 171
  central to evolution, 170
  Essence Value, 171
  higher, invoking, 255
  middle word of Synthetic Triplet, 169
  Sirius, source of, 170
Mind of God
  the Plan, 4
Mispaginations
  First Folio, 125n.2
Monas Hieroglyphica, 27-28
Moon and Earth chains
  numbers 3-4-5, 256
  recapitulation, 256
Moon chain
  disruption of The Plan, 257
  failure of, 256
Mortlake
  courtiers, 28
  Dee's academy, 28
Mottos of Francis Bacon, 156
  ESC values, 157
  gematria interpretation, 156-157
  Master R is veiled in, 157
Much Ado About Nothing
  acrostic of Bacon, 32
Multi pertransibunt & augebitur Scienta

conclusions concerning, 72-73
  ESC values of, 72
  modern AN and RAN values, 72
  RAN value, 238
  relation to "The door of Initiation", 73
  translation, 72, 73
Muse of Bacon, 62
Mutable Cross
  four signs of, 201
  Hidden Christ, 202
  incarnation of Sanat Kumara, 203
  signs, 202
  AN value, 203
"My Essence is Silence"
  AN value, 139
Mysteries
  Masonry, 215
Mysteries hidden in plain sight, 13
Mysteries of Initiation, 244
  Sirius, 139
Mystery Schools
  description of, 131
  Sirius, 131

Napier, John
  logarithms, 65
Napier and Briggs, discussion of the zero in
  logarithms, 67
Nature of the Soul
  Cedarcrans, Lucille, 37
  Selah, 82
New Atlantis, 25
  College of the Six Days' Work, 25
New Group of World Servers
  definition, 11
  seven fields of service, 11
New Zealand
  Michael Taylor meeting, 14, 15
  trip to conference, 14
Non-celibate key words, 115
  symbolism of, 117
November 11, 1919
  Coded date given by Djwhal Khul, 209
Novum Organum, 24
Number clues
  Master R, 125
Numbers
  means of communication, 219
Number symbolism
  Fixed Cross, 205
  genesis, 221
Numerology
  Djwhal Khul, use of, 54n.3
  gematria and, 46
  master numbers, 47
Numerology and gematria (see next page)

Numerology and gematria
  difference between, 46

Occult pattern
  number 113, 226
Offspring key words, 115
Old professor
  American flag, 36
  Declaration of Independence, 36
One About Whom Naught May Be Said,
    205
  planes of consciousness, 221
One Life
  division from 3 to 7, 220-221
Osiris, Isis, and Horus
  Egyptian trinity, 103
  gematria relationship, 103
Owen, Dr. Orville W.
  Bacon's word cipher, 30
  cryptographic birth story of Bacon, 29-30

Pallas
  Greek Gematria value, 60
Pallas Athena Parthenos
  Greek gematria value, 60-61
Parthenos
  515, 61
  symbolic meaning, 61
Periastron
  Sirius A and B, 131
Physical races
  Sanat Kumara and, 249
The Plan
  climaxing phase, 7
  definition, 2
  establishing Will, 195
  five masters involved, 254-255
  free will, 3
  general evolution, 2
  Great Invocation, 7
  higher Intelligences, 4
  Mind of God, 4
  Moon chain disruption of, 257
  next phase of, 188
  number 113, 220
  our solar system, 4
  phases, 3
  purpose, 3
  Renaissance, 235-236
  since 1500, 10
  technology, 3
  telepathic interplay, 3
  twentieth century phase, 11
Planes of consciousness
  divisions of, 221
  One About Whom Naught..., 221

"Planetary Christ"
  AN value, 202
  Sanat Kumara, 202-203
Planetary Hermes
  Sanat Kumara, 214
Planetary Logos
  Custodian of the Will, 195
  cycles of, 204
  Fixed Cross, 203
  incarnated as Sanat Kumara, 189
  Lord of Sirius, 189
  path of the Solar Logos, 215-216
  ray One, 193, 195
  rays of, 193
  relationship to Lord of Sirius, 210
  Sanat Kumara, 203
  Sirian track, 215
  Solar Logos, 192
  on two tracks, 215-217
Planetary Scheme, 221-222
  343 world periods, 222
  globes of, 222
    seven root-races, 222
Poetic meter of Great Invocation, 68
"The Precipitator of the Cross"
  ray Five, 148
Promus, 25
Psalm 46
  Bacon, 86
  Baconians, 82
  centurion symbolism, 87
  connection to Great Invocation, 155
  Elizabethan spelling of, 81
  first and last words of, 155
  Francis and "age of restoration of what
    has been broken by the fall", 238
  honorificabilitudinitatibus, 161
  Janus epigram, 83
  Mediocria Firma, 80
  middle symbolism, 54
  middle word "mooved", 84
  number 287, 161
  number 303, 161-162
  number 457, 161
  number 55, 86
  number 67, 84
  number key 46, 81
  number of words in, 82
  shake and speare, 81
  Shakespeare, 86

"The Queen of Heaven"
  AN value, 70
  Argo, 74
  Athena, 70
  Isis, 70

Rakoczi
  83 38 pattern, 94
  AN and RAN values, 94
  "God of Light within", 175
  "The heart of the Lion", 160
  number 132, 119, 173
  number 249, 171
  number 383, 171
  spelling of, 95
  See also Master R
Rakoczi and Djwhal Khul
  83 38 pattern, 95
RAN
  method defined, 46
  method explained, 46
Ray Five
  266, 148
  creation of humanity, 149
  final five words, 148-149
  Great Invocation and "A Word from the
      Master", 148
  " The Precipitator of the Cross", 148
  "The Rose of God", 148
Ray Four Ashram, 230
Ray One
  Leo, 193
  planetary Logos, 193
Ray Two
  500 year cycle, 134
Ray Seven
  description of, 182
  Master R, 137
  Master R and Great Invocation, 181
  Thoth-Hermes, 166
  Thoth-Hermes-Mercury, 137
  workers described, 164
Ray Three
  Master R, 137
  manifestations, 20
Recapitulation
  Moon and Earth chains, 256
Redemption
  Christ, 57
  initiation, 215
Redemptive experiment
  Earth, 204
Redemptive process
  Fixed Cross, 204
  Sanat Kumara, 204
Regulus
  AN value, 158
  deeper meaning, 160
  Great Invocation and Psalm 46, 159
  Law of Correspondences, 158
  Sanat Kumara, 216
  school for solar Logoi, 216

Regulus and Leo
  "A Word from the Master", 136
Renaissance, 11
  aspect of the Plan, 235-236
  awakened esoteric philosophies, 167
  cultural effects, 11
  spread of, 11
Restoration and Instauration, 57-58
Restoration process
  humanity, 239
Restore
  AN value and Francis Bacon, 238-239
  Essence Value, 239
  link to Master R, 235
  Synthetic Triplet, 239

"Restore the Plan on Earth"
  AN and RAN values, 143
  branch-race five, 250
  implications of, 236
  interpretation, 143
  number 555, 143
  phrase serves two purposes, 240
  RAN value and Sirius, 240
Revelation, 3
Risen Christ
  Cardinal Cross, 202
RKC
  letter values of, 51
  origin of, 50
Root-race five
  plane 5-5-5 of mind, 249
  present time, 247
  true mental race, 249
Root-race five, sub-race five
  mental development, 248
Root-races
  not all in space/time, 244-246
Root-races, sub-races, and branch-races,
      239
Root value
  method explained, 46-47
Rose
  AN value, 58
The Rose, 56
  Great Invocation and Athena, 61
  meaning of, 57
Rose and cross
  CRC, 35-36
Rose Cross, 57
  Great Invocation, 58
"The Rose of God"
  ray Five, 148
Rose symbol summation
  Great Invocation, 59
Rosicrucian Kay Cipher, (See RKC)

Rosicrucians
Fra. Rosi Crosse, 101
symbol of, 57
Rosicrucian/Sirian Cross
names coded into, 109
Rosy Cross
Great Invocation, 58
Royal Arch degree, 78n.25
Masonry, 74
"the door of Initiation", 74

Sacred Science
Science of Thoth, 167
Sacred vessel
Great Invocation, 75
Sacred Vessel of the Mysteries
cover and Dee's titlepage compared, 76
meaning of title, 69
theme, 13
Thoth, Hermes, Mercury
Hermes Trismegistus, 168
St. Augustine on Mercurius, 168
threefoldness, 168
Trismegistus, meaning of, 168
Thoth, Hermes, Mercury, explanation of,
167-168
Saint-Germain
hyphenation, 144-145
See also Master R
Sanat Kumara
3-3-3 and incarnation of, 241
5's and 6's, 105
arrival on Earth, initiation, and Great
Invocation, 228
Cosmic Man, 105
description, 207, 212
Earth substance tainted, 187
fourth cosmic initiation, 189, 227
Gemini, role of, 215
God of Light, 186
Great Invocation and Fixed Cross, 206
"The Great Sacrifice", 101
Hermes Trismegistus, 211
Hermetic Agent, 208
Hermetic Messenger, 215
Hermetic number symbolism, 186
highest Light, 183
human initiation, 230
incarnation of, 186
keynote of sacrifice, 187
Leo and number 189, 192
Leo-Scorpio and number 247, 211
Moon chain, 256
mystery of, 191
numbers 2-2-2 and 4-4-4, 228
numbers 2, 3, and 4, 226

numbers 5 and 6, 183
original Avatar, 186
physical races and, 249
planetary Avatar
Gemini, 200
planetary Christ, 203
planetary Hermes, 214
planetary Logos, 203
pupil in school of cosmic Will, 216
purpose of, 185
ray One, transmission of, 193
reason for intervention, 187
redemptive process, 204
Regulus, 216
response to highest Light, 210
Sirian Agent of Initiation, 215
Sirius and Gemini
Christ Consciousness implanted in
humanity, 203
Sirius and number 247, 211
Sirius and Scorpio-Leo, 210-211
Solar Logos, 216
tawny lions, 216
transfer to Earth chain, 227
Venus connection, 227
Will energy, 216
Sanat Kumara incarnation
controlling factor, 214
Sanat Kumara's transfer to Earth
diagram explained, 223-224
School for solar Logoi
Regulus, 216
Schwaller de Lubicz
Sacred Science, 167
Schwaller de Lubicz, R. A.
fall of Cosmic Man, 105
The Human Canon, 105
number 19, 104
numbers 5 and 6, 105
Temple of Man, 104
Scorpio
humanity tested by, 213
Scorpio-Leo and Sirius
combined with Sanat Kumara, 210-211
numeric relationship, 210
The Second Cryptographic Shakespeare
comments on, 64
spelling of Bacon, 178-179
The Secret Doctrine
ship metaphor, 69
Secret societies
Isis veiled, 138
Selah
meaning of, 97
Septenary unfoldment of creation, 220-221
Sevenfold divisions of Ageless Wisdom, 221

The Seven Rays, *283*
Shakespeare
  Bacon, 6
  manuscripts of, 26
  no library, 26
  Psalm 46, 86
Shakespearean literature
  Bacon and, 21
Shakespearean plays
  philosophical ideas within, 26
Shakespeare's signatures
  Hall, Manly P. comments, 26
Shamballa ray One energy release
  year 1975, 193-194
  year 2000, 194
Shekinah
  Athena and Elizabeth I, 76
  Brahma third aspect, 76
  feminine archetype, 76
  "The light which ever shineth in the
    East", 76
  "The High Priestess", 137
Ship metaphor
  Argo, 74
  ark, 74
  Athena and Isis, 69-70
  immaculate vessel, 75
  Isis and Athena, 69
  Isis and Sirius, 69
  The Secret Doctrine, 69
  vessel of wisdom, 75
Signature of Sirius
  AA signature, 62
  analysis of, 64
  Dedication decipherment, 68
  forms infinity sign, 68
  "the Great White Lodge on Sirius", 64
  "The Light of God", 64
  link to Bacon and Master R, 68
  number 136, 68
  Sirius, Great Bear, Pleiades, 199-200
  Sonnet 136, 68
  Word loop, 64
  zeros, 68
  "The God of Light", 64
Silence
  esoteric meaning of, 139
Silence and God, 169
Sirius
  1.9. and 9.3., 127
  above Scorpio, Leo, and Gemini, 213
  AN value, 91
  "A Word from the Master", 136
  AN and RAN values, 211
  channels for energy of, 203
  Cosmic Christ aspect, 131

cosmic Hermes, 214
creation of humanity, 170
distance, 4
Earth relation, 98
fundamental points regarding, 130-131
  cross symbol, 131
  initiation, 130
  karma, 130
  Masonry, 130
  our solar system, 130
  Sanat Kumara and individualization,
    130
Great Invocation connection, 98
"the heart of the Lion", 194
Hermes, 208
Hierarchy of Earth, 99
"The High Priestess, The Star, The Sun",
  166
initiation, 139
key words of Great Invocation, 143
Law of Karma, 138
Leo, 158
Masonry, 99, 198
Master R, 15
middle of Great Invocation, 88
Mystery Schools, 131
number 19, 105
plan of described, 254
"restore the Plan on Earth", 240
rulership symbolized, 91
Sanat Kumara and number 247, 211
solar system, our, 4
source of mind, 170
spiritual Hierarchy, 131
star of initiation, 91
"The Star", 87
Sirius, Lord of
  our planetary Logos, 189
Sirius A and B
  1993, 131
  astronomical relationship, 131-132
  closest degree of separation, 132
  periastron, 131
  year 1993, 132
Sirius and Gemini
  Masonry, 215
Sirius and Sanat Kumara
  veiled behind The Sun, Jupiter, Venus,
    195
Sirius and Scorpio-Leo
  numeric relationship, 210
Sirius B
  50 year orbit, 132-133
  500 year cycle, 133
  description, 132
Sirius, Great Bear, Pleiades (See next page)

Sirius, Great Bear, Pleiades
  Signature of Sirius, 199-200
  supreme cosmic triangle, 199
"Sirius the Cosmic Christ"
  number 105, 196
"Sirius the Great White Lodge"
  AN value, 99
Sixth Line Word Cipher, 31
  acrostics aspect, 31
  Bacon's name in Shakespearean plays,
    32
  Edward D. Johnson, 31
  explained, 32
Solar Logos
  role of our planetary Logos, 192
  Sanat Kumara, 191, 216
solar system, our
  Sirius, 4
Solomon's Temple and 33, 176
Sonnet 136
  logarithms, 67-68
  number 136, 68
  Signature of Sirius, 68
Sonnets
  Dedication page, 65
    decipherment result, 66
  mystery of, 65
Sothis
  Isis, 69
Space/time illusion, 244-246
Spear-shaker
  Athena, 60
  Shakespeare, 60
  Verulam, 60
spiritual boundary
  18 and 19, 106
Spiritual success, 231
St. Alban
  287 A.D., 101
  Bacon, 87
  description, 20
  Masonic link, 86
  Master R, 20
  year of martyrdom, 86
"The Star"
  Isis Unveiled, 166
  middle of Great Invocation, 88
  Sirius, 87
  Tarot card, 87
Star of initiation
  Sirius, 91
"The star Regulus, the heart of the Lion"
  AN value, 171
Star systems and sub-systems, 190
"The Star" Tarot card
  91, 87-88

Sub-planes
  18 and 19, 106
Summation
  113 branch-races, 252
  113 unit cycle, 252
  113 words of Great Invocation, 252
  avatars, 252
  fourth cosmic initiation, 252
  Great Invocation, 253
  Great Invocation and Shamballa, 252
  Great Invocation, a cosmic mantram, 253
  The Great Sacrifice, 251
  Masters R and DK, 253
  the Plan, 252
    last 500 years, 252
    new phase, 253
  planetary Logos, 251
  reappearance of the Christ, 252
  Sanat Kumara, 251
  Venus, 251
The Sun, Jupiter, Venus
  AN and RAN values, 195
  Individualization, 195
  Leo planetary triangle, 195
  linked Sirius and planetary Logos, 196
  Sirius and Sanat Kumara, veiled behind,
    195
Synthetic Ashram, 64
Synthetic Triplet
  first and last words of, 168
  first, middle, and last words interpreta-
    tion of, 170-171
  first, middle, and last words of, 169
    AN value, 173
  locating middle letter, 172
  locating middle word, 169
  meaning of 417 letters, 167
  middle Essence Value of, 171
  middle word of, 169
  mind is central, 170
  mind is central in, 170
  number 139, 165
  number 383, 171
  number of words in, 165
  restore, 239
  synopsis, 172-173
  three middle words of, 171
    Master R, 171

Tarot Arcanum
  The High Priestess, 137
Taurus
  Fixed Cross, 213
  Great Invocation, 205
  light will emerge later, 213
  veiled, 205

Taurus-Scorpio, 207
  AN value, 207
  The High Priestess, 207
Tawny lions
  Sanat Kumara, 216
Taylor, Michael
  honorificabilitudinitatibus, comments on, 101
  presentation by, 14
  "A Word from the Master", 139-140
Technology
  the Plan, 3
Templar cross, 18n.4
  Master R, 17
Temple of Man
  Schwaller de Lubicz, R. A., 104
The Advancement of Learning, 24
The Great Instauration
  meaning of title, 57
The Masters and the Path
  Master R, 20-21
The Synthetic Ashram
  description, 37
  headed by Masters M, DK, and R, 37
The Tempest
  Boteswaine used as a code, 112
  coded page numbers, 112
Third animal kingdom
  branch-race three of Lemuria, 247
Thoth
  link to Christ, 139
  meaning of names, 138
  Science of, 167
Thoth-Hermes
  AN value, 165
  function of, 166
  magician, 166
  number 139, 166
  ray Seven, 166
Thoth-Hermes-Mercury
  AN value, 146
  "A Word from the Master", 136-137
  numbers 11 and 22, 146, 178
  ray Seven, 137
  RAN value, 178
Three middle word-positions
  of Great Invocation, 69
Three middle words
  of Synthetic Triplet, 171
Three Works
  common source of, 163
  cosmic meaning, 197
  first, middle, and last Essence Values, 161-162
  first, middle, and last words, 162-163
  "the heart of Rakoczi", 160

Hermes, 168
  interwoven by number 189, 156
  linked by number 52, 152-154
  Mediocria Firma and Janus techniques, 154-155
  Master R veiled in, 157
  Middle concept, *Mediocria Firma*, 168
  number 132
    cosmic meaning, 196
    incarnation of Sanat Kumara, 196
    Rakoczi, 173
  numerically balanced, 156
  points of interrelation, 155-156
  reasons for codes in, 181-182
    develop synthetic thinking, 181
    teach and inform about the Plan, 182
  results of analysis, 164-165
  three major themes, 165
  weaving process, 154
The Tibetan
  See Djwhal Khul
Tomb
  Bacon's, 25
Transhuman Hermes
  Masters R and DK, 214
A Treatise on Cosmic Fire
  Path to Sirius, 98
Trinity concept
  Ageless Wisdom, 169
Trinity, zodiac, and the seven rays
  number 22, 146
Trip to New Zealand
  soul searching, 14
Twenty-one key words
  Bacon's alphabet, 114
Twenty-one letter alphabet
  Bacon's use of, 66, 110
Twenty-one letters
  Great Invocation and Bacon, 142

Unnamed Master
  Christ, reappearance of, 96

"Veiled"
  AN value, 60, 92
Veiling, Master of, 92
Veiling factor
  The High Priestess, The Star, The Sun, 166
Veil of Athena, 60
Venus
  Sanat Kumara connection, 227
  Logos of and initiation, 227
Venus and Earth
  chains and globes, 219-220
  numbers 2 and 4, 226

Venus and Mercury
  meaning of names, 197
Verulam
  Bacon, 60
  spear-shaker, 60
Vessel of wisdom
  Argo, 75
Virgo
  Great Invocation, 75
  guardian of the Wisdom, 75
"The voiceless fragrance of a Rose"
  RAN value, 157
Way of the Higher Evolution
  planetary Logos, 215-216
Weaving process
  in Great Invocation, 154
  Three Works, 154
Western civilization
  fifth sub-race, 247-248
White Lodge
  Masonry, 197-198
Will
  establishing, 195
  Leo, 193
  Planetary Logos custodian of, 195
Will, cosmic
  lion symbolism, 192
Will energy
  Sanat Kumara, 216
Wisdom Impressions, 37
  The Synthetic Ashram, 37
  year 1993, 133
Wither, George
  Bacon contemporary, 82
  Collection of Emblemes, Ancient and Moderne, 82-83
  Janus epigrams, 83, 84
Word loop
  analysis of, 64
  "the Great White Lodge on Sirius", 64
  Signature of Sirius, 64
Word placement
  cipher methods, 52
  King Henry IV, 117-118
  Love's Labor's Lost, 112
  Psalm 46, 112
Word placement technique
  honorificabilitudinitatibus, 100
Word-position
  explained, 53
Word weaving message, 160
World Period
  definition, 233n.4
  root-races, 239
  seven root-races, 222